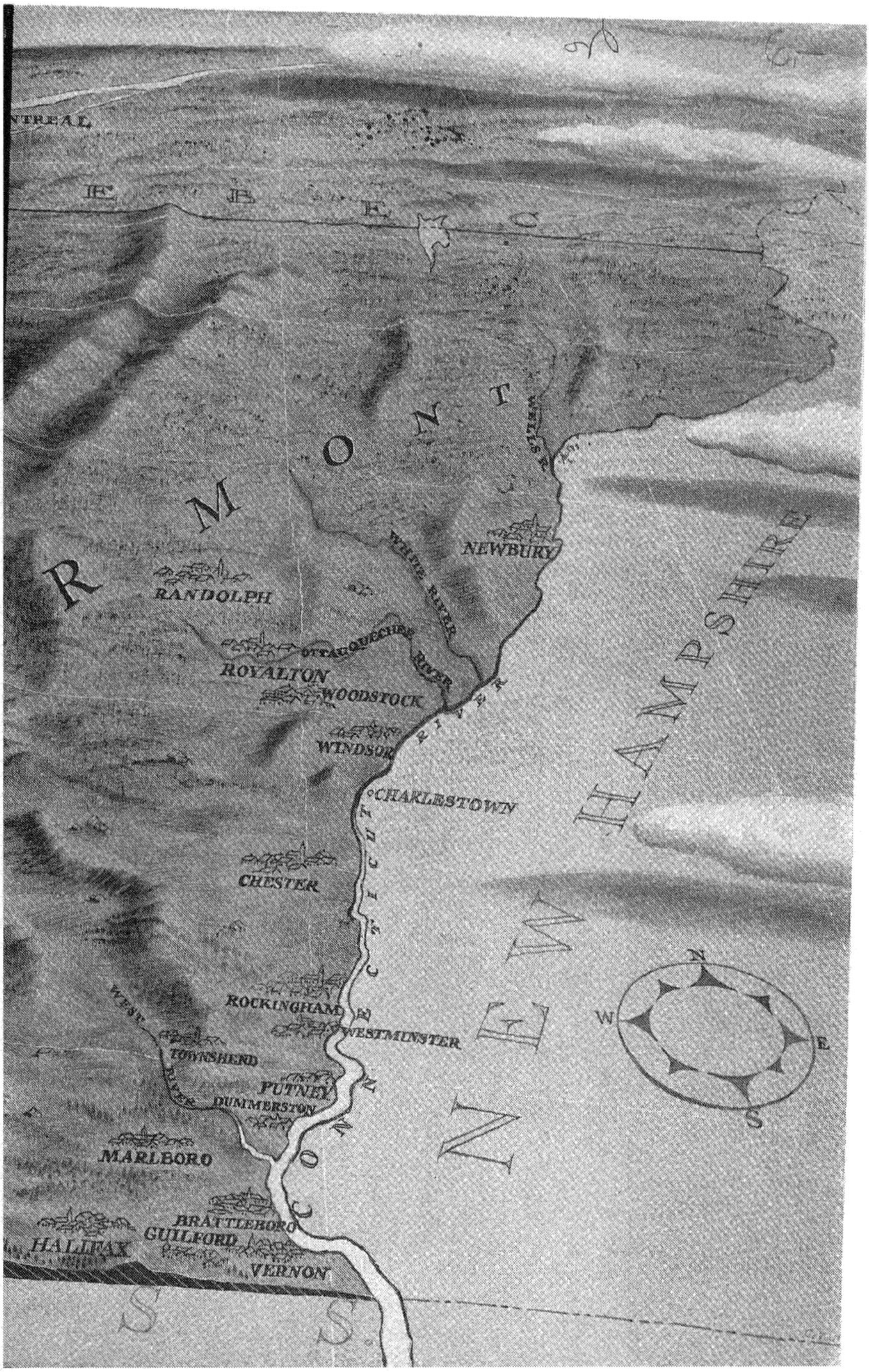

R M O N T
NEW HAMPSHIRE
NEWBURY
WHITE RIVER
RANDOLPH
OTTAUQUECHEE RIVER
ROYALTON
WOODSTOCK
WINDSOR
CHARLESTOWN
CONNECTICUT RIVER
CHESTER
ROCKINGHAM
WESTMINSTER
WEST RIVER
TOWNSHEND
PUTNEY
DUMMERSTON
MARLBORO
BRATTLEBORO
GUILFORD
HALIFAX
VERNON
N
W
E
S

THE RELUCTANT REPUBLIC

Books by

FREDERIC F. VAN DE WATER

RUDYARD KIPLING'S VERMONT FEUD

A HOME IN THE COUNTRY

WE'RE STILL IN THE COUNTRY

FATHERS ARE FUNNY

THE CIRCLING YEAR

THE RELUCTANT REPUBLIC

THE FAMILY FLIVVERS TO FRISCO

ELMER 'N' EDWINA

STILL WATERS

PLUNDER

THE REAL MC COY

THUNDER SHIELD

GLORY HUNTER: A LIFE OF GENERAL CUSTER

HIDDEN WAYS

THE FIRST SIX TITLES LISTED ABOVE ARE PUBLISHED
BY THE JOHN DAY COMPANY

The
RELUCTANT
REPUBLIC ·

Vermont 1724·1791

FREDERIC F. VAN DE WATER

Illustrated

THE JOHN DAY COMPANY
NEW YORK

To Eleanor

WHO BORE WITH ME

Foreword

THIS BOOK UNEARTHS few hitherto unknown facts, proclaims no important historical discoveries. It reassembles matters long established, and it is candidly parasitic in that its material has been drawn from a multitude of earlier annals and from the minds of more erudite men.

The narrative has seemed worth retelling in the hundred and fiftieth year of Vermont's statehood, not only for its innate drama, but also for its possible significance in an era of despairing minorities. It has been the book's intention to lighten a shadowed chapter in American general history and to emphasize the implausible attainments of a remarkable and independent people.

Debts contracted while working on such a volume are difficult to acknowledge adequately or even to list entire. More than ordinary gratitude is due to Charles E. Crane of Montpelier, author of *Let Me Show You Vermont* and other Green Mountain volumes; to John Gale of Guilford, historian; to Miss Agnes K. Lawson, secretary of the Vermont Historical Society; to Mrs. Hazel B. McTighe of Dummerston for invaluable secretarial aid; to John Spargo of Old Bennington; and to the patient and long-suffering officials whose names properly should head this acknowledgment—Miss Florence L. Pratt, Mrs. Florence Greenwood, and Mrs. Jean Hebb of the Brattleboro Public Library. These profusely pestered and incredibly responsive persons must be even more relieved that a long period of research and source-seeking has ended than is their recent chief affliction,

FREDERIC F. VAN DE WATER

West Dummerston, Vermont

Contents

Illustrations

PART ONE

COLONY

We value not New York with all their powers,
For here we'll stay and work; the land is ours.
                              —THOMAS ROWLEY

1 The Land Withheld

LONG AFTER the first white man saw it, the land lay empty. For a hundred years, to east and west, north and south, cabins were raised and towns were born, yet no ax touched its forest, no plow its soil. The land stood aloof from the brawl of settlement, the ruin of clumsy wars. Those who, at last, came to hold it thereafter defended their own with the jealous passion of men accepted after long thwarting.

This is the story of that defense and its tardy triumph. It is odd that land destined to be so greatly contested should have lain for generations ignored. Yet this was so. The European who first set eyes upon its distant beauty accorded it only a careless glance.

The long war canoes moved down the lake, July 4, 1609. The last of the islands dropped behind the noisy flotilla, and Samuel de Champlain looked to his left across brilliant water.

> Continuing our route along the west side of the lake, contemplating the country, I saw on the east side very high mountains, capped with snow.

Thus he and his two French companions discovered Vermont. Champlain was indifferent to the finding of still more land. Already there was too much of it—more than Europe could possibly populate in a thousand years. He may have been a slovenly observer, too. Snow, in this era, does not crown Mansfield and Camel's Hump during July, yet there is some warrant for the belief that the earth was cooler, the seasons more rigorous in Champlain's day.

The explorer's red allies told him that the distant territory was theirs. Their vague title was no better, no worse, than the many over which, in years to come, white men would strive. Actually the land was virginal. It had been no man's sure property.

Champlain shrugged. The paddles dipped again, and the war party went on up the lake to that small, half-comic battle that was to bring untold woe to New France.

The short matchlocks of the white men roared, the advancing Iro-

3

quois broke before the fell miracle of firearms, and the screeching Hurons rushed in to kill the panic-smitten. The human wolves of the Long House never forgot nor forgave the terror and the shame of that day. Champlain and his allies returned in triumph down the lake that now bears his name. He had contrived the frequently ingenious deaths at Iroquois hands of a host of Frenchmen yet unborn.

There is no record that the explorer turned aside to inspect more closely the lake's east shore. It was wilderness. He left it thus. So for a long and violent time it remained—a lovely and an empty land.

No living man has seen its like. Today, the same hills move inward from either border, gathering up the land, lifting each fold toward the culminating central ridge, but these ranges wear only a sleazy imitation of their former clothing.

Streams, clean and quick, still follow old courses, but their flow has dwindled to a half, a third, of its former strength. There are meadows and pastures now where swamps once sponged up the lavish water.

A puny progeny succeeds the trees that covered the Green Mountains then. Thick rugs of spruce, pine, and hemlock lay across the knees of the hills that were splotched, too, with the lighter hues of giant oaks, maples, ashes, and birches—members of an incredible forest.

These ancients stood shoulder to shoulder, great trunks soaring branchless a hundred feet or more to spread at last an unbroken roof of foliage that summoned the rain and held moisture beneath its canopy. Occasional arms of sunlight groped down through the green dimness of the lower forest, and in these depths endured the musty, aromatic smell of fallow mold.

Scant undergrowth could exist in this damp gloom. Ferns grew thick on the ledges, and across the forest's floor the mushrooms' pale discs were scattered; but only spindling saplings stretched vainly for sunlight, and of lower brush there was almost none. The crooked aisles between the great tree boles were so clear that a man might ride a horse unhampered and prowling creatures could move unbetrayed.

Only the wind, moving overhead, and, perhaps, the continual soft voice of never-far-distant water disturbed the vast quiet. The air hung still in these depths. Birds were few and mute, for lovers of sunlight and song shunned this damp dusk. The shadow-hued life of the wilderness moved like shadows. Moose and deer woke no sound from the sodden earth by their passage. Bear, panther, and lynx ranged the hushed precincts. Those and lesser mammals—beaver and otter, fisher, mink, and their brethren—those and the dull-hued birds were the land's natives.

Yet there were trails through the woods, not worn by hoofs and paws. Along river banks, up and over the ridges and down again beside contrary-flowing rivers ran paths that padding moccasins had made; and, where the earth was hard or rock slopes intervened, saplings bent into arcs and tied to the ground pointed the course of the Indian roads. Highways follow them today across the state. They led to no long-established villages within the land. They were the shortest and easiest ways across territory too wild for even the redmen to covet.

The forest wholly covered the land. Save for rocky peaks, occasional open glades, and the vast jumbles of the windfalls where tornadoes had overthrown trees, the high green roof, the rugged lichened pillars that upheld it, ran unbroken between the river and the lake.

This lake and this river long had been Indian roads to war. The elm-bark canoes of the Iroquois went down Champlain and through its outlet, the Richelieu River, for raids on the Algonquins and Hurons of Canada and, later, upon their allies, the French.

Mohawks and other tribesmen of the Five Nations traveled overland to the Connecticut and followed its course to spread terror among the Abanakis and their neighbors. When King Philip's revolt against New England crumbled, the broken fragments of his host fled upriver. Some at last joined the village Greylock, the grizzled chief of the Waranokes, established where the waters of the Missiquoi pour into Champlain. Others went on into Canada and settled at the Indian community of St. Francis. This town became a catchall for fugitives from the vengeance of English and Iroquois alike and an enduring curse to the New England frontier.

Thereafter, the lake and the river became the greater and the lesser pathway of a serial seventy-four-year conflict that was a shabby and more savage imitation of Europe's political wars.

From 1689 to 1763, with three intervening periods of peace that were only pauses for breath, war's tide ebbed and flowed along the water roads, sweeping away the feeble settlements of reckless folk on the edges of what was to become Vermont, driving the French from their houses and stone windmill at Alburg on the lake, abolishing log dwellings and palisaded forts on the Connecticut's west bank; by destruction keeping the land inviolate.

There was no cause native to the New World, where populations still were small and acreage apparently limitless, for these paroxysms of violence. They were born of imported hatreds. They were reflexes, responding to trans-Atlantic quarrels for the eternally toppling Balance of Power. Thousands died, valiantly or cravenly according to their texture, and frequently with extreme ghastliness, in no better cause.

England enlisted the Iroquois; France, the Algonquins and Hurons and the bitter remnants of New England's ousted tribes. None of these was of any sure aid in open conflict. Both sides used the redmen, not for their weight in battle, but as specialists in their own ghastly version of war. The Indians were employed to shatter by terror civilian morale.

That morale shrank and wavered on the New England northward-creeping border, but it never wholly broke. When the raid had passed in screechings and flame, those who had survived fled from smoke-filled valleys where their homes had stood and caught their breaths and numbered their dead and, in the pause between the involved chapters of the war, faced about and came again and often fled once more with the war yell's echo dinning in their ears.

War ebbed. The late fugitives—the hopeful, the valiant, the monu-mentally stubborn—gathered reinforcements and went north over trails still reeking with the stale scent of terror—a drab, a fearful, a foolish, a not unheroic people.

Men had reached the southern border of the land that was to be Vermont before the first tempest blew from overseas. In 1669, explorers sent out by the General Court of Massachusetts Bay worked their way north along the Connecticut River as far as the rolling and fertile land where the domelike lodges of the Squakheag Indians' chief village stood amid squaw-tended fields of corn, beans, and squashes.

Two years later, the Squakheags sold their land; and in the year following, 1672, cabins were built and called Northfield. The town had a miserable infancy. Three years after its establishment, it went up in flames during the last days of King Philip's War. Its surviving residents returned, rebuilt, and were attacked again by Indians in 1688. Six persons were killed, but the population was even more radically cut by the many settlers who gave up their holdings and sought more peaceful farmsites elsewhere.

The conflict which the English, with a light disregard for its sundry other participants, call "King William's War" broke in the next year. It was not William's exclusive property. He and England had for their allies Spain, Holland, Sweden, Denmark, Austria, and some Italian and German states. Their expressed purpose was to preserve the

Balance of Power; their actual, to humble Louis XIV, who had managed to acquire more strength than the rest of Europe could endure to see in any one man's hands.

The war in Europe resolved itself into the floundering of armies in the bloody mire of the Low Countries. The reflex war in America was no more decisive. Schenectady perished in a manifold screeching with flames that painted the February snow an appropriate scarlet. The Maine frontier was charred and blood-stained. New England struck back. Phips's fleet of armed merchantmen wallowed up the coast, with an expeditionary force of seasick farmers. They took Port Royal, reduced Acadia; but their leader's vainglorious intention to capture all Canada died out in blundering and fumbling before Quebec. In revenge for Phips's presumption, the French seared the New England frontier a second time.

The Peace of Ryswick left affairs and boundaries in Europe much as they were at the war's beginning. Port Royal and Acadia were returned to France.

The Balance of Power was shortly in question again. Philip, grandson of Louis XIV, succeeded to the throne of Spain. This jolt to a precarious equilibrium alarmed most of the monarchs of Europe, including Queen Anne of England, whose grateful subjects named the subsequent war after her. This time, Spain and Bavaria were the allies of France. Opposing them were England, Portugal, Austria, Holland, Denmark, and some German states.

American response to the mother countries' conflict began to show traces of routine. Another army was raised in New England to capture Quebec but was obliged to disband when Britain diverted the expected reinforcements and ships to Portugal instead. Another expedition was sent, this time with a Royal Navy convoy, against Port Royal.

The provincials, aided by marines from the fleet, performed their task with skill born of practice. The affair was adorned by polite letters framed in chivalry's best spirit that shuttled between besiegers and besieged, and when the town surrendered there was much concern for the comfort of the ladies of the garrison. It was a polite war in America, elsewhere than on the frontier.

There, New England suffered the resourceful fury of French and Indian terrorism. No raids were launched against New York, lest the terrible Iroquois be roused to strike the war post again. New England had no red allies to protect the single cabins, the mean clusters of huts, that had sprung up during six years of peace. Presently the frontier was blackened and empty once more.

Major Hertel de Rouville, with two hundred French, one hundred and forty-two Indians, and dog-teamed sledges for his train, marched down Champlain's ice and by the Indian road up the Onion (later the Winooski) River, over the divide, and down the White. The Connecticut River was frozen and buried deep in snow. De Rouville's snow-shod raiders made good time. They had to wait, shivering in a pine grove, for the first pallor of dawn, February 29, 1704.

Thereafter, they went forward toward the unguarded palisade and the great drift that had climbed unheeded almost to its top. Deerfield slept until the first musket boomed and was followed by a dozen explosions. One war yell sired a hundred. There were cheers and screams and the Indians' high yowling, jets of flame in the twilight, banging and smoke, and the sliding fall of smitten fugitives. Gun butts and tomahawks beat upon splintering doors that gave at last, and rooms lately calm were filled with brief fury. Then silence fell that seemed immune to outside clamor, and the living whom the redmen bound were as stark and still as bodies sprawled on the floors.

Forty-eight persons were killed at the taking of Deerfield, and 119 captured, of whom only an even hundred survived the frigid three-hundred-mile return journey. The wife of the Rev. John Williams was a fragile and ailing woman. It was plain to her Indian captor that she could not endure the march. Before the first day's travel ended, he butchered her before her husband's eyes.

The Rev. John Williams did not go mad. Neither did he question the justice and mercy of the Lord God Jehovah. That first Sabbath of the bitter march he preached to his fellow captives and chose as his text Samuel 1:13—"The Lord is righteous for I have rebelled against his commandment; hear, I pray you, all people and behold my sorrow; my virgins and my young men have gone into captivity."

The little river at whose mouth they halted for the first Protestant service held in Vermont still bears his name.

For what was done at Deerfield the fat old Indian fighter, Captain Philip Church, captured and burned Grand Pré. In reprisal de Rouville came again and fired Haverhill on the Merrimac, killing forty-odd and taking many prisoners.

These events had import that set them apart from the uncelebrated small tragedies and humble agonies that beset and at last left almost wholly desolate the New England frontier. Year by year, the savage round of violence continued—ambushes, murders, burnings, abductions, cattle maimings. There was no sure defense against the tactics of Indian warfare—the wolflike attack, the swift flight. Ranger companies were organized to grope through wilderness. They killed a few men and lost a few men. The raiding continued.

Massachusetts' settlement of her Indian problem had been too thorough; her eradication of the native redmen had been too complete. One friendly tribe in the Commonwealth's employ would have saved its frontier much woe. The French had been wiser. The French were more merciful, too, than their adversaries. An English prisoner delivered approximately intact at Quebec had a higher market value than his scalp. New England drew no such distinctions. It paid £50 for Indian scalps and no questions asked.

In Europe ten years of war burned to ashes. By the Treaty of Utrecht, England won from France Newfoundland, Acadia—thereafter Nova Scotia—and an indefinite region around Hudson's Bay. In America militia regiments were disbanded, and still another plan for the invasion of Canada was laid aside. Peace had been declared, but none of its soft blessings were discernible to the haggard folk of northern Massachusetts. The French Indians kept on with their own variety of war.

Years of day-long nightmare were to drag past before settlers found relief. No man took his hoe to the cornfield without a gun in the other hand. No one lay down at night with surety that he would see another morning. When respite at last came, it did not spring from a victory over the marauders or reinforcements sent by the smug and the safe folk of the interior towns. The frontier was preserved and peace was restored largely because a number of eminent gentlemen got themselves involved in a real-estate deal and could not profit thereby unless their property was reasonably free of Indians.

To the early colonists, their patrons and proprietors, the land had seemed as boundless and inexhaustible as the sea appears to a porpoise. There was too much land even to estimate. Careful surveys, therefore, were a vain and unnecessary expense. This dangerous indifference was complicated and made additionally hazardous, not only by the inaccurate geography of the time, but also through the open-handed granting by a succession of kings of charters with the vaguest and sometimes most ridiculous descriptions of boundaries.

Not infrequently, as a consequence, when the supply of land proved to be limited after all and settlers were muttering for more, it was found that by His Majesty's most gracious condescension the boundary of one province considerably overlapped the frontier of a neighbor or that one colony had sold land that actually belonged to another. In 1713, it was discovered that Massachusetts had made the latter error on no small scale.

A survey, more accurate than its predecessors, to fix the Massachusetts-Connecticut boundary revealed that 107,793 acres which Massachusetts had sold to settlers for cash actually lay within the province of Connecticut. Worse than this, the Bay Colony already had spent the money it had received.

Before the defrauded wails of Connecticut grew too loud, Massachusetts agreed to a compromise. It could not pay its aggrieved neighbor in currency, but it could and would let Connecticut sell an equivalent amount of Bay Province land and keep the proceeds. Most of the territory Connecticut was to auction lay on the other colony's western marches, but 43,943 acres were below what was then believed to be Massachusetts' northeast frontier where Indian forays still were retarding any building boom.

There was some doubt whether this land in the upper Connecticut Valley actually was Massachusetts territory. The Colony and New Hampshire already had had more than a little dispute over the question, but if Massachusetts let Connecticut auction off land and Connecticut did so and got the money, what could either province lose? If anyone suffered in the transaction, it would only be the ultimate purchaser and therefore in accord with tradition and propriety.

Sale of the "equivalent lands" awarded to Connecticut was held at Hartford, April 24-26, 1716. It yielded a total of £683, New England currency, which was turned over to Yale College by the recipient. Purchasers of the faintly debatable acreage on Massachusetts' northern border were three gentlemen of Boston, William Dummer, Anthony Stoddard, and John White, and the Rev. William Brattle of Cambridge, who died shortly thereafter and was succeeded in the Company by William, his son. For some unannounced fraction of £683 they acquired almost all of the territory now included in the river towns of Brattleboro, Dummerston, and Putney. It was wilderness, primeval, absolute, boasting only a transient population of Indians going to or returning from forays.

These visitors were no advertisement for the Dummer-Stoddard-White-Brattle subdivision, but its promoters were influential. Dummer soon was to become acting governor of Massachusetts. There was a something to their complaints of Indian ravages that carried them further into official ears than appeals from the suffering frontier folk had been able to penetrate in twenty-five years. With each new foray, the repute of the Dummer and Company Equivalent Lands fell lower, and the anguished voices of its owners went higher.

In 1723, Indian outrages and the plaints of the Equivalent Lands' proprietors reached apogee. Accordingly, the Massachusetts legislature voted, December 27, to establish for the protection of citizens and real-estate developments "a blockhouse above Northfield in the most convenient place." The fact that Mr. Dummer of the Equivalent Lands firm now was acting governor of the province may have been purely coincidental. So may have been the oddity that, when Colonel John Stoddard of Northampton chose the site for the blockhouse, he set it on Dummer & Co.'s property.

The fervor that ownership of real estate quickens in men is surprisingly intense. Vermont was first settled, finally established, and resolutely maintained by men who were passionately concerned for the land they held.

With oxteams and sledges, carpenters and an escort of militiamen, Lieutenant Timothy Dwight set out from Northampton February 3, 1724, to build the fort. Axes rang among pines that clothed the flat land between the hills' beginning and the shallow bluff that was the Connecticut's west bank. The work moved swiftly. Before summer ended, the structure, which received with propriety the name of Fort Dummer, was finished. The first permanent white settlement of Vermont was under way.

It was no redoubtable fortification, even by the standards of 1724, but to the bedeviled people of the frontier it was Gibraltar's first cousin. Its walls of locked pine logs ran approximately 180 feet each way, forming an uneven square. Within were barracks, storehouses, officers' dwellings—all slanting, salt-box fashion, with low rears toward the parade ground and faces of the logs which formed the fort wall.

There was a well, not too plentiful, within the fort, but water for other than drinking purposes was drawn from the Connecticut, just below the post's eastern exposure. A swivel gun was mounted at each of the wall's four corners. There was a larger cannon too—"the great gun"—which was fired only to alarm settlers—the infatuated land-hungry, who, now that at least equivocal protection was afforded them, began to creep northward once more.

Their return was no eager folk movement into new land. They came back slowly and a few at a time from the havens whither flight had sent them; creeping beyond Northampton, daring to pass even what remained of Deerfield, settling in Northfield, reclaiming, one by one, their homesights on the scorched frontier.

There still was cause for alarm. The new fort had not completely awed the Indians. The distant thunderclap of the great gun rocked settlers' hearts and sent them scurrying from half-built houses to Dummer for protection. When the danger was past, they turned about and worked again upon their houses.

They spoke of the dwellings they raised as "forts"—Burke's fort, Hinsdell's fort, Bridgman's fort. They built for protection, not only from the weather, but also from homicidal redmen. The structures generally were two-story log houses, heavy-doored, loopholed, with the upper story overhanging the lower. There were traps at the outer rim of the second floor through which muskets might be fired directly downward upon attackers below. A platform on the roof's peak was occupied by a sentinel in time of danger.

Gradually about these "forts" newcomers raised less formidable dwellings. These they deserted and fled to the strong house when peril hovered. Thus towns were born. On the chief eminence in each settlement a sentry box was built, and men watched there while their fellows worked in the fields. Settlers spoke of this post as "the mount."

Already Fort Dummer had been worth the building. On December 15, 1725, Massachusetts concluded formal peace with the hostile tribesmen, a truce that lasted nearly a generation.

Gradually the garrison at the fort was reduced. Captain Timothy Dwight and his wife went back to Northampton, taking with them their son, Timothy, born on Vermont soil, May 27, 1726. The baby's mother was Mary, daughter of Jonathan Edwards. Her child's son and great grandson, Timothy Dwight III and IV, were presidents of Yale.

War's forthright brutality was over for a time, and men turned from its straight road into the more devious and involved ways of peace. Traders invaded the lately perilous land to compete against French brandy with English rum. The stream of the northward-moving home-seekers grew deeper and more clamorous. Wilderness that lately had seemed an unmitigated affliction since it had produced only Indians suddenly possessed a cash value. Bickerings over boundaries, suspended during the war, were resumed again with waxing heat.

Above the Equivalent Lands, Massachusetts established a town on the Connecticut's west bank. All such surveyed tracts of wilderness

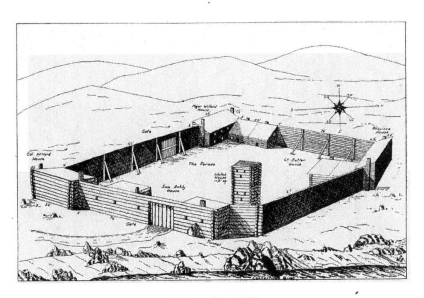

FORT DUMMER

The First Permanent White Settlement in Vermont—From a Drawing
Made in 1747 (Courtesy, Bennington Historical Museum and Art Gallery)

were called "towns," even when they still consisted, like this, only of virgin forest.

This town was chartered in 1737 to citizens of Taunton, over the objections of New Hampshire, who claimed that Massachusetts was invading her territory. The purchasers christened their property New Taunton. Later it was renamed Westminster.

Deaf to the increasing wails of New Hampshire that she was being robbed, Massachusetts serenely established four town sites on the Connecticut's east bank. These temporarily were designated Towns Number One, Two, Three, and Four. The last, and the fort built there, enjoyed no other name for years.

New Hampshire continued to yell. She flourished her charter, which undoubtedly proved by its provisions that Massachusetts was trespassing. Massachusetts in turn waved her own documents, which demonstrated, equally indubitably, that no trespass had been committed. Thanks to the lighthearted disregard of land's inelasticity, the Massachusetts north boundary, the New Hampshire south, lay, if their respective claims were to be believed, widely overlapping each other.

There were attempts to compromise in 1737, but the fine old New England fervor that stirs most effervescently when a Yankee thinks he is being cheated prevented calm discussion of the problem. Compromise failing, the matter was referred to that fount of all knowledge, George II of England, for final judgment. Meanwhile, Massachusetts continued blithely to survey and charter additional towns.

In 1740, crumbling Fort Dummer was repaired. Two bastions were built on opposing corners, and additional guns were mounted on its walls. There were more settlers to protect than when the fort had been built. Furthermore, the Balance of Power in Europe was reeling again. The spirit of prodigious mass murder and colossal larceny which men dignified by more grandiose names once more was loose overseas.

Frederick of Prussia, with Spain, France, and Bavaria as accomplices, had embarked on the theft of however much he could steal from Austria's young queen, Maria Theresa. England was growing worried lest a too-successful robbery make the robbers too powerful.

While the little fort on the Connecticut was being strengthened for whatever might befall, King George, after consulting no man knows what authorities, made known his will regarding Massachusetts' northern and New Hampshire's southern boundary. The decision shocked and delighted New Hampshire as much as it shocked and dismayed Massachusetts.

His Majesty placed the dividing line twelve miles further south than New Hampshire's claim, forty miles further south than Massachusetts'.

The Bay Province lost twenty-eight surveyed towns and much unmapped territory by this scratch of the royal pen. The first of the involved boundary disputes out of which Vermont was born and in which her infancy was passed had been decided. There was no further argument. Massachusetts had scant time to mourn her bereavement, for in 1744 the long American truce ended, the land quaked responsively to explosions overseas, and that installment of the serial conflict, called in America King George's war, got under way.

In Europe it was known more ornately as the War of the Austrian Succession. Its continental phase was chiefly memorable for the general ineptitude of Austria's allies, including Great Britain and Holland, and for the display by Frederick the Great of a startling genius for assault, both military and felonious.

Europe's renewed struggle launched the usual complementary war in America. The conventional expedition, organized to capture Canada, was spectacularly mismanaged and disbanded without accomplishment. A New England army and a royal fleet besieged the great French citadel of Louisbourg, built on Cape Breton Island after the last war at a cost of 30,000,000 livres. Yankee artillerymen blew up a number of themselves by overloading their cannon, but they also managed to blow in a portion of the fortress wall. To the amazement of the British and to their own no small astonishment, they captured Louisbourg.

In reprisal, the French struck again at the most available and vulnerable portion of the colonies, the Massachusetts frontier where a line of defense hastily had been strung from Fort Dummer in the east to Fort Massachusetts, built in a meadow just beyond the present city of North Adams, in the west.

The French struck; and the old nightmare, the grisliness with which children had been frightened for twenty years, returned, intensified. Shots rattled from ambush, men dropped in the furrow, oxen shook their horns and rolled their eyes as dark figures burst whooping from cover with scalping knives gleaming.

For an intense instant between slumber and oblivion, the suddenly awakened saw the door go down and paint-blotched, screeching furies pour in.

This was not a war of purposeful, frontal assault that the resolute might withstand. It was an ordeal of sudden violences and enduring

terror, an unending, nerve-straining game of homicidal hide and seek
—stealthy approach, patient waiting for the inadvertent moment, then
clamorous slaughter, dazed prisoners plodding north, and small blue
flames fluttering over the embers that had been a house.

A tormented frontier cried aloud. The anguish was sorer, the lamentation greater, than heretofore. There were more cabins to burn now,
more settlers to capture or destroy. Trails to the older and safer towns
filled with dreary men, women, and children, burdened, beating gaunt
cattle along before them. The fugitives glanced back often at the stain
upon the sky—cloud by day, fire by night.

The Indians smote and vanished and came again, dodging the attempted reprisals of militia who yesterday were farmers. Into the terror there crept an inappropriate, sardonically amusing theme that was
a protracted Yankee dickering. Massachusetts strove with New Hampshire and again was worsted. The latter colony had made a fortunate
deal and was prepared to squeeze therefrom the last possible advantage.

Massachusetts, having repaired Fort Dummer, pointed out tartly
that the post now was her neighbor's responsibility. By the king's late
boundary decision, Dummer lay wholly within New Hampshire territory. It was that colony's duty to maintain and garrison it.

New Hampshire hemmed and hawed. She didn't know 'baout that.
S'portin' one fort a'ready upriver, she was—Fort Number Four, in the
taown laid aout by Massachusetts 'fore the baoundary decision. Didn't
have no real use for another fort, seemed 's'if. No New Hampshire
settlement in fifty miles of Dummer.

Massachusetts retorted that if the fort wa'n't helpful to New Hampshire settlements, it was keepin' Injuns aouta interior New England.

"Ehyah," New Hampshire admitted. "Keepin' 'em aouta Massachusetts. Let her s'port the fort then. Her business."

There was relish in the answer that comes into New England speech
only when the speaker is sure he has his rival bested. Massachusetts
angrily threatened to abandon the fort, since New Hampshire didn't
want it.

"Abandon her an' welcome," New Hampshire replied. "Ye don't
dare."

Massachusetts truly did not dare even to pretend to fulfill her empty
threat. The final peace of 1763 found the Bay Province unhappily and
fumingly still supporting Fort Dummer.

Even with this post garrisoned, the frontier bulged and cracked. The
enemy ranged calamitously its entire length, striking, slipping away,

striking again. Vaudreuil came down the Pownal Valley with a thousand men and abolished Fort Massachusetts. The settlers fled from New Taunton. Putney's infant town on the Connecticut was abandoned.

The dark citizens of St. Francis whom New Englanders had ousted from their homes had a score to pay. They discharged it, two hundred cents on the dollar. Under French leaders or guided by their own simple zest for slaughter, they bewildered, hoodwinked, confused—and slew—the blundering farmer-soldiers or, when these kept too close to the forts, preyed upon farms the stupid or resolute still maintained.

There were men of all substances among those who, despite terror and reiterated punishment, kept the reeling frontier from collapsing entire and held a horde of deft and eager killers back from the interior towns.

There were valiant men, like William Phipps, who was hoeing corn in Putney's new settlement, beyond the fort, when the Indians came. They captured him and dragged him toward the woods, but Phipps clung to his hoe and in the split second offered by chance, swung it. He halved one captor's skull and killed the other with his first victim's gun. Then Phipps ran for the fort, but the raiders shot him down before he reached its gate.

There were many of Phipps's breed. There were others as scant of heart and brain as Captain Eleazar Melvin and his scout of eighteen men. These, retreating toward Fort Dummer before a larger Indian force, tarried by a West River pool near the present town of Jamaica, not to ambush their pursuers, not to sell their lives dearly, but to shoot salmon.

This artless self-advertising had almost immediate results. The Indians fell upon the sportsmen, who fled, save five of their number, who after the first volley lay among the slaughtered salmon. John Petty, sorely wounded, was helped along by his comrades for a little way.

In the van of the fugitives Captain Melvin ran earnestly yet right awkwardly. A tomahawk blow had severed his belt so that he had to hold up his breeches while he galloped. Even thus handicapped, he reached the fort, thirty-odd miles away, ahead of all his men but one. The wounded Joseph Petty was not among the survivors. He had been left on a pallet of pine beside a spring "to live if he could." One record says that his body was recovered and buried; another, that it never was found.

There were men of no more fortitude than Melvin and his command. There were men like Captain Humphrey Hobbs, whose patrol, while it ate its noon meal in the forest that now is Marlboro, was jumped as Melvin's had been. Outnumbered, it fought for two hours behind trees and rocks and at last drove off its attackers.

There were many folk of normal fiber whom frontier violence cowed or destroyed. There were men of incredible toughness like young Samuel Graves of Hobbs's command.

He, an old record recites, was shot through the head by a musket ball during the Marlboro skirmish, so that the missile emerged behind his left ear "bringing with it almost two spoonsful of his brains, by which unhappy accident his life was in very great danger and almost despaired of but through divine, undeserved goodness his life is continued but under great difficulty, by reason of the fits of the falling sickness [dizziness] which render him incapable of business."

Four years the raids endured, launched from the ever more flourishing nursery of Indian violence at St. Francis, waxing in savage ingenuity as they progressed, continually hammering the thin line of frontier blockhouses but never quite smashing it. They became so intolerable that General Joseph Dwight wrote a little wildly, urging the enlistment of a thousand men for the forts' defense and a price of £1000 per Indian scalp.

Though the forts still held, the land above them that was to be Vermont had been swept bare. Most of those who had settled there had fled. The rest had died defending their homes, which now were ashes, in clearings where saplings sprouted.

In 1748, the nightmare ended. Europe temporarily had fought itself to a standstill, and the reflex American war had been halted, with the Continental, by the Peace of Aachen, whereby Frederick of Prussia was permitted to keep stolen Silesia, and none of the other contestants won much but a dubious glory.

Louisbourg, so surprisingly captured, was returned to the French. The Indians withdrew to St. Francis with their last batch of scalps and prisoners. In the sudden silence, men drew breath, assembled their families, and moved north once more, into the land where brambles and fireweed and scorched trees marked the sites of cabins.

It was not, though the returning folk tried to believe otherwise, the ordeal's end. It was not to be, despite their hope, even a long truce. While the deserted towns—New Taunton, regranted by New Hampshire as Westminster, Putney, and a few others—were revived; while new towns were made on the wilderness's rim, the serial, colonial struggle had only paused before moving on toward its climax.

This climax, the French and Indian War, had a quality and a purpose lacking in its forerunners. Precedent was overthrown. The conflict actually began in America, not Europe. Friction between French and English in the Ohio Valley, where an overzealous and rawboned young Virginia colonel surrendered Fort Necessity on a morning of dismal rain, supplied the detonating spark.

The small flame kindled here grew and merged belatedly with the European conflagration called the Seven Years' War, wherein Austria, France, Russia, Sweden, and Saxony strove to overwhelm Prussia in the interests of the Balance of Power; and Frederick with some aid from England, his late antagonist, withstood them all.

In America still further precedents were jettisoned. This was not to be a repetition of earlier haphazard and inept maneuvers by Colonial militia. It was England's purpose to drive France from the Atlantic seaboard. To this task she summoned professionals. Not all of them respected the American way of war, as the remnants of Braddock's army, wallowing in flight across the bullet-lashed Monongahela ford, attested.

Fort William Henry below Champlain fell to Montcalm, whose Indians raged hideously among the prisoners of war. Colonel Ebenezer Marsh's Connecticut militia, marching to the post's relief, turned about at tidings of the surrender and marched home again. In Captain Lyman's company there was a large and noisy stripling called Ethan Allen.

Abercrombie, whose unadmiring army called him "Aunt Nabby Crumby," sent his carefully ordered scarlet ranks marching to slaughter before the abatis of Fort Carillon at Ticonderoga. Montcalm was quick and deft, but there was growing weight behind the British blows.

Amherst with an army, Boscawen with a fleet, besieged Louisbourg. The grenadiers and light infantry went cheering through the surf of Fresh-water Cove, led by an ardent young brigadier named James Wolfe. The fortress fell. In America two captures seemed necessary to ensure permanent possession of important French posts.

Amherst and an army moved down the lake, retracing the course of Abercrombie's retreat. Ticonderoga fell, Crown Point was abandoned. The path into Canada was clear. Then, on a showery September morning, musket volleys crashed in Abraham Martin's lofty field under Quebec's walls. Bayoneted lines moved forward, the High-landers ran in, claymores swinging, and Canada's citadel fell with Wolfe dead before it and Montcalm hastily buried within the town. In a year the war ended, and Canada was lost to France.

The war ended; but before the peace, the old, the wretched convulsions afflicted the New England frontier once more. Warriors from St. Francis, strangely merciful, raided up to the gates of Number Four, taking Ebenezer Johnson, his wife, and six others prisoners. On the return march up Black River, the girl child, Captive Johnson, was born. For a little thereafter, the mother rode a stolen horse. When food gave out she kept her baby alive with strips of that horse's flesh. Both woman and child survived.

Westminster was abandoned again. The fort that had replaced Bridgman's in Vernon was burned. Then all at once the hornet attacks from the north came no more. Major Robert Rogers and his rangers, attached to Amherst's army, had marched at the infuriated general's orders against St. Francis.

Amherst's choler had been brought to the boil, not by what was happening to the New England frontier, but by a more unpardonable offense. One of his officers had been taken and detained by the St. Francis Indians despite the fact that he had been proceeding under the sanctity of a flag of truce.

To avenge this outrage Rogers sacked St. Francis, killing two hundred of its inhabitants and recovering more than six hundred white scalps. The source of innumerable border woes was abolished. Henceforth, though guns still spoke along the St. Lawrence, terror faded from the New England frontier.

Garrisons of the harried forts saw how the raids dwindled and died away and how something resembling peace, as clearly as frontiersmen could recall her face, came down from the north. Hundreds looked doubtfully upon the vision, then reassembled what belongings war had left them and, turning backs upon the settlements, went outward again toward their blasted homes.

A whisper came to the ears of hundreds more. It told of good land, well watered, splendid with timber, that waited, unpeopled. Excited voices flung the tidings further, altering for wistful or disheartened eyes the future's whole aspect. Men, hearing the news, lifted their heads; and suddenly the interior roads, the dim further trails, carried a drab and struggling host out from the border, out from safety into adventure, out from a solidified society to the fluidity and freedom of a wilderness.

A people were on the march, meagerly, shabbily, bent beneath burdens, tramping into new land. This land had lain empty since, long ago, the first white man had seen it. The thwarted folk who, at last, came up permanently to possess it were a peculiar, a special people.

II   Axmen in the Clearings

THE LAND, so long withheld, had been released. War that had abolished the first feeble settlements along the east border, and by its very violence had preserved the wilderness, at last had ended. Dread had vanished from the forest. In its place fortune spoke, offering fertile soil, abundant water power, and timber's vast stands, waiting unharvested. Responsive people moved out past the frontier forts.

No tumult, no pageantry accompanied them. Men, singly or in small groups—lean men, with packs and axes strapped between their shoulders and muskets in their fists—followed the narrow roads that dwindled into blazed trails that, in turn, faded out upon the forest's uncharted floor. Behind them whole families plodded northward, thrusting indignant cattle along, pausing with reproachful clamor for the smallest burdened youngster to catch up.

Up the Housatonic Valley from Connecticut's thin-soiled frontier; along the "Great River," that had been war's own road; afoot, ahorse, in rowboat, dugout, and canoe, the shabby, unordered procession moved while at its sources, as the tidings spread, more of the eager gathered and swelled its flow, marching north to claim their homesteads, to "make a pitch" on either flank of the wilderness.

As a Yankee enterprise, the progress was typical; as a spectacle, sad-hued and barren of ostentation or excitement. No sound or fury of a land stampede accompanied it. Here was none of the drama of groaning oxen, shouting men, and wagon sails beating outward. This was the unobtrusive trickling, the intensely preoccupied movement of weathered people into a new, yet not unfamiliar land.

Gradually, almost imperceptibly, the dingy tide flowed up along the edges of the wilderness. More deliberately still, it seeped inland toward the dividing ridge of the Green Mountains. ·

Old settlers, returning after Indian eviction, were the first of the invaders. These already had been tempered in frontier fires. They were the advance's cutting edge, yet those who followed were not of the rash, the raw substance that has made most American folk movements tumultuous and tragic.

These were eager folk, ambitious folk; but they knew what they would find in the forest and what to do when they met it. There were no tenderfeet, no soft-minded, soft-handed men among them. The invaders were repeating a familiar routine. Men from the longest-settled portions of New England faced in the Vermont wilderness the problems their fathers or grandfathers had solved. Men from the Connecticut, the Massachusetts frontier towns, merely were moving to a more promising land to continue what they had been doing all their lives—clearing the forest away, building cabins, routing out stumps, plowing, seeding, hunting, trapping.

The people were skilled in woodlore, familiar with toil and privation. They were bred to the smooth-bore musket, and the ax to them was a third and defter hand. They fitted into the wilderness as a foot slips into a well-worn shoe. Dreamers were few among them, and outcasts and ne'er-do-wells fewer still. The invaders cherished no glamorous hope of easy wealth at their journey's end. No promise of gold, or oil, or fat prairie brought in Vermont's people. The purpose behind that migration were more sober if no less compelling.

Strongest of these was the normal human yearning for land, not to barter but to possess. This third oldest of mankind's hungers could not be gratified adequately in settled lower New England, where there were too many would-be farmers for the farms at hand. The best agricultural soil already had been occupied, and the young and the restless who had settled on the western boundaries of Connecticut and Massachusetts found only a grudging earth, hardly worth the clearing. News of fertile and open territory to the north blew upon the coals of desire.

Vermont settlers, driven from their homes by war, published the tidings. New England militia who had served with Abercrombie and Amherst in the Champlain Valley spread them further. These men were sensitive to promises uttered by magnificent forests and tumbling streams. In the last years of the final war, troops had cut a military road across Vermont. It was little more than a blazed trail, cleared of underbrush and leading from Fort Number Four on the Connecticut to the lake shore opposite Crown Point, but those who made it praised, on returning home, the enormous wealth of timber, the depth of the fallow mold at its roots.

Others than Yankee soldier-farmers were impressed with the land's fertility. Men of the Highland regiments looked upon and coveted it.

Repatriated, they spoke of the delectable country to folk on the starved farms of Perthshire. The only considerable immigration from overseas directly to Vermont was composed of Scots who came to Ryegate and Barnet. Nineteen-twentieths of the settlers elsewhere were Anglo-Saxons with Old Testament names and New England fortitude.

There were adventurers among these men; but they, too, bore New England's imprint. They were not swashbucklers, not fortune-hunters, but odd, contentious folk who found true happiness only in striving with untamed land. Once the pioneer phase had passed, they itched for further wilderness to conquer. The challenge Vermont uttered drew them into the migration's current. They were not typical, yet they were not conspicuously rare.

Thomas Chittenden, Vermont's first governor, had been proprietor of disciplined acres at Salisbury, Connecticut, and an established and honored citizen. He forsook his home for no better apparent reason than to match his big body once more against the strength of the frontier.

The craving for a new land to fight was one of the forces which, eighty years later, drew so strong and depleting a stream of Vermonters westward. Even before the state was wholly settled, those whose delight it had been to wrestle with the frontier were looking for antagonists elsewhere.

Daniel Foot of Middlebury, eighty years old, longed to join once more in such a contest, even as worn Ulysses yearned for the sea wind and the thresh of galley oars. At last, deaf to protest and entreaty, Daniel portioned the six hundred cleared and profitable acres of his farm among his descendants, girded himself, and set out for western New York and one last struggle with the wilderness. There he died, as he had wished, in a place so primitive that they buried him in a wrapping of elm bark in lieu of a board coffin.

Such men were the extremists. Most of the northward-plodding multitude had humbler desire—to gain land they might have and hold.

Associated with the wish for that most binding of unions, that cleaving of man to the soil of his choice, was an itch for more room, mental, physical, and spiritual, than the land of their birth afforded—or approved. This yearning is an accompaniment of all movements wherein men by masses get up and go elsewhere.

Folk who had been underprivileged in Connecticut and Massachusetts were irked by the Puritan society's rigidity. Liberty, for them, was not an abstract noun but a daily essential. Insurgence became, when combined with the soil of Vermont, an explosive mixture, easy to detonate and of astounding power once it was fired. It was to grow in time and under pressure into an intractible, immensely vigilant love of freedom, a passionate adherence to the belief that each man was the. only proper proprietor of himself.

No active persecution drove these homeseekers with their sun-darkened skins and faded clothing and big competent hands to seek haven in the wilderness. Some who made the march bore Puritan mores and religion along with them, practically intact. More deemed these unnecessary burdens to pack all the way north and left them behind.

These were the young—and the bulk of the migration was young—who had struck no deep roots into an uncordial soil, who had girded with youth's intemperance against the stringent laws and the diverse enforcing authorities with which the New England theocracies were more than adequately equipped. These people had been the implicit, if judiciously muted, antagonists of all arbitrary officialdom, from the town constable up to and including Jehovah Himself as interpreted by His ministers of the Congregational Church.

Already the future rebels were tinted with the freethinking and libertarianism that was floating about the eighteenth-century world. The substance of the wilderness, its space and air, would intensify that hue and make it indelible.

Vermont, it seems, was to be a safety valve for pressures and bubblings that went on beneath the tightly clamped lid of Puritan New England. First and last, it blew off a good deal of steam but with definite, if noisy, intent. It was not the sober, the experienced elderly who founded and defended the Republic of Vermont. It was the uproarious, disorderly, irreverent, hard-drinking, hard-minded young hellions, who substituted for a number of arid and uncomfortable virtues esteemed in Massachusetts and Connecticut an almost uxorious devotion to the soil they owned and a jealous pride in the state that preserved their titles.

So intense and truculent a loyalty gave their more conventional neighbors an inordinate amount of trouble, but even in the crises which came with the recurrent inevitability of thunderstorms the pilots of their small nation's destiny seem to have enjoyed themselves. Probably no men in all New England's history had as much fun as the turbulent young leaders of young Vermont.

What piety and decorum the new colony acquired centered itself through geographical circumstance in the southeast corner of the land, where hills roll back, crescendo, from the Connecticut Valley. Among the folk who followed the river upward into the wilderness were many who had absorbed in Connecticut's long-settled regions too much Calvinist doctrine and had acquired too many Puritan standards ever to get wholly rid of either. These were a solid and indigestible element, provocative of many pains and gripings in the infant state. They were godly folk in a generally irreligious land—contentious and excessively stubborn. Most of them settled in the state's southeast corner. Their influence was not commanding, but by adhesion to ancient virtues in a region which, generally, held these in little regard, they made a deal of trouble.

They might have been converted or absorbed in the general hurly-burly of the settlements if geography again had not intervened. Between them and their more rowdy fellow citizens who were a majority on the western slope, rose the long spine of the Green Mountains, making communication difficult and delaying any continuity of culture.

Ten years after towns were permanently established on both slopes of the range, its ridge was still unbroken wilderness. By the time close contact between the Eastside and the Westside became possible through the establishment of roads, the Eastside already was solidified in its dissenting opinions. Much effort, parliamentary, judicial, and military, had to be expended before it surrendered.

As missionaries the Eastsiders were not successful. The rest of the land, including much of the eastern slope, went riotously on its way. Twenty years after its establishment in Vermont, nineteen of the Republic's twenty-one Congregational communions were east of the mountains.

Early settlers of western Vermont merely moved from one frontier to another. They were, like their neighbors over the ridge, chiefly from Connecticut, but not from the long-established areas. They were reared on the still-raw border, and the border's forthright rowdiness accompanied them into the new land. Baptists were among them and also Separatists, opponents of a state-supported church. There were many, too, who used their religion chiefly for squabbling purposes—Freethinkers, Deists—and a great number with too great a zest for current living to bother themselves about any religion at all. These made their first pitches in the lovely valley running north from the Massachusetts border between lofty mountain walls.

Agnosticism and downright atheism flourished early in the soil from which Mormonism, the Oneida Colony, and other more fantastic faiths later sprang. The bulk of the human stream that the Green Mountains split, so that it flowed along either side of the wilderness, was concerned with matters more immediate than salvation. Here was the country of which they had been told, rich in promise; withheld, so it seemed, for the advent of a people fitted to take and hold it. They had no doubt, then or later, that they were the appropriate, the ordained, people.

There was warrant for this belief. The qualities required for conquest of this land were theirs. They were a skilled and ingenious people, able with ax and auger as their only tools to build a log cabin, roof it with slabs of elm bark, and fashion the rough furniture it required. By immense labor, infinite contriving, and only primitive tools, they let spreading pools of sunlight into the forest's gloom, and in their centers established the bare necessities that might keep a family alive. They were inured to such enterprises. They solved with dexterity what unfamiliar problems this new wilderness presented.

Men from Salisbury, Connecticut, led by John Chipman and carrying their supplies by oxcart, moved up the Battenkill Valley in 1766 to explore the land for farmsites. When windfalls and second growth blocked their vehicle's further progress, they did not turn back. They cut a path along the river bank, burdened themselves with the cart's contents, thrust the cart itself into the water, and let the oxen tow it upstream, past the obstructions.

Actual settlement was slow, for the winters were long and bitter. The terrific toil of hacking a home out of the primeval woodland seldom could be accomplished in a single summer. Sometimes an entire family launched itself into the wilderness and by united effort contrived at least some variety of house before the first snows fell.

Such a family were the Meads, who made their pitch in Rutland and, until their home was built, lived all together in a lodge they had bought from a wandering group of Indians.

More often, two or three years passed before the household moved out of older New England. Meanwhile, each spring, the man went north, and, until the snows returned, used each moment of daylight for stubborn heavy work.

Normally, he established the site of his house upon a hill where the trees were a little more sparse, a little less formidable of girth. The air, he believed, was healthier, too. The valleys were marshy, and in them one acquired the fever and ague swiftly. Most settlers contracted it, soon or late, anyway. Until the lowland swamps were drained, malaria was a chronic frontier affliction.

When languor and the creeping sense of cold warned the lone man in his clearing that a seizure of "the shakes" was imminent, he drank— if he were affluent enough to possess it—a brew contrived by steeping ash berries in liquor. This ardent concoction burned his interior so heartily that it served, at least, as a counter-affliction to his chill.

If he lacked such medicine, he lay in the sun and quaked until the seizure passed. Then, if the subsequent fever did not unsteady him, he rose, picked up his ax and swung it once more, dropping further trees with sibilant swoops and leafy crashings, hewing away their tops, piling these for burning, cutting the trunks into proper lengths, notching them, and, finally, laying them on the brown walls of the cabin.

Each day the pool of sunlight in the forest's depth was a little wider, and the dwelling's sides had climbed a few inches. Meanwhile, when darkness forbade further work, the owner of the farm-to-be crept into the leanto he had raised for himself. This was clad on three sides with elm bark. A blanket, hung on the fourth, served for door. A hole in the slanting roof let out a portion of the fire's smoke.

The man who wrought in the slowly dilating clearing lived off the wilderness on which he warred. Game was unbelievably plentiful. The streams were quick with trout. Salmon in dusky companies, shad in great schools, made their annual voyage up the larger, eastern rivers. These, with deer and bear, partridge and duck, were the pioneer's fare. They sustained him through toil too heavy for distaste at the food's monotony, too intense for loneliness to penetrate.

When the cabin walls were at last complete, with doorway and, if this were a luxury-lover's effort, a window to be filled later with oiled paper cut therein, the labor was not half done. Rafters must be raised, a roof laid, chinks filled with mud, a stone fireplace built, and, above this, a chimney constructed of wattled clay. Then when the deft ax had wrought bedstead, table, settles, and a door of hewn slabs, the dwelling was ready for its occupants. Sometimes an uneven floor of puncheon logs was laid. More often, the leveled and packed earth served.

Jacob attained Rachel with less real labor than the Vermont pioneer spent to win his farm. Twice, sometimes thrice, the warning whisper of the first snow drove him away from his task before the new home was ready.

Then a household bade farewell to old neighbors and began the journey north. At whatever season of the year the home was completed, they moved. If it were finished in the fall, winter did not deter them. Swamps were frozen, the ice of rivers made smooth roads. Whenever, however, they came, hardship accompanied them.

If they were more than ordinarily fortunate, a horse bore the bulkier items of the family property, a cow lurched on ahead under frequent proddings. If they were no better off than most settlers, they strapped their more portable goods on their backs, along with packets of corn, apple, turnip, bean, and pumpkin seeds and, thus burdened, walked implausible distances.

They were strong people, from whom grimly just existence had abolished weaklings; a tall, long-limbed, ungainly, tireless people; and they accomplished as a workaday task marches that today would wreck a crack infantry regiment.

Ira Allen and four others, surveying the wilderness that was to be Colchester, ran out of provisions and in four days walked seventy miles to Pittsford through difficult country on no other nourishment than one meal and three additional partridges.

A settler of Poultney plodded thirty miles to Manchester with one hundred pounds of iron on his back—bar iron was a prevalent if cumbersome medium of exchange. On the morrow he returned home, under one hundred pounds of meal.

The children, those who survived, were as toughly fibered as the men. Deacon John Burnap of Lebanon, Connecticut, made his pitch in Vermont on the outskirts of Norwich. Thereafter, Deacon John went home and assembled his six offspring, burdened each according to his or her capabilities, and, bearing the weightiest pack himself, set the pace for them to follow. His gifted family footed the whole distance, which was about one hundred and forty miles in airline and no one knows how much more by the twisting roads and trails of that day.

These settlers were a poor people. Horses were not plentiful among them. Until calves grew into oxen, folk had to depend upon their own muscles for the grueling task of merely keeping alive. Corn for daily use was pounded into a rough meal in a plumping mill. This was a wooden mortar fashioned by burning and scraping a hollow in a hardwood stump over which was hung a rock pestle dangling from a bent sapling. By jiggling this up and down, the grains in the mortar eventually were shattered.

Winter supplies of meal were obtained by carrying the corn unlikely distances to the nearest grist mill and packing the meal home again. Folk on the frontier did their own and draft animals' work. Men drew the crank for the first sawmill at Newbury, eighty miles from Manchester, New Hampshire, by hand sled.

The punishing toil bodies endured without breaking—the tale of the labor men and women did, despite the lack of what seem in a soft age the most necessary tools—sound legendary now. Homes a little better than burrows, raiment inferior to furry pelts—these and an ax and a gun and an obstinate industry and an abiding ambition were all that distinguished many of Vermont's early comers from the creatures already in possession.

Reuben Bratlin of Colrain, Massachusetts, marched over the hill to his pitch in Whitingham, Vermont, with all his goods on his back. The journey was no great feat in those days, for the distance was only twenty-odd miles, nor was the Bratlin burden heavy. It consisted of one medium-sized iron kettle. During the family's first year in their new home, that kettle was the entire household equipment—water bucket, milk pail, and cooking pot.

The more ornate mansions of the frontier possessed, besides oiled paper in the window, split logs on the floor and a plumping mill beside the dwelling, a stone oven in the front yard. Dry wood was burned therein until the interior was thoroughly hot. Embers then were raked out with a fire slice, the oven was swept with an oven broom, and loaves were thrust in with an oven shovel.

Even possession of all this elaborate equipment did not always insure a family enough to eat. In the first years of settlement starvation perpetually stood just behind men's shoulders. There were times when the normally swarming game inexplicably vanished; there were others when the last charge of powder had been spent. Then, folk raised on sound New England cooking were compelled by their pinched bellies to eat whatever could be swallowed and kept.

Hard-pressed pioneer families dined on mussels, woodchucks, turtles, roots, weeds, acorns, washed down with milk from the essential, the life-preserving cow. During one household's first year in Vermont, the normal menu was cornbread and milk for breakfast, boiled herbs for dinner, milk sweetened with maple sugar for supper.

As settlement progressed and the first crop had grown among the stumps of the clearing, the stringency eased. Beans, corn, turnips, parsnips, and pumpkins now were included in the family diet. Pumpkins, baked for eight hours and served with milk, were a substitute for porridge. Where folk were putting on airs, wooden trenchers were used. More generally the entire household dipped for provender into one common bowl. Tea and coffee were unknown. A broth made of roasted beans or corn took their places.

As the obdurate land surrendered under the never-relaxing human attack, and the back-breaking, joint-springing labor of tearing stumps from the clearings was completed, wheat, barley, and buckwheat were sown, potatoes planted. These meant more food in flat stomachs but not respite from labor. The fields already accomplished must be hoed. More must be won. The dawn-to-dark hours of labor, first established by the lone man hacking away at the original clearing, still were observed by him, his wife, his sons and daughters.

They were not only a determined people but also a folk of quiet and unposturing courage. They could not have been otherwise and have survived the toil of the first home-making years. A great self-possession, not to be distinguished from heroism, was to be found within them when the emergency arose.

Amos Story, clearing his pitch in Salisbury, was killed by a falling tree. His wife buried him and then took up his ax herself. With the help of her children, she made her fields and finished her house and dwelt therein, an ardent patriot, through all the Republic's stormy years.

Betty Whitney, the thirteen-year-old daughter of Samuel, who had settled in Marlboro, was left with the responsibility of a motherless household upon her shoulders when her father fell ill one winter. Soon after he was smitten, the home's fuel supply ran low. The child thereafter regularly, until her father recovered, yoked the oxen, hitched them to a sled, drove to the woods, felled trees, chopped them, and brought firewood home.

Fortitude was the common virtue of these worn people, who smelled of sweat and wood smoke and the earth in which they endlessly labored. They accepted its presence in each other with what seems, now, a breathtaking presumption.

Edward Aiken came from New Hampshire to clear a farm in Windham. He fell ill and sent word to his wife. She mounted a horse and, with her nursing infant cradled in an arm, rode almost a hundred miles through wilderness to her husband's side. Aiken recovered. The next summer, he returned to his clearing, taking his twelve-year-old daughter and son of ten with him. The three together raised a cabin.

Thereafter, Aiken went back to New Hampshire for the rest of his family, leaving the children to keep house while he was gone. For six weeks, which must have seemed the shadow of eternity to them, the boy and girl maintained their father's property, two lonely atoms in the forest's vast depths. Then the rest of the Aikens arrived, and the reunited family resumed work upon its farm.

Vitality and a resolution that it was hard to distinguish at times from downright stubbornness were the heritage of this people. It was not the exclusive possession of the young. The aged shared in it.

George Gardner, of Hancock, Massachusetts, moved up into Pownal and made himself a new farm at an age when most men are contemplating a one-way journey to a more permanent abiding place. Gardner was eighty-five when he joined the Vermont pioneers. The fashion in which he cleared his land proved that his body still was sound; but it was plain, so his neighbors muttered to each other, that his mind was gone. Why should a sane person of his age subdue a difficult soil when it was probable that the Reaper would garner Gardner before the oldster could harvest his first crop?

When Gardner, having sowed and cultivated his first field, felled the trees and dug the stumps from another, and in his newly won precinct planted apple seeds, the only reason why his neighbors did not lead him to an asylum was that there wasn't any.

The seeds sprouted, the saplings grew, and still Gardner disconcertingly endured. He continued to cumber the earth long after his orchard came into fruition, and died, having eaten of its fruit and drunk a deal of its fermented juice, at the reputed age of 114.

The land itself prescribed the qualities its owners were to possess. Few of weak will or tender fiber made their way into this region, and those who did were swiftly destroyed, or else they turned about and fled. The men who came and stayed fitted themselves to the stark pattern of existence. They endured toil's circular routine and were tested and weathered by privation, yet these ordeals neither warped nor soured them. They did not become the crabbed, cantankerous folk that most of America still believes inhabit New England's hinterland.

Something of the spaciousness of the country they had married swept into and enlarged the settlers, abolishing Puritan strictures, stamping receptive minds with the boldness of mountains, the freedom of winds blowing and water flowing. Few men remain unmarked by the land in which they live and whose soil they possess.

No leader directed, no pastor decreed, this transformation. Most of the pioneers had outdistanced parsons and statesmen and had learned the exciting advantages of unsupervised existence. Thereafter, they never accorded their ecclesiastical shepherds any vast amount of obedience, and they set up their own secular leaders as the need warranted.

In earlier-settled New England, the Church, fully organized and vigilant, had moved in with the colonists. In Vermont it commonly arrived only after a people who had paid little more than technical attention to its gospel on the other side of the border had managed to get a pagan warmth into their blood that the coldest winter henceforth could not abate. By the time the prophets of Jehovah's vengeance and imminent hellfire found their lost sheep, many of them had strayed too far and too gleefully ever to be recalled.

Such fugitives from the fold became a boisterous, an unruly, a vociferous and ebullient folk, who got, despite the rigors of existence, an enormous satisfaction out of being alive and free. The Puritan esteem for rum, which has been stubbornly overlooked by decriers of grim, bleak New England, had not been abated in these immigrants.

Strong drink played an indispensable and enlivening role in their lives. It was a prime element in the rite of hospitality. The man who had none when a guest came felt that by this lack his face was blackened. All political and social gatherings were enlivened and accelerated by the quaffing of innumerable toasts. Liquor refilled bodies drained by toil, defended them against winter's cold, accompanied the sealing of bargains, made gestures more eloquent.

Thus, Timothy Lull, paddling his family up the Connecticut in a dugout canoe toward the first pitch made in what became the town of Hartland, steered into a creek and paused at its mouth to christen it by smashing a bottle of rum upon a jutting boulder. The little river still bears his name.

The first Vermonters were an intemperate but not sodden people. There was an instinct for moderation in all they did, however violent it might appear. Furthermore, those who dissipated their substance in a region where that small substance was the only barrier against extinction, speedily were extinguished. Men in the earliest days drank rum and brandy when they could get it. When their farms began to flourish, they drank hard cider, perry, a distillate of pear juice, and spruce beer, reputedly a health-giving beverage and having, if current versions are authentic, no other possible virtue. From honey they made metheglin, a descendant of the ancient Saxon mead; and, as their resources and their ingenuity developed, they contrived a number of fell mixtures—punches, slings, and mulled flips brewed in huge bowls that then were passed from man to man.

Few who entered into partnership with the land deemed too high the price they were paying for that freedom. The grimness of men who find that they have spent much for little did not oppress Vermonters. Early travelers through the region found a wild, rough, irreverent but a hearty and a friendly folk. They were lanky, soiled, unkempt, and, to Calvinistic strangers, dismayingly pleased with their lot. Their swarm of shock-headed, barefooted children were not cowed by the biblically prescribed rod, but were a brawling, noisy crew who strove with each other like bear cubs and displayed toward their parents the scant reverence these parents themselves accorded still higher authority.

The single-roomed, dirt-floored log hovels wherein large families packed themselves always had a warm and eagerly cleared space for the wayfarer. All that the cabin contained was placed at his service with unreticent hospitality. The bed might be verminous, the food bad, and the drink worse; but the simple cordiality with which these were offered atoned for some of their blemishes.

The land had let loose among its invaders a stimulating belief in a new life with elating possibilities. The dream was seen entire by few, yet all had caught phrases of its promise and flashes of its splendor. Wherefore, they were to become a self-confident, forward-looking people, difficult to awe, almost impossible to bully. Folk such as they were not likely to look back with any wistfulness or a great amount of respect upon older New Englander's taboos or deity. The first Vermonters were wholly certain they themselves would fashion a gayer, freer, better society.

As the forest was driven back and the stump-studded clearings spread, as the clearings themselves gradually were transformed into disciplined fields, food became a surplus. The specter of famine was thrust still further away. Grass sprouted in dying woodland between the girdled trees and supplied frugal grazing for stock.

The scrubby cattle, at whose dwarfish, angular aspect modern Vermonters would gape, roamed at will, a constant provocation to marauding bears. Calves were penned but not weaned until snow came. Their hungry twilight bawling called the cows home. Sheep had to be more closely herded and were folded each night lest wolves slaughter whole flocks.

Oxen and horses assumed some of the toil that heretofore straining human muscles had performed. Their employment did not diminish labor but extended and speeded it. Hardwood plows, sometimes elegantly shod with strips of iron, tore the forest mold apart.

Life was becoming something a little beyond the blunt question of survival. Each homestead remained a practically self-supporting unit, but its activities no longer were a savage, simple struggle to get enough to eat.

Clothing, once stomachs were adequately filled, became the pressing necessity. Yankee frontiersmen, save for a few wastrel woods-runners, seem never to have been at ease in deerskin raiment. They wore it when the need was sore, but discarded it as soon as possible. The beaded buckskins to which the Far West clung affectionately did not appeal to New Englanders, possibly because better materials soon were available—wool of their own shearing, flax of their own growing.

From these raw substances each family contrived its own clothing, carding, spinning, and weaving the wool, weaving the flax fibers into linen "tow cloth" for summer garments. These were slow and toilsome processes. The fabrics were harsh and would have been unendurable to less leathery hides. By the most elementary modern standards few of these people were ever adequately clothed. The materials were stiff, the fit of the garments deplorable; but they kept their wearers from freezing, which was their chief purpose.

Men wore heavy boots or shoes—when they did not go barefoot—fashioned from homegrown hides with a rough impartiality that made no distinction between right and left foot. Stockings were of wool, knitted by the womenfolk. Knee breeches were of woolen home manufacture, too. A coarse linen shirt and a coat or, more frequently, a "frock"—a smocklike garment reaching to the knees—completed the costume of the early Vermont farmer.

Black and white wool, mixed and woven with a double thread, was the common cloth for winter wear. This gray fabric was thick and stiff as tar roofing and as impervious to wind. Other cloth was dyed varying shades of brown by butternut juice or steepings of sumac berries.

Women wore the same materials. Children were less adequately covered. They inherited hand-me-downs their elders had outgrown or discarded, and generally went barefoot, winter and summer alike.

The entire average family moved about unshod save on formal occasions. Folk attending church or town meeting frequently tramped thither with shoes under one arm and put them on just before public appearance.

Hats were rare among the Vermont pioneers. Children went without them and so, for the most part, did the women, who covered themselves with home-woven shawls or poke-bonnets. Men commonly wore fur caps. The hats they had brought with them from the settlements were cherished articles. They were of felt with wide brims that shielded the wearer's face from sun and rain and, when not so employed, were pinned up on three sides into the familiar tricorn of colonial costume.

The guns that had been imported from the lower settlements were smooth-bore firelocks, the old "Queen's arm" of the Indian wars. Fiction and poetry to the contrary, rifles were extremely rare in the Vermont wilderness, or elsewhere in New England.

Men used their muskets only in times of great necessity. Powder and ball were extremely expensive and hard to get. Animals taken for their meat or their pelts—bear, deer, and smaller creatures—were killed in deadfall traps. These were so efficient that the deer herd dwindled rapidly.

Cash was even scarcer than gunpowder. "Salts" was the chief product of early commerce. This was the ash of hardwood trees, leached and boiled until the resultant lye was thick enough to carry in baskets. It was sold, through a number of intermediaries, to manufacturers of soap and glass. What soap the Vermont farmsteads used was made from lye and grease upon the premises.

Books were rarer than gunpowder or cash. Until the individual clearings had coalesced into organized towns, there were no schools whatever, and illiteracy was epidemic.

Such were the folk who peopled the land. Outwardly, there was little to recommend them save the enduring frenzy of their labor and the important fact that they represented in their privation and squalor, not an end, but a beginning. These were not oppressed and sinking men and women. They were a free people, rising through travail.

Upheld by their still, deep passion for their land, controlled by the provocative, half-understood purpose that muttered in their ears, these willful self-exiles, with their stump-filled clearings and their reeking huts, were to face long and complex danger. Already its shadow lay upon them. They rose, incredibly, to withstand protracted and continually shifting peril. Their defense entailed much that such folk could not be expected to possess—worldliness, intelligence, dexterity, skill in statecraft and delicately involved diplomacies, monumental patience, colossal persistence.

All these were to be demanded of them; all these they were to supply from some unapparent store the lank, sure-stepping men brought north across the border with their axes and their muskets and their hopeful packages of seeds.

III   His Excellency the Realtor

His Excellency Benning Wentworth was a graduate of Harvard College, a merchant of acumen and wealth, royal governor of the province of New Hampshire from 1741 to 1766, and the grandfather of Vermont, since he created the complex brawl from which a small nation at last was born. No man ever was a less wishful forebear. All the while he actually was grandsiring a state, he believed he was doing only a smart job of promoting.

His Excellency had a fine tall house in Portsmouth, power, riches, and a craving for more. He suffered from gout, as a man might whose portrait displays so wide and concave an expanse of waistcoat. Above this precinct were a tight mouth, hooked nose, and clever eyes in a fat, long face.

The Governor of New Hampshire loved pomp, particularly if he might be its center. The progress of his gilded chariot through the streets of Portland was the town's major spectacle. Red-coated postillions rode two of the four horses. Harness jingled and flashed, dust streamed behind; and lolling upon the cushioned seat, the center of splendor, rode Benning Wentworth himself, wrapped in a necessarily vast crimson velvet cloak. The pageantry quickened more admiration than disapproval in the hearts of Portsmouth folk. This was not some plundering sprig of British aristocracy thrust upon them by His Majesty. This was Benning Wentworth, of their own people—the local boy who had made good.

The Governor had an abiding devotion to Bual Madeira, old rum, fair women, good food, brilliant raiment, money, influence, and Benning Wentworth. He was a vigilant advocate of New Hampshire's interests, a crafty bargain driver, a man who could see his own interests a long way off, and, by standards removed from the spacious corruption of his day, just a bit of a crook.

No slinking craft, no niggardliness, tainted the deals His Excellency accomplished. These were fulfilled with blandness and a childlike audacity. When his or his province's interests were in the scales, Went-

worth's disregard for his own pledges or his king's instructions was
so simple and so complete that it left the gentlemen of the British
Board of Trade and the Colonial Office open-mouthed and gasping.
They could not believe he really could be aware of his own flagrant
and profitable disobedience.

This tranquil audacity had served New Hampshire well before the
serial French war had finished its final installment. By quibble and delay, and downright deafness when the order was delivered particularly
loudly, Wentworth had saved his province men and money.

Massachusetts had begged that he take over the defense of Fort
Dummer. Great Britain had sternly pointed out that the fort, now that
the boundary had been adjusted, lay within New Hampshire and had
ordered him to maintain it. Wentworth explained and temporized and
did nothing until the British government believed he could not have
understood what had been said.

Possibly His Excellency's attention was held by one particular clause
in Britain's command to the exclusion of the others. Fort Dummer was
on the west side of the Connecticut River, yet the government had
just insisted it was in New Hampshire. That outwardly simple remark
was an inwardly eloquent statement. It opened up vistas for exploita-
tion and profit, not while war was pulling everything apart, but later.

Peace must come at last, and then men of true ability would prosper.
Governors of inconspicuous provinces might vastly extend their influence and power. Britain had declared flatly that New Hampshire's
dominion extended over the river, into the territory on the west shore.
Well, then!

In a calm, cool room of his stately dwelling Governor Benning
Wentworth took a pinch of snuff, a sip of Madeira, and a deal of
thought to himself. Possibly he consulted maps; probably he read with
close attention, and consequent mental confusion, the boundary descriptions contained in the charters of the several New England provinces. He was specially interested in their westward limitations and in
New York's eastward.

This was reading that might have unsettled a less acute mind than
Benning Wentworth's. Under their respective charters, Connecticut's
western boundary was the Pacific Ocean; Massachusetts' extended to
the same water. New Hampshire's west line was more vaguely limited.
Wentworth's province extended "till it meets with our other governments."

All that was reasonably clear. But New York's charter, bestowed in

1664 by Charles II upon his brother, the then Duke of York, pronounced that province's eastern frontier to be the Connecticut River.

His Excellency Benning Wentworth took more snuff and smiled and hummed a little tune to himself. The whole problem was a confusion, a welter of conflicting claims, but men who fished in troubled waters proverbially were rewarded. It looked like good fishing weather.

Connecticut ran all the way to the Pacific, and New York extended to the Connecticut River. There had been trouble over that contradiction that several times had been quelled on the crumbling verge of war. Finally, a compromise had been made that seemed destined to stand. By its terms Connecticut's west line ran north and south approximately twenty miles east of the Hudson River. Thereafter, leap-frogging over New York's extent, Connecticut continued its triumphant, unmapped, unexplored, unpeopled way to the Pacific.

Wentworth laid the New York and Connecticut charter copies aside and took up Massachusetts'. The Bay Province's west line was not scar tissue of a dispute finally healed. It was an open wound. Massachusetts was many miles across the Connecticut and still thrusting westward, confirmed in her advance by her own charter. New York was beginning to snarl at the Bay Province's encroachments. New York owned everything Massachusetts now was settling. The Duke of York's charter said so.

Wentworth leaned back in his chair, swelling his jowls above his lace stock. His clever eyes were narrow, his heart beating faster. Opportunities for a man of parts with a fine business mind were not too plentiful in this new world. Opportunities for the governor of a small frontier colony were scanter still. One must not ignore possibilities; one must take eagerly whatever chance offered. If a governor was to make his province stronger, and himself wealthier, he could not afford to split hairs or weigh eyelashes—not if he intended to go into the wholesale real-estate business.

The plan in all its scope and profitable complexity already was taking form in his mind. This was not to be a piddling enterprise such as the Equivalent Landholders had undertaken. They were petty operators who, even now, were paying no attention to business, but instead were plaintively asking the parent government to what province, under the recent New Hampshire-Massachusetts boundary adjustment, they now belonged. Wentworth scorned quibblers. The successful man moved ahead and let others protest.

Land was the sole commodity the new country afforded in which a deft and daring promoter could make much money quickly. Agriculture gave a toilsome, small yield. Commerce was slow and hazardous. Of land there was a limitless supply. Among the folk who were overpopulating the lean farms of Connecticut there was a growing demand. Once the wars were ended and two-thirds of the perils of settlement thus abolished, there would be a scramble for land, an authentic boom. The wise, the clever man would prepare for that now.

His Excellency flicked snuff from his lace with a pudgy hand and considered ways and means. He thought comfortably of Great Britain's instructions. These had bidden him grant land to settlers. He considered, and at once resolved wholly to disregard, the parent country's additional and hampering instructions—no grants to any but genuine settlers; no more than 50 acres per person to any one family; no towns to be granted until fifty families each had cleared five acres therein; no towns to be finally established until one hundred families were in residence. These were Britain's restrictions. They were inconvenient. Wentworth would ignore them all.

The thing, to be profitable, must be done in a big way. Dickering with individual settlers would bring in only a slow trickle of cash. Better to sell whole towns outright to men with funds, adding enough free grants to men of influence to make the venture safer. Sell to proprietors and let them peddle their lots as they pleased. The country was painfully short of money, anyway. Rights to new lands would take the place of scant coinage. The enterprise would stimulate business. Wentworth would be the whole country's benefactor. All he needed now was land good enough to sell.

His Excellency thought of the virgin, unnamed territory across the Connecticut, where ranges climbed in uneven blue steps from the river to the central ridge—lovely, well-watered, empty land with deep forest mold that, once the woods had been cleared, would yield enormous crops. This would be ideal territory for the development he planned. All that was required for the great enrichment of New Hampshire—and of himself—was title to the tract. It need not be an absolutely airtight and inviolable title; even a moderately shaky would do.

The Governor's thoughts had gone a full circle. Now he was considering again that peremptory, easily ignored order from Great Britain, bidding New Hampshire to maintain Fort Dummer. Since that post was west of the Connecticut it should be New York property, but the British authorities proclaimed that it lay within New

Hampshire. What better guarantee than this, the relayed voice of His Majesty himself, could a keen operator want? If only this blundering war would cease!

That chapter of the conflict endured long enough for Benning Went-worth's plan to be well ordered before peace came in 1748. The following year, His Excellency granted his first town beyond the river and thereby kindled a bonfire that was to blaze with changing intensity on a variety of fuel and to the severe scorching of a number of persons for the subsequent forty-two years.

By accident, or maybe by design, New Hampshire's governor established his initial grant in the worst possible place to escape New York's attention.

The future Republic of Vermont was not designed by nature to be an independent state. The upthrust of the Green Mountains' backbone cut it longitudinally in half. One flank sloped down to the Connecticut, inviting settlement by New Hampshire; the other rolled without any geographical demarcation into the settled precincts of the Province of New York. Topographically, the country seemed destined to be split along the mountain's culminating ridge between the two neighboring and already organized colonies. Frequently in the coming years it seemed that such division could not be delayed much longer. A stubborn people were the only pins that held the two halves of their state together.

When Wentworth, in 1749, granted the town of Bennington to sixty proprietors, there was doubt whether New Hampshire could properly claim the eastward slope of the land. Her right to the western watershed was still more questionable. Despite this, it was in the west and as close as he could conveniently get to the north-south line twenty miles east of the Hudson, already Connecticut's west boundary, that His Excellency caused his namesake town to be established. Thus, he challenged New York authority. He had put his worst foot forward. Thereafter, he waited to see what would happen.

The charter creating Bennington was typical of all such documents issued subsequently by New Hampshire's governor. In ornate and misspelled periods these granted plots, usually six miles square, to proprietors of Wentworth's choosing. To compensate the Governor for getting much resounding eloquence into legal documents, the fortunate gentlemen paid a fee of about £20 sterling.

They also, directed by their charters, divided the land into as many lots as there were proprietors, plus six. These extra were distributed as follows: one lot to the Society for the Propagation of the Gospel in Foreign Parts; one to the Church of England; one to the first minister to settle in the town; one for the benefit of a town school; and two lots, not the worst of them, to Benning Wentworth himself.

His Excellency had already pocketed his fee. This was a most reasonable amount. He seems from the outset to have determined to issue many grants cheaply, rather than a few expensively. Cash payment was not enough. The Governor insisted upon a part—usually about five hundred acres—in each venture. He wished to be speculator as well as bank of issue.

The allotment of land to the Gospel Society and the Church was not a mere charitable gesture, either. These were powerful organizations. It was well to have them concerned in Wentworth's enterprise, in case—as just possibly might happen—the titles he had granted eventually should be disputed. Under such distressing circumstances it would be well to have influential allies like the Society and the Church helping in a fight against annulment.

The quitrent, or permanent tax imposed upon the land, was as moderate as the initial fee. It amounted to one shilling yearly for each hundred acres held. Wentworth's liberality in this regard cost him nothing and won him customers. The quitrent did not go to him, or to New Hampshire. It was tribute paid to the King himself.

His Majesty, who technically granted these charters "By and with the Advise of our Trusty and well beloved Benning Wentworth Esq our Governour and Com'ander in Chieff," made the usual reservation of all pine timber as future masts for the Royal Navy. Theoretically, none of this could be felled without a special permit from the Surveyor General of His Majesty's Woods. In fact, it was cut down regardless —if a man's pitch was pine-timbered how else could he clear his land? —and the surveyor general only winked, unless he had at the moment some grievance he needed to work off.

As for the royal warning against issuing grants to any but actual settlers and the limitations imposed on the establishment of towns, His Excellency blandly forgot all about those. He was perfectly satisfied to have the proprietors sell their shares if they wished. How were you to establish a market for securities if you did not get them into circulation? Meanwhile, he was waiting to see what New York would do about this townsite of Bennington established practically on its doorstep.

New York did nothing. New York ignored the whole matter so

long and so consistently that worry stirred in the oversize breast of Benning Wentworth. He had made his trial flight; he had prepared his test case; and he had obtained no reaction, no enlightenment, whatsoever. He could not go ahead comfortably with his project until he · learned how severely New York regarded it. When the continued silence became unendurable, he had to write the neighboring province and ask for information.

Quill pen scratching, wig a little awry, His Excellency contrived a letter that seemed more than adequate. It was gracious, smooth, and had just the proper casual air. He addressed the missive and forwarded it to George Clinton, His Majesty's Governor of New York.

The delicately composed communication enclosed a copy of Wentworth's royal commission, empowering him to grant unimproved land to settlers, and extending the province's western boundary "till it meets with our other governments."

In his accompanying letter, His Excellency spoke with patient forbearance of the number of persons who daily were pestering him for land grants and of his charitable wish to accommodate them. He also stressed his great unwillingness to intrude upon New York's domain and with affecting confidence asked Clinton what he had better do with these urgent applicants for land, "it being my intention to avoid as much as I can consistent with His Majesty's instructions, interfering with your government."

The correspondence, thus hesitantly launched, proceeded thenceforward more briskly. Clinton consulted with his council and by his reply on April 2, 1750, sowed seeds of strife from which another George Clinton, a later governor of New York, was to reap an abundant and supremely distressing harvest.

This first Clinton was the son of an English earl and an officer in the Royal Navy. His letter to Wentworth was as uncompromisingly blunt as a punch in the nose. Under the patent issued to the Duke of York by Charles II, New York's boundary extended to the Connecticut River. Thus Clinton wrote with an obvious desire not to discuss a settled matter further.

Wentworth regained his breath and balance quickly. He was too wily to force an open quarrel, too tenacious of his plan and its rich possibilities to surrender. His response was placating, with an air of wide-eyed ingenuousness.

Perhaps Clinton was right. Wentworth had no wish to argue with one who seemed so positive. Wentworth, as a matter of fact, would never have brought up the subject at all if he had not been genuinely puzzled. If, New Hampshire's governor asked, New York's territory extended to the Connecticut, how did it happen that Connecticut province's west boundary was so far to the west of that river? How did it happen, also, that Massachusetts' settlements were far across the stream and still moving west? Wentworth was not disputing; he was just asking.

This appeal for enlightenment, so guilelessly phrased, had no appreciable softening effect upon the Governor of New York. Clinton's return letter was dry and uncompromising: Connecticut's west boundary had been established by negotiation; Massachusetts had no business to be where she was. She was trespassing. And speaking of that, Wentworth would be pleased to get his newly granted town of Bennington out of New York territory. He was trespassing, too.

The Governor of New York clearly was a person on whom blandishments were wholly wasted. Wentworth's next letter, June 22, 1750, was pitched in a different key. He wouldn't withdraw the Bennington grant. He was not satisfied that it was upon New York land. Since the whole matter was confused, he suggested that the King be asked to clear it. Wentworth must have smiled to himself as he set this proposal down, remembering comfortably the partiality to New Hampshire His Majesty had displayed in the Massachusetts' boundary dispute.

Let the question rest, Wentworth urged, until the royal will could be made known. Meanwhile, he would make no more grants pending the decision. He did not think it worth while to mention that already, on May 11, he had granted the town of Halifax on what Clinton claimed was New York property.

Thus the matter hung. The governors agreed to submit their contentions to George II and his privy council, and to furnish each other with copies of their claims. Wentworth, somewhat bruised and disheveled mentally by his collision with Clinton, returned to consideration of his plan.

An ordinary man might wait for his king deliberately to settle his problems for him. An unambitious, or overpunctilious, might ignore the potentially profitable fact that the clamor for land was waxing among a farm-seeking people—and speculators as well. The demand echoed continually in Wentworth's ears, and there across the river lay an unlimited supply.

To be sure, His Excellency of New Hampshire had promised His Excellency of New York to establish no more towns in the debatable territory until its ownership was royally established. There were urgencies that rose above the limitations set by promises. More grants should be, must be, made for the good of an eager people, for the good of New Hampshire Province, for the good of Benning Wentworth.

In 1751, tentatively, almost furtively, the towns of Marlboro and Wilmington were established. These, like Halifax, lay to the east of the land's long summit where New York would not be likely to notice them. They were experimental, a hesitant poke in New York's ribs to see what the reaction would be. There was none. Wentworth paused, wondering how much further he might go. Reassurance from overseas all at once heartened him.

This was not the divine voice of the King, uttering unbreakable mandates. Royalty, for some inexplicable reason, never got around to adjudicating the New Hampshire-New York dispute until years thereafter. The new encouragement was a lesser, yet heartening, decision of the monarch's minor ministers. It was delivered, not at the behest of Wentworth, but of the holders of the first Vermont real-estate development, the Equivalent Lands.

Following the royal re-establishment of the New Hampshire-Massachusetts boundary, whereby their property had been taken out of the Bay Province's jurisdiction, the proprietors of the Equivalent Lands had moaned in bewilderment and had voiced increasingly loud cries for reassurance. Their holding was no longer in Massachusetts. Where was it then? In New York? New Hampshire?

The harried landlords could obtain no finally authoritative decision from colonial officials. In desperation, they appealed to the King, who deemed this a matter so trifling that his lawyers best had settle it and referred the question to Attorney General Sir Dudley Rider and Solicitor General Murray.

The findings of these gentlemen enlightened the proprietors of the Equivalent Lands and immensely comforted and stimulated His Excellency Benning Wentworth. The territory in question, Rider and Murray proclaimed, "is become a part of New Hampshire."

Thus, Governor Wentworth's province had been twice confirmed in its right to land west of the river—first by the royal assertion that Fort Dummer was within its domain; now, through the confirmatory finding by legal giants that the Equivalent Lands were her territory also.

Greatly reassured, Wentworth in 1752 granted two towns—Rockingham and Westminster—and in 1753, seven. His promise of abstinence to Clinton was but a dim and fading memory; and Clinton, having been recalled to England in the latter year, was in no position to remind him of it.

What prodigies of town granting, what immediate wealth in fees received and vast acreage in "Governor's rights" Wentworth planned for 1754 will never be known, for in that year came the culminating paroxysm of the French and Indian War. Five years later, His Excellency was waiting, impatiently, for the convulsions to subside. In 1760, to celebrate the fall of Quebec and the rubbing out of the Indian headquarters at St. Francis by Rogers, Governor Wentworth granted one town, Pownal, as deep in the territory New York claimed as Bennington had been. It was the first raindrop of a shower.

With the frontier freed at last, the clamor for farms began again and swelled as the land-hungry moved north. With one wary eye on New York, which seemed, inexplicably, to have gone to sleep, Wentworth went into action.

His Excellency granted sixty-three towns in 1761. Settlers received directly some of the lots. Speculators, who had no more idea of going to the frontier than to China, got more and proceeded at once by the eighteenth-century version of high-pressure salesmanship to develop a lively market in shares of the New Hampshire Grants.

Proprietors sold their rights to jobbers, who sold them to retailers, who peddled them throughout the colonies. Of the ninety-four proprietors of Ryegate, only one ever even visited his property. The canny and the guileless, the reckless and the prudent, succumbed to this first of America's Get Rich Quick campaigns. Rumors, carefully circulated, pushed up the prices of shares of certain towns. Disheartening reports, equally purposeful, depressed the shares of others. Pools were organized. Companies were formed.

The tide of migration was setting in strongly now. There was an increasing number of shabby folk who sought for land as fair, as fertile, as closely resembling paradise, as the gamblers' word pictures of Vermont. The ambitious and frequently defrauded ultimate consumers kept up the prices of the rights. Frequently they bought good land. As often, they purchased ledges or swamps. They, the actual settlers, were the eternally exploited folk—people with a little money and the hope to improve themselves.

Tales circulated by the speculators inflated the prices of rights to ridiculous extremes. One of these engaging gentlemen got the ear of President John Witherspoon, Princeton College's head, who invested heavily in shares of the New Hampshire Grants and suffered the usual losses of ministers who play the market.

Tidings spread by defrauded settlers, who bought title to land and on subsequent inspection found it worthless, disheartened the purchasers of property in the same townsites, making them willing to sell out for whatever they could get. Even some of the proprietors themselves set small value upon the rights Wentworth granted them. Jonathan Willard bought the shares of many of the grantees of Pawlet at the price of a new hat to each shareholder. He got more of them for a mug of flip apiece.

These were extreme cases of discouragement. In general, the market boomed, and the source of all this fevered and personally gratifying commerce was His Excellency Benning Wentworth himself, who for each town he granted received about £20 cash and two land shares. He was thriving on the sale of clouded titles.

The Governor cut down his output in 1762, possibly for fear of glutting the market, and only established nine towns; but he seems to have been reassured quickly, for in 1763 he granted thirty-seven more. He was doing very well indeed, and there was a lot of land still left. So far, he had distributed less than half of the territory of Vermont, and most of this was situated in the present southern counties of Bennington, Windham, Windsor, and Rutland. Business was good, speculators were active, and Wentworth was protecting himself against whatever retribution might overtake him, should the King calamitously decide that his "Trusty & well-beloved Governour" had sold a vast amount of property that belonged neither to him nor to the province he ruled.

Not all of the grantees were settlers or professional speculators. Many were persons of influence whom it would be well, in case trouble loomed ahead, to have on Wentworth's side. Upon these gentry the benevolent Governor literally crowded title to Vermont land. He gave it to such New England worthies as Thomas Pownall, former governor of Massachusetts, and Francis Bernard, the current governor; Meshech Weare of New Hampshire and Harrison Grey of Massachusetts, politicians; Eleazar Wheelock, founder of Dartmouth College, and Edward Holyoke, president of Harvard; Jonathan Edwards, theologian; Major Robert Rogers, Captain John Stark, General Timothy Ruggles.

The Governor's bounty was not restricted by geography. He stretched it to include many New Yorkers. Some of these had names of great value to a tricky promoter. Alsops, Schuylers, Governeurs, Schermerhorns, Ten Eycks, and Van Wycks were among the grantees. There was also a host of Burlings and Bogarts whose connection with Wentworth is obscure. They may have been debtors whom he paid off in this fashion. There were other folk who may have been dummies. Colonel Joseph Blanchard was proprietor in twelve towns; Captain Sam Robinson in ten; Samuel Averill in twenty.

His Excellency's charity, if it did not begin at home, spent a good deal of time there. He was not a man to neglect his friends and family, particularly as he might have need presently of both. Most of the leading men of New Hampshire received free grants. All of Wentworth's kin must have, unless he was singularly equipped with relations. He granted land to Samuel Wentworth of Boston, Samuel Wentworth of Portsmouth, and Samuel Wentworth, Jr.; to Major John Wentworth, John Wentworth, Jr., and Captain John Wentworth; to Ebenezer, Thomas, Foster, Daniel, Joshua, Hugh, and Hunking Wentworth.

The florid person in the crimson velvet cloak and the overfilled waistcoat rewarded friends and made others, discharged debts and established credit, enlisted influence and seduced opposition by offering all who might henceforth be useful or profitable to him opportunity to make money in the vast new real-estate development. By the time incredibly heedless New York roused itself to protest, Wentworth's beneficiaries had received title to almost half Vermont, and the thread of traffic in granted land had run in and out of New England's social and political structure until it would prove painfully intricate work to disengage it.

Beneath this impressive and potent assemblage of proprietors and their jackals were the folk who had bought the advertised and peddled titles in order to own the land these represented; who even now were clearing and grubbing in that soil which they were pathetically certain was to be theirs forever.

They had no knowledge that trouble was piling up ahead of them. Wentworth twitched, and the proprietors he had made flinched nervously when, in 1763, New York suddenly woke up to what was happening to land she held to be hers and spoke against the invasion. The men who swung axes in the clearings, the men who hoed in the newly made fields never heard the initial protest.

Cadwallader Colden uttered it, and he was a gentleman almost as remarkable as his name—a Scottish-born physician, mathematician, botanist, physicist, ethnologist, author, and inventor; a less benign reflection of Benjamin Franklin, whose friend he was; a forward-looking scientist and a reactionary politician; an aged, acid man.

Colden had been appointed lieutenant governor of New York in 1761. He was to hold that office all the rest of his life, at intervals running the colony when no royal governor was in charge. Ascetic, irascible, intellectual, he was the antithesis of the flamboyant Wentworth—a lean person with high sloping forehead, eyes heavily browed, a domineering nose, and a small, intemperate mouth.

The cold scorn in which he held the now audible colonial mutterings against edicts of the new king, George III, was visited, too, upon the equally insurgent and even more dubious land operations of Benning Wentworth. Colden wasted no time in dickering with New Hampshire's governor. He referred the case to authority with scientific directness, complaining of encroachments, not to His Excellency, the wholesale encroacher, but to the British Board of Trade. Colden did not content himself merely with citing the Duke of York's charter. He reinforced his appeal for decision of the boundary question in accordance with that document by a recital of his prejudice that was also an appeal to Britain's.

The Acting Governor compared the dangerous republicanism stirring in the New England colonies with New York's fine, loyal, conservative government "established as nearly as may be after the model of the English Constitution." He then asked the Board of Trade—the body directing the all-important commerce of Great Britain and its dependencies—whether, in the light of the political virtues of New York and the increasing sins of New England, it could "be good policy to diminish the extent of jurisdiction in His Majesty's province of New York to extend the power and influence of the others?"

Having misidentified Wentworth's shady real-estate enterprise as still another evidence of New England's irreverence, Colden rested his case. It was difficult, though, to sit remote and scornful while New Hampshire towns were popping up all over territory rightfully New York's. The thirty-seven grants made by Wentworth in 1763 were more than Colden could endure in silence, but when he spoke, he still ignored New Hampshire's governor and addressed his proclamation exclusively to New York officials.

Colden indirectly attacked His Excellency, the realtor, by informing all New York "judges, justices, and other civil officers" that their authority extended east to the Connecticut River "notwithstanding any contrarity of jurisdiction claimed by the government of New Hampshire." His tone then grew ominous, and he bade the sheriff of Albany County to furnish the New York government with the names of "all and every person or persons" who were squatting on New York land by New Hampshire's false authority. These persons were to be listed "so that they may be proceeded against according to law."

This was on December 28, 1763. News traveled slowly if at all through a snow-buried wilderness. Pinched folk in the cabins on what men were beginning to call "the New Hampshire Grants" were too concerned with the elemental possibilities of freezing or starving to pay heed to abstract jurisdictional disputes, but in his magnificent Portsmouth dwelling, Wentworth suddenly found that the Madeira was rank and his gout was worse.

He rallied quickly. New Hampshire had been embroiled in boundary litigation before and had emerged triumphant. He had also the Fort Dummer and the Equivalent Lands decisions to comfort him, but this dismal bookworm in New York should not be permitted to make such statements unchallenged. They were an affront to the dignity of Benning Wentworth and New Hampshire, his province. Besides, they would have a bearish influence on the share market.

Wentworth's counter-proclamation was designed to reassure proprietors, speculators, and settlers; but it had the windiness of an uneasy man. He found Colden's contention "of a very extraordinary nature." He scoffed at New York's claim of jurisdiction to the Connecticut and pointed out that "she never laid out and settled one town in that part of His Majesty's lands since she existed as a government." This was not precisely true. New York had issued patents to lands along the Walloomsac and Hoosic rivers, in what is now extreme southwest Vermont. The townsites of Bennington and Pownal, granted later by Wentworth, intruded upon these.

His Excellency, however, found this no time for hesitation over facts. His proclamation announced that the Duke of York's charter was obsolete and further insisted, without clear warrant, that whatever happened, however the King decided the joint appeal of New York and New Hampshire that had been lying on the royal desk for almost fourteen years, His Majesty certainly would confirm grants already made by his "Trusted & well-beloved Governour."

Wentworth echoed Colden by ordering his own civil officers to consider the New Hampshire Grants within their bailiwicks hereafter and "to deal with any persons who may presume to interrupt the inhabitants or settlers on said lands." Thereafter, to show that his natural forces had not abated, he granted before the autumn of 1764 the towns of Hubbardton, Wardsboro, Readsboro, Corinth, and Dover.

This marked His Excellency's final appearance in the real-estate field; this was his swansong. It was choked off in mid-verse by fell tidings from overseas. The King and his Privy Council at last had got around to considering the long-delayed question of the New York-New Hampshire boundary line. His Majesty, it was announced, July 26, 1764, at last had made up his mind and "doth accordingly hereby order and declare the western banks of the river Connecticut from where it enters the province of Massachusetts Bay, as far north as the 45th degree of north latitude, to be the boundary line between the said two provinces of New Hampshire and New York."

One hundred and thirty-one towns established by Wentworth thus were pronounced illegally granted; countless gamblers in rights found that these had become worth no more than their weight in paper and ink; hundreds of settlers in the already established handful of towns learned, as the dire news slowly spread, that they had paid something for nothing and had bent their shoulders and cramped their hands to improve land they never had owned.

His Excellency Benning Wentworth, having sowed the wind, endured in office only a brief time longer. He does not seem to have been ousted or even reproved for his blandly unscrupulous raid upon New York's real estate. He retired in 1766 of his own volition, full of years and self-bestowed grants amounting to 65,000 acres; and his nephew, John Wentworth, governed New Hampshire in his stead. By the time the uncle resigned, the whirlwind of his planting already had begun to rise.

The storm gathered with the deliberation of tempests that are to be long enduring. New York made no immediate move; Wentworth had no argument to offer. His Excellency's career as a promoter of real estate was over.

The proprietors were stunned. They also were ruined. Or were they? They sought for a loophole, for a toehold that would support a quibble, with the frantic intensity of desperate men, and at length found one. It was slight but it might serve.

The King had declared the west bank of the Connecticut "to be the boundary line between the said two provinces." "To be!" There was ground for at least faint hope in that infinitive. Surely it had a flavor of futurity. Did it not mean "to be henceforth"? If so, it did not blight earlier land grants. It secured them and merely restrained New Hampshire from making further.

To this tenuous argument the proprietors henceforth clung. "To be" was a small straw, but it must be their cause's support. Seldom have four letters of the alphabet been foundation for as much subsequent strife.

While these resolutely hopeful gentlemen tried to fortify themselves on scant provender, those who actually were settling the land heard with indifference of the transfer of its ownership.

That stolidity beneath indefinite menace was to be their abiding attitude in the years ahead. Not until the danger became material, not until they felt its actual impact, would Vermonters gird themselves and move to meet it. They were not, now or later, sluggards or neutrals, as their enemies charged, but very simply a folk who were not to be bothered by empty threats or hidden menaces.

They learned early how spendthrift and purposeless concern over formless things could be; how frequently problems, if left alone, solved themselves. Always they waited until they could see clearly the peril's actual outline before they moved against it. Roused at last, they were purposeful, tenacious, and extremely deft.

These people waited now. There was gossip in the settlements, talk in the cabins, but when the event moved forward it was New York that pushed it.

Months after the King's decision, on May 22, 1765, Colden spoke. His utterance was typically oblique, for he addressed, not the folk who had settled the Grants, but his own surveyor general. The Acting Governor admitted the obvious, pointing out that the ousting of people who had bought their farms from New Hampshire "might be ruinous to themselves and their families." He bade the surveyor general not to survey for the purpose of establishing New York towns on any land where men already were actually settled.

This was encouraging, but Colden was one of the two-sided men who limit their probity to their social and intellectual avocations. The benevolence that flavored his instructions was tempered by the fact that the day before he uttered them he had issued to a dummy list of patentees a town of 26,000 acres in the Battenkill Valley to be called Princetown. This sprawling tract overlapped the New Hampshire-granted towns of Arlington, Manchester, Sunderland—all of which already had been settled.

In Arlington, numerous occupied farms and the land on which the lank, sandy Indian fighter, Remember Baker, was building saw and grist mills had their titles shot out from under them, not by contesting settlers from New York, but by land gamblers; for the dummy patentees had transferred their holdings at once to Attorney General John Taber Kempe, James Duane, and Walter Rutherford, notorious speculators.

This was an age when political appointment was considered a larceny license, and Colden seemed to find no difficulty in reconciling his tolerant announcement with his rapacious action. Before the month had ended, he had sold further improved land in Bennington town to a Rev. Mr. Slaughter, who immediately filed ejectment suits against its occupants. Colden also had issued patent for 10,000 more Bennington acres to a malodorous Irish manipulator, Crean Brush.

The Acting Governor's staunch loyalty to his sovereign, his dislike of New Englanders and their rebellious tendencies, was responsible for much of his subsequent ruthlessness. The Stamp Act now was quickening disorder throughout the colonies, and the reactionary Cadwallader's scant sympathy for republicanism was not heightened by the fact that a mob besieged him in his New York mansion, November 1, hanged him in effigy, and burned his stable and contents, including the governor's state coach.

There was also the matter of military grants to temper still further Colden's expression of original benevolence. At the close of the last war, the King had awarded gifts of land to discharged soldiers—5000 acres to a field officer, 3000 to a captain, 2000 to a subaltern, 200 to a noncommissioned officer, and 50 to a private. Discharged veterans had some difficulty in turning this promised bounty into actual land. No fees for governors came out of these military grants. They were free gifts from a grateful monarch, and the colonies' heads were not particularly interested in giving away land out of which they themselves would get nothing.

The military grants, incidentally, were only another phase of the real-estate racket which had passed from New Hampshire's hands into New York's. At the time of the still-long-distant settlement of strife between Vermont and New York it was determined that, of three hundred and twelve military patents issued by the latter state in the territory of the former, only five still stood in the names of the original patentees. All others had been sold to gamblers.

There was further reason for Colden's waxing hostility to the settlers on the Grants. This cause was close to his heart, for it was financial and he was a Scot. Wentworth, upholding a system of small profits and mass production, had charged in the neighborhood of £20 sterling— the price varied a little—for each town he established. These towns averaged 15,000 acres. The quitrent, which went to the King, not the Governor, was one shilling yearly per hundred acres. The fee New York imposed was £14 sterling per thousand acres, or better than ten times Wentworth's price for the same amount of land. Quitrent for a hundred acres was two shillings, sixpence.

It hurt Colden's thrifty soul to see people whom he did not like enjoying such bargains. The pain was intensified by the fact that they were depriving him of much cash. The fee for a New York patent was distributed among several office holders, but the governor or acting governor got most of it. The King, too, was losing money at the rate of one shilling, sixpence yearly on New Hampshire-granted land.

If Colden let the settlers alone, he felt they would be getting too much for their money and he would be getting nothing at all. He determined to squeeze a New York fee from them or else to transfer their holdings to the old soldiers who were clamoring for the land their king had promised them. Under this system either patriotism or New York's governor was bound to be rewarded.

Avarice, vindictiveness, and expediency all combined to stiffen Colden's antipathy to the intrusive New Englanders. In June, 1766, with the smell of his burned stable still in his nose, he grimly ordered all holders of New Hampshire grants to appear "as soon as may be" before himself and his council with their titles and attorneys and receive justice.

This was ominous, but it was the New Hampshire proprietors, not the settlers, who first took alarm. There was much feverish scurrying about by these gentlemen and the circulation of a round robin which received what the proprietors said was a thousand but actually was 648 signatures. Power of attorney was accorded by this paper to a group of nineteen who were to prepare a petition to the King. Of these nineteen, ten were citizens of New York, six of Connecticut, and only three —Captain Samuel Robinson of Bennington, Ebenezer Cole of Shaftsbury, and Jeremiah French of Dover—were actual settlers on the Grants.

The petition, as eventually formulated, mourned over the high fees demanded by Colden for reconfirmation of New Hampshire titles and begged His Majesty, with the pained earnestness of gentlemen about to lose a lot of cash, for a restoration of the grants to New

Hampshire jurisdiction "as every Emolument and Convenience, both publick and private, are in your Petitioners' humble Opinion clearly and strongly on the side of such Connection."

Weathered old Captain Sam Robinson, Bennington's first settler, was chosen to present this document to the King. Pitt, the apostle of appeasement as far as the unruly colonies were concerned, was back in power when Robinson got to London, and Colden had been succeeded in New York by another royal governor, Sir Henry Moore.

Captain Sam did not look upon His Majesty's countenance, but he did gain the ear of Lord Shelburne, Minister of State for the Colonies. What he poured in drew from Shelburne a blistering letter to Moore, warning him not to molest actual settlers on the Grants and terming the fees New York was trying to squeeze from them "so unjustifiable that His Majesty is not only determined to have the strictest enquiry made into the circumstances of the charge, but expects the clearest and fullest answer to every part of it."

There was a plea in the Robinson petition to which no one seems to have paid special attention at the time, so filled was that document with justifications of the grant-holders and accusations against New York. Toward its end, the petition begged not only for ratification of the Wentworth grants but also suggests "that the said Country may be erected into a distinct government."

The small straw pointed, unheeded, the course of an impending wind that was to blow long and blow high. Robinson was an actual settler, and already these settlers' wish to own themselves had been born. If, the petition continued, the Grants could not be made a separate colony, its people would be content with inclusion in the Province of New Hampshire. The time was near when this alternative no longer would interest them. Freedom was an early crop in the Grants' newly cleared soil, and it grew fast.

The Robinson petition was echoed by a protest from the Society for the Propagation of the Gospel in Foreign Parts against New York's high-handedness. Wentworth's pious charity in cutting the Society a slice of his melon thus yielded its expected dividend.

Moore, a gentleman of no great fortitude, prepared with the aid of James Duane, a leading speculator in Grants Lands, a vague and voluminous reply wherein he blamed the Stamp Act disorders for his failure to confirm the settlers' titles, denied demanding fees from anyone, and charged that Robinson never had been a captain but only "a driver of an ox cart for the suttlers." This last was no more accurate than the rest of Moore's response, for Robinson had led a company with honor in the last two French wars.

Bush fighting pleased Captain Sam better than London diplomacy, for he wrote home: "It is hard to make a man believe the truth when there is ready money on the other side" and, having delivered this inclusive comment on statecraft, fell ill of smallpox and died with his mission uncompleted.

He had sowed good seed; for, July 24, 1767, the King published an order in council forbidding New York to regrant any New Hampshire titles "until the King's further pleasure should be known."

This encouraged the proprietors and moved speculators to look with a little less remorse upon their unsold parcels of rights. Also, it slackened the slowly gathering, long-enduring Yankee wrath of the settlers themselves, but only briefly.

Most of the folk who had paid their painfully hoarded money for land they were even more painfully clearing were from Connecticut and had a naturally acquired dislike for the Province of New York, which had a remarkable gift for making itself offensive to its immediate neighbors.

Strife over the New York-Connecticut line, which had been settled and reopened again with heart-burnings and hot speech and gestures that verged upon outright war, and then settled once more, had burned into tough, retentive spirits abiding suspicion of Yorkers and all their works. It would not be overhard to quicken the coal of resentment into flame, and New York was to furnish an abundance of wind and fuel.

If Benning Wentworth was the grandfather of the Vermont Republic, New York was its actual and detested sire, for New York impregnated a young land with an abhorrence that eventually solidified loose and divergent elements into a state. Hatred of Yorkers was the prime, unifying passion of Vermont. Antipathy to Great Britain was milder and more unwarranted.

During the colonial period, the mother country repeatedly intervened on behalf of the Grants settlers. The people, holding land under dubious titles, were regarded with sympathy and heard with patience by the British authorities. The folk of the Grants had no legitimate grievance against Great Britain before the Revolution. The governors of New York, the land speculators of New York, were the oppressors, not King George III.

His Majesty's order in 1767 that the people of the Grants be left alone awed Moore and won brief respite for the settlers. Sir Henry, obedient to the command, devoted his talents thereafter more to organization than to plunder. He incorporated the region about Bennington into Albany County and established a new county, Cumberland, to include all other settlements. In 1769 Moore died, and during the year that elapsed before the arrival of Lord Dunmore, his successor, Cadwallader Colden again was acting governor. Almost at once the horse that Moore had ridden lightly began to buck under the aged politico-scientist's intractable weight.

Colden's scant fondness for Yankees had not been increased by the waxing disregard for royal authority displayed throughout most of New England. He was eighty-one years old now and, though age had impaired his memory so that he seems to have had no recollection of His Majesty's warning to leave the Grants settlers in peace, his appetite for patent fees, his energy in distributing land, would have been worthy of a much younger man. In the thirteen months before Dunmore's arrival he issued patents for 600,000 acres.

Deaf to the wails of New Hampshire proprietors who saw their property swept away, blind to the stiff, narrow-eyed faces of settlers whose titles he was abolishing, Colden encouraged the haling of the disputes into the courts. He wanted a test case; he wished this mare's-nest in the Grants settled, legally and finally.

James Breakenridge had bought a farm in the town of Bennington under New Hampshire title. His property was also the property of New Yorkers under the earlier Walloomsac patent. A writ of ejectment was issued against Breakenridge by New York authorities.

Isaiah Carpenter of Shaftsbury occupied a farm granted by Wentworth in 1765. His land was included in a military patent issued by Colden in 1769 to Major John Small, late of His Majesty's 42nd Highlanders. Carpenter was served with an ejectment writ, refused to obey it, and Small brought suit against him in the Albany Courts.

Recipients of New Hampshire's grants—proprietors, gamblers, and settlers alike—were smitten by this action. Men of large holdings who saw their fortunes about to be abolished by law banded together once more to frame protests and compose petitions. The folk who lived in little houses on half-cleared land also moved to meet the peril—by a different and straighter road.

Proprietors whose titles were menaced directly by the suit of Major Small met several times in Shaftsbury and Canaan, Connecticut, and discussed ways and means of saving their investments, without arriving at any clear method. It appeared that the law would take its disastrous course. They were intimately concerned in the fate of Carpenter, but they did nothing effective at first beyond contributing each man of them two shillings for the man's defense.

No funds were needed for James Breakenridge. The writ of ejectment had not been served on him. Breakenridge had placed his faith, not in the proprietors of Bennington, but in its settlers. He had turned to his neighbors for aid. The obdurate wrath that was to distinguish aroused Vermonters already was kindling.

John Munro, New York justice of the peace in Shaftsbury, a stubborn and truculent Scotsman who was to uphold New York's cause in subsequent disorders with considerable wear and tear to himself, rode out from Albany, October 17, 1769, with the ejectment writ in his pocket and in company with a surveying crew who were to prove the illegal situation of the Breakenridge farm.

There was a splendor of leaves on the little rolling hills as the party jogged up the winding Walloomsac Valley, and the warmth of a pleasant duty about to be performed lay in the Justice's heart. He held his Yankee neighbors in small regard. It would be a distinct gratification to order James Breakenridge off the farm he had made.

Hoofs drummed across a small, solid bridge. Ahead was the square house Breakenridge had built himself, and in the field its owner and his hired men were shocking corn. The Justice grinned. Little did James know what was about to happen to him and his corn and his house and his farm. Little, for that matter, did Justice Munro.

Breakenridge and his helper were not alone in the field. A group of men lingered in the middle distance conspicuously doing nothing at all. They looked intently at their feet, or inspected the sky. They were drab and lean and inexplicably idle, there in the bright October sunlight; and cradled in the arm of each was a long, well-kept firelock.

Some of the zest for his legal duty left Munro's spirit as he and his surveyors dismounted. Breakenridge looked up from his work. Then he and Samuel Robinson, son of Captain Sam, came forward to meet the intruders.

What happened then never has been wholly established, so divergent are the tales of those involved. Breakenridge and Robinson went to Portsmouth after the affair in the hope of enlisting New Hampshire's aid and there made affidavit that they approached the surveyors and asked them politely not to go to work.

They attested further that Munro displayed his credentials, but that they told him, still very politely, that they were commissioners of the town of Bennington and that no survey by New York could be permitted there. After that, Breakenridge and Robinson swore, they went quietly into the house. They couldn't remember what became of Munro and his party.

Colden published another version. It was contained in the wrathful proclamation he issued, ordering the arrest of James Breakenridge, Samuel Robinson, Jr., Moses Robinson, Nathaniel Horner, Henry Walbridge, and the Rev. Jedediah Dewey, pastor at Bennington. These men the acting governor accused of being "authors and actors in a riot."

The details of the alleged riot are blurred, but Colden's proclamation insists that the participants "interrupted and opposed" the New York officials, that they behaved "tumultuously and riotously," and "by insults and menaces" scared the Yorkers so thoroughly "that, apprehensive for the safety of their persons, they found it necessary to relinquish any further attempts to perform the trust so reposed in them"—which is probably the most ornate way of saying that they ran.

None of the authors and actors in the riot was ever arrested for his alleged violent misdeed. Breakenridge, when Munro had ridden away, went back to his corn again. His armed audience hemmed and hawed and at last decided that mebbe they'd go home. They believed there was small chance of the Justice's immediate return. If he kept up the rate at which he had started, he most probably was clear all the way to Albany by then.

Carpenter and other like unfortunates were in the toils of the law and were about to be haled into court. They had been patient, unresisting men, and look at what happened to them. Jim Breakenridge was free still, wasn't he? Maybe patience could be carried too far. Maybe you had to work on a Yorker to make him see sense.

So the talk ran in the small houses of the Bennington settlers; so the heretofore-unresisting who had made their pitches in good faith on the New Hampshire Grants began to move slowly, half-blindly, thrust on by events toward a yet-undiscerned goal.

Meanwhile, the proprietors interested in the Carpenter case were holding more meetings and getting nowhere in particular. What they needed, they decided at length, was some one man who would take the whole matter of defense in hand and manage it competently, forcefully.

If forcefulness was their chief need, there was a person living in Salisbury with an abundance. He was not a proprietor, it was true, but he had trumpeted his opinions of New York and its acting governor at the proprietors' meetings. He knew the Grants, too. During the winter of '67 he had wandered, hunting, up one side of the land and down the other.

He was a noisy person, yet a crafty—not as slick perhaps as his young brother, Ira, yet nobody's fool. The proprietors decided to entrust the defense of Carpenter to his hands. There would be compensations, even if he did not prove the ideal man for the job. At least there would be more peace in Salisbury with him out of it for a spell. The proprietors offered their candidate the post, and Ethan Allen accepted it eagerly.

IV Portrait of Two Brothers

MARY BAKER ALLEN rode the horse and carried her firstborn son in her arms. Joseph, her husband, drove the cows along before them, following the blazed trail twenty-five miles northwest from Litchfield to Cornwall. There, in the Connecticut frontier village—a huddle of log houses squatting on half-cleared land beside the falls of the Housatonic—Joseph, in the summer of 1740, made his pitch.

The man, who was a great grandson of that Samuel Allen who came to America in 1632, found immediate favor among his fellow settlers. He was moderator of Cornwall's first town meeting and thereafter selectman all his life. It is doubtful whether his neighbors' impressions of his baby boy were as pleasant. The infant must have possessed even then some portion of his mighty adult voice and the willingness to use it on slight provocation. He bellowed all his days. He had been practicing for a year and a half by July, 1740. Ethan was his name, signifying in the Hebrew "firm." It was an appropriate title, though possibly a little inadequate.

Seven more children, six of them biblically christened, were born to the Allens in the fifteen last years of the father's life—Heman, Heber, Levi, Zimri, Lydia, Lucy, and Ira. They needed all the sanctification Scriptural names could afford them, for they were a vital and turbulent brood, weaned on strife and craving it all their days. Amid the rigors and the brutal realities of the New England frontier, mortals had to battle with bodies and minds to exist at all. The weaklings died early. All of the Allen children survived.

"My mother," Ethan is supposed to have said, excluding himself with unwonted modesty, "and Mary Magdalen are the only two women who ever were delivered of seven devils."

The epigram is apochryphal; but then, so in part is the man. He is half stalwart and violent flesh, half myth. Legends, which have a disconcerting habit of surpassing dry historical record in actual verity, clung to him. They still dangle from every angle of his person, magnifying his raw-boned breadth, his six feet, two inches of height into

60

the stature of the demigod, so wholly racial, so typical of his people that today Ethan Allen has become almost indistinguishable from the state he served with such vehement dedication. He and Vermont, in some odd way, are so nearly one that you cannot think of the land without also thinking of the man.

This is more remarkable because no actual physical portrait of Allen exists. It is strange that this should be. Vanity never was one of his deficiencies, yet he left us no material picture of himself. His intemperate deeds, his furious speech are all he bequeathed posterity. Like Jehovah, whose active enemy he was, his face is hidden. There remain only the thunderous echoes of a voice.

Insurgence was Ethan Allen's foremost characteristic. It was his instinctive reaction to existence. He was too crammed with vigor of body and mind for peace or decorum to bridle him. He fretted under compulsion; he fought against authority, whether it were the local selectmen, New York, the British Government, or the Lord of Hosts. His terrific vitality could not be slackened by the hard and demanding life of the frontier.

When he had performed labor that would break the average man today, there was still an excess of steam in his boiler, and the fires beneath it could not be drawn. The diversions of his age did not suffice. Drinking, brawling, hunting, forest-roaming, horse-breaking were not enough. He continually itched and fretted for adversaries more worthy of the attention of Ethan Allen.

His brain was as truculent and as difficult to appease as his robust frame. His thoughts ran far beyond the endless contriving and the heavy routine of managing a farm. He had the trader's instinct without which no Yankee of his day was born and long survived, and an immense and bellicose vitality boiling over. From boyhood on, he was entangled in business enterprises, but rarely were these conducted with the forethought and gravity typical of his breed. Most of his earlier ventures yielded the minimum of profit and the maximum of disorder.

Whether he were dickering for pigs, swapping acreage, or forming a company to exploit a lead mine, the transaction proceeded in a sulphurous cloud of quarrels, denunciations, law suits, personal assaults, and an astounding obligato of profanity. Ethan was canny. He could build and see clearly the outlines of a satisfactory deal, but personal prejudices—no one ever was equipped with more—got in the way of smooth fulfillment. He was disappointed if business was not attended by riot.

His profanity was spectacular even in a day when men were more resourceful in such matters, though trespass against the Third Commandment was a statutory crime. This may be one reason why Ethan swore so wholeheartedly and with such a gift for improvisation. His prowess is legendary. Apparently, he lifted blasphemy to the level of an art that since has degenerated into the piddling, ejaculatory cursing of today.

His was a performance requiring a preliminary deep breath and subsequent uncommon powers of imagery. Few of his oaths have come down to us entire. Auditors, deafened and aghast, would have considered it a mortal sin to perpetuate them on paper. One early effort, however, got itself embalmed in a law suit at Cornwall, outcome of a quarrel with the selectmen who reported that Ethan said:

"By Jesus Christ, I wish I may be bound down in Hell with old Beelzebub a thousand years in the lowest pit of Hell and that every little insipid devil should come along by and ask the reason of Allen's lying there, it should be said in cool blood that he would have satisfaction of Lee and Stoddard and did not fulfill it." '

Later, no doubt, he improved considerably upon this youthful essay.

Cornwall, it appears, produced no mortal adversaries worthy the efforts of his avid, contentious mind. There remained, however, the Head of New England's theocracy—Jehovah Himself. Lacking other worthy opponents, Ethan assaulted Him.

Dr. Thomas Young, Yale graduate and newly made physician, had come to the settlement there to serve the equivalent of a modern internship. It was his purpose to try out his skill in purging and blood-letting upon hardy frontiersmen before taking his proven art to more profitable climes. In Young, Ethan found a fellow spirit, a companion mind. The physician was steeped in deism and eighteenth-century freethinking. His and the restless young giant's iconoclastic conferences must have been prototypes of ten million subsequent "bull sessions" in a thousand college dormitories. This was Ethan's nearest approach to a formal education.

Young and his crony pored over the Bible, not with reverence but to dig out of its context apparent inconsistencies and impossibilities. They considered the performances of the Hebrew tribal deity with a daring and, to them, a delicious scorn. Together and in secret they commenced a manuscript. This was to proclaim to the world the frailties of Scripture and the far more estimable beliefs of Young and

Allen. The physician departed, seeking more profitable practice, before the script was finished. He took it with him.

A quarter-century later, Allen encountered his boyhood friend again in Philadelphia. Young gave him the uncompleted book, preserved all these years. Allen took it home to Vermont with him, revised, expanded it, and presented it to the world under the title—he was never modest or brief about such matters—of "Reason, the only Oracle of Man or a Compendious System of Natural Religion, Alternately Adorned with Confutations of a Variety of Doctrines incompatible to it; Deduced from the most exalted Ideas which we are able to form of the Divine and Human Characters and from the Universe in General."

Publication of this turgid and, to modern minds, intensely tiresome heterodoxy was a stench and a scandal in 1784 when a printer in Bennington, more valiant than many of his trade who had declined the task, finally produced it. It brought down on Allen's head the curses of the religious, which he was used to by then, and the enmity of all ministers of the Gospel. He was inured to enmity, too.

He was prodigiously proud of his book. It proved what he had been proclaiming to the skeptical for years: that he was by nature and inclination a philosopher. He was no such thing. He was a sensationally full-blooded man of action—a hard rider, a hard drinker, a hard worker, and a hard swearer. He was a woods-running, pot-tossing, sword-rattling braggart, who, when the pinch came, in some baffling way managed to fulfill his boasts. His quarrel with Jehovah was not intellectual. In life's unfortunately recurrent periods of calm, the God of Israel was the only available adversary.

No one—certainly no one in supposedly grim and prim old New England—ever lived with greater zest for life than Ethan Allen. No one indulged that appetite more indiscriminately or with less regard for the feelings of prudish bystanders. In all things he was vehement— in speech and writing, in brawling and tippling. To only one indulgence of full-blooded men he seems to have been immune or, until late in life, indifferent.

His first marriage, to a woman six years his senior, was accomplished with hardly more formality than the rutting buck observes, and he paid her little more subsequent heed than the doe receives. Mary Brownson was a mild, a complaining, a wholly illiterate wife. She was a trial to him; he was an affliction to her. No reflected glow of his fiery personality warmed her. She bore him children as she performed the other heavy chores that were a frontierswoman's duty. When she died, her husband does not seem to have mourned her. Possibly, she missed existence as little.

Allen was forty-six and had lived through enough activity to supply the lives of half a dozen ordinary men when love came to him, apparently for the first time. Fanny Montresor Buchanan was the sprightly widow of a British army officer and the daughter of an energetic twice-widowed mother who had recently taken herself a third husband. In the winter of 1784, the older woman, who was now Mrs. Patrick Hall, came to Westminster, Vermont, from New York City to locate lands left her by an earlier spouse, and Fanny accompanied her mother. They boarded in the big square home of Stephen Bradley where, since the legislature was in session, sundry leaders of the state also lodged.

Here the gay and accomplished young woman from New York met General Ethan Allen, until recently commander in chief of all the armed forces of the Vermont Republic. How often she encountered him and what was the nature of his wooing, no man can say.

On February 9, 1784, the judges of the superior court breakfasted with Stephen Bradley. They hailed Allen as he entered, but he tramped through the room and into an adjoining chamber where Fanny, standing on a stool, rearranged china in a cupboard. Even now the man's voice was not tempered. The judges heard him announce that he was leaving Westminster for his home in Sunderland.

"So," he added briskly, "if we are to be married, now is the time."

The stool creaked as Fanny climbed down.

"Very well," she said at last, "but give me time to get my joseph."

A few minutes later, wrapped in her joseph, a brilliant cloak, and ready to travel, Fanny appeared with Allen before the still-breakfasting judges.

"This young woman," her escort told Judge Moses Robinson, "and I have concluded to marry each other and to have you perform the ceremony."

"For myself," he pursued, fearful lest they deem him subservient to convention, "I have no great opinion of such formality and from what I can discover, she thinks as little of it as I do, but as a decent respect for the opinions of mankind seems to require it, you will proceed."

Robinson floundered through the service, far more agitated than the bridegroom, who was co-operative until the Judge asked him whether he promised to live with this woman "agreeably to the laws of God."

"Wait," Allen bade, then scowled and muttered to himself, staring through the small-paned window at the white glare of the wintry morning.

"The law of God as written in the great book of nature?" he asked at last. "Yes."

When the ceremony had ended and Fanny's baggage and guitar had been stowed in his sleigh, her husband drove her across the mountains to her new home.

They were a queerly matched pair, this forty-five-year-old animate explosion and the gay, civilized wife who was twenty-one years his junior, yet she seems to have found in him tenderness that no one else had discovered. She quickened the one passion in his extensive stable that had not already been wind-broken by hard riding. She learned to manage him, and he loved it and her. She even modified his drinking habits.

Fanny drove a nail into their bedroom wall, and upon this Allen was to hang his watch when he returned late at night from his frequent sorties "on affairs of state." If the timepiece dangled therefrom in the morning, she accepted his boast that he had come home sober; if it lay on the floor, he had no excuse.

So ardent was the warrior's devotion that it overflowed on one occasion into surprising verse. On the flyleaf of the first copy of his *Oracles of Reason*, he wrote:

This Book is a present from the Author to his Lady

> *Dear Fanny wise, the beautiful and young,*
> *The Partner of my joys, my dearest self,*
> *My love, pride of my life, your sexes pride*
> *And partner of sincere politeness,*
> *To thee a welcome compliment I make*
> *Of treasures rich, the Oracles of Reason.*

Ethan liked his book. He admired everything he ever did.

Psychologists may find in his belated love an unreliable key to his character. It may be that his vast vitality, the immense store of energy packed and fretting inside him, unduly protracted his emotional adolescence. Certainly, the things he prized most in his life were those in which youth places the highest store. Young men followed him because he had what they wanted most.

He was a skilled woodsman and a mighty hunter, using his smooth-bore firelock with riflelike accuracy. His stamina and resource were phenomenal even among the tough forest rangers of his time. Once, hunting in what later became the town of Poultney, he killed a deer, dressed and skinned it, and hung carcass and pelt in a tree, placing his hat upon the trophy so that the human scent would keep bears, panthers, and crows away. Thereafter, he slew another deer and, after adorning the hung body with his jacket, hunted further. The third he shot was protected by his shirt, the fourth by his breeches and, shod but otherwise naked, he followed a fifth until he killed this. Wrapped in the freshly taken skin, he returned to his camp for aid in recovering his meat and his wardrobe.

Late one autumn, night overtook him in the woods, fireless, shelterless. Rain that had drenched him turned to snow, and waxing cold froze his wet clothing. He was lost, and he knew that until the morrow he would be unable to find his way. Already numbed and ice-sheathed, he prepared to spend the night where he was. In a clearing he tramped a circle on the snow, and for twelve hours stubbornly trod that ring.

The hissing storm tried to blow him down. Trees looked upon the weary giant slogging his circuit, falling to be revived by the sting of snow upon his face, rising to lurch forward once more. Dawn found him thus. Landmarks revealed themselves, and Ethan, his outer clothing cased in ice, made his way back to camp.

His body was the ideal tool for the strong, erratic spirit within it, incredibly tireless, immensely vital. He could grip a bushel bag of salt in his teeth and fling it backward over his head with a heave of his mighty torso. There was no horse he could not ride, no man he could not outwrestle, no draught of flip or sling, perry, metheglin, or punch too deep for him to drain.

He lived heroically according to the standards of his day; and, in whatever brawl, predicament, or adventure he was involved, saw himself surely as its hero. He had, however, a rough and salty sense of humor, though, like most exhibitionists, he never directed it against himself.

While Mary Brownson, his first wife, still lived and nagged, Ethan one night mounted his horse with considerable difficulty before Stephen Fay's tavern in Bennington. It was apparent that the "affairs of state" that he had discussed in the low, wide room, where the legend "Council Chamber" was cut on the stone above a fireplace, had been plentiful and potent. Fellow tipplers had noticed his condition and, begging sheets from Landlord Fay, had stolen out to the graveyard past which they knew that Ethan must ride.

Ghostly figures rose from among the gravestones, and Allen's horse shied at the hollow sounds they uttered, but its rider reined in. He bellowed to the apparitions:

"If ye be angels of light, I fear ye not; if ye be devils from hell, come home with me and welcome. I married your sister."

When the affronted colony of New York set a price upon his head and promised eagerly to hang him if he were taken, Allen wrote to a well wisher who had warned him: "A late account from there [Albany] informs me that by Virtue of a Late Law in Province, they are Not Allowed to hang any man before they have ketched him."

The raw drama of early Vermont in which he played a leading role was not enough for him. He strove to heighten its spectacle, to adorn its crudities with romance. Somewhere he had learned about Robin Hood. To his mind he was that hero's reincarnation—though it is questionable whether Robin would have shared Ethan's interest in land speculation. The Green Mountain Boys were, to Allen, successors of the greenwood's merry men.

He added his own flavor to their exploits. He captured and locked up two bailiffs from New York in separate rooms overnight, promising each that he should go free on the morrow but that his partner must hang. Each wretched prisoner was taken alone from his chamber in the morning and released, after being shown a distant tree from which dangled an effigy that the captive devoutly believed to be the body of his companion.

Not until the two supposed corpses met face to face on an Albany street did they realize the jest, and it is probable that they did not appreciate it even then.

Robin Hood himself would have relished his disciple's dealings with the squad of regulars from Crown Point who arrested him and Eli Robards, a friend, in the cabin of one Richardson at Bridport. It was night, and Ethan proposed that they while away the hours before he must be marched to prison in a little temporarily friendly drinking. The punch bowl passed and repassed. Captives and captors sang together, and presently in the midst of a chorus the prisoners rose and tiptoed out. Richardson's daughter passed them their pistols and muskets through a window. It was some time before the thoroughly befuddled redcoats missed them.

Allen glozed over sordid matters with the grotesque vividness of his speech. The punishments dealt interloping Yorkers were not to him mere beatings with tree branches. He spoke of this vengeance as "the beech seal," or "chastisement with the twigs of the wilderness." The burning of an unhappy settler's house was "a sacrifice to the gods of the world."

It was inevitable that so vehement a romantic should not be content with a verbal recital of his exploits. He fancied himself, with some justice, as an author, as well as patriot, soldier, philosopher. Whether he were writing his own exploits or composing a political counterblast to the perfidious machinations of the foul enemies of Vermont, he at least was vivid.

His spelling was haphazard; punctuation was beyond him. Half the work of publishing him must have been spent in correcting his scripts, but some of the vigor of the man got into his work. He used words largely by ear, employing them more often for the sake of sound than sense, but that, too, was of his essence. It was the way he talked.

Ethan Allen was a more rugged Quixote, tilting at obstacles infinitely more dangerous and resentful than windmills; a coarser-fibred Cyrano, a less fantastic Munchausen. His narrative of his British captivity, the fragments of his autobiography are spacious and lusty, if marred by a faint reek of implausibility that fades when one remembers how implausible was the actual man. Some of the sensational adventures that he says befell him certainly did happen. Many of them, possibly, were inventions.

Maybe, as he writes, he paused in the dawn twilight on the beach below Ticonderoga to deliver to his Green Mountain Boys an inspiring and lengthy address; maybe his attack on Montreal failed through the perfidy of his ally; maybe, when he was captured and brought before General Prescott in Montreal, he really bared his breast and offered it as a substitute target for the thirteen prisoners he says Prescott had ordered bayonetted for no clear reason. Possibly Prescott promised him he should hang at Tyburn. Maybe, during his imprisoned voyage to England, he became so enraged that he ripped the stout iron staple from his handcuffs with his teeth.

One may question whether enthusiastic crowds actually thronged the quays at Falmouth to see him disembark, or whether, while he was imprisoned in Pendennis Castle, the wit and beauty of England flocked thither to argue with him and ply him with punch. One may doubt his claim that, when the frigate bearing him back to America touched at Cork, the devoted citizenry presented him with a purse, rich raiment, wines and liquors, hampers of delicacies, and a dagger.

He may have amused himself at Halifax by pretending to be mad; he may have been offered at New York wealth and station if he would turn traitor. When he had been exchanged and rode to Valley Forge, he may, as he holds, have made his journey between enraptured multitudes who "voiced the acclamations of a grateful people."

All of it may have been true, or none of it. His narrative of his captivity has one indestructible virtue: its hero never gets out of character. Because the exploits he says he performed sound exactly like the sort of thing Ethan Allen might have done, you cannot scoff at the implausible tale. After all, he was that sort of man, and things like that did happen to him. George Washington wrote after Allen's Valley Forge visit: "There is an original something in him that commands admiration."

He never lost this quality. In the complex and continually altering strife of Vermont's birth years, that Original Something was alternatively the people's diversion and the Republic's salvation. He was worshiped and extolled, hated and feared. No one could regard him impersonally. All who knew him were devotees or enemies. To the strict older man and to the insurgent minorities of Vermont he was Satan's agent. Half his opponents were sure that his big military boots concealed cloven hoofs. The other half would not have been surprised if a spiked tail had lashed out from beneath his resplendent uniform coat.

He frightened the rebellious out of their wits. One look at his infuriated person, one bellow of his tremendous voice, and lately determined men broke and fled. He was Ethan Allen, and there was no withstanding him.

It was not only his lung power, but also the strangely conglomerate verbal missiles it launched which daunted his hearers. His was an unscrupulous and unique collection of language. Legend has preserved a limping version of its rhythm and a shadow of its grotesque imagery. His speech is reproduced, with scrupulous policing, in the mass of pamphlets he wrote, but these records must be only faded and formalized versions of the authentic Ethan Allen, purple-faced and going full blast. A contemporary has left a tribute to and description of his powers.

Alexander Graydon, a British officer, who met Allen and found him "a robust, large-framed man," wrote in his *Memoirs*:

> I have seldom met a man possessing in my opinion, a stronger mind, or whose mode of expression was more vehement and oratorical. His style was a singular compound of local barbarism, Scriptural phrases, and oriental wildness; and though unclassic and sometimes ungrammatical, it was highly animated and forceful.

It is hard for us who have inherited only the dubious record of his deeds, who catch across a century and a half only his garbled and muted echo, to understand why Vermonters, who still are a folk not too easily impressed, held him in such awe.

For all his blustering and sword-flourishing, his accomplishments were not dire or blood-soaked. Compared to his tumult and his shouting they were mildly anticlimactic.

As a soldier he was beaten ignominiously in two skirmishes he fought against the British; as a leader he was refused command of the regiment raised in Vermont for the Continental service; as guerrilla and outlaw he never fulfilled a tithe of his tremendous threats. The worst punishment he ever administered was a sound whipping. There is no sure record that, in all his tumultuous career, this vociferous swashbuckler ever actually killed anybody.

Yet he browbeat, and on occasion completely subjugated, a particularly turbulent people, employing no weapon more deadly than apocalyptical predictions of what would happen in another moment if they didn't behave. It may be that he was compelled so seldom to employ genuine force because his enemies knew full well how thoroughly he itched to use it. No one called the bluffs that Ethan Allen bellowed because in the back of their minds lurked the uneasy belief that he would, in all probability, take a ferocious glee in fulfilling them, if challenged. His Original Something was potent.

If he shocked the old, he fired the young. He was anathema to the pious and mature. To the youthful, whom the land and the spirit abroad in the land were molding into a special people, he was the tribal hero, the champion, the myth-maker. No one was quite like him. He represented an ideal. He was all that the young men who had not so wholly shaken themselves free from the pious strictures of the older New England wistfully would have liked to be. He warmed and lifted them up. In a gray, grim pioneer way of life, he was a blaze of color and a great sound.

Always, at his name, the young men rose and followed. That name by itself won conflicts and overthrew rebellions. He raised Vermonters, weaned from an earlier allegiance, in the way that they should go; in the way that, largely, they still move. He was, with the explosions smothered and the tinsel stripped away, the personification of Vermont freedom. The Republic survived because he flavored and colored it.

He was not an American; he was a Vermonter. No other colony, state, or nation ever obtained his full allegiance. He fought New York, New Hampshire as enthusiastically as he battled against the British. He and Ira, his brother, defied and thwarted the Union itself when it threatened Vermont. Ethan Allen lived and he died a Vermonter. Despite that narrow loyalty, there are less secure niches in the national Pantheon than his own.

Ethan was the oldest of the eight Allens, and Ira was the youngest. The brothers were at opposite ends of their generation and of the spectrum. Ethan was a flaming red; Ira, a decorous violet. Ethan was forthright and blustering; Ira, insidious and devious. He shunned display, he hated ostentation. He had not a single grand gesture to his name. Oratory was beyond him; posturing, abhorrent. He best accomplished his purposes by pressure on an elbow and a voice that spoke mildly in another's ear. His was the puppeteer's vocation. Obscured, ignored, he guided the movements, supplied the speech, of those upon the stage.

The brothers were unlike in form and substance, yet they complemented each other. We lack Ethan's portrait, but we have a miniature painted of Ira when he was in his forties. Gray hair that once had been brown has retired from a high, narrow forehead. Maturity has swelled the cheeks and thickened the flesh about the rounded chin. The pictured Ira has a poet's eyes, large, dark, and luminous; but his other features are strong antidotes for this inappropriate dreaminess. If the eyes indicate the idealist, the nose is the hawk's and the mouth belongs to a chairman of the board—small, with a faintly pouting lower and a tightly drawn upper lip.

He was a small, compact person whose family nickname was "Stub" —brown, sleek and lambent-eyed as a seal, with a seal's sinuous deftness in troubled water; and, still like a seal, it was his wont to dive into conflicting currents and to emerge at last, blinking his large brown eyes, with his quarry in his jaws.

In the internecine brawls of the Allen brothers, Ira and Ethan never seem to have been opposed. They had all their mature lives a common objective—the welfare of Vermont—though they moved toward it by divergent ways.

A tale is told—it may be verity; it certainly is good parable—of a wager that Ira and Ethan made in their youth. They engaged to race to a tree that towered over brush on the other side of a swamp. Ethan went straight toward the goal, stumbling over hummocks, slipping in mire, scratched by brambles, whipped by twigs. Muddy and breathless he reached the tree at the very second that Ira, who had circled the swamp, arrived, unsoiled, composed.

Ethan had a share of the tight, bargaining instinct without which few on the New England frontier survived; but Ira was a trader unsurpassed. He was resourceful, he was slick, and his life is the tale of one difficult deal after another, smoothly, if obscurely, consummated. When they roamed the wilderness together, Ethan bore his musket and sought for deer and bear. Ira was better pleased to carry a surveyor's compass and estimate the land. His eyes made him dream of towns and mills, forges and farms; his tight small mouth muttered of grants and rights, of buying for a shilling and selling for a pound.

He infected Ethan with his own enthusiasm for promoting enterprises. Ethan woke in Ira reciprocally that intense, obdurate patriotism the northern wilderness gave so abundantly to those who learned to know it. In time, the twin passions became in each brother infinitely tangled and twined, so that no one now can say whether many of their deeds were the outcome of their love of country or their craving for acreage. Their service to the Republic was always part idealism, part concern for their own real-estate investments.

By instinct, Ira was a speculator; by profession, a self-taught surveyor. He, like his brother, was a canny woodsman, proud of his skill. His vanity was as intense as Ethan's, but he never let it get in the way of his own prosperity. He shared, too, Ethan's birthright of intense vitality and had the physical egotism of all woods-runners.

On a trip of a day or so, he admits that Ethan could walk him down; but on longer journeys he insists that he could outstrip his brother. It pleased him in later years to recall how much farther he could go than most men on a slice of raw salt pork and a hunk of bread; how Remember Baker, his cousin, once when supplies ran out dared him to complete the survey they were making on no better sustenance than suckers speared in a brook, and how he emerged from that ordeal in better shape than tough, slab-sided Remember himself.

He recollected, too, with the sharp pleasure that only a Yankee wholly could relish, the tricks and commercial dodges of his youth.

When proprietors of a certain grant promised him pay for the survey, only if it should prove to be good land, Ira discovered that it was forested in spruce, indicating a sour soil. He reported to his principals that the territory was covered with "gum trees." And what were "gum trees"?

"I told them all straight trees that had gum much like the gum on cherry trees."

For this survey and his promising report, his reassured employers paid him ninety pounds "which I considered of more consequence than the whole town."

"Having closed this business satisfactorily to myself, I returned to my brother's and had a hearty laugh with my brothers Heman and Zimri on informing them respecting the gum wood."

He never underestimated himself, but his ego fed for choice on provender that Ethan's scornfully rejected. He took great relish in unpublicized exploits that his brother would have considered insipid. Ethan charged down, roaring, upon opposition; Ira overwhelmed by persuasion.

No man ever lived who knew the intricate, obstinate natures of Vermonters quite so thoroughly. He was of their baffling race; he spoke their language, persuasively, enticingly, and when he had won his point, was indifferent thereafter who had the credit. The inner consciousness of the victory seems to have been for him an adequate reward. Ethan found no exploit worth while unless it was accompanied by applause, even if he had to supply it himself.

Ira Allen was damned in his day as a Jesuit, a trickster, a straddler, a would-be traitor to America and the Revolution. Perspective of a century and a half has brought these matters into a more comprehensible grouping. The man, in some odd, instinctive fashion, was a diplomat of no small skill. He had patience, tact, a gift for dissembling, ready argument, potent persuasiveness. These carried him through infinitely delicate negotiations, not only with men of his own breed and background, but also with cultured, experienced citizens of the world.

During a long and intricately perilous time, Ira Allen was the emergency man, the trouble-shooter of the Vermont Republic. If danger loomed more portentously than usual, if it appeared at last that the game was wholly lost, distracted leaders called on Ethan when force was necessary; on Ira for negotiation. Thereafter, for a space there was a similitude of peace.

The sleek brown man had his enemies. No one existed in Vermont during this period without a lavish supply. There seems to have been little vindictiveness, small instinct for reprisal, in his relations with his adversaries. He was less tolerant during the frequent family brawls, maybe because his eldest brother usually was ally in these upheavals, and Ethan supplied the vehemence.

One squabble, growing out of the complex land deals of the Allen family, roused Ira's and Ethan's wrath against their brother Levi to the point of vengeance. They accused him of being a Tory and used their political influence to bring about the confiscation of all his property.

The dispute dragged its way through the courts, but the ordinary dreariness of the proceedings was enlivened by Levi's challenging Ethan to fight a duel and, when friends persuaded them to abandon this enterprise, by Levi's further assault upon his kinsmen in verses published in the *Connecticut Courant* and entitled "The Three Brothers." Here they are:

Ethan

Old Ethan once said over a full bowl of grog
Though I believe not in Jesus, I hold to a God,
There is also a devil—you'll see him one day
In a whirlwind of fire take Levi away.

Ira

Says Ira to Ethan it plain doth appear
That you are inclined to banter and jeer,
I think for myself and I freely declare
Our Levi's too stout for the prince of the air.
If ever you see them engaged in affray
'Tis our Levi who'll take the devil away.

Levi

Says Levi, your speeches make it perfectly clear
That you hath been inclined to banter and jeer,
Though through all the world my fame stands enrolled
For tricks, sly and crafty, ingenious and bold,
There is one consolation which none can deny
That there's one greater rogue in this world than I.

Ethan and Ira
"Who's that?" They both cry with equal surprise.

Levi
" 'Tis Ira, 'tis Ira, I yield him the prize."

This effort apparently relieved Levi's system of most of his indignation, and the brothers eventually entered into amicable business relations again.

None of the little group of obstinate, competent men who founded and defended and finally established the Vermont Republic were rich in education or in worldly experience. There were a few frontier lawyers, a doctor or so, among them. The rest were hard-handed, hardheaded farmers.

Untrained for either statecraft or diplomacy, they drew from some inner source the ability to look calmly at enormous odds against them, to estimate the dimensions of a hazardous and complicated task, to hitch up their breeches, spit on their hands, and in workaday fashion to proceed with it, employing for the job no more erudite equipment than common sense, monumental stubbornness, Yankee skill at bargain-driving, dickering, trading—drab qualities that still, when the need grew sorest, were shot through, time and again, by lightnings not to be distinguished from flashes of genius.

There was scant magnificence to the statecraft or the persons of these men, yet no infant commonwealth ever had more attentive obstetricians or more careful nurses. They hoodwinked and thwarted determined enemies. They blocked invasion and quelled internal rebellion with no more lethal weapons than a vast amount of bluff and a good deal of conversation.

They played threatening forces off, against each other, with uncanny dexterity and all through the years of confusion and peril clung to their purpose until at last they saw, with no more exultation than faint twitchings of grim lips and the deepening of wrinkles about keen eyes, that long-held purpose completely fulfilled.

Among these lank, shabby statesmen who talked through their noses and, ill-advisedly, were derided by their more worldly adversaries, the Allen brothers stand first—Ethan, the whirlwind, the earthquake, and the fire; Ira, the still small voice; Ethan, who stamped the impress of himself deep upon the state he served; Ira, who is the very substance of that state itself.

v "The Gods of the Hills"

ETHAN ALLEN, AGENT GENERAL for the Honorable Proprietors of the New Hampshire Grants—he must have invented for himself some such grandiose title—leaped upon a horse and rode off to Portsmouth. He was an important person now, and he had been ready for years to act the part. Thereafter a Jovian pose, an air of being crammed with unutterable affairs of state, rarely deserted him. Even in his sleep, he must have seemed to be accomplishing a portentous and delicate mission.

In Portsmouth, Allen came in upon Governor John Wentworth, Benning's nephew and successor, as a wind blows a door open. Wentworth welcomed a new and promising ally in the undercover war he was waging when opportunity offered against New York. Outwardly, Governor John displayed only courteous warmth toward New Hampshire's next-door colony and wrote neighborly letters to its authorities, but inwardly he found it hard to pardon New York for getting back what Uncle Benning had grabbed, nor had he wholly given up hope of regaining at least part of the Grants.

Wentworth was not above stirring up trouble or doing a smooth job of double-crossing when he had the chance. Only recently he had accomplished a little of both with excellent effect.

His Majesty had conferred upon New Hampshire's governor not only Benning's discreetly vacated office but another with a more resounding title. Nephew John had been created "Surveyor General of His Majesty's Woods in All and Singular of His Majesty's Colonies," which meant that his was the decision whether pine trees might be cut down by settlers or should be left to grow into masts for King George's warships. One such decision, lately made, had started a brawl on the east slope of the Grants that still was proceeding, moved on by the wrathful and clashing beliefs of men.

The Eastside settlers were conglomerate. Among them were sober, righteous, and orthodox people, and many that were none of these. Their politics were as various as their ethics. Here were Tories, Whigs,

Yorkers, New Hampshiremen, supporters of Massachusetts, and those who wished a wholly separate government for the Grants. Discord already was perceptible, and it was growing.

New York was a milder affliction to the East than to the West. Between the Connecticut Valley settlements and the land-gambling ring in Albany lay not only the already insurgent Westside but the additional barrier of the mountains. Since the Eastside territory was remote and not so easy to exploit, many of the settlers there already had had their New Hampshire grants confirmed by New York patents. These, and others, preferred to be governed from Albany rather than from Portsmouth. The most vehement Yorkers had settled in the southeast corner of the Grants, at Guilford, Vernon, Marlboro, Halifax, and Brattleboro.

Even now, Guilford, one of the largest settlements in the Grants, was trying with much persistence and no success to surrender its New Hampshire charter in exchange for a New York. It had petitioned the latter province in 1765, 1766, and 1767 and had received only polite acknowledgments. Indifference did not daunt the Guilfordites. It only increased their peculiar loyalty.

Other towns did not share this fervor. Common New England origin was practically all the region did share. The noisiest of the contending factions were folk who disliked the New York officers imposed on the land when the county of Cumberland had been established.

The tough-minded folk of the Eastside had largely ruled themselves in their native New England towns. They had accepted, with grumbling, royal appointment of certain high officials; but they, the people, had chosen all lower officers in democratic and acrimonious town meetings. Furthermore, the voters had set their own taxes. Where government hurt most, they had managed it themselves. Under New York, this had been changed.

Officials—sheriffs, judges, justices of the peace, and the like—who heretofore had been elected by the people now were appointed by New York's governor. Taxes for their and the courts' support were levied arbitrarily. There were too many officials, in the Eastside's opinion, and these comported themselves as the governor's, not the people's, representatives. There were too many taxes; the fees demanded for reconfirming New Hampshire grants were too high; and money was still as scarce in this new land as wholly cleared farms.

Discontent already had reached the petition-making stage. Various groups had begun to complain to His Majesty of a variety of wrongs and to beg a wide assortment of reliefs. These appeals continued to pour down upon London until the Revolution.

The Eastside's political and social structure was an equilibrium precariously kept. The diverse elements regarded each other with latent hostility. Knotty and intractible persons jostled each other, and contact bred heat. Wentworth, in January of 1769, overset the barely maintained balance, apparently for gratification of his own immediate spite and the eventual advancement of New Hampshire's influence. The consequences of his act still were marching tumultuously on when Ethan Allen visited him early in 1770.

His Majesty's Surveyor General of His Majesty's Woods while inspecting the timber stands of the Eastside had found that William Dean and his sons, settlers in Windsor, were cutting down mast pines regardless of the needs of the Royal Navy. Such violation of the law was practically universal on the frontier, and usually Surveyor General Wentworth shut his eyes or looked the other way. The Deans, however, were not only flagrant in their sinning, but they were also obstreperous and influential Yorkers. Wentworth ordered the arrest of the Deans.

Father and two sons were taken to New York and tried, to the dismay of the Eastside's New York element and the glee of all others. The Deans were fined, but they professed themselves destitute. Technically they were penniless; for, counseled by John Grout, a New York attorney, they had conveyed all their property to Samuel Wells of Brattleboro, a New York judge.

This slick subterfuge did little to increase the esteem of the anti-York elements for the Eastside's courts or for the lawyer who had saved the Deans from paying a fine. Just how Grout was made aware of popular disapproval is not wholly clear, but only a little while before Allen visited Portsmouth, a warrant had been issued for the arrest of Nathan and Simon Stone, Joseph and Benjamin Wait, all of Windsor in the Grants, for "a violence committed upon one Mr. John Grout."

John Wentworth had reason to be pleased with himself as a fomentor of discord. He had no cause to be dissatisfied with his large, loud visitor, Agent General Allen. If this picturesque person acted as forcefully as he spoke, New York was to have still more trouble with the settlers on the Grants' western slope.

To further this pious end, the Governor furnished his visitor with copies of all documents supporting the title of the defendant in the impending Westside case of *Small* vs *Carpenter* and urged that Allen engage Jared Ingersoll of New Haven as counsel. John Wentworth had some of Uncle Benning's contagious enthusiasm for Grant's real estate. Allen, before rushing off from Portsmouth, bought a right in the town of Poultney for £4 and paused long enough in Springfield on his way to New Haven to purchase a Castleton right for £6. Thus he showed faith, that Wentworth possibly had inspired, in the future of New Hampshire titles; thus, too, he infected himself with the land-gambling fever and from it never wholly recovered.

The Agent General was prodigiously busy the rest of the winter. He rode furiously about. He bought a right, Benning Wentworth's own, in Panton town, for £8. He wrote denunciations of New York and all its works for the *Connecticut Courant*. Some of them, edited and respelled, got printed. He appeared often, travel-worn, mud-stained, but still vociferous, at Captain Stephen Fay's tavern in Bennington.

This gaunt, oblong building, with a hipped roof and thick chimneys, stood on the brow of Bennington Hill. New York's governors deemed it a nest of rebels. It was, with equal accuracy, the prototype of Vermont's capitol. About the fireplaces of its taproom and the more exclusive "council chamber" above, gathered in the winter and spring of 1770 uneasy men whose investments were threatened, more bitterly wrathful men who actually were losing their hard-won farms.

Their grievances were eased by recital and the bowls of flip and hot punch that passed through the shabby half-circles before the hearths. Rum's aroma mixed with the smell of steaming clothing. Pine walls cast back sour Yankee voices. Above them all, more insurgent than most, louder and more blasphemous than any, blared Ethan Allen's.

Light from the council chamber's fire lay on the strong faces of humble folk whom the years were to entangle in the myth and history of Vermont. Here were Gideon Warren, Samuel Safford, and the younger Sam Robinson, who had chased the surveyors off Jim Breakenridge's farm with, according to his story, consummate politeness. Here was Moses, Sam's brother, a calmly determined person who was to be Vermont's chief justice, governor and United States Senator. The landlord's sons were present—John, whom a Brunswick mercenary was to kill on a little hill above the Walloomsac River; Joseph, a competent and cautious man; and Dr. Jonas, whose bedside manner would serve him well at a republic's birth.

Here was tough, swaggering Robert Cochran and Peleg Sunderland, Indian fighter and hound fancier, who bred dogs of great stamina and tenacity on a trail. Here, too, was the Rev. Jedediah Dewey, hard-bitten pastor of an unruly Separatist flock, who made no distinction between the minions of New York and those of the Prince of Darkness. With all these sat the already well-regarded members of the Allen clan.

Seth Warner, a grave young giant, listened to his kinsman Ethan's bawling with what seemed to some people a trace of cousinly dislike. Leathery Cousin Ebenezer Allen grinned and nodded approval. Cousin Remember Baker, a rawboned, sandy-haired woods-runner, scowled as he spoke of how New York strove to rob him of his two half-built mills in Arlington. Heman Allen was there, and with him Ira, smallest, youngest, most thoughtful of them all. He was a scant twenty years old, yet was not present by sufferance. Already older men had found substance in his speech that made them thoughtful.

Old Captain Stephen Fay drew the mulling iron from the coals. It boiled as he plunged it into the flip. A stir ran through the half-circle when he brought the bowl to Ethan. Dewey spoke sharply against the toast to the confusion of New York that the big man shouted. Dewey had no objection to what Ethan said about Colden, who had calmly disregarded His Majesty's command and again was issuing patents to New York speculators. The Rev. Jedediah did object to the way Ethan dragged the Almighty into the controversy.

The bowl passed toward Ira, who watched the successive drinkers with large, bright eyes. They were undistinguished folk, all of them, and, save for Dr. Jonas Fay, uneducated, unworldly, with shoulders already sagged by labor, with hard, half-closed hands that had been bent since childhood to toil with ax and hoe.

They came to Fay's tavern because, after swilling flip and airing their woes, they felt better. They must have had no further conscious purpose, all the lank, angry young men, than to hold their land against threatened confiscation.

"The bowl, Stub," Remember drawled, and Ira roused himself to take it. If any of that company actually knew that they were drawing foundation plans for the Vermont Republic, it was Ira Allen, who was by trade a surveyor.

FAY'S TAVERN

Vermont's First and Unofficial Capitol (Courtesy, Bennington Historical
Museum and Art Gallery)

Ice was breaking in the streams' swifter reaches, and osiers on their banks were turning crimson when inspiring news came over the mountains to Bennington. The Eastside's antagonism to New York authority had moved out of the talking stage, thanks to the original impulsion by Governor Wentworth of New Hampshire.

That indefinite violence which had been committed by the Wait and Stone brothers upon the person of John Grout, attorney for the pine-cutting Deans, had gone long unpunished. In March, 1770, Sheriff Daniel Whipple of Cumberland County arrested the quartette. He held his prisoners extremely briefly. Their Windsor neighbors, large, uncompromising men, surrounded the sheriff and took his captives.

Such crass defiance of his dignity and office was more than Whipple could bear. He assembled a posse and returned to the assault. His late prisoners came forth to meet him, and they had forty men armed with clubs at their backs. When the scuffle was over, it was the unhappy sheriff and his posse who had been taken.

They were locked in Joseph Wait's house for several days before they were let go. For this mockery of Cumberland County's, New York's, and His Majesty's law, Joseph Wait and Nathan Stone again were indicted. They were not arrested any more. No one seemed eager for the job.

News from Boston came north with the spring. It roiled men's tempers and split Grants factions further. Rowdy snowballing of a sentry on Brattle Street had swelled into purposeless riot. Muskets of His Majesty's 29th Foot had spoken, and when the smoke had thinned four men were dead and seven more had been wounded in the Boston Massacre.

June came. Flowers and a vernal crop of Colden patents appeared on the face of the New Hampshire Grants. Cumberland County Court summoned Stone and Wait to Chester for trial. In Albany, the New York Supreme Court prepared to hear the cases of settlers under New Hampshire's grants who had refused to be evicted by holders of New York titles. The Eastside and the Westside were marching, for a rare moment, in step.

Jared Ingersoll of New Haven and Peter Sylvester of Albany appeared for the defendants in the Supreme Court, and Ethan Allen himself came also. He had no opportunity for verbal fireworks. The defense which he had been planning for months fell apart almost at once. The thing was accomplished as deftly and painlessly as a surgical operation.

There was an instant of triumph for the settlers at the proceedings' beginning. The case against James Breakenridge was nonsuited. It appeared that his farm had not been surveyed by the plaintiffs. Therefore, no actual trespass could be proved. After this setback, the prosecution moved with the expedition of a machine, which it may have been.

The impartiality of the learned Robert Livingston, chief justice, may not have been swayed by the fact that he already held title to 35,000 acres of Grants land under New York patent. The efforts of James Duane and Attorney General Kempe, prosecutors, may not have been influenced by their leadership in the New York gambling ring.

The refusal of the court to admit any of the documentary evidence collected by Allen may have been wholly legal, and the verdict directed for the New York claimant to Isaiah Carpenter's farm may have been the logical outcome of the proceedings. All this may have been simple justice. Neither Allen, nor the defendants, nor the people of the Grants found it so.

No more suits were brought after the usurping Major Small's successful action against Carpenter. The court had made its attitude plain. Further trials would have been a waste of time. The Carpenter verdict bluntly canceled the rights of all settlers under New Hampshire Grants to the land they had cleared.

It was over—finished. The Grants belonged wholly to New York patentees. This was complete victory, yet there was something in the faces of the defeated as they filed out of court, there was a swollen and ominous look about Ethan Allen as he accompanied them, which seems to have worried the victors. Three big shots of the New York ring—Kempe, Duane, and a gentleman with the surprising name of Goldsbrow Banyar—called on Allen that night at his inn.

With fair words and just the least trace of worry, the three begged the Agent General to tell his people they were whipped and to urge them to make the best possible terms they could with their conquerors. Allen drew a mighty breath. He thundered:

"The gods of the hills are not the gods of the valleys."

This was one of the cryptic utterances characteristic of him. They sounded blasting and profound until someone tried to find out what they meant. In this instance, the pardonably bewildered Kempe inquired, and Allen answered no more lucidly:

"If you will accompany me to the hill of Bennington the sense will be made clear."

Thereafter, he called for more punch.

Though the west flank of Grants resistance seemed to have been shattered, the Eastside's revolt had been more successful and much more spectacular.

On June 5, when the county court met in the shack dedicated to its sessions at Chester, the indicted Stone and Wait appeared. They seem to have had a habit of keeping appointments, but they always brought along a number of friends armed with clubs. This time Stone brought his sword, too.

The self-returning prisoners placed themselves before the bar of justice while their companions hung about in the background, making a hushed and ugly noise. Instead of submitting to trial, though, Wait and Stone proceeded to try the court, challenging its authority, contesting the legality of the newly established Cumberland County, and demanding the disbarring of John Grout, attorney.

The court was indignant, then bewildered, and then, as Wait's and Stone's escort continued to utter unpleasant sounds, openly scared. The judges preserved what dignity they might by refusing to argue and adjourning hastily until the morrow. They retired. The Stone-Wait party retired too, and in the midst of their column marched that miserable lawyer, John Grout, whom they had taken along with them as a souvenir.

Mr. Grout was pushed around a good deal by his captors, and repeated demands were made that he promise to abandon his nefarious profession and become instead a good York-hating farmer. To all these urgings, he reports that his only answer was that he felt unwell, which was probable.

The kidnapers took him to the tavern in Charlestown, New Hampshire, where the lawyer, who seems to have been a mild and dyspeptic man, spent a wretched night, alternately plied with punch and arguments, neither of which agreed with him.

On the morrow, he was moved to Nathan Stone's house in Windsor; and several days later, he still proving ailing and obstinate, he was conveniently permitted to escape. The court, cautiously reassembling at Chester on the day after its dispersal, issued warrants for the arrest of a number of miscreants, none of whom was brought to trial.

Meanwhile, in the west, Ethan Allen had ridden back to Bennington from Albany, and in the council chamber of Stephen Fay's tavern had bawled his tidings to the tight-lipped men hurriedly gathered there. By the court decision, all New Hampshire-granted land, cleared and uncleared, the farmhouses, the dwellings in Bennington, Landlord Fay's hostelry, even the meetinghouse, no longer were the property of their holders. They belonged to New York. Chief Justice Livingston had said so.

The volatile giant whose own holdings in Grants property were recent and slight was probably the most openly excited and certainly the noisiest man present.

Soberly, cannily, wasting no time in curses now, the group that heretofore had gathered to tipple and complain rolled back its sleeves and went to work. There was always an antidote for disaster if you strove hard enough to find it. The Anglo-Saxon instinct not to disperse but to close ranks under danger's pressure swayed these farmers now. The frontier-bred resourcefulness, whereby men had learned to contrive out of materials at hand a solution for any emergency, was their aid.

By the time Allen had run out of breath, the group had ceased to be a loose gathering of convivial spirits and had become a unit. The news from Albany had been an additional pinch of salt dropped into an already saturate solution, and crystallization had begun.

There must be a committee of safety to oppose the court's decision. They established it. There must be, too, an army raised to meet invasion should Colden call for bayonets to spike Chief Justice Livingston's decision down upon the Grants. They raised it. Out of someone's brain, quite possibly Ethan Allen's, sprang the name this defensive force should bear.

It would be an orphan organization, dutiful to no established power —neither to New York nor New Hampshire nor even His Majesty himself. It would protect many harried people but no single ruler. The land would be its cause—the fair and threatened mountainous land, now green with June. The troops were called the Green Mountain Boys.

There was no question in anyone's mind—least of all in Ethan Allen's—who was to be this regiment's colonel. The roster of captains was composed quickly. It was drawn from those who had passed the bowl in earlier less tense sessions in the council chamber—Seth Warner, Remember Baker, Robert Cochran, Peleg Sunderland, Gideon

Warren. Others were added later. The "Colonel Commandant" was Ethan Allen.

It was a lucky choice. Fortune was Vermont's chief ally now and in the troublesome years ahead. So detractors said. It may be, though, that Fortune was not chiefly involved, and what the disparaging misidentified was, instead, simply an intense, earthy craft which enabled the Republic's leaders to read with clarity the natures of men, the texture of their purposes.

There could have been no better chief than Allen for men like the Green Mountain Boys and the task that was to be theirs. Such insurgent groups had been formed ever since men first had governed one another. Ethan Allen's command was ancestor of innumerable later vigilante and regulator and night-riding bodies, but the Green Mountain Boys themselves had a long line of forebears. They were original only in that their leader had an Original Something.

Allen was a propagandist born before his time. He would have been wholly at home in the current warfare that strikes more heavily at civilian morale than military objectives. In actual battle, he was valiant and comically inept. In the task to which he dedicated his first command, he was superb. Continually he spoke, then and later, of the valor and gallantry of his Green Mountain Boys. They probably had an ample store of each, but he never permitted them to display much of either. They fought New York with other, more potent, weapons.

No tougher, better material for soldiers ever existed. A military man could have trained the forest-roaming, close-shooting youngsters into a force that could have withstood any equal number of troops in the world—and eventually would have been rubbed out by New York, as Governor William Tryon had abolished the regulators in North Carolina by killing and wounding two hundred and hanging six leaders for treason. Ethan Allen was not a military man. He was only— when he stopped to think—an extremely intelligent.

His first act as Colonel Commandant was to order that exalted officer a self-designed uniform. No detailed description of that has come down to us. We only know that it included a startling cocked hat, a large amount of gilt braid, many brass buttons, an immense sword, and enormous military boots. Whatever its color and its cut, it was successful. Enemies dreaded Allen in regimentals as Israel feared Goliath and his brazen armor.

While the uniform was being made, Ethan organized his Green Mountain Boys. Here, the Original Something had full sway. His men had no uniforms at all. A sprig of evergreen on their hats was their only identifying badge. The members of this force were inured by personal experience, or the example of the recent war, to slaughter; they never killed anybody. They were bred to firearms; they used them for no purpose but intimidation. They enlisted to defend their land against New York; they accomplished this, not by conflict, but by making persistent pests of themselves.

A man less forceful than their chief never could have held these wild men in check. A person with smaller genius for leadership could not have succeeded in bending such a group of young hellions so wholly to his purpose.

That purpose was strangely modern. By a native shrewdness, which he kept most of the time successfully hidden, Ethan Allen knew that he could not hope to defeat New York, but that it would be possible to annoy that more powerful province into hysterics. He knew that a dead man may be a cause of war, but that a humiliated is almost certain to be a joke. He was aware that threats delivered with the bellowing candor of which he was capable were infinitely more frightening than bullets, and that a thoroughly terrified person was bound to infect others.

These were the principles on which he formed his command. These were the theories that became their practice. The uniform arrived, Ethan put it on, and he and his Green Mountain Boys were ready to go to work.

No job immediately offered itself. While the Westside towns formed their individual committees of safety, while delegates from these met frequently in Bennington and a rough system of government was formed by the pressure of events, there seemed to be nothing for the Green Mountain Boys to do but listen to Ethan Allen.

The possibility of peace grew brighter that summer when the British Board of Trade again warned Acting Governor Colden that settlers under New Hampshire title should be left alone and "in entire possession of such lands as they have actually cultivated and improved." The Board also directed that the proprietors of undeveloped towns should be permitted to keep their rights, pending survey.

England apparently had not heard of Chief Justice Livingston's decision, and age seemed to have deafened Colden completely to the Board of Trade's command. Between September, 1769, and October, 1770, he issued patents to 600,000 acres of Grants land.

The unsettled strife over ownership had not checked the stream of migration, though its character had changed. Farm seekers still were trudging in, but with them now came gentry who deemed life on a disputed and wild frontier—and the wilder the better—preferable to precarious existence in better-policed areas.

Even in the depths of the forest primeval, these persons managed to attract attention to themselves and became so notorious that the northern part of Cumberland, their chief hide-out, was reorganized into Gloucester County to protect respectable settlers there who were "exposed to rapine and plunder from a lawless banditti of felons and criminals who fly thither from other places."

Kingsland, now Washington, was chosen as the county seat of Gloucester; John Taplin was appointed judge, and his son, John, Jr., sheriff. The banditti of that region may have been nefarious, but they were not exactly overpopulating the county; for in February, 1771, the Taplins started on snowshoes from their home in Bradford to hold court at Kingsland and, though they searched the snowy wilderness for two days, could not find the town.

Weary and frostbitten, the officials yet were faithful to their trust. Before plodding back to Bradford they paused in the forest to hold court, and at the rite's conclusion Sheriff Taplin entered in the record: "The court, if one, adjourned over until the last Tuesday in May."

The summer of 1770 ripened into fall peacefully enough, while Colonel Commandant Allen instructed his shabby legion in his own version of warfare and delegates from sundry committees of safety met frequently in the council chamber of Fay's tavern. This had a new signboard.

On a gallowslike standard twenty-four feet high perched a badly stuffed catamount who snarled in the direction of New York where His Majesty was changing governors again, still seeking an administrator with a gift for something more constructive than issuing land patents. Colden was retiring, and as his successor came John, Lord Dunmore, a penniless Scottish peer with no intention of remaining so if the supply of land to be patented held out.

With Dunmore's advent the swooning dispute revived. The New York claimant to James Breakenridge's farm made another attempt to survey it. Jim and his neighbors met the surveyors with more of the politeness that had welcomed their predecessors. The expedition returned to Albany, bruised and angry, and Dunmore issued a warrant for the arrest of Simon Hathaway, Moses Scott, Jonathan Fisk, and Silas Robinson, members of the Breakenridge reception committee.

The indefatigable Justice John Munro of Shaftsbury, stool-pigeoning for Albany's sheriff, finally brought about Robinson's capture. He was arraigned, indicted, released on bail, and never tried. Jim Breakenridge got the rest of his harvest in that fall without further interruption.

Isaiah Carpenter, defendant in the fateful suit, was less fortunate than Breakenridge. Munro, who was taking increasing zest in hunting New Hampshire settlers, entered the Carpenter farmhouse with a writ of ejectment. Isaiah, a mild man, made some vaguely threatening motions with a gun, which Munro and his aid confiscated and found to be loaded with nothing more lethal than a powder charge and a handful of kidney beans.

Munro, the assiduous servant of New York—and of his more profitable employers, Duane and Kempe—prevailed for a time because Ethan Allen's mind had been pulled away briefly from military affairs by financial. Something had happened this spring which had opened pleasing and profitable vistas for the Colonel Commandant of the Green Mountain Boys.

Thanks to reiterated British disapproval of New York land-grabbing, thanks also to stiffening of resistance in the Grants, the market for the New Hampshire rights had turned bullish; and Allen, who had bought his share in Castleton for £6, now sold it for £24. Patriotism, it was clear, had its rewards. You not only served Freedom's fair cause by defending the Grants; you could also make money.

How much this discovery swayed Ethan Allen hereafter, he himself probably would have been unable to tell. Certainly, it had influence. He must have seen that victory over New York by the Green Mountain Boys would enrich anyone who furnished himself now with plenty of New Hampshire rights. If he didn't see this himself, Ira Allen pointed it out to him. He and Ethan bought thirty-two Hubbardton and four more Castleton shares this spring. Thereafter, resistance to New York authority grew brisker.

Dunmore, in the rare moments when he was not selling patents, considered reports from his officers concerning the violence, the fright, the humiliation they had undergone while trying to enforce New York law in the Grants. Something strange had happened. The land was no longer simply populated by farmers. It bore at the most unexpected moments sudden and extremely rough mobs that seemed to pop up from nowhere and, after a painful interval, vanished whence they came.

These intemperate and unpredictable persons surrounded York Constable Samuel Willoughby, who had just served a writ of ejectment on Thomas French of Arlington, and, flourishing clubs, threatened to knock Sam's head off a little at a time unless he withdrew the writ. Sam withdrew it.

Constable Samuel Pease, a person of sterner fiber, who came from Albany to arrest French for complicity in the Willoughby riot, was fired upon from the woods as he advanced and found so many armed men at French's house that it seemed better to fall back upon Bennington. During the night Pease tarried there, his horse was killed, leaving him afoot and far from home in a dismayingly hostile land.

The disorder spread, not sporadically, but as though there were a purposeful system behind it. York settlers as well as York constables suffered. Fences mysteriously fell down, cows showed amazing skill in getting into gardens, haystacks on windless nights blew over and scattered themselves about wide areas.

"Every person," industrious Justice Munro reported to his principals, "that pretends to be a Friend to this Government is in Danger of both Life & Property."

The Colonel Commandant of the Grants army had sent his troops into action. The Green Mountain Boys were testing Allen's theories of effective guerrilla warfare and were finding that they worked. Dread, they were learning, was a far more powerful weapon than any musket. It routed invaders almost by itself.

Thus, William Cockburn, a New York surveyor who had been commissioned by Duane to map the recently patented town of Socialborough, overlapping already settled territory in Rutland and Pittsford, lost his way and lost his nerve and fled, pursued only by his fears.

Hostile men had replied to his request for directions with the promise to shoot him if he did not go away. One, more garrulous than his brethren, informed the unhappy surveyor that Ethan Allen and his men, all dressed as Indians and with their faces blackened, were waiting for him in the woods. Cockburn faced about and scuttled back to Albany. "By all accounts," he wrote to Duane, "we should not have been very kindly treated."

New York officials were frightened, New York settlers increasingly wretched; but the New York patent business still was booming. Dunmore, in the eight months of his administration which now was ending, had issued titles to 450,000 acres more of Grants land. His Majesty was transferring him to North Carolina and bringing William Tryon, that province's governor, to New York. Dunmore protested bitterly. Business was excellent here in New York, and in any province over which Tryon had had control there would be few pickings left even for an industrious Scotsman. On June 9, 1771, Tryon arrived and Dunmore departed.

William Tryon was a soldier who had married wisely into the family of a British colonial secretary. This union had obtained him a place in the government. He was not a person who left opportunities undeveloped. His administrative abilities had won for him, among other things, a £15,000 governor's palace in Carolina. They also had roused a rebellion which he had smashed flat, and he looked forward to settling the Grants revolt as finally. There had been no Ethan Allen in Tryon's former province.

The new governor determined to clear up unfinished business before starting new. There was the Breakenridge affair still dangling. Jim, though New York had tried twice to oust him, still was farming the same old place. The expeditionary force now mobilized against him was a tribute to his staying powers.

Sheriff Henry Ten Eyck of Albany assembled a mounted posse of two hundred men, including Mayor Cuyler and other town notables, and marched against Jim. On July 18, 1771, the advance guard of the column reached the Walloomsac bridge, a half-mile from Breakenridge's home, and found seven men waiting there, quiet men with guns. The bridge, its guard said, was closed. After argument, Mayor Cuyler, who led the advance, and Abraham Lansing were permitted to cross and talk to Breakenridge.

Jim, they found, had even more visitors today than usually were calling when New York authorities appeared. Forty, well-armed, lingered in a field on one side of the road, near a fold of land that would make an excellent breastwork. One hundred and fifty more of Jim's guests were behind a ridge on the opposite side of the highway with only their heads—and their muskets—visible. Twenty additional friends of Mr. Breakenridge accompanied him when he came out of his house to talk with Cuyler. They explained they were the dwelling's garrison.

The town of Bennington, Breakenridge told the mayor, had appointed a committee to protect his farm. The men in the field, behind the ridge, from the house, were all committee members. They didn't want him to surrender his farm to New York, and he guessed he wouldn't. Cuyler gave him a half-hour to change his mind and went down to the bridge where Ten Eyck and his forces now waited. The guards had retired. When Jim sent word that thirty minutes were spent and his mind was unchanged, the sheriff commanded his army to advance.

There was something in the prospect of the distant, overpopulated farm that made most of his followers deaf to his orders. Only part of them crossed the bridge, and only twenty accompanied him as far as the house. The men in the field were forming in its hollow, the men behind the ridge were uncomfortably still. Breakenridge and his house guests had vanished. The dwelling's door was barred, and there was stealthy movement and a glint of musket barrels behind its windows.

While his handful of companions fidgeted, the sheriff demanded the farm's surrender. Breakenridge refused. Argument, persuasion, threats, brought no more profitable reply than indecent noises from the garrison.

Ax in hand, Ten Eyck threatened to break in the door. He was promised death if he tried it, and the assurance sounded sincere. The aspect of the party behind the ridge and the other force in the field now became so threatening that the sheriff gave up. He and his remaining followers rode back to Albany to inform Tryon that it wasn't as easy to evict Breakenridge as the Governor had said it would be.

Tryon could be pardoned for underestimating the people of the Grants. No troops quite like the Green Mountain Boys ever existed elsewhere. They were loosely organized, sketchily drilled, and incredibly apt. The tactics that Ethan Allen had prescribed for them could only be performed by men with ice-cool heads. Adventures like the Breakenridge incident were dangerous. One rash movement, one finger inadvertently pressing a trigger, might turn them into shambles.

Resistance to New York was not a sport. It was a matter of deadly earnest, of constant peril; yet it demanded, as sports do, deftness, resourcefulness, a sure, firm touch. Open combat would have required far less than the Green Mountain Boys' system entailed. The miracle of their success is dwarfed by the even more prodigious fact that in all their scuffles, their brawls, their violences, they never killed anyone but Constable Pease's horse; they never permanently injured any man.

Each of the enterprises of Allen's men teetered on tragedy's thin edge; yet each, by the Colonel's boldness, skill, and immense self-possession, toppled back at last into comedy. The men whom the Green Mountain Boys misused were conscious thereafter that even their friends secretly were laughing at them, as Sheriff Ten Eyck's associates must have laughed when his discomfited column returned to Albany.

Dr. Samuel Adams, not the Boston rabble-rouser but a contentious resident of Arlington, had supported the Grants cause at first but thereafter, for no man knows what inducements, had turned his coat and begun to uphold New York at the top of his voice. When neighbors warned him, Adams put a brace of pistols in his pockets and dared them to stop him.

He may have been a loud-mouthed eccentric. It is just possible, though, that he was courting violence which New York would be compelled to answer in kind. This thought seems to have been in the minds of Allen's irregulars. They made Adams hush his noise, but not by threats or injury.

The doctor was captured, taken to Bennington, and trussed in an armchair which was hauled aloft on the standard before Fay's tavern. There, to the intense delight of the spectators, Adams hung for two hours, just beneath the stuffed catamount which glared toward New York less shamefacedly than the culprit surveyed the crowd below him. When at last he was lowered and dismissed, his voice was no more heard in the land.

Internally, Allen's men were intensely disciplined—or inconceivably lucky. Externally, they looked more like the "rioters" or "the Bennington mob," which were New York's more printable names for them, than they resembled the Green Mountain Boys of poetry and fiction.

They were a wild-eyed, shaggy, bawling rabble, and the costumes they contrived for their raids were utterly undignified and wholly deplorable.

In blackface, in Indian blankets, handkerchief masks, horsetail whiskers, women's mob caps, they came riding through the woods to frighten invaders or fell upon York surveyors like rum-maddened Indians. They looked less like heroes than children who have spent a rainy afternoon in Grandma's attic.

On the surface they were a barbaric, uproarious rag, tag, and bobtail, who broke surveyors instruments, burned Yorker's cabins, and on rare occasions thrashed the defiant with stinging bunches of twigs, "the beech seal of the wilderness." Actually, they were unique soldiers on whom their leader had stamped his own impress.

Each of the unnumbered clashes with New York authorities was conducted in the very presence of death. The ghastly threats, the blasphemous epithets the Colonel Commandant roared in action, and his followers echoed, were insulting enough to move even mild men toward homicide.

Instead of provoking strife, these objurgations seemed to quench it. Allen and his followers possessed the inestimably precious ability to scare their enemies into paroxysms. The tale of these triumphs by lung power is not from their own lips. It is contained in the complaints that the victims of the Green Mountain Boys sent to Tryon in ever-increasing volume.

Charles Hutchinson and the Todd brothers, Yorkers, took land that Robert Cochran owned in the New Hampshire-granted town of Rupert. There Hutchinson built a cabin and the others a leanto.

They looked up from their work to find their clearing full of horsemen who seemed, because of the violence they used and the much more horrid predictions they made of what was going to happen in another moment, abnormally large and deadly. The biggest and the most blasphemous of them all, Hutchinson deposed in Albany later, was Ethan Allen. Two of his companions were Remember Baker and Robert Cochran.

These intemperate persons smashed the leanto and set fire to Hutchinson's cabin as a burnt offering, Allen informed its owner, "to the gods of the world." He added to Hutchinson:

"Go now and complain to that damn scoundrel, your governor. God damn your governor, laws, king, council, and assembly." And when his victim reproved him for swearing he bawled:

"God damn your soul, are you going to preach to us?"

"Deponent," Hutchinson's affidavit primly adds, "is also credibly informed said Allen denies the being of a God and that there is any Infernal Spirit."

This complaint and a mounting babble of similar tidings from the Grants distracted Tryon from profitable work at hand and wore upon his no great store of patience. He was following the custom of other New York governors and issuing patents with a complete disregard for the British Government's reiterated orders. Allen and his accomplices were a nuisance and a growing detriment to the real-estate business, yet nobody seemed able to abate them. Perhaps if a reward were offered, the problem might solve itself.

Tryon replied to the hearty ill wishes that Hutchinson had relayed to him by issuing a proclamation, promising £20 each for the capture of Ethan Allen, Robert Cochran, and Remember Baker.

The gentlemen singled out for this evidence of His Excellency's regard seemed more pleased than irked. They posted Tryon's placard in Fay's tavern for all to see and presently set beside it a companion piece indited by Allen, which read:

TWENTY-FIVE POUNDS REWARD

Whereas James Duane and John Kempe of New York have by their menaces and threats greatly disturbed the public peace and repose of the honest peasants of Bennington and the settlements to the northward, which peasants are now and ever have been in the peace of God and the King, and are patriotic and liege subjects of George III, any person that will apprehend these common disturbers, viz James Duane and John Kempe, and bring them to landlord Fay's at Bennington shall have fifteen pounds for James Duane and ten pounds for John Kempe, paid by

> ETHAN ALLEN
> REMEMBER BAKER
> ROBERT COCHRAN

The only other response Tryon's offer brought him was a further complaint against Allen, embodied in an affidavit by one Benjamin Buck of Albany, an unfortunately tactless man. Buck deposed that he had stopped at the Fay tavern in Bennington and was overseen reading His Excellency's and Allen's companion proclamations by the author of the latter, who demanded what Buck's politics were. Buck swore that when he declared for New York, Allen cuffed him three times and said:

"You are a damned bastard of old Munro's. We shall make a hell of his house and burn him in it and every son of a bitch who takes his part."

No actual attempt was made to capture the Colonel Commandant. The pay Tryon offered was deemed ridiculously small for the job, but rumors of kidnaping plots did float about, and one of them must have come to the ears of Colonel Philip Skene.

Skene was a retired army officer and a man of wealth who lived in lordly splendor, with a stone manor house, tenants, indentured servants and slaves, on a 30,000-acre tract of land granted him directly by the British Board of Trade. He called his estate Skenesboro. It is now occupied in part by the village of Whitehall, New York. The old soldier seems to have been a person of tastes and alcoholic capacity akin to Ethan Allen's. The manorial magnificence of Skene's holdings impressed the "honest peasant of Bennington," and he visited there frequently. Perhaps already he was discussing the plan that later he furthered.

This project was the establishment of the New Hampshire Grants as a separate province with Skene as the royal governor.

At any rate, when Skene heard of the rumored plot, he wrote Allen, warning him that he was in danger and that it might be wise to leave the Grants for a time and go home to his family in Connecticut.

The Colonel Commandant's reply breathed defiance and resolution. His letter, from which valiant emotion had banished any vestige of punctuation, began:

> Tho I Cannot Dispute Your Friendship to me Yet I Now Inform You that I Cannot Flee to Connecticut I have a spirit above that I shall stay in Your Neighborhood I hope Till I Remove to the Kingdom of Heaven.

So Allen wrote and then sent this indomitable profession to Skene from Salisbury, Connecticut, to which haven he already had retired. This may have been the Colonel's idea of humor. More likely he was so completely, so boisterously, fearless that he could not imagine anyone might deem him afraid. It was a resounding letter, and he meant Skene to have it, no matter from where it was sent. The Colonel Commandant was a remarkable man.

VI Storm Winds

IN THAT TIME, troublesome winds blew through America. Old loyalties were suspect, and the new, derided. Long-cherished reverences crumbled. Mobs marched toward the Millennium with no clear idea of its direction. Anger bred anger, and demagogues fed insurgency's fires with whatever fuel came to hand.

Men had reached the feverish state in which they talked only of theories and ignored their practice. They fumed, not over the weight of taxation, but its principle, and made a mighty issue of a petty impost on tea. Clumsy government attempted placation which was empty of conciliation and cast this aside to adopt an obstinacy which was barren of wisdom.

Pioneers of the New Hampshire Grants heard the winds' far hooting with the abstraction of folk who still strove with simple, urgent, concrete things. They had no time to savor new political doctrines. They were holding fast, stubbornly, desperately, to their own land.

Tryon, in New York, ignored the blast and its sound of omen. Despite the repeated warnings and prohibitions of Britain, he was issuing more patents to Grants territory. In the year ending June, 1772, he bestowed 542,450 acres, some unoccupied, some already settled by New Hampshire title holders. He was a masterly ignorer.

In Salisbury, where he wintered with his family, Ethan Allen, too, was immensely occupied. He was writing pieces for the paper reciting, as far as the not too stiff strictures of the *Connecticut Courant* would permit, the iniquities of Tryon and all his governing predecessors, upholding the rights of New Hampshire claimants, who included, in a rather large way now, himself and brother Ira. These diatribes, signed "A Friend of Liberty & Property" or "A Lover of Reason & Truth" may or may not have irked Tryon, but they surely gratified Ethan Allen. In moments of stress he always was quite as likely to run for his pen as for his sword.

Others besides the Colonel Commandant were taking to paper and ink. Throughout the Grants, earnest groups were petitioning the

King, calling attention to the wicked chaos brought about by all factions but their own, begging that Britain delay no longer in announcing a decision of the quarrel, and appending their own prescription for a really just settlement.

The growing blizzard of appeals had little effect upon London. Decision, continually promised, never came. The amazing deliberation of His Majesty must have weaned many settlers from their original loyalty to the Crown, yet the delay was pardonable.

King George and his ministers were being presented with more problems than they could adequately decide. They had no time at all to give to a wild frontier land and its scattered population of 7000. A cat fight in the kitchen is ignored when the rest of the house is ablaze.

His Majesty simply never got around to refereeing the contest between the Grants and New York. The British Government's major contribution to a solution was an occasional and austere request that the fighting parties try to behave themselves.

The first month of 1772 saw strife resumed where it had been left off at the end of the previous year. Even in Allen's absence, the Westside rebellion continued, and in January there was a brief upflaring on the Eastside that indicated insurgency also was at work there. The East's rebellion, like its forerunner in which John Grout had been involved, was aimed less at Tryon than at the New York court which had been imposed on Cumberland County.

This court, which was considered by many an expensive and arrogant and increasingly pestiferous institution, awarded damages to Jonas Moore of Putney in his suit against Leonard Spaulding of Dummerston, who refused to pay. The court then authorized Moore to levy on his adversary's chattels.

The successful litigant had small opportunity to use Spaulding's belongings. Armed men burst into Moore's house on the night of January 27, took the property, and returned it to Spaulding. What they said to Moore and the earnest way they said it choked off any subsequent protest. Matters in Cumberland County had reached that dangerous stage when some men believe they themselves are justice's only servants.

Revolt still was unorganized on the Eastside. In the West, it had become a business. There, only officials of the stoutest spirits and most robust constitutions dared represent New York at all. A few of those obstinate zealots who are the scoundrels of a losing cause and the heroes of a successful, still carried on—men like John Munro, Shaftsbury's justice of the peace; Judge Benjamin Spencer of Clarendon; the

Rev. Benjamin Hough, Anabaptist parson and justice of the peace in Socialborough. Through perversity or patriotism they kept up the fight. The rest of their associates, including Sheriff Ten Eyck, had quit.

Even now, John Munro, whom threats did not awe and an occasional beating up did not unduly depress, was planning a coup both spectacular and profitable. He had a spy watching Remember Baker's house in Arlington. Sooner or later Baker would return; and he was worth, thanks to Tryon's proclamation, £20 on the hoof. On March 20, the spy, Bliss Willoughby, sent tidings to Munro. Before daylight on the morrow, the Justice and a following of Yorkers smashed in Baker's door.

There was thumping and bellowing in the torchlit dusk, a rush of men, a flourishing of swords, and a loud screeching from Baker's wife and little son, who had got in the way, and both were slightly wounded. Remember was a hard man to take. He had jumped for his ax as the door went down and now stood, back to the stairs, deaf to demands for surrender, swinging his weapon through the cleared space before him. Someone slashed at him, nearly severing his thumb. He yelled, whirled about, and went up into the attic like a squirrel.

While Munro's men hesitated to follow, they heard the crashing thump of the ax, the splintering of wood, brief silence, and then, from outside, a hearty howl. They rushed forth and captured Baker, raging but helpless. He had battered a gable out of his dwelling, leaped, and landed armpit-deep in a snowdrift. He was extracted, bound, thrust into a sleigh, and the party started for Albany. They did not know that already Caleb Henderson was flogging his farm horse down the road to Bennington.

After sixteen cold miles in which there was no visible pursuit, Munro's party stopped at an inn. Meanwhile, there had been an early-morning shouting in Bennington's street and much swearing about Fay's tavern as, one by one, the horsemen came in. When ten had arrived they would not wait for more, but galloped hell-for-leather by a shorter road than Munro had taken toward the Hudson ferry. They got there first, and, turning, trotted their blown horses back along the way by which the Justice and his party must come. When they saw these advancing, a dark blot upon the snow, they charged.

"All run for it," Munro lamented later to Duane and Kempe, "but the two constables."

These and he were taken back to Bennington with Baker. They afterward were released. This was an odd yet common practice. It may have been part of the Allen system. If Yorkers were eliminated by imprisonment or exile, life would have been dull for the Green Mountain Boys. So Munro went free, but he was not happy, for he wrote thereafter to Tryon that all New York officials had been wholly cowed by the Baker affair and that he himself was "almost wore out with watching."

His vigilance did not prevent the pardonably aggrieved Remember from visiting Bliss Willoughby, the spy, and using him "in a barbarous fashion."

Munro's own troubles were approaching climax. That usually moderate man, Seth Warner, girded on his sword, mounted his horse, and rode to Shaftsbury. There he demanded that the Justice turn over to him Remember Baker's gun, taken during the raid.

Munro refused, gripped Warner's bridle, declared him under arrest, and yelled for aid. Seth forgot decorum sufficiently to draw sword and clout the Justice over the head so vigorously that the weapon broke. It was dull, and Munro's skull was hard. Though he fell, he was not seriously hurt. Warner's assault seems to have pleased everybody but Munro. The grateful town of Poultney voted to settle on Seth one hundred acres of land "for his valor in cutting the head of Esquire Munro, the Yorkite."

Ethan Allen was back from Connecticut, too. Tidings from the Grants had distracted him from further literary composition. It is probable that he called on Munro to discuss the Esquire's misuse of Cousin Remember, for soon after Allen's arrival, Munro reported to his principals dismally: "Since my last to you and my other friends, the rascally Yankees spoiled my best hat and sword coat with their Pumpkin sticks," and with that valedictory fades out of the lively picture.

This grew continually more active as the spring advanced. So many New York officials had been manhandled, so many surveyors from Albany had been chased back home, without ensuing reprisal, by vehement persons who had bawled that they were "sons of Robin Hood" that the insurgents grew worried. This apathy of the enemy must mean that something dire was brewing. When news came that troops were moving up the Hudson, the Grants at once identified them as a punitive force.

There were panicky twitterings in the Committee of Safety when it met in Bennington to consider the menace, but the strong voice of Ethan Allen blew terror away. He mocked at the older men's faltering suggestion that they send a flag of truce to Tryon and ask for terms. If the Governor ordered war, the Colonel Commandant would oblige him.

Expresses rode to muster the scattered elements of the Green Mountain Boys. Cannon were hauled up from the old fort at Williamstown. They were rusty relics with scant powder and no ball available, but their presence stiffened morale. Young Ira Allen was sent out on his first recorded official mission. Ethan bade him go to Albany and determine the strength and purpose of the expedition.

If Tryon led it against the Grants, Ira was to move before the column until he made contact with five other marksmen the Colonel Commandant would supply. Their duty then would be to lurk in ambush and do their skillful best to shoot the Governor out of his saddle and, thereafter, to abolish as many other officers as possible.

Ira departed and returned swiftly, laden with anticlimax. The troops were destined, not for the Grants, but to relieve garrisons at Oswego, Niagara, and Detroit. The Safety Committee adjourned. Ethan Allen's army returned to its regular enterprises, but their preparation for war may not have been wholly a futile gesture.

It is possible that the plan to knock over William Tryon may have reached His Excellency's ears and have inspired, in part at least, the letter that he wrote, May 19, to Parson Dewey and his neighbors.

Tryon, the stern governor, the enemy of disorder, who had brutally stamped out rebellion in North Carolina, spoke gently, almost appealingly, to the insurgents of the Grants. He must have gulped a little while he wrote. He chided them like an uncle for their past misdeeds. He professed himself suddenly and immensely concerned over their grievances and urged them to send him emissaries so that he might discuss and remedy their woes.

He would be glad to see anybody from the Grants except—here his benevolence cracked for a moment—except a few unpardonable miscreants: Ethan Allen, Robert Cochran, Remember Baker, Seth Warner.

The Committee considered this offer with some justifiable suspicion. Landlord Fay and his son, Dr. Jonas, at last were appointed agents to confer with the Governor and his council. They bore a letter from the Committee, setting forth the Grants' case, and another on behalf of the four untouchables. This was written by Ethan Allen, who, stung by such discrimination, had leaped at once for a pen.

Allen's missive was in his most unrestrained style, which, whatever else it lacked, had the grandeur of chaos. It had been respelled and

punctuated by some purist, but it still contained sentences as daunting
as this:

> We do not suppose, may it please Your Excellency, we are making
> opposition to a government as such; it is nothing more than a party
> carried by a number of gentlemen attorneys (if it be not an abuse of
> gentlemen of merit to call them so) who manifest a surprising and
> enterprising thirst of avarice after our country; but for a collection
> of such intrigues to plan matters of influence of a party so as to even-
> tually to become judges in their own case and thereby cheat us out
> of our country appears to us so audaciously unreasonable and ty-
> rannical that we view it with the utmost detestation and indignation
> and our breasts glow with a martial fury to defend our persons and
> fortunes from the ravages of these that would destroy us but not
> against Your Excellency's person or government.

Recollection of Allen's design to shoot him off his horse may have
tempered whatever comfort Tryon took in that final assurance.

The Fays left for New York. Quiet, unfamiliar yet soothing, which
might ripen at last into peace, brooded over the Grants. In the East,
events favored Tryon. Guilford town, after successive petitions, had
taken matters into its own hands, ignoring its New Hampshire charter and, in the absence of any substitute, simply declaring for New
York and letting it go at that.

An election had been held in Cumberland County, and two representatives—the slippery Crean Brush, now of Westminster, and Samuel
Wells of Brattleboro, both pro-Tryon—had been seated in the New
York Assembly. A statelier house for the Cumberland County court
had been built at Westminster, which now became the county seat.

The spring's soft air was full of promise. Even tidings from the south
that told of the burning of His Majesty's eight-gun schooner *Gaspé*
by Rhode Island insurgents could not mar the hope and half-assurance
that hung in the Grants' sunny weather.

The prospect of peace was not lessened by a letter Tryon received
this June from Lord Hillsborough, the colonial secretary. The heavy
cargoes of petitions exported from the Grants to London and the general tenor of their complaints had stirred suspicion in the noble lord
that William Tryon was plundering again.

Hillsborough's letter had edge and point. It warned Tryon to leave
the Grants settlers alone and to issue no more patents to land there on
any excuse whatever, and it cut deep enough into his insensitive hide
to bring about a temporary obedience.

The Fays, arriving in New York, found His Excellency in a placating mood. The truce that they and he worked out seemed likely to serve. Meanwhile, men could only hope that Britain would get around to deciding the strife once and for all. By the agreement, all suits of private individuals, all suits on behalf of the Crown, were to be suspended, settlers were to remain undisturbed, and those Yorkers who had been chased off their land permitted to come back.

Bennington, on the morning of July 15, witnessed an unprecedented sight. The "Bennington Artillery" that had been brought to repel Tryon's dreaded invasion was fired off in his honor. Seth Warner's company delivered three volleys in the same cause. Bells were rung, and Landlord Fay's punch bowls, so lately devoted to toasts wishing His Excellency all possible and painful ills, were raised now to pledge him health and happiness.

The Grants agents had returned and reported to the Committee the success of their mission. There was a new spirit abroad in Bennington's streets. The New York lion and the Grants obstreperous lamb were about to lie down together.

Such periods of popular relief and rapture seldom last long and usually end in extreme disillusion. Bennington's endured more briefly and concluded more calamitously than most. In August, Tryon wrote the folk who recently had been extolling him, thanking them for their courtesy and asking with some bitterness why their conduct immediately after the celebration had involved flagrant "breech of faith and honor."

The Governor cited the complaint of William Cockburn, the surveyor whom Allen already had frightened from the Grants. He charged that Seth Warner and Remember Baker had found Cockburn running a line in the Onion River country and had chased him forth again.

Lieutenant Colonel John Reid, late of the 42nd Highlanders, "The Black Watch," and persistent claimant to a tract of land in the New Hampshire town of Panton at the falls of Otter Creek, where his settlers and New Hampshire settlers alternately had been pushing each other out for some time, now charged that Baker and Warner had evicted his people once more.

No one seemed better fitted to reply to Tryon's embarrassing accusations than Ethan Allen, and he got the job. He explained the inexplicable and justified the unjustifiable so eloquently and so turgidly that all Tryon seems to have got out of the letter was the general opinion that it was "highly insolent and deserving of Sharp Reprehension."

The Governor's temper was not improved by the receipt at this time of another letter, this from Lord Dartmouth, new Secretary for the Colonies, who accused Tryon of crass "deviations" from the King's instructions and warned him against committing any more. Henceforth, the truce fell quickly to pieces. The Green Mountain Boys resumed their well-tempered outrages while New York patentees and settlers reached out again for whatever they thought they could hold.

In October, when all traces of the recent compromise had vanished, delegates from the Westside towns assembled in convention at Manchester and prepared another petition to the King which they determined to send by the hand of James Breakenridge. This petition, though personally escorted overseas, seems to have done nothing more toward speeding the royal mind to a decision than its forerunners, and Breakenridge returned to the Grants with only the conventional promise of a speedy settlement.

Meanwhile, the Allen brothers—Ethan and Ira—had spent a vacation together in the Onion (now the Winooski) River country. Ethan intended to hunt, but Ira, who had prospected this region before, guided him astutely into another enterprise by pointing out the magnificent timber of the hills, the water power going to waste, the fertility of the valleys. They emerged from the wilderness with few deer but many plans.

Most of the Onion River land was held under New Hampshire title by the Burling family of White Plains, New York, who, considering the riotous state of affairs in the Grants, would be certain to sell cheaply. Ethan and Ira assembled other members of the Allen clan— Heman, Zimri, and Remember Baker—formed the Onion River Land Company, and with every shilling the concern's members could assemble journeyed to White Plains and purchased 45,000 acres.

They were committed now. They had invested the family's last penny in the future integrity of New Hampshire grants. If patriotism consists of an attachment to one's land, the Allens were superpatriots.

Theses have been written on less entertaining subjects than the influence of the real-estate business upon the birth of the American nation, not forgetting the Father of His Country's involvement in the Ohio Land Company. Revolution, to grow satisfactorily, must root deeply in a soil.

The Allens' speculation on Onion River was not the least potent of the forces that created the Vermont Republic. The company, as it sold its property, did not pocket the profits. Instead, it turned them back into the concern, buying still more acres, pyramiding its holdings, until presently the cause of the Grants became permanently entangled with the safety of the Allens' whole fortune.

No one can say with authority how much of Ethan and Ira Allen's immense service to the land of their adoption was pure patriotism—if that ever can be a wholly refined substance—and how much was a more materialistic concern for the large fragment of the Grants which they precariously owned.

The Allens were not entirely mercenary men. They had enlisted to defend the integrity of the New Hampshire Grants before either of them had made any considerable cash investment in the territory. They had striven for the safety of poor and threatened farmer folk with creditable lack of self-interest. Now they were directors of a real-estate concern with continually increasing acreage, and were bound to work more passionately still for freedom. They had got themselves into a position from which they could move only in one direction—toward independence.

They had to get the country clear of New York. If the Grants became part of that province, the Allens were ruined. They could not possibly pay the patent fees New York would demand. If the patent fees were remitted, they could not pay the quitrents.

They must also keep the Grants from becoming part of New Hampshire. Even the moderate rents demanded by this province would wreck their enterprise.

They must have the exactly right sort of government—a government that imposed no taxes at all; a government that moved along a narrow channel, avoiding Scylla to the east, Charybdis to the west, and steered, because it could not exist otherwise, toward independence; a government by the Grants people, for the Grants people—and Ethan Allen & Co., Realtors.

The troublesome winds which ranged the colonies that winter had a shriller, more ominous cry; but the Allens scarcely heeded it. They were intensely busy, not for the public weal, but for their own eventual profit. Each man labored, according to his gifts. All of them sold land and looked for further promising purchases. Ira, the astute and plausible, was promoter and sales manager; Ethan was advertising manager and, as Colonel Commandant of the Green Mountain Boys, chief of the company police as well.

Advertisements extolling the virtues of the Onion River "with a diversity of all sorts of excellent fish particularly the salmon" and not underpraising the surrounding territory—"There is no tract of land of so great quantity between New York and the government of Canada that in a state of nature can justly be denominated equally good"—appeared in the *Connecticut Courant.*

The Allen Company began to sell and with the cash received went forth and bought more. In the spring, Ira built a "road" to the development. Like all thoroughfares of the region and the time, it was merely a blazed trail that a man on foot or a horse might follow. Settlers began to move north along it.

> Thus [wrote Ira smugly, later] in a short time I led a people through a wilderness of seventy miles; about the same distance that took Moses forty years to conduct the children of Israel.

Distracting matters kept Ethan from active participation in the real-estate business this spring. The strife between New York and the Grants had emerged from hibernation a little uglier, a little more menacing, than it had been the previous fall.

From Clarendon, the York judge, Benjamin Spencer, was complaining:

> The tumults have got to such a height both in Socialborough and from Bennington to Manchester that I cannot travel abroad to do any lawful business, indeed I cannot travel safely two miles from home.

In Socialborough, the Rev. Benjamin Hough was uttering similar cries of outrage and appeals for aid. The tumult that caused this distress may have been due to the solution of the Grants-New York disputes, advanced this spring by Tryon. This had at least the virtue of simplicity.

The Governor proposed that Great Britain declare all New York patents valid, all New Hampshire grants void; and that actual settlers under the latter be allowed for their confiscated farms "liberal equivalents out of the wastelands and such other indulgences by a suspension of quitrents as His Majesty shall think equitable."

It was not a tactful solution under any circumstances, and at that moment it was particularly ironic. On May 12, New York's dispute with Massachusetts over that province's western line had been settled by negotiation. It had been agreed that the boundary should run, like Connecticut's, parallel to the Hudson River and twenty miles to the east of the stream. Once more, New York had abandoned her claim of jurisdiction to the Connecticut River, but she still imposed it on the Grants.

That imposition became increasingly difficult to maintain. Ethan Allen's soldiery were more active this year. The wails of ousted New York settlers, the more piercing clamor of patent holders who found they had acquired possession of nothing but a document, were a continual buzzing sound in the Governor's ears. There must have been many times when he wished that New York never had laid claim to any land east of the Hudson. That must have been the way Colonel John Reid, New York claimant in Panton, came to feel about it, too.

After his repulse of the previous year, Reid had enlisted a number of Scottish immigrants and had established them on the property again. They built a mill and began the construction of a village. On August 11, 1773, Ethan Allen, Remember Baker, and Seth Warner, with a hundred Green Mountain Boys, abolished the settlement.

They came out of the woods, yelping and lashing their horses, and went to work with the skill of long practice. They turned their mounts into the standing grain. Their aspect, the threats they uttered, the outrageously familiar terms on which they seemed to be with the Deity, scared most of the simple peasants speechless.

One of the still-articulate demanded a warrant for this invasion, and Baker, lifting his thumbless hand, bawled, "Here is my warrant!" and Allen, raising his firelock high, bellowed, "This is my law." He laughed when the Scots threatened him with New York authority.

"We are a lawless mob," he shouted, "and our law is mob law. I have run these woods for seven years past, and I never have been catched yet, by God."

Smoke blew through the clearing from the kindling houses. Haystacks were cones of fire, and Warner, having found a bolt of cloth somewhere, was hacking it into pieces with his sword and tossing fragments to the men to be worn in their hats as "cockades of victory." The settlers fled. One, when he reached safety, wrote to Colonel Reid:

> Our Houses are All Brunt Down The Gristmill is All Put Down The Mill Stones Brock and Throne into the Crick The Corn is all Destroed by There Horses and When it was Proposed That We Should build houses and Keep Possion They Threatened to Bind some of us to a Tree and Skin us Alive.
>
> Therefore [the writer continues with excellent logic] we think it Imposable To us To live hear in peace.

This was Colonel Reid's last attempt at settlement. The fragments of the Put Down grist mill were reassembled into a stout blockhouse for the protection of New Hampshire residents in the town of Panton, where Ethan Allen held a share.

Insurgencies as spectacular as this were rare, yet day after day the guerrilla war went on. Day after day Tryon read dismal reports from his agents in the Grants.

These tidings were forwarded to the Governor by his hard-pressed officials, the Rev. Mr. Hough and Judge Spencer. Then Spencer's reports ceased. Whatever comfort Tryon might have got from this elimination of calamitous news was blighted by Hough's account of how his associate had been hushed. This enclosed an affidavit by the Judge, which seems to have been his final report.

Several attempts had been made to lay hold upon the elusive Spencer before at last they got him. He wakened, in the night of November 20, to feel he still was in the dire grip of a familiar dream. It seemed that Ethan Allen and several other grim persons stood beside his bed and bade him rise. Spencer gaped. Then, as Allen whacked him over the head with a musket barrel and repeated his command, the judge appreciated that this was not a nightmare, but worse.

His unsought guests discussed what they should do with him when he had finished dressing and made frequent awful promises to Spencer of what would happen right away if he did not hasten. When the quaking jurist had got his clothes on, he was bundled aboard a horse and taken to the dwelling of Thomas Green, where he was held under guard from Saturday till Monday.

On Monday, a detail of Green Mountain Boys took the prisoner back to his own home, explaining to him cheerfully that he had best be tried there since they were going to burn down the dwelling afterward anyway.

A "Judgment Seat" was established before Spencer's home and, after an oration by Allen, he, Cochran, Warner, and Baker sat themselves upon it and demanded that the prisoner stand before them bareheaded. A half-circle of the Grants' army used musket butts when needful to keep back the crowd that watched the proceedings with awe or delight, depending on their politics. Spencer was found guilty of serving New York at the expense of the Grants and urging his neighbors to buy New York titles to their land.

In punishment for his sins, Baker, still seeking revenge for his maimed hand, urged that Spencer be flogged, but the other judges were more merciful. The prisoner was sentenced to watch his house burn, and the roof actually was kindled; but the wretched man begged so hard for his property that the flames were put out.

The roof was then torn off "with great Shouting of Joy and much noise and tumult" and, after Spencer had promised to raise his dwelling's cover again under Grants jurisdiction and had pledged himself to buy a New Hampshire deed to his property, he was set free.

To compensate the audience for the lack of spectacle, the court adjourned to the house of another Yorker, Simpson Jenny. He was discreetly not at home, and they burned that structure down.

Tryon's was not a heart-warming character, yet he must have seemed when he got the indefatigable Hough's report a rather pathetic man, pulled several ways and able to go none of them. Allen, by the prankish, infuriating war he was waging, had almost unsettled the Governor's mind. This was not stabilized by the reiterated commands he was receiving from the home government to stop oppressing the Grants people until the King had decided the dispute. Already, Tryon had ignored that order to the extent of appealing to General Frederick Haldimand for troops to quell the spreading revolt, and this appeal had been coldly turned down by the general, then commanding the soldiers quartered in Boston.

There was no place, Haldimand pointed out, where a large number of troops could be barracked during the winter. Fort Ticonderoga was rotting to pieces; the Crown Point fort had burned down the preceding April. Furthermore, the general—a Prussian-trained officer who had had no more experience with the Allen variety of warfare than he had had with airplanes—spoke cuttingly of Tryon's plea that His Majesty's regulars were needed to put down a few bush bandits.

William Tryon was a most unhappy man. When, in December, he learned that a Boston mob, in spite of scornful General Frederick Haldimand's presence there, had dumped all the India Company's tea into the harbor, he must have known the rare delight of a hearty chuckle.

The winds, that winter, blew over the land with a still sharper note of menace. They cried through Salisbury, where the Allens, home temporarily from the wars, considered the present state, the probable future, of their real-estate concern and found both good. They whistled through the Grants, quiet now under the truce the snow imposed, and dinned about the chamber where the New York Assembly considered at Tryon's instance Hough's latest report and debated how best to put down the waxing revolt.

No more original or effective expedient was evolved by legislative minds than the offering of larger rewards for the chief miscreants. The Governor agreed. He was in a state to try any possible remedy. The prices he set upon the offenders demonstrated how pestiferous they had become since the day when Tryon had considered £20 adequate pay for the capture of Ethan Allen.

The Colonel Commandant was now quoted at £100 and so was Remember Baker. Seth Warner, Robert Cochran, Peleg Sunderland, Sylvanus Brown, James Breakenridge, and one John Smith, whose iniquity is obscure, were worth £50 apiece to the Governor.

Meanwhile, representatives of the Westside towns, meeting March 1, 1774, at Manchester and later in the month at Arlington, summoned the Colonel Commandant, not to war but to literature. Allen was chosen head of a committee that was to prepare for publication in the *Connecticut Courant,* the *Hampshire Gazette,* and later embody in pamphlet form, a new statement of Grants' grievances.

This eventually appeared. It was titled "A Brief Narrative of the Proceedings of the Government of New York Relative to their Obtaining the Jurisdiction of that Large District of Land Westward from Connecticut River Which antecendent thereto had been patented by his Majesty's Governor and Council of the Government of New Hampshire" and proportionately was no shorter than its title, for it ran to two hundred pages.

Allen was distracted briefly from the composition of this justification by the pressing and hot need to write another document. On March 9, Tryon proclaimed his new set of rewards. On the same day the legislature passed an act which those most intimately concerned immediately named "the Bloody Law."

This provided that anyone henceforth embroiled in riot against New York authority or attack upon the property of New York adherents in the Grants should be considered a convicted felon and suffer death without trial or benefit of clergy. Furthermore, the act stipulated that if Ethan Allen, Remember Baker, and the other evil doers cited in Tryon's proclamation did not surrender themselves in seventy days, they should suffer a like fate.

It may have been that some of the Colonel Commandant's subordinates were awed by this vengeful move, which practically amounted to the declaration of a permanent open season on all of them, but not

Ethan Allen. Defiance breathed from every word of the reply he immediately leaped to write. There was an embattled snort in every line. The Bloody Law was not a political move. It was immensely personal. It was an invitation to anyone to take a shot at him. If Tryon had hoped to frighten Allen, he simply didn't know his man.

The "remonstrance" which Allen composed spoke for all the outlaws, with or without their consent. The Colonel Commandant was never deficient in or particular about adjectives. He used them now as though they were rocks and New York the target. He found in all New York officials "insatiable, avaricious, overbearing, inhuman, barbarous blood-guiltiness of Disposition and Intention." He dared them to come on, authorities and land gamblers alike.

> We flatter ourselves that upon occasion we can muster as good a regiment of marksmen and scalpers as America can afford and now we give these gentlemen above named [Duane, Kempe, Banyar] together with Mr. Brush and Colonel Ten Broeck and in fine all the land jobbers of New York an invitation to come and view the dexterity of our regiment and we cannot think of a better time for that purpose than when the executioners come to kill us. . . . Come on we are ready for a game of scalping with them for our martial spirits glow with bitter indignation and consummate fury to blast their infernal projections.

Any officer, the writer pursued, quill sputtering, ink flying, who dared to arrest a single one of the Green Mountain Boys would be killed, either immediately by his prisoner or later by the captive's friends.

Those were his sentiments. The Westside convention echoed them by passing, April 12, a resolution branding any person in the Grants taking or holding a commission from New York an "enemy to their country and the common cause."

Tryon must have been surprised by the Grants' explosive response to what he certainly had believed would be terrifying measures. All the way through its history, persons who mistook Vermont's patience for weakness, eventually picked themselves up, bruised and gasping, if they picked themselves up at all. Even then, the Grants people were folk whom it was extremely hard to bully successfully.

New York's perplexed governor had no time to consider this new aspect of the problem, for in April he was called back to England to explain the waxing tumult in the Grants—an enterprise that must have been extremely intricate—and Cadwallader Colden temporarily reigned in his stead. Colden was now eighty-six, but age had not withered him. He resumed the granting of patents where Tryon had left off, and in a year had issued titles to 379,100 acres.

The wind of trouble blew more strongly now. Its blast was keener, its course more sure. In this same month of April, Britain attempted disastrously still another solution of its difficulties with the colonies. Punitive acts were established—closing the port of Boston, annulling the charter of Massachusetts, providing for trial in England of Crown servants who killed persons in America, extending the system of quartering troops on the people, granting religious freedom in Canada, and advancing its frontier behind the seaboard colonies to the Ohio River.

Black clouds were gathering at the back of the wind, and there was thunder whose distant echo shook the Grants. On the Westside the proscribed leaders continued their scandalous pursuits apparently unhampered by the prices set on their heads, and the stipulated seventy days elapsed without any of them surrendering. On the Eastside, men felt the waxing strength of the wind, and discord between factions there moved toward violence.

In May, the Committee of Correspondence that had been established to draw the threatened colonies closer, wrote to the supervisors of Cumberland County asking what stand the people there would take against further British aggression. Months elasped before an answer was returned.

The supervisors, being cautious and lukewarm men who felt that their county already was sufficiently supplied with provocations to strife, simply sat upon the committee's letter and made believe, as long as they might, that they never had received it.

It was almost impossible then—it still is today—to keep public business secret in that region. Rumors flew about and left more wherever they lit. There were questions that quickly became demands; mutterings that swelled into open threats; and the unfortunate supervisors found that by trying to avert trouble they actually had created it. At last they gave up the letter; it was circulated through the Eastside towns, and a convention was summoned to meet at Westminster, October 19, and prepare an answer.

Meanwhile, on the Westside, New York officials and settlers led lives replete with contusions and lacerations, and the Rev. Benjamin Hough lamented like Jeremiah, and Acting Governor Cadwallader Colden, who had looked with intellectual scorn on Tryon's surly blunderings, began to wonder whether that scorn had not been rather too ample.

In September, he followed in the footsteps of his predecessor and cried as loudly as ever Tryon did for troops. General Gage refused them as bluntly as Haldimand had. The Province of New York should be able to keep order within its own boundaries.

Whatever remnants of tranquillity still had clung to the Eastside were fleeing now. The county convention met in the fine new courthouse at Westminster and framed unusual resolutions, declaring in one breath unwavering loyalty to that benign and righteous monarch, George III, and in the next announcing its purpose to treat "enemies of American liberty as loathsome animals not fit to be touched or to have any society or connection with." This dissonant profession was sent to the Committee of Correspondence.

Popular comment on the crisis was less ambivalent. Out of the growing brawl of disputing voices, only one still sounds clearly, and that belongs to Leonard Spaulding of Dummerston, who cursed his King so giftedly for his recognition of the Catholic Church in Canada that they shut him up in the courthouse jail, charged with high treason. Spaulding remained there eleven days, and then armed men gathered and marched to Westminster.

Dr. Solomon Harvey, "practitioner of physick" and clerk of Dummerston, adorned that town's records thereafter with his version of what happened:

> The plain truth is that the brave sons of freedom whose patience was worn out with the inhuman results of the imps of power grew quite sick of diving after redress in a legal way and finding that the law was made use of only for the emolument of its creatures, the immesaries of the British tyrant resolved upon an easier method and accordingly opened the gaol without key or lockpicker and after congratulating Mr. Spaulding upon recovery of his freedom dispersed every man in peace to his respective home or place of abode.
>
> The foregoing is a true and short relation of that wicked affair of the New York, cut throatly, Jacobitish, high church, Toretical minions of George the Third, the Pope of Canada and tyrant of Britain.

Thus the year ended in tumult and dismay, in gropings toward rebellion, in the clashing angers of men, and another still more fateful came in. It was young when a semblance of peace again fell upon the Western Grants. The voice of the Rev. Benjamin Hough, so long attuned to the utterance of woe, was heard no more in the land.

The Anabaptist minister had been warned and had not heeded. He had been pursued and stalked but hitherto had escaped. On the morning of January 26, his luck ran out. Allen's men caught him at his home, hustled him into a sleigh, and drove him fifty miles to Sunderland town. He was prisoned there until January 30, when men with drawn swords haled him before the Judgment Seat, where Ethan Allen, Seth Warner, Robert Cochran, Peleg Sunderland, James Mead, Gideon Warren, and Jesse Sawyer were chaired.

By the prisoner's own account, there was none of the racket and blustering, none of the rowdy extravagance, that had marked earlier forays of the Green Mountain Boys. The trial was conducted with gravity and a semblance of form.

Hough was charged with being an informer for the government of New York; with dissuading people from joining the Grants cause; with defying the Grants' newly established law by exercising the office of New York Justice of the Peace within Grants territory.

When the indictment had been read to him, the prisoner was told by Ethan Allen that he might plead his case. Hough asked whether he had done injustice as a magistrate, and his judges said, "No." Seth Warner added:

"I would as willingly have you for magistrate as any man whatever."

"Have I intermeddled with land titles?" Hough demanded.

"No," Allen answered. "You are not charged with that."

It may have been that Hough mistook the court's decorum for mildness. He boldly admitted that the charges brought against him were all true. The judges then retired and came back several hours later to pronounce sentence, which Allen read from a paper.

This decreed for the prisoner banishment from the Grants, until the procrastinating British had judged the controversy, and two hundred lashes before he departed and five hundred more if he returned.

Hough was stripped, tied, and, under Cochran's supervision, four men thrashed him in succession with a rope scourge. Thereafter, "deponent being very faint was put into the care of one Doctor Washburn who conducted him into a house."

Later the same day, the minister was sent on his way into banishment. Before he departed on foot he received the following safe conduct:

Sunderland, January the 30th day, 1775.
This may certify the inhabitants of the New Hampshire Grants that Benjamin Hough hath this day r'cd a full punishment for his

crimes committed heretofore against this Country and our Inhabitants are ordered to give the sd Huff free and unmolested Pasport toward the City of New York or to the Westward of our Grants he behaving as becometh Given under our hands this day and date aforesaid.

ETHAN ALLEN
SETH WARNER

Hough's trial and punishment was the climactic and probably the final action of that singular regiment, the Green Mountain Boys, in their unprecedented warfare against colonial New York. Romancers, who have equipped Ethan Allen's regiment with rifles as well as a number of equally mythical heroisms, have done that organization disservice. It was not designed for battle. Its members did not strive to hack the Grants free from New York. Theirs was an almost bloodless surgery and an infinitely skillful, requiring, not marksmen and scalpers, of whom their colonel delighted to bluster, but intelligent, deft men.

The factual accomplishments of the Green Mountain Boys surpass the tritely romantic deeds with which fiction has credited them. For almost five years they fought a more powerful adversary—an enemy with more men, more munitions, and more trained leaders. Allen's men defied and outwitted a series of governors; they chased alien officers out of their country; they ousted New York settlers or bent them to Grants law.

That five-year defense was triumphant, and it was won at the most trivial cost. A few frontier cabins were burned, a few persons were jostled and threatened, a half-dozen were whipped. Hough, the most savagely treated of them all, was able to walk out of the Grants when his punishment was over.

New York called Allen's men brutal savages. They actually were physically merciful. The hurt they dealt New York was almost entirely mental. They were immune to reprisal. Remember Baker's severed thumb was the sole recorded wound suffered by the regiment in five years of action. A minor automobile accident of today can wreak more bodily damage than all the Green Mountain Boys and their adversaries incurred.

Allen's command were extremely able and level-headed men, but those qualities were not enough to insure their fantastic success. They followed a system that their leader had invented.

Those who have portrayed Ethan Allen as a flame-breathing warrior, those who have pictured him as a headlong, blundering favorite of fortune, all are wrong. Luck, or valor, or both could not have kept his regiment of young rapscallions intact, unhurt, neither bloodied nor blood-guilty through five years of rough-and-tumble campaigning.

Their commander had something more—something much more— than valor and fortune's favor. He had the Original Something that Washington discerned. No one before or since possessed it in even re- motely similar quantity.

Hereafter, he was to be often a bungler, sometimes a comic; but in his own field and time, in that crisis for which he was apparently de- signed, he was superb. He established the rhythm, he set the pitch, for his people's future resistance to civil threats and injustices. Thence- forth, the Grants and the republic the Grants became, would deal with these in the Ethan Allen way.

Those who would disparage his deft and punctual genius should consider what happened a few weeks after the Rev. Mr. Hough's punishment, when Yorkers and their opponents clashed on the East- side without benefit of Ethan Allen's presence or influence.

VII   Men March to Westminster

FORTY WORRIED MEN RODE, early in March, 1775, to the home in Chester of the Cumberland County Court of Common Pleas' Chief Justice Thomas Chandler and urged him to omit the impending spring term of the court.

These volunteer counselors were not the heated, defiant folk who, at the time of John Grout's kidnaping, had broken up a court session. These were grave elders, sound and sure of themselves. Chandler, a politician, was neither.

The mud-spattered callers voiced their plea with such solemn anxiety that the Chief Justice found himself unable to be convincingly indignant. It was true that they asked for the suspension of a government function, but there was scant insurgence in their speech.

It would be better, Chandler's visitors insisted, for the authority of New York Province, for the safety of Cumberland County people, for the safety, even, of the judges themselves, if the court did not sit this March.

Their mission was simple. The causes that, joining one another, had impelled these men to ride on such an errand were more complex. There was tension in the Eastside's atmosphere, and on men's minds lay the haze and the heat of spiritual earthquake weather. People lived in calamity's shadow without quite knowing its actual form or substance.

The factions in the Connecticut Valley were striving at cross purposes, each cherishing a fine New England certainty of its own political rectitude and the chicanery or worse of all other cliques. Tories damned Whigs, who reciprocated with interest. Upholders of New Hampshire authority bickered with advocates of Massachusetts, and both these latter groups assailed Yorkers and their doctrines.

Each man had his own personal set of grievances and a growing anger in their possession. A general feeling of wrath toward each other was the Eastside's chief common possession. The disturbances and the sense of looming general disaster which afflicted the rest of the colonies were felt, though faintly, even on the frontier, and did nothing toward keeping the precarious peace.

The first Continental Congress had met in Philadelphia. The Cumberland County Convention of October, 1774, had been followed by another, meeting also at Westminster, November 30. While Tories had jeered, this second gathering had endorsed the proceedings of the Congress, including the nonimportation proposal—a suggested boycott of British goods. The New York Assembly rejected this boycott, thereby making the fissure between Yorkers and their antagonists in Cumberland County wider still.

The third Cumberland County Convention met at Westminster, February 7, 1775. This was about a month before the forty horsemen rode to warn Judge Chandler. The meeting's action foreshadowed their mission. It petitioned Acting Governor Colden for relief from the burden of the county court. Dislike of this body, a suspicion of its integrity, had been growing ever since it had been instituted.

The convention's petition was framed by Charles Phelps of Marlboro, a fat, bald giant of astounding loquacity, a monumental gift for trouble-making, a bewildering dexterity in saving a hide frequently imperiled by his own contentiousness. The fact that he stood then as a protestant against New York is sardonically noteworthy. Most of his subsequent extremely pestiferous life was devoted to upholding that same authority.

Phelps's petition was long, for brevity was not in him. It recited in chaotic periods the grievances against the court that were discussed daily by humble folk in taverns and farmhouse kitchens. They were many. Chandler's uninvited visitors repeated them all while the Chief Justice fretted under the droning of accusatory nasal voices.

The court was imposed on Cumberland County, not chosen by its people. It was expensive, holding too many sessions, requiring too much money for operation, dragging away from their work as many as seventy farmers at a time to sit in petit and grand jury panels.

The travel-worn critics may have muted their opinion of the court's membership out of consideration for their involuntary host. They may not have announced the prevalent belief that Chief Justice Chandler was a slick and slippery politician with a desire to appear on both sides of every question that might affect his future; that Joseph Lord, associate justice, was supposed to be insane; that Noah Sabin, his colleague, was a harsh, ambitious man; that Sheriff William Paterson was an Irishman and Samuel Gale, County Clerk, an Englishman—which made them both "foreigners" to New England eyes.

All these were minor complaints. The dry voices grew more strident as they launched into their principal grievances. These were neither political nor personal; they were economic. The court had become the ally of the rich, the oppressor of the poor.

Money never had been plentiful in Cumberland County. It was almost nonexistent now, thanks to the cessation of commerce in the seaboard colonies. The court had become the instrument whereby creditors wrung their due out of impoverished debtors. The court ignored the plea that there was no money abroad wherewith debts could be paid, and proceeded to collect them anyway.

The properties of penniless debtors were put up at auction and sold for the benefit of the creditors. Men may be deprived of cash with only an internal woe, but when they see their livestock, their land, their homes, jerked away from them, protest becomes vocal and is disinclined to stop there. For long, people had been complaining of the court. Now they were threatening. The March calendar was crammed with actions for replevin, collection of promissory notes, foreclosure of mortgages. These, with popular temper so hot, were explosives that a spark might set off. Therefore, Chandler's volunteer counselors urged him to omit the March session.

When they had ended, the Chief Justice nervously cleared his throat. He sympathized with them. He did, indeed. He saw their point, but he could not do all they asked. As for civil suits, it might be possible to omit consideration of these at the coming session, but the court must convene. It was the law; and he, as chief justice, must uphold it. Furthermore, there was a murder case that must be tried. The court would limit itself to that business.

He ended and looked appealingly at his unimpressed audience. Someone predicted that if that Irish Sheriff, Billy Paterson, acted in his usual high-handed fashion and brought armed deputies to the session, there'd be trouble.

None of the court officials would be armed, Chandler assured hastily. The session would proceed quietly and in good order. He would guarantee that.

With this promise his visitors had to satisfy themselves. Their original worry, as they mounted and rode off through the brown slush, had not been appreciably abated. Chandler's assurance, which they relayed to their more vociferous associates, did not convince the hot-heads.

The session of the Cumberland County Court of Common Pleas was to open at Westminster, Tuesday, March 14. On Sunday, March 12, Sheriff Paterson was extremely busy in Brattleboro and elsewhere south of the county seat, enlisting an armed posse to go to Westminster on the morrow.

Early Monday morning, folk who set no great store in Chandler's promise, gathered at Rockingham, north of Westminster, and marched. All that Chandler's visitors had dreaded was now on its way to accomplishment.

Westminster, the second oldest settlement in the Grants, lay then as it does today along two of the few entirely straight miles in all Vermont's roads. It was a raw, new town in 1775. The grace that is the common belonging of the state's early-maturing, long-enduring villages dwells in Westminster. Its oldest elms were saplings on that long-ago Monday when wrathful men invaded it. The violence they wrought there is now only a mellow memory and the still voice of a gravestone.

Then, as now, the village lay on two levels. The straight road went north across an elevated plateau, dipped sharply downhill, and pursued its undeviating way over a lower flat. Below the hill stood a log schoolhouse, the home of Captain Azariah Wright, the dwellings of other settlers, and John Norton's hostelry, which enemies of its patrons called "the Tory Tavern."

On the upper level were more homes, and at the hill's crest, looking north, stood the Cumberland County courthouse. This was a two-story building with a sentry box at the peak of its gambrel roof. Its upper, unfinished chamber, where beams and studding still were bare, served as court. A broad hall divided the lower floor. Two jail rooms faced one side of the passage. On the other were a kitchen and a taproom, maintained by the jailer for court officials, lawyers, and litigants. A more narrow hall between these chambers led to a side door.

The building was empty when the hundred men who had met at Rockingham came sloshing over the mired road into the village through the strong spring sunshine. Folk cheered or jeered their drab, uneven ranks, according to the spectators' political faith. The column did not advance at once upon the courthouse but paused at the foot of its hill.

The shabby marchers milled in squelching boots about the log schoolhouse. Their purpose was clear; the fashion in which they should follow it, still dim. Out of the buzz of uncertain talk rose cries for another meeting to lay final plans. The schoolhouse was too small to hold the crowd. It trailed away into Captain Wright's larger dwelling.

Meanwhile, Sheriff Paterson, girt by his sword of office, and the twenty-five defenders of the court whom he had enlisted and armed with staves, were plodding north from Brattleboro. Paterson had sounded the alarm thoroughly. At crossroads and farmhouse entrances, other men waited to join his column until fifty were marching, fourteen of whom carried firearms.

The meeting in Captain Wright's adjourned at last and came streaming uphill. Each man bore a club that he had chosen from the Wright woodpile. Some residents of Westminster joined them as they advanced upon the courthouse, entered, and took possession with hoots of defiance.

Hereafter, the record is blurred. There is no impartial account of the subsequent contest that, step by step, mounted toward tragedy. There were no impartial witnesses in Westminster.

The afternoon wore on while the invaders kept possession of the courthouse, with a possibly dampening lack of opposition from anyone. Guards were posted at the building's doors, but they had nothing to do but keep out inquisitive children and dogs. The rest of the self-appointed garrison wandered through the building or gathered in the upstairs courtroom for the loud talk of men who try to keep their courage high, or else sought remedy for failing determination in the courthouse taproom. It was sunset when a call from the guards drew them together again.

Paterson's leg-weary column was marching into Westminster. There was momentary hesitation when the newcomers saw the courthouse already occupied. Then they wheeled from the road and advanced toward the building, staves at all angles, patience worn thin by the long up- and downhill tramp. Uncomplimentary sounds greeted them. These swelled as the sheriff, stepping before his huddling command, bade the courthouse occupants disperse.

The retorts, shouted from the guarded doors, squalled from the windows, did little to ease an Irishman's temper or still the anger of men whose feet hurt; but Paterson drew out the King's proclamation whereby court always opened and began to read it. When he had finished, irreverent voices recommended a number of impractical things he might do with the document. Paterson's anger got away from him. He bawled:

"I'll give ye fifteen minutes to quit the courthouse, and then I'll blow a lane through ye."

Wrath was mounting, danger was waxing as twilight closed in: Cooler heads among the garrison sensed its presence and called for a parley. A few of the sheriff's force echoed the appeal, but Samuel Gale, the English county clerk, thrust his way through the uncertain crowd. He flourished a pistol and cried:

"Damn parley with such damned rascals as you are. I'll hold no parley with such damned rascals but by this."

His ire was not contagious to men who had walked a long way, and Paterson may have felt the irresolution.

"I'm warning ye all," he squalled, "if ye persist in biding in the courthouse, ye'll all be in hell by morning."

Through the responsive hooting, one member of the garrison, Charles Davenport, carpenter, of Dummerston called:

"Try to come in and ye'll all be there in fifteen minutes."

After this, the sheriff and his force withdrew. Derisive yells followed them as they plodded downhill through the dusk toward John Norton's tavern and its promise of solid and liquid sustenance for the journey-worn.

Darkness thickened, lighted windows in Westminster's houses uttered their promise, and the glee of recent squabbling faded, leaving the garrison a milder, more uncertain host that welcomed Chief Justice Chandler with something akin to relief when, at seven o'clock, he entered the courthouse.

Chandler felt their more temperate mood and profited by it. He was deaf to all pleas that he refuse to hold court on the morrow. That was His Majesty's business, he said severely, and it must be accomplished. However, he would be glad to consider, after court had opened, any grievances the invaders cared to present, and grant redress if possible.

Some purblind partisan reminded the Chief Justice of his promise that no arms should be brought into the courthouse; and Chandler, tactfully ignoring the clubs and other weapons of the garrison, deplored the sheriff's decision to bring an armed posse and pledged himself that this would be remedied in the morning. Since it was clear that the invaders would not give up the building, he said graciously that they might continue to hold it.

Chandler left. The more earnest of the courthouse occupants set about framing a list of grievances by candlelight. The hungrier and less vehement drifted away to seek hospitality behind the alluringly bright windows of the houses. The most resolute remained on guard.

They were all weary men, spent by marching and meetings and excitement. There was a frosty scent in the night air. A lopsided moon came up over the New Hampshire hills, and one by one the lights of Westminster went out, until at last only the windows of the Tory Tavern still were bright. Shouting drifted from the hostelry and an occasional snatch of song. Otherwise, the night was still.

In Norton's inn, the sheriff and his thwarted men passed the bowl. Fervor mounted as the punch went down. Weariness had vanished; thought of sleep had been thrust aside; memory of their repulse that afternoon no longer shamed the revelers, but only reminded them that a task from which they earlier had turned away still was to be finished. It appeared more urgent and pleasurable each time the bowl went round. At eleven that night they moved toward its accomplishment.

Sheriff William Paterson led the way. Behind him, his uncertain posse climbed the hill with stumbling, swearing, and some hysterical tittering. The thing from which they had withdrawn while sober now seemed praiseworthy. Drink quickened memories of partisan grievances and urged them forward.

It is possible that their plan, if they had one, was to approach the building undetected and swarm in before resistance could meet them. The clump of feet, the hushed voices, the black mass advancing through the moonlight woke the drowsing sentries. There was a stir and clattering in the courthouse as the garrison roused. The doorway was filled with armed men when Paterson approached it.

Exactly what happened then is no clearer or more certain than the subsequent stories of any men who have clashed in a midnight riot. The most competent testimony asserts that the sheriff advanced, climbed the courthouse steps, and demanded entrance. He was shoved back, made a second more furious advance, and was clubbed down by an unidentified someone, from which attack, perhaps, was born the ancient and long-lived query, "Who hit Billy Paterson?"

Repulse such as this was more than an Irishman in the sheriff's then condition could endure. He screamed at his men: "Fire, God damn ye; fire."

They were less ardent than he and, besides, they had not been clubbed. Two or three muskets banged, but the balls went high. A clatter of shots from the doorway answered them. Benjamin Butterfield of the attacking force was grazed along the arm by a ball, and his son Benjamin's coat was scorched by pistol flame. William Williams was wounded in the head.

Then a half-dozen of the posse fired, together and more purposefully. Yells rose through the fusillade's echoes and became an anguished screaming. The dark bulk of the attackers rushed in through the powder cloud, staves and musket butts swinging.

There was a violent instant of thudding and outcry at the courthouse door. Through this worrying press, Philip Safford of Rockingham, club in hand, beat his way to freedom. Paterson's sword slashed him as he passed.

The strife thrust inward along the building's main hall. In the darkness, there was a brief screeching fury while the defenders still fought, and the attackers, according to the deposition of Dr. Reuben Jones, a witness, "did most cruelly mammoc several more."

Resistance broke. Fugitives packed the smaller hall between kitchen and taproom and burst through the side door into the night where powder haze was pale beneath the moon and lights in Westminster's houses were rekindling.

In the main hall, someone held a candle high. The faint light shook over battered men who lurched to their feet and were thrust by panting captors into the jail. The candlelight dwelt on wounded men whom others raised and on two members of the garrison who lay appallingly flat and still. Daniel Houghton of Dummerston had been shot through the body. Young William French of Brattleboro, wounded in the calf, thigh, mouth, forehead, and behind the ear, still was breathing.

Ten prisoners, the whole, the wounded, and the dying alike, were placed in the two jail rooms. Physicians were permitted to attend the injured. The victors, awed in spite of themselves by what they had done, trooped into the taproom where Pollard Whipple, the jailer, served them. French died just before daylight. Houghton died nine days later.

Court opened on the morning of the fourteenth at the appointed time. It was neither a well-attended nor a stately opening. There were stains in the lower hall that scrubbing had not wholly removed. There were men to whom the Chief Justice had promised undisturbed possession of the courthouse in the jail below. There were others, the wounded, who had been borne to Captain Wright's house. There were still more, who had not been in the fight, but now gathered in small groups throughout Westminster town and talked in low voices.

On the bench, the judges themselves were pale and nervous. They ignored the court calendar and instead made inquiry into the tragedy. When they had prepared a statement, they adjourned until 3 P.M. There was something in the air, in the hushed speech and stiff faces of Westminster's men, that troubled them. It bothered Paterson's posse, too, whose members began to disperse and hurry home.

Before noon, the storm that folk already had sensed was beginning to gather. All that morning, lathered horses had carried messengers to the neighboring towns. Muskets had been snatched down from over fireplaces and hard-faced men had gone striding from their farms to the mustering places.

Captain Azariah Wright's company of Westminster militia already was patrolling the village. The angry voices were louder now. They swelled; they broke into cheering as other militia companies tramped in—Captain Stephen Sargent's from Rockingham, Captain Benjamin Bellow's from Walpole, across the Connecticut.

Westminster was filling with a wrathful buzzing noise. Pursuit parties galloped out to overtake the fleeing members of Paterson's posse. There were ugly and growing crowds before the dwellings of York sympathizers, and again and again cheering rose savagely above the scuff of feet and the slanting firelocks as more militia came in.

When court reconvened at three o'clock, it hastily adjourned again and by that action, though none of its members knew it at the time, passed permanently from existence.

Before the door through which Paterson and his posse had forced their way a few hours earlier, a mob was gathering with the earnest intention of burning the courthouse and shooting the judges, sheriff, clerk, and all their associates.

Captain Bellow's company held them back, and its commander by argument and appeal quieted them. The prisoners all had been released. The judges now were arrested, along with Sheriff Paterson and County Clerk Gale. They were held in the courthouse, and whatever members of the posse the patrols picked up were added to the worried company.

Tumult dwelt in Westminster all that night, and on the morrow it rose still higher, but there were distractions now that turned men's minds away from violence. A coroner's jury returned a verdict that

Paterson and his posse had been guilty of the death of French. Dr. Solomon Harvey, town clerk of Dummerston, marched a company into town with a drum banging at its head and four members of the posse as prisoners.

William French was buried that afternoon with military honors in the Westminster graveyard. Already, he was not just an unfortunate young man who happened to get in the way of an inordinate number of bullets during a riot, but a martyr. Later, when the Eastside's temper had altered, when there were prospects of conciliation with the new State of New York, and Britain seemed for the moment the more dreaded foe, poor French's role was recast. His gravestone attributed his death, not to the blind volley fired at the order of a York sheriff, but to some obscure animosity on the part of George III. It read:

> In Memory of William French
> Son to Mr. Nathaniel French Who
> Was shot at Westminster March ye 13th
> 1775 by the hands of Cruel Ministerial tools
> of George ye 3rd in the Courthouse at 11
> o'clock
> At night in the 22nd year of His age
> Here William French his Body lies
> For Murder his blood for vengeance cries
> King George the third his tory crew
> tha with a bawl his head Shot threw
> For Liberty and His Country Good
> he lost his life his Dearest blood.

Revision, for accuracy's sake, might have been applied to both recital and spelling.

Rumors innumerable ran all day long up and down the village's straight street where so many armed men swarmed that the town had neither adequate food nor shelter for them. New York was sending an army to rescue its court; the Yorkers of Guilford were planning an attack; regulars were coming from Boston. None of these reports had the least foundation, but the hoarse, lowing sounds they wrung from the crowd dinned unpleasantly in the ears of the courtroom prisoners.

There was no need for a tenth the force that had assembled, but late on the afternoon of the fifteenth, no single one of the militia who lined the highway and suddenly cheered so fiercely felt that his presence there had been futile.

Forty men on mud-caked horses rode up the hill to the south of town and into the village. In their hats were sprigs of evergreen. Muskets were poised on thighs or carried across the saddles of weary mounts. These tired, grinning strangers were Green Mountain Boys, a detail of Ethan Allen's own men; and at their head, sword in hand, two pistols in his belt, rode Robert Cochran.

Captain Cochran seemed able to swagger even while straddling a horse. The sixty-mile ride had had no effect upon his vigor or his voice, as he bawled that Tryon had placed a £50 reward on his head and invited any Yorker present to try to collect it.

His command rode the length of the village street and between outbursts of cheering Cochran could be heard proclaiming with more enthusiasm than biblical knowledge that he had come to find out "who is for the Lord and who is for Balaam."

As spectacle, the arrival of the Green Mountain Boys was uplifting; as reinforcement, wholly unnecessary; as a portent of the future, immensely significant.

Heretofore, the Eastside and the Westside of the Grants each had gone its own way, divided by the central ridge, kept apart by the divergence of their problems. Now, in the travail of the eastern half of the Grants, the western had sent men to its aid. Cochran's column was a visible first step toward unity. There were to be many slippings and grievous toe-stubbings before that union finally was attained.

On the morrow, the sixteenth of March, a committee examined all persons present who were charged with complicity in the affray which already was known, with no more accuracy than marked Cochran's biblical quotation, as "the Westminster Massacre."

It was no massacre, but a clash of headstrong, overheated folk, and its cause was violent intolerance, not of His Majesty George III, but of the more immediate and, as far as the Grants were concerned, far more offensive, government of New York.

The conduct of New York's governors, past and future, not of Britain's kings, was to temper and whet the Grants' passion for freedom. The short-sightedness of New York, province and state, not of Great Britain, was to found and maintain the reluctant but persistent Vermont Republic.

The examining committee, which actually was an unofficial court, seems to have been guided more by the general popularity of its prisoners than by their participation in the recent affray. Thus, Thomas Chandler, who as chief justice surely could have forbidden the sheriff's attack, nevertheless was released on bond along with others. On the other hand, Justice Noah Sabin, whose chief crime seems to have been that his neighbors didn't like him, was held. So were Sheriff Paterson, County Clerk Gale, and several more.

These miscreants were marched off, on the seventeenth, to North-ampton, Massachusetts, jail under a guard consisting of twenty-five Green Mountain Boys, commanded by Cochran, and twenty-five New Hampshire militia, headed by Captain Butterfield. None of the prison-ers was tried, and several eventually returned to the Grants.

Justice Sabin, when he finally came back to his home in Putney, was not welcomed by his fellow citizens. He was marooned on his farm with the assurance that he would be shot the instant he trespassed be-yond its borders. The esteem in which his neighbors held him was such that many spent their spare time with their firelocks in the brush about the boundaries of the Sabin farm, waiting hopefully for the justice to step out of its confines in an absent-minded moment.

New York's reaction to the Westminster riot was milder than it might have been if the Westside's Green Mountain Boys already had not weathered that province to insurgent violence. An express sent by Yorkers of the Eastside rode to New York City and acquainted the provincial legislature in session there with the details of the upheaval. The assembly, March 30, voted through a vague measure providing that something should be done "to enable the inhabitants of the County of Cumberland to reinstate and maintain the administration of justice."

This was the colonial New York government's last futile finger-shaking at the Grants' tumultuous people. Tryon, returning from Brit-ain in the following year, found that his province had been pulled out from under him and that his sole safe seat of government was in the cabin of a man-of-war in New York's lower harbor. While presiding over this limited dominion, he continued to issue patents to land in the Grants. The habit had become practically unbreakable.

In March, 1775, the sands almost had run out. The hourglass was about to turn. Fat Samuel Adams and the elegant John Hancock, evading Gage's clumsy attempts to arrest and ship them to England to stand trial for treason, had left Boston for Concord and Lexington. Gage was planning an expedition to catch them there and burn in-surgent stores.

These were matters of impersonal interest to the hardbitten farmers of the Grants. The strife at Westminster had been related only dimly to the brewing rebellion. It was simply another evidence of how universal had become resistance to irksome authority throughout America.

Enthusiasts have seen in the blind volley fired at the courthouse by not-too-sober posse members the first blow in the first war against Great Britain. They have hailed William French as the proto-martyr of the revolution. He has received the somewhat immoderate consideration which comes to him who is first to die in any period of mass slaughter.

Since New York's courts were also remotely those of George III, the Westminster affray, by stretching every point to elasticity's limit, can be considered an extremely indirect rebellion against royal authority.

More sanely, the riot was merely another incident in the Grants' strife against New York, and the strife was not finished when that province turned itself into one of the thirteen states. It was to endure thereafter, pull-Dick-pull-devil, for another sixteen years. While other enemies of the Vermont Republic were persuaded, or overawed, or beaten in the field, New York remained the constant, the omnipresent, adversary.

The epitaph above French's grave becomes a peculiarly flagrant distortion of fact when matched against the resolutions passed by delegates from Cumberland and Gloucester counties at the convention held in Westminster, April 11—less than a month after the "massacre."

In a week from that convention's meeting day, Paul Revere and William Dawes were to ride out of Boston on a mission for which Revere, thanks to the fact that there are many rhymes for his name, gets all the credit from posterity, though Dawes did most of the work.

No hint of the colonial crisis elbowed its way into the Westminster convention's resolutions. They proclaimed it the duty of all Grants inhabitants "to wholly renounce and resist the administration"—not of "Cruel Ministerial tools of George Ye 3rd," whom the French epitaph accuses, but "of the government of New York."

With most loyal reverence, the petition also begs that "His Most gracious Majesty" in "his royal wisdom and clemency" will remove the Grants out of the clutches of New York. French's epitaph was not only inaccurate; it was a mortuary afterthought.

The convention wove a second strand into the still-tenuous bond between Eastside and Westside. It voted that a remonstrance be drawn up against "the unjustifiable conduct" of New York, and that its framers be Colonel John Hazeltine and the garrulous Charles Phelps of Cumberland County and Colonel Ethan Allen.

But Colonel Allen never scratched a quill in this particular cause.

Before tidings of his appointment reached him, a volley had crashed on Lexington Green, dead men lay beneath the drifting powder smoke at Concord bridge, and a brawl of gunfire like a deliberately exploding string of firecrackers moved back with the redcoats along the road to Boston.

Temporizing was over; appeasement was at an end; and Ethan Allen, who had no love for either, already was neck-deep in a project that appealed even more to his peculiar gifts than the composition of another pamphlet defaming New York.

PART TWO

ALLY

Had ye no graves at home across the briny water
That hither ye must come like bullocks to the slaughter?
If we the work must do, why, the sooner 'tis begun,
If flint and trigger hold but true, the quicker 'twill be done.
                                        —*Bennington Battle Song*

VIII "In the Name of the Great Jehovah"

PLODDING FEET pounded dried mud to dust. The sad-colored companies moved through perceptible shade cast by the small beginnings of leaves, for it was an unwontedly early spring. Something beyond vernal elation filled the air as the uneven files went by with crookedly sloping firelocks and field officers jouncing on plow horses. Men knew, now that the peril's face was clear before them, that relief which is rapture's odd kinsman. It marched with the drab militia host, hay-footing-strawfooting it to Boston town.

Sixteen thousand of them at last lay about the city where the regulars of the scandalized and still incredulous Gage were penned. The harsh ecstasy that had impelled this farmer army moved on, filling at last even the yet-raw clearings of the New Hampshire Grants.

In the histories of an embarrassing species, fidelity to abstract virtue is justifiably suspect. Self-interest is human idealism's attendant, but in the Grants men were turned toward Freedom by motives disconcertingly pure.

The quarrel that had become war at Lexington was not of the Grants' making. More could be gained by staying out of it than by going in. From Ethan Allen down to the dweller in the newest log hut, settlers had found New York the obstructionist and the adversary; Great Britain the dilatory friend.

The Grants people had no material reason to join the revolt and the prospect of much profit by remaining aloof. They need risk nothing for the moment and still be paid for it. Their mere neutrality had its value. The price they might demand for alliance with either the colonies or Great Britain already was high and bound to go higher.

These matters were clear to acute folk who were by nature bargain drivers. This was heaven's own opportunity for a much-harried people at last to get all for which they plaintively had begged in deaf ears —secure possession of the land they held, a government of their own choice. They blinded themselves to these probabilities. Months before rebellion flamed, its sparks were kindling the north. A bare three weeks after Lexington, the Grants were actively in the war, without stipulation or demand for preliminary guarantees.

Investment in a venture where the risks were so tremendous and the possibility of dividends excessively remote was against New England principles, or the best material interests of a people; but these were a peculiar folk whom the very word Freedom and its implications made a little drunk. Freedom had come up over the border with them into the new land. In some strange way, the climate, the soil, the contours of that land itself, had nurtured—still preserves—that disconcerting passion.

The Grants' deliberate embroilment was against all dictates of common sense. It violated all trading standards. Adherence to the colonies' cause could not possibly gain anything negotiable that disavowal would not more probably win. This was the obvious time to dicker and swap and contrive. Attack on Britain most certainly would bring a wide variety of disasters down about the settlers' ears, and theirs was a scant and almost defenseless population. They planned immediate attack.

The water roads of war washed either flank of the land, and the British could move from Canada easily along one clear way, or both. On a frontier far from succor, a handful of farmers, each with a handful of powder, prepared to smite Britain where it would hurt most; to strike, as volunteer allies of the revolting colonies, an extremely sensitive ganglion of the Empire's nervous system; to take the garrisoned forts that guarded the narrows of Champlain's smooth, blue highway to war.

This was the crazily valiant decision that leaders in the Grants, themselves led by Ethan Allen, had made before the first guns spoke to the south. None risked so much in this reckless enterprise as the Colonel Commandant himself.

The properties of Ethan Allen & Co. lay along the lake's east shore, wholly exposed to whatever counterattack the British might launch. The concern had bought 77,622 acres, of which it still held 60,829; and now its president was about to take the extremely probable risk of losing these. More actually and largely than most patriots, Ethan Allen was pledging, not only his life, but also his own and his relatives' entire fortunes. He was always an unusual and, at moments, a noble person.

No greater military knowledge than the Colonel Commandant possessed was needful to see the importance of the Champlain forts.

Whoever held them possessed the northern gate to colonial defense, the southern portal through which a successful advance against Canada must move.

They guarded a waterway that ran with minor obstructions clear from Quebec to the harbor of New York—the St. Lawrence, the Richelieu River that was Champlain's outlet, the lake itself, into which Lake George poured its overflow. At the foot of the second lake's narrow length, a ten-mile march reached the Hudson, geographically splitting the revolting colonies in half. Were Britain to hold this entire fluid road, the revolution's jugular would be cut. Almost half of the waterway already was in her hands.

Both forts—Crown Point where Champlain's lizardlike length suddenly pinches into a thin tail; Ticonderoga, twelve miles further south beside Lake George's outlet—already had been hallowed by battle and thoroughly baptized in French and English blood. Their former and now suddenly revived importance had magnified them in American eyes. To Colonials, they seemed the counterparts of Louisbourg or Gibraltar. Actually, they were something considerably less. Glamour was their most redoubtable strength.

Two years earlier, Crown Point had burned. A shelter had been contrived out of the fragments that remained; and here, in the spring of 1775, Sergeant Alexander Nairns and nine of His Majesty's 26th Foot led a dreary existence in which their most martial enterprise was to chase away Grants people who paddled across from the east shore to grub among the embers for precious iron nails.

Ticonderoga was going to pieces more deliberately than her sister fort, but with a growing promise of equal imminent ruin. Here were quartered forty-three men of the 26th and two officers—Lieutenant Jocelyn Feltman, waiting wistfully for the arrival of Lieutenant Wadman, who was to relieve him, and Captain William Delaplace, a justifiably mournful man who kept reporting to his superiors the progressive rotting of his post.

Neither the presence of his wife and children nor the farming enterprises he maintained in his spare hours were able to cheer Captain Delaplace, and for his deploring outlook there was adequate excuse.

In the preceding August the commissary room had fallen in upon itself. Half his force were elderly semi-invalids fit for only light duty, and most of the rest during the summer months were smitten with malaria, which their commander blamed, not upon the swamps about the fort, but on the pellucid and ostensibly poisonous lake water. The food was bad, and there was not enough powder to serve the vast array of cannon.

Further afflictions fell upon the captain in the spring of 1775. His letters to his superiors complained of the number of persons from the Grants who crossed the lake at night to snoop around the fort, an enterprise from which Delaplace believed no possible good could come.

Already the dismal reiterations of his woes had begun to wear away official indifference. Gage in Boston, General Guy Carleton in Canada, were making deliberate plans to abandon Ticonderoga, letting it go its brief remaining way into absolute ruin, and to build a new fort at Crown Point which would be adequately garrisoned. Britain at last was moving, but Ethan Allen moved first.

It is probable, though not provable, that the project of taking the forts was his original idea. It may have come to him in a moment of illumination while he and his associates in Landlord Fay's council chamber were, as the Colonel poetically puts it, "tossing about the flowing bowl." There is indirect evidence that he was cherishing the project early in 1775.

In February of that year, the Massachusetts Committee of Safety sent John Brown, a Pittsfield lawyer, on a mission to Canada. He bore credentials signed by Samuel Adams and Joseph Warren and was to sound out Canadian attitude toward the Continental cause. Peleg Sunderland, one of Allen's captains, guided Brown, presumably at the Colonel's direction.

Due to the floods of early spring, they had a physically miserable but otherwise successful trip; and from Montreal, March 24, Brown wrote to Warren and Adams, reporting that Canadian temper seemed favorable and adding:

> The fort at Tyconderogo must be seised as soon as possible should hostilities be committed by the Kings' Troops. The people on N. Hampshire Grants have ingaged to do this Business and in my opinion they are the most proper Persons for the jobb.

If the idea was Allen's original possession, a number of persons soon acquired it. In late April, a headlong ex-apothecary, Benedict Arnold, captain in the Governor of Connecticut's Foot Guards, was urging the attack upon the commanders of the troops besieging Boston. On April 27, the project was discussed in Hartford by Silas Deane and

. other Connecticut leaders, who thereupon translated their debate into action.

Deane and his associates drew £300 from the provincial treasury on their own responsibility and, on April 28, sent Noah Phelps and Bernard Romans, an engineer, north to raise the Grants. Captain Edward Mott, Epaphras Bull, and four other Connecticut men followed their trail the next day.

The second party overtook the first at Salisbury where Phelps and Romans, who was a tiresomely disputatious person, had tarried to consult with the Allens. Ethan, they learned, already was in Bennington advancing his plan and steaming and bubbling at the objections offered by the cautious. After a night conference in Salisbury, Levi joined the party and Heman rode ahead to tell his brother that he could stop being indignant and start to raise his men, since Connecticut had authorized the taking of the forts.

The urgency of their mission led the travelers to violate New England law next morning and journey on the Sabbath as far as Pittsfield. They stopped at the inn of James Easton, a neighbor of John Brown, and when they hurried north on the morrow, Easton, Brown, the early advocate of the plan, and one Captain Dickinson rode with them.

Easton was colonel in Massachusetts' militia. He suggested that reinforcements for Allen be raised from his command; and his companions, awed by the legendary might of Ticonderoga, agreed. No force could be too large to assail so strong a fortress. Thirty-nine Berkshire County men marched with the emissaries into the Grants.

In Bennington they found the fuming Ethan Allen. He had his uniform on, his horse saddled, and was lingering no more comfortably than a chained bear, only because Heman had bade him wait. Here Romans, who had become increasingly contentious, grew angry and left the expedition, to the relief of all concerned. A council, held in Fay's tavern, was brief. The Colonel Commandant needed no instructions. The thing had been clear in his mind for weeks. In the shortest possible time, he was rocketing away to the north, to muster his Green Mountain Boys against a new foe and for the last time.

The rest of the party proceeded more deliberately to Castleton. When they reached the frontier village, the first of the summoned troops were coming in, and their Colonel Commandant, who had appropriately chosen Zadock Remington's tavern as his headquarters, was thundering greetings to them between occasional flowing-bowl-tossings.

Seth Warner had arrived, and more of the Green Mountain Boys were on the way. The martial spirit was high and extremely noisy. Patrols had been sent out to guard all roads to the west with orders to turn back travelers toward Crown Point and Ticonderoga and to bring to Castleton for questioning all men coming from the forts.

By Monday, May 8, a hundred and sixty of Allen's regiment were assembled at Remington's, either in, or trying to get into, the taproom —leathery and irreverent men in worn attire but with well-oiled muskets and so vast an enthusiasm for their commander that the heads of the expedition, seeking comparative peace in which to lay final plans, had to move out of the inn to the home of Richard Bentley.

There, with Mott acting as chairman, all things were made ready. The time for the attack was set for Wednesday, the tenth, before day-break. Allen was confirmed as leader of the expedition. Easton was chosen second in command and Warner, third. It was discovered in this advanced moment that everyone had been too absorbed in contemplating imminent victory at Ticonderoga to spend thought or action on the problem of how the force was to get across the lake.

No one seems to have been particularly concerned over this omission. It was resolved that Mott, Captain Samuel Herrick, and thirty men should march to Skenesboro, capture the place, and bring back whatever boats they should find there.

They might not return in time, but the Colonel Commandant was naïvely resourceful. He sent Captain Douglass to Crown Point to see if he could not prevail upon the troops there to rent him boats for their own undoing. Having solved the transportation problem to his own satisfaction, Allen, on the afternoon of the eighth, galloped off with most of his officers to Shoreham, where more Green Mountain Boys were assembling, leaving the men at Castleton to follow when they got their legs under them.

The column still was trying to form itself, a maneuver beset with difficulties, when a strange officer appeared. He was a small man on a fine, big horse; and, since he wore a red-coated uniform, the Green Mountain Boys, if they had felt a little better, might have taken a speculative shot at him—which would have saved everyone a deal of immediately subsequent trouble and have done America an equivocal favor.

The officer was well groomed, darkly handsome, and haughty. His

.appearance was an offense to swimming eyes and democratic hearts that the attendance of a respectful orderly compounded. The boys most intensely did not like the splendid stranger, and it was clear from the way he surveyed their disheveled persons that he had small esteem for them. The announcement—it was more like a proclamation—he made forthwith did nothing to increase his popularity. Instead, it started what promised to be a most earnest mutiny.

"Captain Benedict Arnold," the intruder barked, "of the Connecticut Foot Guards. Where are your officers? I am in command here."

Arnold was used to militia insubordination, but the sounds these rumpled persons made, their gestures, the impossible suggestions they bawled, affronted and daunted even him. It was clearly hate at first sight. Something, the few cool heads present knew, must be done before the lurid dissenters exhausted improvisation and turned to action. Someone hastened after Edward Mott, who had marched off with the Skenesboro detail.

When the breathless Mott returned, Arnold lifted his voice above the waxing uproar to justify his demand. The Province of Massachusetts had joined the rapidly increasing host that wanted to capture the lake forts and had commissioned him to lead the enterprise.

("That Goddam popinjay? Claw my guts if I'd foller him anywheres. Ethan's our Colonel.")

Mott asked the red-coated and now red-faced stranger for his credentials, and Arnold produced them.

("Let's take them pretty pance offen him, Seth. Le's hang him onto 'em, b' God. Old Ethan's a-leadin' us.")

The Massachusetts commission seemed to Mott entirely in order. It empowered Arnold to raise and command a force not exceeding four hundred men for the reduction of the forts. That was all very well, Mott demurred, but where were these men? Arnold's face grew redder still.

("Jeezes, Obadiah, what we waitin' here for? Ethan told us to march. March then, I say, so's we don't have to breathe this perfume-stinkin' so-and-so no more.")

The rapidly empurpling object of these attentions told Mott stiffly that he had no army with him. Captains Oswald and Brown were recruiting a force. He himself, hearing that another expedition was under way, had hurried on to lead it.

("Well, b' God, if he wants to keep them whoreson clothes of his on him, he better keep right on a-hurryin'. Come on, boys; le's march after Ethan. Le's go find old Ethan.")

Feet shuffled. A few of the more determined shouldered firelocks and moved out. The rest of the column followed. In its straggling rear, a wooden-faced and probably secretly delighted orderly rode behind the still fuming Arnold.

He had no one to argue with now, for Mott had been obliged to stay behind. The column had stormed away so indignantly and with such distaste for food that they had ignored entirely their provisions. Mott had to assemble these, find horses, pack the rations upon them, and herd the animals forward himself. It was a hard and long job, but he persevered. His forethought and the delay it caused robbed him of participation in Ticonderoga's capture.

At Shoreham, the men from Castleton found Colonel Allen and a hundred more Green Mountain Boys who glared at the brilliant Arnold with suspicion that their newly arrived and still insurgent comrades quickly intensified. The brusqueness of the commander of Massachusetts' non-existent expeditionary force sat no more pleasantly in Ethan Allen's stomach than it had in Mott's.

This was a Grants enterprise, furthered and financed by Connecticut. Let Massachusetts skin her own pork. The ambition that was to raise Arnold high and cast him down made him persist in his claims now, oblivious to the dangerous lowing sound that rose from the eavesdropping men. The noise dinned, too, in Allen's ears, and he broke off the argument to roar:

"Silence, you numbskulls—all of you. Whoever leads you, you'll get your pay."

Purposefully or not, he stung them. Harsh voices rose in clamor; muskets were shaken.

"Goddam the pay. We want you or no one. You lead us, or b' God, we club firelocks and go home."

There was a scornful look on Arnold's face, but Colonel Allen, surveying his obstreperous army, swelled with pride.

Land went down in a tree-filled trough to the crescent of gravelly beach in Hands Cove. Wind from the north blew May's young leaves above two hundred and thirty men who squatted in the slanting grove and thought wistfully of the food they had left behind in their angry haste.

The red-coated intruder and his orderly sat a little apart. Arnold, still with scorn upon his face, watched Allen as the giant in the pre-

posterous uniform went down to the beach and scanned the empty
water and returned to bawl at his men orders to be quieter, and rest-
lessly tramped down to the beach again to look once more.

No boats were waiting for the column when it reached the cove,
save a few inadequate dugouts and canoes. None were visible on the
rough blue water that was darkening toward sunset. The Colonel
Commandant fretted and blasphemed to himself. There had been no
word of the Skenesboro expedition. Douglass had returned from his
artless errand to Crown Point with tidings that the garrison there was
not renting its boats to anyone. He had heard that there was a scow
at Bridport that might ferry a small fraction of the regiment across,
and the Colonel had sent him off to find it.

The breeze was freshening as the sun went down. Fires were forbidden, and the hungry men quaked. Color faded from the lake, and
the hills to the west grew black. Allen stood on the beach again peering into the dusk, and Arnold, watching him, was irked by the growing futility of this waiting, yet pleased by his adversary's plight. This
hobbledehoy had no soldierly equipment whatever save a garish uniform and the devotion of his men. He had led them hither without
rations, without providing for transportation; and Ticonderoga was a
wet two miles away.

Hours dragged by, each darker and colder than the last. The wind
still whistled and dug chill fingers into the bodies of wretched men
whose mumbling voices accompanied the sibilant clatter of waves on
the gravel. The moon's crescent first quarter made the shadows blacker
still and struck faint gleamings from the Colonel's gilt-adorned coat
as he strode to the beach once more and returned, groaning. Arnold
smiled at the sound.

"Hush that noise," Allen bade in a stifled bellow. His men looked
at each other suspiciously. All now were aware of the sound, yet none
of them had uttered it. Someone was singing. Not here. Out on the
lake. Someone whose cares had wholly left him was caroling uncer-
tainly out there on the rough water. The tumult grew louder. Now
the listeners also could hear the slap of water on a boat's side and the
steady thresh of oars.

Allen blundered hastily down to the beach. He gave a cautious
hail. Voices responded as warily, and the singer, breaking off in mid-
bar, shouted "Hallelujah!"

The luck of Douglass, the unsuccessful searcher for boats, had
changed at last. He had hurried away toward Bridport and the scow

supposed to be there, with Allen's parting admonitions still reddening his ears. At the farm of one Stone, he had paused to make known his errand and ask for aid. The sound of voices in the farmhouse kitchen woke the hired men, James Wilcox and Joseph Tyler, who entered blinking and straightway took fire at the mention of Ethan Allen's name.

B' God, if Ethan wanted a boat, they knew where there was one, a thunderin' big one, too. Colonel Skene's row galley was moored off Willow Point with her crew aboard her. Maybe they could take her. They'd try, anyway.

Douglass blessed their project and hastened on to find the Bridport scow. Wilcox and Tyler dressed, armed themselves with muskets and a gallon jug of rum, and marched to Willow Point, enlisting four other young men on the way.

Jack, Skene's slave, and his crew of two listened with scant enthusiasm when Wilcox and Tyler babbled of a hunting party that was gathering at Hands Cove and begged to be rowed thither. The unstoppered jug uttered more eloquent sounds. The smell of rum was exquisite perfume on this raw May night. Jack, still dubious, invited the hunters aboard. They gave him the jug. Presently, he bawled for his men to get out their oars.

The galley's head came round. She moved toward Hands Cove. After a little, her captain began to sing. There seemed to be an inordinate number of hunters at the cove, but already Jack had begun to distrust his eyes. There were moments when these told him he was holding several jugs. By the time stupor had abolished his delight in song, Douglass had brought in the Bridport scow.

The moon had set, and the blackness that comes before dawn warned that night was waning. If the thing was to be done at all, it must be accomplished at once, yet there was room in the assembled boats for not more than eighty of thrice that many men. The eighty clambered aboard while their colonel called their and the deity's attention to the need for silence and beat down Seth Warner's protest at being left behind with the remainder of the force while Easton accompanied it, and at last, to avoid further squabble and delay, permitted Arnold to embark.

The boats pushed off. They turned clumsily toward the blackness and the few dim lights that marked Ticonderoga. The oars' measured splashing, the singing wind, and the smack and slobber of water under blunt bows were the only sounds. It was a long row, those dark two miles, while Allen watched the further shore and waited for the red cannon flash that would be disaster's prelude.

He may not have been fearful; he could not have failed to be anxious. The mountains were more sharply outlined in the east when the boats grounded with what seemed terrific tumult on the beach below the darkly looming fort. Men held their breaths, waiting for challenge. None came.

They assembled on the shore in a formless huddle that once more curled Arnold's intemperate lips. The silence magnified the stir of feet, the men's hard breathing, the small, curt sounds of cocking muskets. This moment of peril needed a soldier, not a brass-bound mountebank, to master it. Arnold stepped forward. Again he demanded the right to lead the assault, and again Allen refused with hushed fury that his followers found contagious. For a moment it appeared that the attacking force might turn itself into a lynching party. Easton and other peacemakers smothered the quarrel. Allen agreed that Arnold might walk beside him and prepared to lead his mountaineers forward.

He turned and faced his deplorably unmilitary force. His glittering figure, while he spoke, grew more distinct in the quickening pallor from the east, as though the radiance of his imminent exploit already lay upon him. Above was the fort, vast and boding in the twilight. Each second wasted here on the beach doubled the peril, brought agonizingly nearer the instant of discovery, the challenge, the alarm and the annihilating burst of grapeshot; but Colonel Ethan Allen, by his own account, addressed his troops in resounding periods as follows:

"Friends and fellow soldiers: You have for a number of years past been a scourge and terror to arbitrary powers. Your valor has been famed abroad and acknowledged, as appears by the advice and orders to me from the General Assembly of Connecticut"—the General Assembly had had nothing whatever to do with the matter—"to surprise and take the garrison now before us.

"I now propose to advance before you, in person, conduct you through the wicket gate, for we must this morning either quit our pretensions to valor or possess ourselves of this fortress in a few minutes, and, inasmuch as it is a desperate attempt which none but the bravest of men dare undertake, I will not urge it on any contrary to his will. You that will undertake voluntarily, poise your firelocks."

That is what he says he said. No one since then has deemed to contradict him. Thereafter, he relates, all the firelocks were satisfactorily poised, though it is a mystery why he found this assurance necessary from men whose only possible chance of safety lay in going forward as quickly as possible. Allen then turned and, with Arnold walking beside him, led his invasion through the wicket.

Those close behind the leaders marched in decorously. Others in the rear broke ranks and scrambled over the low wall in which the gate was set. A sentry, apparently suffering from eye and ear trouble, belatedly discovered the advance when it was almost upon him. He snapped his piece at the giant in surprising regimentals who led it, but he either had neglected to load his gun or it misfired. Allen charged him, whooping, sword waving. The sentry fled, yelling for help, with the vast military boots pounding close behind and a tremendous voice promising him a peculiarly horrid immediate future.

All semblance of military order was thrown away as the column ran after its leader. The chase roared through a covered way and stormed out into the parade. The sentry ducked like a rabbit into a bomb-proof and vanished. The screeching invaders fanned out and galloped across the clearing with Allen still in the lead.

Another sentry, white-faced and gasping, pointed a wavering bayonet toward the Colonel, who clouted him across the head with his sword. The musket dropped. Allen roared in his prisoner's ear demand that he point out at once where the commandant's quarters lay.

No shot had been fired. The awful screeching of the Green Mountain Boys, the ghastly threats they squalled, seem to have paralyzed resistance. Part of the mob followed Allen as he ran for the officers' quarters on the west side of the parade. The rest surged up to the barrack doors and began earnestly to beat them in.

Lieutenant Jocelyn Feltman of the 26th Foot awoke from a dream of Indian massacre to discover that something of the sort actually was progressing on the parade below his chamber. Shrieks and squallings of "No quarter!" began to be accompanied by a terrific pounding sound and a surplus of most reprehensible speech.

Lieutenant Feltman sprang from his bed. The racket unsettled his mind only gradually. He had got his uniform coat and waistcoat before his self-control gave way entirely. Thereafter, he ran out to the stairway's head. His purpose was to inform his commander, Captain William Delaplace, who dwelt with his family on the far side of the passage, that something was the matter—an obviously unnecessary mission.

Feltman knocked on Delaplace's door, but before it was opened there was a great bellowing and a thunder of boots upon the steps, and the lieutenant turned alone to face overwhelming odds in the best tradition of His Majesty's service. He went to the stairhead and looked down.

A prodigious, bawling figure in a strange uniform, another and more decorous in a proper red coat, were rushing upward at the head of a wild-eyed, savage, most distressingly vocal rabble. The advance was checked, silence clapped upon it, as Feltman stepped into view. He looked down upon the invaders with what sternness he could muster.

They gaped, in their turn, at the apparition whose upper half wore the yellow-faced scarlet coat, the white waistcoat, and silver gorget of His Majesty's 26th Foot and the lower only the unadorned and intimate integument of Jocelyn Feltman. It was a thoroughly surprising encounter, and from its temporary paralysis Ethan Allen recovered first.

He raised the sword that he had almost dropped for an instant, resumed his climb and, waving his weapon, roared at the lieutenant:

"Come out of that, you goddamned old rat" (or "skunk" or "bastard"—there are several versions).

Feltman did not move. His extremities, quailing in the breeze, had made him suddenly aware that he was more than far enough out already. He faltered a question in a weak voice; it is difficult for a man to be resolute who has just discovered that he is trouserless. Allen's sword sung about the subaltern's ears. He bellowed, as Feltman reported it later, demand for the "immediate possession of the fort and all the effects of George the third [these were his words]."

The bandits who had followed their leader had halted, two-thirds the way up the stairs. They now aimed their muskets at the increasingly uneasy figure of the lieutenant while the giant's voice ran on proclaiming that, if any resistance whatever were offered by the garrison, no man, woman, or child could be left alive in Ticonderoga.

The slight dark figure in the coat of the same hue as Feltman's and an enviable pair of breeches protested this threat in what the lieutenant found was "a genteel manner." He also told the subaltern that he was Captain Arnold and had with Allen "a joint command" in the attack.

The moment was too intense for anyone to gag over this heresy. Captain Delaplace, correctly attired, now issued from his quarters; and Allen, turning upon him, demanded the fort's surrender.

"In whose name?" the dazed commandant inquired.

"In the name," Allen thundered, "of the great Jehovah and the Continental Congress."

The resounding lines of history are automatically dubious, but there is no real warrant for disbelieving that these were the Colonel's actual words. They are far more in character than those he said he uttered in his preposterous address on the beach. He himself set them down as his speech, and others who were witnesses confirm him.

The barrack doors had gone down. The whooping maniacs had swarmed in upon the elderly and infirm men who had cowered behind them. All these now were prisoners. Delaplace surrendered. His post already had been captured.

Lieutenant Feltman was locked in his room. The captain accompanied Allen to the parade. There in the dawn's shadowless light, the Colonel Commandant looked with tolerance, Arnold and Delaplace with horror, at the squalling irresponsibles who cavorted about with wild demands that they be allowed to fight someone and more earnest requests for liquor and loot.

The boats which had gone back for more men brought over Seth Warner, Peleg Sunderland, and eighty more, who immediately doubled the riot in the fort, and went back for the remainder.

This person, Ethan Allen [Feltman's report reads] and Warner are as great villains as any on earth.

The last men to be ferried over were accompanied by Edward Mott, who had brought up the pack horses and the rations just after Allen had left Hands Cove. The Green Mountain Boys at the moment showed no appetite for solid food. Two hundred-odd ingenious, uninhibited, and intensely thirsty persons now were in Ticonderoga and seemed to overcrowd it. Allen appropriated ninety gallons of King George's rum for the refreshment of his command. This was a niggardly allowance of something more than a quart per man, but the elation of victory atoned in part for the lack.

The sun [the Colonel Commandant writes] seemed to rise that morning with a superior lustre and Ticonderoga and its dependencies smiled on its conquerors who tossed about the flowing bowl and wished success to Congress and the liberty and freedom of America.

Others found nothing whatever uplifting in the jubilation. The British officers were aghast at the plundering, in the course of which

Captain Delaplace, according to his later complaint, lost the entire population of his personal farm, including forty-five sheep and eleven cattle.

Arnold sympathized with him and, striving again to exert authority, forbade further looting. The response of the looters only bruised further his already sore self-esteem. With considerable resource and much apt imagery, the men he strove to discipline told him where he could go. They added that he wasn't their commander and that the moment he became so he could keep the damned fort by himself; they'd all march home.

This was mutiny; this was more than an officer should be forced to endure. Raging, Arnold sought Mott, Easton, and the Grants leaders and brought up the matter of commissions again. He flourished his own and argued childishly that, since he had written authority and Allen none, he himself should be placed in command. Mott was compelled to write a commission for Allen then and there before the furious man could be stilled.

Warner, too, had a plea to make. He had been left out of the Ticonderoga affair. Now he demanded that he be permitted to take Crown Point's fire-blackened shell. He set out on the afternoon of May 10 and returned on the morrow with Sergeant Nairn and his small command, who seemed to have been so frightened by Ticonderoga's fall that they surrendered eagerly.

Other aftermath tokens of the triumph continued to pour into the riotous fort. Remember Baker and his company appeared from the Onion River country with two boats they had captured fleeing down the lake toward St. John's, the Canadian town on the Richelieu River just beyond Champlain's outlet.

Lieutenant Wadman, the unfortunate Lieutenant Feltman's tardy relief, was taken as he landed at the head of Lake George with four men and brought to Ticonderoga. Word came from Sam Herrick that he had captured Skenesboro, Colonel Skene's two daughters, his son, Major Philip Skene, fifty tenants, twelve slaves, and a schooner, already rechristened *Liberty*.

The spoils of war that fell into American hands at Ticonderoga and Crown Point were tremendous when matched against the puny garrison at either place. More than a hundred good cannon and many decrepit, mortars, swivels, howitzers, coehorns, tons of musket and cannon balls, and a small amount of poor gunpowder were taken.

The ordnance was to be a godsend to the civilian army besieging

Boston. Its magnificent quantity filled Colonel Allen's mighty chest with pride, but he had no time to gloat. He was an extremely busy man and, as always, a furiously ambitious.

For the moment the Colonel was too preoccupied to notice Arnold's sneers and, also momentarily, both men's purposes had blended. Neither had the easily satisfied spirit which sits by the deed accomplished and looks no further. The forts that were the southern gateway to Canada had been taken. St. John's was the sole remaining defense below the St. Lawrence. With this captured, the way would be clear. Determined, energetic men might push on to Montreal and Quebec. There were two such men in Ticonderoga.

John Brown hurried off to Philadelphia, bearing tidings of the victory and the royal colors that had been taken. He was to urge an immediate expedition into Canada. Arnold wrote to the Albany Committee of Safety that he himself had taken the fort—with a little help from Allen—and asking that five hundred men be sent him at once. He was bound to get a command of his own, somewhere. Allen wrote Governor Trumbull of Connecticut a letter beginning: "I make you a present of a Major, a Captain and two Lieutenants in the regular Establishment of George the Third" and confiding a plan, already under way, to take St. John's and the British sloop based there, which would wholly clear Lake Champlain of the enemy. Ticonderoga, after years of placid decay, hummed like a disturbed hive. On May 13, its chief disturbers left it.

Arnold, with thirty-five men, in the rechristened schooner taken at Skenesboro; Allen with ninety more in bateaux—scowlike, blunt, and flat-bottomed craft with square blanket sails and oars for motive power—set out to reduce St. John's. This was supposed to be a joint expedition. It became at once a race in which the swifter *Liberty* outdistanced Allen's sweating and much-cursed oarsmen until, May 16, the wind died into utter calm with Arnold's schooner still thirty miles south of St. John's.

Allen's part of the expedition was far behind. Arnold did not wait. He thrust his men into boats, rowed the thirty miles, took St. John's, its garrison of a sergeant and twelve men, His Majesty's sloop with her crew of seven, burned five bateaux, and departed on the captured sloop with his ego considerably repaired. This was a feat in which that pestiferous oaf, Ethan Allen, could claim no share. This was demonstration of how able a leader was Captain Benedict Arnold when freed from obstinate clodhoppers in funny uniforms.

The sloop, renamed *Enterprise*, sailed back toward Ticonderoga and met, not many miles up the lake, Allen's bateaux, whose oarsmen still were tugging at the sweeps and glaring at their impatient commander. Victory had made Arnold generous. He fired a salute in his rival's honor and invited him aboard the sloop. There the late enemies absorbed "several loyal Congress healths" while Arnold told how he had taken St. John's. There was no need of Colonel Allen's going further. The objects of the expedition had been accomplished.

Colonel Allen, by God, begged to differ. Captain Arnold had taken St. John's. Very well, Colonel Allen would press valiantly forward and capture the town also. There was another installment of the serial squabble in the cabin of the *Enterprise*. Then Arnold sailed on south, and Allen's oarsmen rowed on north.

St. John's submitted to being taken again with a pious patience. Allen found a French trader, one Bindon, who consented to carry an appeal for reinforcements and supplies to James Morrison, a sympathizer with the Colonial cause in Montreal. In the letter the Colonel Commandant spoke of his handful as the advance guard of a large American force and promised, if Morrison would aid him, speedily to reduce all Canada. Arnold was not going to outstrip Ethan Allen while paper and ink were handy.

Bindon departed and returned even more hastily, reporting that he had run into Captain Anstruther, who was moving with two hundred regulars and six field pieces to recapture St. John's. Colonel Allen's army bivouacked that night on the beach at the town.

Something—it may have been the enormous amount of rowing—made their slumbers so deep that the field battery arriving on the Richelieu's far shore got into position before anyone woke. Thereafter, St. John's second captors ran for their bateaux through a brisk shower of grapeshot and rowed out of range. When their commander recovered enough breath to call the roll, he found that three of his slumberers had been left behind, still asleep, but it was too late to try to rouse them then.

The triumphant Arnold, with his prisoners, schooner and sloop, the discomfited Allen and his weary oarsmen reached Crown Point, May 19 and 21. Only once during their subsequent discordant sojourn there were they ever as close together in any enterprise.

Congress had scarcely reassembled in Philadelphia when John Brown arrived with what Allen had deemed glorious, and the assembled legislators considered decidedly disconcerting, tidings. Theirs were the feelings of mild gentlemen who had asked for a small steak and had received instead a large, rampageous bull.

Revolt against His Majesty was certainly justified, and a little semi-loyal shooting of redcoats about Boston was perhaps permissible; but to capture, without warrant from anyone, the gracious king's forts with such a large amount of ordnance was, Congress thought nervously, going just a bit too far.

Immediate orders were issued commanding a careful inventory of all George III's property so precipitately taken—or all that possibly could be replevined from the Green Mountain Boys—so that it could be politely returned to its original owner upon "the restoration of the former harmony between Great Britain and the colonies so ardently wished by the latter."

A little later, the amateur strategists in Philadelphia decided to abandon the forts and to concentrate all the captured stores at the south end of Lake George. The outraged howl from Allen, Arnold, and all other officers with a glimmer of military sense impelled them hastily to rescind these instructions.

At the forts, the rival leaders employed their voices chiefly in quarreling with each other over command of the post. The militia that Arnold's agents, Captain Oswald and Brown, had enlisted belatedly were beginning to come in, and Allen's men were beginning to go home. They had left an almighty lot of farming undone, and besides there was nothing now to drink at the fort but water, and that beverage was even more notoriously poisonous here than elsewhere.

They were bored as well. The job was finished, and they didn't like the discipline of soldiering. Most especially, they didn't like Arnold. A couple of them shot at him playfully, just to see him jump, but Arnold and the other officers raised an inordinate amount of fuss over that. It was time to catch up on their spring plowing. Even Old Ethan couldn't hold them longer. He kept promising to lead them into Canada, but nothing happened except more squabbles with Arnold, who wrote to Massachusetts:

"Colonel Allen is a proper man to lead his own wild people, but entirely unacquainted with military service."

Allen was doing more than merely making promises. He was writing appeal after appeal for permission to raise more men, for orders to go forward. Nothing he had seen of the British, save the unfairly early field battery on the Richelieu, had given him cause to respect them, and the best military strategy he knew was to keep striking at an enemy who already was off balance.

On May 29, he informed Congress that if it would only send him five hundred men he would guarantee to capture Montreal. On June 22, he was less optimistic but equally urgent. He asked then for fifteen hundred troops and "a proper train of artillery" to do the job. As far as moving Congress was concerned, he might as successfully have been yelling down a well. He looked elsewhere for aid, valiantly swallowing the aftertaste of old hatred. He wrote to the New York Provincial Convention offering to raise a "small regiment of rangers" commissioned by New York and financed by that province.

Few outlaws ever have been more willing to let bygones be bygones. Allen got no more response to his suggestion than Congress had vouchsafed. The only person who would answer him promptly, it seemed, was Benedict Arnold. The enduring squabble between them had now become three-cornered.

Colonel Hinman appeared at Crown Point with a thousand Connecticut men and orders to take command. Arnold refused to recognize him as a superior officer, and the strife between his men and Hinman's grazed the verge of open battle. Seldom has a great scoundrel-to-be more thoroughly advertised the spiritual defects that were destined eventually to overthrow him.

The summer advanced; the troops grew semimutinous while their officers quarreled. The broad water highway to Canada still lay open, though the British frantically were fortifying St. John's, and still Congress did nothing. On June 10, officers to whom inactivity and constant bickering had grown unbearable held a meeting, of which Major Samuel Elmore of Connecticut was chairman, and prepared a petition to Congress, begging that body to unscramble the puzzle of divided authority at the lake forts and urging employment of the troops garrisoned there.

The deputies chosen to carry this plea to Philadelphia were Seth Warner and Ethan Allen, whose persistent letters had brought him 'no satisfaction. He was to try now whether his voice might prevail where his pen had failed.

ix   Brief Millennium

THE AMERICAN REVOLUTION, like all catastrophes, stilled small rivalries beneath the pall of a common plight. It created momentary, bizarre, and faintly millennial associations. Idealism burned with an ardent and fleeting glow. By its brief light, lately antagonistic colonies were met together; New York and the Grants had kissed each other.

While the radiance endured, it illuminated the most unlikely sights. Men of the Grants, by taking the lake forts, were protecting the frontier of their prime enemy; the discordant factions of Cumberland County were meeting in a state of practical harmony; Ethan Allen himself was about to appear before and be welcomed by the legislature of New York. Men identified the fair light as the dawn of a new and better day. It was all very inspiring and transitory.

The paroxysms of war continued and increased. The face of earth, the outline of human beliefs, were changed. The bright fervor burned itself out; and mortals, surveying a dislocated world, sought in the chaos for personal advantage. New patterns of conduct were established; new alliances, defensive and offensive, were formed; new goals were sighted. The crusade was turning, as all high human endeavors will, into a business enterprise.

In the clash and shuffle and interplay of intentions released by revolution, the Grants' ambitions seemed elderly and stable. They were barren of glitter, unadorned with novel phrases. Their very simplicity made men, at first, ignore them. This was a mistake that it took a number of years to repair.

The substance of the aspirations that had begun to take their final and extremely durable form in the minds of raw farmers had come up across the border with the first pioneers. The already crystallizing ideal was nothing more exalted in that time of flamboyant oratory than the humble but stalwart desire which already had cost the Grants a decade of strife. It demanded for a people complete and unchallenged possession of their own land and the right of freemen to govern themselves.

These were elemental requirements, but also solid. They stood obdurately in the way which others were to travel, and many who were to try to kick them scornfully aside were destined to hop about, holding one foot with an intensely concerned expression.

That modest immobility and the anguish it caused quickened the ire of the injured until, presently, the Grants were to find themselves confronting, instead of their original single external adversary, no less than fourteen, implicit or explicit. The reluctant but obstinate Republic would have to deal with the hostility of Britain, the enmity of New York, the original adversary, and to confront as well the varying antipathies or disapprovals of twelve other newly established commonwealths.

No other state in this time of peril was so physically weak or so heavily outnumbered. No other was afflicted with so wide an assortment of intestine rumblings, cramps, and spasms, created by obstreperous factions within the political body. No other state through the intricate, embattled years ahead was to hold so steadfastly to its purpose or in the end was to gain so completely all its original objectives.

These still were obscure and considerably scrambled in the summer of 1775 when Ethan Allen and Seth Warner journeyed to Philadelphia as emissaries from the military anarchy that seethed at Ticonderoga and Crown Point. There was apparent unity on the Grants' Westside. There had been a promise of harmony on the Eastside that already was beginning to relapse into the more familiar discord, not of bewilderment, but of assorted certainties. Here, all men knew exactly what they wanted; but few of them wanted the same things.

The primal flame of idealism had blazed brightly. It had revealed the town of Guilford so far shaken in what its detractors deemed its pigheaded loyalty to New York that on April 7 it had insisted that all officers holding commissions from Governor Tryon resign them.

The sublime fire had illuminated the enveloping enthusiasm for New York which briefly had swept through all Cumberland County communities when, on May 23, a patriot Provincial Convention, meeting in New York City, had supplanted the royal legislature. Zeal for liberty was so high on the Eastside that no one paused for the moment to ask just what this new convention's attitude would be on Grants land titles.

Cumberland County held still another of its meetings at Westminster, June 6, and sent resolutions to the convention enthusiastically damning British oppression and pledging loyalty to the new legislative body. The meeting's fervor was emphasized by the election of three delegates to sit in that convention—Colonel John Hazeltine of Townshend, Dr. Paul Spooner of Hartland, and Major William Williams of Westminster.

Acknowledgment of New York's authority was stressed still further . by the Westminster gathering. It asked the Provincial Convention for aid in re-establishing a county government and begged for arms and ammunition, adding, "We have many brave soldiers but unhappily for us nothing to fight with." For the moment, it also seemed that recently simmering Cumberland County had nothing to fight over, either.

Hazeltine, Williams, and Spooner were seated in the New York convention on June 21, four days after the remnants of Howe's and Pigott's regiments had swarmed cheering over the Bunker Hill trenches in a victory more costly than most defeats, two days before Ethan Allen and Seth Warner appeared in the Continental Congress in Philadelphia.

Colonel Allen, the one-man spectacle, and his more sober associate had been well received in the city. He and Warner·had sent to Congress the letter they bore. They had been entertained by an enthusiastic citizenry who had found the Colonel one hero who in vehemence and physical dimensions lived up to his reputation.

Here, while he awaited a summons from Congress, Allen met again his youthful crony, Dr. Thomas Young, whose liberalism had not abated with maturity and who now was as violent an enemy of George III as he once had been of God. Dr. Young became a convert to the cause of the Grants and thereafter favored the leaders of that region with a steady stream of letters on a variety of subjects.

Congress at last called the emissaries before it. Colonel Allen seems to have appeared, not only as a witness to the disgraceful conditions at the lake forts and the need for the immediate invasion of Canada, but also as an advocate of the interests of Ethan Allen; for at the conclusion of the interview Congress sent recommendations to the New York Provincial Convention that the Green Mountain Boys be . formed into a ranger regiment with officers of their own choosing.

Such advice was bound to cause shock and pain to New Yorkers, but the millennial spirit still ran high; and when, on July 4, Allen and Warner, the recently infamous outlaws, appeared at the convention's portals, it was voted eighteen to nine to admit them. The capture of Ticonderoga had absolved the erstwhile miscreants of their sins.

The conference was cordial, and from it Warner and Allen emerged with authority to raise in New York's name and at her expense a battalion of not more than five hundred men, to be officered by residents of the Grants. These were to be known—so large was New York's forgiveness—as the Green Mountain Rangers, and uniforms of green faced with red were ordered for them.

Such magnanimity was contagious, and Colonel Allen on returning to the Grants wrote a resounding letter to the convention predicting a speedy reconciliation between the late insurgents and New York and "assuring your Honours that your respectful treatment not only to Mr. Warner and myself but to the Green Mountain Boys in general in forming them into a battalion are by them duly regarded."

Folk had small time to marvel at the spectacle of Ethan Allen making epistolary bows and scrapes to a recently detested enemy. Another and still not wholly understood marvel was to claim attention.

The safety committees of the Westside towns met, July 27, at Cephas Kent's tavern in Dorset to elect officers for the new battalion. The colonel chosen was not the man who had formed and trained and led the Grant's unconventional defense force, who was his people's most aggressively martial citizen, whom all the colonies were hailing as the hero of Ticonderoga. Seth Warner was elected the commander of the Green Mountain Rangers. He got forty-one of the, forty-six votes cast.

There is, even now, no complete explanation for the committees' action. They not only took from the Colonel Commandant, retired, the command that he already had regarded as certainly his, but they also wholly ignored him in naming subordinate officers. Samuel Safford was chosen major, Heman Allen a captain, Ira Allen a lieutenant. There was no place at all, save in the ranks, for Ethan Allen.

He seems in the face of brutal and affronting disappointment to have behaved remarkably well. No echo of a roaring and empurpled fit of fury has come down to us. He has supplied the most nearly plausible solution of the mystery in a letter he wrote Governor Trumbull of Connecticut immediately after his rejection. Even this missive, though bitter, lacks the familiar thunder and lightning of Ethan Allen's rages. He wrote:

Notwithstanding my zeal and success in my Countrys Cause the old Farmers on the New Hampshire Grants who do not incline to go to war have met in a Committee Meeting and in their nomination of Officers for the regiment of Green Mountain Boys who are to quickly be raised have wholly omitted me . . . I find myself in favour of the Officers of the army and the young Green Mountain Boys how the old men come to reject me I cannot conceive inasmuch as I saved them from the encroachments of New York.

No one has supplied any better answer to the puzzle. "The old men" did it—the elders who had been steeped too long in the prim and prudent precepts of older New England for the Grants' new freedom and spacious atmosphere ever to absolve them. These had pursed their mouths and had shaken their heads at Ethan Allen and his goings-on, deploring his bawling zest for life, his uniform and his swagger, his capacity for rum and recklessness, his blasphemy and his derision of the Hebrew God. He had been their salvation, but his usefulness was over in the millennium's dawn. He was a trial and a scandal and a deplorable influence on the young, wherefore the old men rejected him and chose in his stead the comparatively moderate, sober, and careful Seth Warner.

It would have been easy for a man of such apparently headlong ambition as Colonel-reject Allen to have torn the Westside apart by the fury of his indignation. The young men were almost as outraged as he and ready to follow him. Warner had extreme difficulty in raising his battalion and never enlisted its full stipulated strength. Yet Allen did not rebel. He went off in unwonted meekness and the hope of a Continental commission to Ticonderoga.

At the lake forts Arnold had resigned in a rage and gone home; and General Philip Schuyler, commander of the northern department, who had arrived to lead the assembling army against Canada, found only twin crumbling cesspools of diseased, drunken, and disorderly troops who displayed more desire to fight their comrades from rival colonies than they did to war on Britain, and had done little toward building the necessary flotilla for an advance down the lake.

Meanwhile, Guy Carleton, Governor General of Canada, was heavily fortifying St. John's, and most of the summer had slipped by. It is doubtful whether the distracted Schuyler considered Allen's advent as a blessing or an added affliction, but he permitted him to remain and, when the army at last moved, on August 28, allowed him to accompany it without a commission. The general had a scarcely higher opinion of the demoted colonel's reliability than Arnold.

> It was not [Schuyler wrote] until after a solemn promise made me in the presence of several officers that he would demean himself properly that I would permit him to attend the army; nor would I have consented then had not his solicitations been backed by several officers.

The general may have shared the Grants elders' opinion of Ethan Allen's soldierly qualities. He had no reason, presently, to esteem the prowess of Remember Baker more highly.

Before the army embarked in its hastily built bateaux, Schuyler sent scouting parties north under Baker and John Brown, now a major, to feel out the British defenses and preach liberty's enlivening doctrine to the apathetic Canadian French. Both patrols were warned to do nothing to stir Indian enmity.

Brown fulfilled his mission. Baker and his men, moving by night toward the lake's north end, hid their boat and crept into the waterside woods to pass the day. Caughnawaga Indians found the craft and rowed it past the scouts' hiding place. Baker squalled a demand that they bring it back and, when they mocked him, slipped behind a tree and leveled his musket. It misfired, and Remember, thrusting his head from concealment to see what ailed its flint, never found out, for an Indian bullet shattered his skull. The other scouts returned the fire and killed two of the boat's occupants. They had supplied adequate grounds for Indian participation in the war, and Schuyler mourned the dead redmen more than he did Baker.

The army at last moved down the lake toward the Richelieu River and the strengthened St. John's. The town that Arnold had taken with thirty-five men beat off the first American attack. The army settled down to a regular siege. Schuyler fell ill and relinquished command to General Richard Montgomery on September 16. That same day, Warner joined the army with one hundred seventy of his allotted five hundred Green Mountain Rangers. Seventy more reported later.

Guns began deliberate speech about the invested town, and lines of raw earth showed where Montgomery had laid out his trenches with the aid, sought or unsought, of Ethan Allen, who was eager to be not only helpful but instructive as well. It may have been this over-hearty spirit of co-operation which impelled the General to send his volunteer aide as a missionary further into Canada with the hope that he might prove equally annoying to the British.

Allen received command of thirty Connecticut militiamen and orders to range the country between the Richelieu and Montreal, converting habitants to the cause of liberty and, if possible, enlisting them as well. The siege proceeded more tranquilly after his departure. Frequent letters of information and exhortation came back from him to Montgomery.

> You may rely on it [he wrote September 20] that I shall join you in about three days with five hundred or more Canadian volunteers. I could raise one or two thousand in a week's time but will first visit the army with a less number and if necessary will go again recruiting.

Meanwhile, it was ex-Colonel Allen's opinion that General Montgomery should take St. John's without delay.

> To fail victory [he informed his commander] will be an eternal disgrace but to obtain it will elevate us on the wings of fame.

The only recruits he actually sent the army were six hogsheads of rum and some flour, purchased from the habitants.

Four days later, Allen was still wandering about Canada with, not five hundred men, but a hundred and ten, eighty of them Canadians whom he had hired at the wages of fifteen pence per day. John Brown and Seth Warner also were roaming through the region with small forces of their own. On September 24, Allen encountered Brown near Longueuil.

Concerning what happened there, and thereafter, we have only the testimony of Ethan Allen's own narrative, written some years later. It is a one-sided story at best, and not wholly watertight. Allen says that Brown proposed that the two forces co-operate in the capture of Montreal, Brown crossing the St. Lawrence to the south of the town, Allen to the north, and both attacking it at the same time. The signal for the assault was to be "three huzzas" uttered by Brown's men when they were in position.

That is the story, or the excuse, of the late leader of the Green Mountain Boys, who soon had a great deal to explain as plausibly as possible if he were to maintain his role of a great and indomitable warrior.

By implication, Allen charges that Brown betrayed him. No contemporary but Ira Allen ever echoed the accusation. In all other crises

Brown showed himself to be an honest man and a good soldier. He and Warner already had asked Montgomery's permission to attack Montreal, and the General had refused it on the ground that their combined force was too weak. The most charitable explanation of the subsequent fiasco is simply that Allen, in the heat and exaltation of the moment, misunderstood the arrangements.

He misunderstood with a devastating thoroughness, ferrying his hundred and ten across the St. Lawrence by night in the few canoes he could find. It took several trips to get his whole force to the north side of Montreal. There he waited for the "three huzzas" signal, and after two hours sent out scouts to see what had become of Brown. He dared not start to move his men back over the river for fear of discovery. So he waited and swore, and soon the British became aware of his presence.

A mixed force of regulars, townspeople, and Indians swarmed out to the attack. Allen had not been conspicuously fortunate in his only other open engagement, but that had been triumphant compared to this. Muskets banged; slugs whistled overhead. Allen's fifteen-pence-per-day soldiery found their wages much too small. They walked out on their employer, fifty of them by the right flank, more by the left.

Thus deserted, Colonel Ethan Allen and his remaining force retreated down the center. He admits, in one of his rare moments of modesty, his dismay in finding that the enemy could run just as fast as he.

Pursuers and pursued galloped over the countryside for the better part of a mile before the leader of the chase, an officer most indefinitely identified as a natural son of Sir William Johnson, got close enough to Allen to shoot at him and miss. The fugitive fired in his turn, but his ball, too, went wide. His marksmanship had left him along with most of his wind. What remained to him he spent, according to his narrative, in an ornate colloquy with his pursuer, both of them presumably still running.

Allen pointed out, between puffs, that he was outnumbered and said he might be induced to surrender. The officer approved of the idea. Surrender, however, would be extremely repugnant to the pursued unless he were treated with honor thereafter. The officer assured him that he would be and promised further that his men would receive good quarter. Thereupon Allen surrendered himself and the well-blown remnant of his command, thirty-eight men, seven of them wounded.

The ordeal was not yet over. Capitulation did not usher in peace and a chance for Allen to get his breath back. The Indians, it immediately appeared, did not recognize the running treaty just established with the British. The first warrior to reach the distinguished prisoner prepared at once to shoot him. The Indian's appearance seems to have· left a lasting impression on the mind of his intended victim.

As he approached near me, his hellish visage was beyond all description, snakes eyes appear innocent in comparison with his, his features extorted, malice, death, murder and the wrath of devils and damned spirits are the emblems of his countenance.

Even the most valiant of men might pardonably seek refuge from such a spectacle, and the only protection immediately available to Allen was the officer who had just disarmed him. The prisoner gripped his captor and hid behind him.

For several minutes a lively and impromptu dance went on, the Indian leaping about and poking with his musket's muzzle to get a clear shot; Allen whirling the loudly objecting officer around to keep this human shield between him and his would-be murderer. Another Indian joined in the pastime, compelling the prospective target to swing his unwilling partner just twice as fast. Other white men, arriving, drove the Indians off, and Ethan Allen released his captor.

The most extreme violence and abuse accompany the narrator through the remainder of his narrative, implausibly, until one considers how constantly each companioned him through most of his career.

Allen relates that, when he was brought before the British General Prescott, that officer threatened at once to cane him and was deterred only because the prisoner thrust his fist under the officer's nose, "telling him that that was the beetle of mortality for him."

Consideration of this cryptic statement apparently deflected Prescott's wrath to the thirteen Canadian prisoners, whom, Allen says, the General ordered his soldiers immediately to bayonet.

I therefore stepped between the executioners and the Canadians, opened my clothes and told Gen. Prescott to thrust the bayonets into my breast.

Foiled again, the General, as Allen heard it, then said:

I will not execute you now, but ye shall grace a halter at Tyburn, God damn ye.

The opponents then parted with mutual expressions of disesteem. Allen was taken aboard His Majesty's schooner of war *Gaspé,* and eventually, in shackles, to England. The Grants were a drearier place during his absence.

Many there doubtless mourned his capture. In the army still besieging St. John's it was regarded with a philosophy kin to relief, and Allen's serio-comic fate was used as a moral for others who valued their own opinions more highly than the purposes of their superiors and fretted under discipline. Washington himself wrote:

> Colonel Allen's misfortune will, I hope, teach a lesson of prudence and subordination to others who may be too ambitious to outshine their general officers and, regardless of order and duty, rush into enterprises which have unfavorable effects to the publick and are destructive to themselves.

The reckless and inept assault on Montreal became inevitable the moment Allen had unsupervised command of men and an enemy stronghold was in sight. To a nature like his, such circumstances would have been a challenge under any conditions. That challenge was irresistible when Allen's own pride so recently had been abased, and Warner was colonel of the Green Mountain Rangers, and he himself only a tolerated and inconspicuous volunteer in the invading army.

If he had, by a miracle akin to Ticonderoga, taken Montreal, he would have cast Cousin Seth into the shade, refuted the old men who had chosen him, and reburnished the sullied fame of Ethan Allen.

Abused, enchained, penned with other prisoners in a stinking hold, the late leader of the Green Mountain Boys was spared final humiliation. His prison ship had sailed for England before Warner won a victory that made more ignominious still Allen's own defeat.

The Green Mountain Rangers, two companies of the 2nd New York Infantry and two field pieces, held Longueuil across the river from Montreal. On October 31, Carleton, with a force of regulars, Indians, and Canadians in thirty-four boats, launched an attempt to relieve the beleaguered St. John's. None save a few dripping prisoners ever reached the St. Lawrence's further shore. Warner smashed the attack in midstream with a loss to the British of fifty men and no casualties of his own.

Captain Heman Allen escorted the captives to Montgomery's camp, and several of them were sent into St. John's. After an interview with them, Major Preston, commanding the town, surrendered his force of one hundred Canadians and five hundred regulars. Among these was a graceful young lieutenant, John André.

The way was clear now to interior Canada. The American army, already shivering in the winds of late fall, stumbled down the Richelieu toward Montreal. The town capitulated November 13 without any attempt at defense. Prescott, Allen's recent adversary, was among the prisoners. Ragged and frost-nipped, with the seeds of the pestilences that were to overwhelm it already in its insanitary body, the army crept on toward Quebec.

Warner and his men did not accompany it. That sober and reliable man disagreed with Montgomery, demanded the discharge of himself and his troops, and, obtaining it, led his Rangers home, away from the already thickening shadow of disaster. The lambent idealism of the spring was guttering out now with a rank smell.

Elsewhere than in Canada the enthusiasm that had possessed men was fading. Harmony on the Eastside of the Grants already was a thing of the past. After brief co-operation, the Yorkers, the New Hampshiremen, the Tories and Whigs and supporters of Massachusetts had split apart along their already established lines and were resuming their old contentious ways.

Unity, when at last it came to Vermont, was amazingly enduring, chiefly because it was obtained through so great a travail. Only folk with monumental patience could have deigned to suffer deliberately until each obdurate, angular element had been shaken down into its proper place, and the infinite varieties of independence, of obstinacy, of cantankerousness had been fitted nicely against each other in one solid whole.

That unity was still a long way off. The grating friction which was to fill early Vermont with its abrasive sound had resumed again, after its brief stilling by war. It was low in the Westside, where the folk from the beginning had been more nearly of one mind and strife against New York had unified them further. It was louder and continually growing on the Eastside. The meeting at Westminster, November 21, 1775, to choose officers for the militia regiments was a sounding board for dissonance.

The candidates for these martial posts and their partisans would have made a redoubtable reinforcement for the flagging army in Canada if they could have been persuaded to carry their numbers and pugnacity into the field. Each faction was convinced that the militia leaders should be drawn from its more than willing ranks and disparaged vehemently the candidates of other groups. There was an abundance of material on hand for every post.

"If they were all commissioned," one Yorker wrote dismally to the New York convention, "about one-third of the men in the county will be officers."

With dissension so heated, it was obvious that the persons finally chosen could not hope for popularity. Most of the successful candidates were immediately accused of being at heart minions of George III, which was the handiest defamation to use at the moment. The regiments were formed on paper, but never approached actuality. The technical members thereof were more intent on fighting each other than on combining against a common foe.

The year wore to its dreary close with the squabble muted but not extinguished. Nothing in the news from Canada served to rekindle patriotism. On the year's last day, the ailing army stormed Quebec, after a feint by Robert Cochran and Ira Allen against Cape Diamond, had failed to distract the defense. The attack collapsed in the falling snow, with Montgomery hiccupping his life out in Aaron Burr's arms and Benedict Arnold severely wounded. The army limped away into encampment up the river, there to spend a wretched and disease-ridden winter; and General David Wooster, on whom its command now fell, appealed to everyone within reach of his dispatches, including Colonel Warner, for more men.

Recruiting for the Green Mountain Rangers began again. At almost the same time, the Westside moved obliquely against an older enemy than the British. The general war was remote—far to the north where smallpox was burning in the miserable army huddled beside the St. Lawrence; far to the south about still-besieged Boston, whither General Knox was hauling by sled cannon captured at Ticonderoga. An older strife was still on the Grants' doorstep. Now that the brief millennial light had burned out, recently dazzled eyes observed that New York preserved in rebellion the identical threatening attitude toward the Grants that had been hers as a royal province.

There were patentees to Grants land in the New York convention. Duane, Livingston, and other vast gamblers in Grants real estate were members of the Continental Congress. Their presence reawakened a people's never more than mildly dormant suspicion, revived their deliberately acquired, dauntingly stable hatred.

They were dubious, then fearful, and finally bitterly hostile once more toward New York and all its works. Congress's early suggestion

that the lake forts, after their capture, be abandoned and the south
end of Lake George be made the line of defense, was deemed by
Grants folk to be the New York members' plot to drive settlers under
New Hampshire titles from the land by exposing them to British
invasion. It is harder to wean a Vermonter from a conviction than to
unbreech a Highlander.

An obstinate consistency held this people to the American cause
despite the offensive fact that their immediate neighbor also had
joined it. The Grants had espoused Freedom, and they stayed monog-
amous, fighting the British madly when the need arose but spending
their more undistracted moments in deliberate, implacable warfare
against New York. That conflict, with none of the picturesque embellishments Ethan Allen had supplied, was resumed after the transitory
truce, early in 1776.

Cephas Kent, deacon and innkeeper of Dorset, received delegates
to a convention of Westside towns at his tavern, January 16. Here
there was none of the heat and flying sparks that distinguished Eastside gatherings. The meeting proceeded with the smooth deliberation
of canny men whose minds were attuned. The petition formulated
for presentation to the Continental Congress was marked by the astute
craft of leaders who had learned their statesmanship in the enlighten-
ing school of horse-trading.

This document reviewed once more the source and progress of the
Grants' trouble with New York. It pledged the Westside's loyalty to
Congress but demurred at spreading that virtue thin enough to cover
New York, too. If the Grants were to promise fealty to the New York
convention, what was to prevent that body from pulling the farms
right out from under their current holders?

Maybe they would and maybe they wouldn't, but the realistic West-
siders were taking no chances. Since, their petition pled, matters between the Grants and New York seemed doomed to abide in an
atmosphere of mutual suspicion, would not Congress decree that
New York was to keep its hands off "until a general restoration of
tranquillity shall allow us an opportunity for an equitable settlement"?

No one can tell how clearly the leaders of the Westside, those long-
headed, long-tempered men, saw the goal toward which this request
was the first, almost imperceptible movement. Ostensibly, it artlessly
asked Congress not to consider the disputed territory as part of New
York but as the New Hampshire Grants, until the war's end. Heman
Allen, the historically obscure but apparently extremely able brother

of Ethan and Ira, was charged with the presentation of the appeal to Congress.

Captain Allen was extremely deliberate in accomplishing his mission. He may have been busy recruiting men for the Green Mountain Rangers, though he did not accompany that regiment when it marched sometime in February, four hundred and seventeen strong, to the aid of the army in Canada, now rotting away with smallpox, dysentery, and other ailments.

Warner's command reached the pestilential encampment March 5, four days after Wooster had been succeeded by General John Thomas. The arrival of the Green Mountain Rangers scarcely compensated for the men who died during that single week. Of the three thousand in Thomas's army only nine hundred were fit for duty. The general ordered a retreat lest the entire force remain in Canada permanently and, leading the agonized withdrawal, himself was smitten by smallpox and died at Chambly. The groaning army staggered on, now under the command of General John Sullivan. Anthony Wayne's and John Stark's reinforcements were scarcely enough to move the ailing living or to bury the dead.

The ragamuffin remnant of the host reached the lake forts at last, as John Adams wrote, "disgraced, defeated, discontented, dispirited, undisciplined, eaten with vermin, no clothes, beds, blankets, or medicines." The drive into Canada had failed calamitously. Britain's counter-thrust was to come. Not even the fact that Washington had forced the British from Boston could abolish the bitter aftertaste of complete defeat.

Heman Allen had no share in this ignominious collapse. In all probability, it was not prevision that restrained him from joining Warner's command in its futile journey to Canada. Something more urgent may have kept him at home and delayed his visit to Congress until trails were drying and leaves stirring and May had come to wipe away memory of a brutal winter.

The leaders of the Westside had dreamed a dream and seen a vision. It was a revelation too startling and unprecedented for them to impart it at once to their followers. So secretly did they discuss it, that to this day no one can be certain who were that particular "four of the leading men of the Grants" to whom, Ira Allen wrote later, enlightenment had come.

Probably, since he speaks with authority of their meetings, one of the quartet was Ira himself. Heman Allen was almost certainly a

second. The identity of the other two still is obscure. They may have
been Dr. Jonas Fay and Thomas Chittenden.

The hope they cherished, the high enterprise they determined to
further, has a trite flavor today. In early 1776, it was radical and
would have been profoundly shocking if proclaimed bluntly to the
Grants' people. It was, simply, that the land which had waited a
century and a half for settlement, the land that earnest farmer folk
had come up to possess, the land they had defended against the intru-
sion of New York, should be forever theirs—an independent nation.

It must not be an appendage of New York, or of New Hampshire
or Massachusetts. It must be, without qualification or higher loyalty,
the property of the folk who now held it and their children and their
children's children—a land of freemen, a republic.

Who first advanced this daring break with tradition, no one will
ever know. It may have been the land itself, its hills and clear streams
and immemorial forests, that sponsored the dream. It may have been
a spirit, born of the need of men, that mysteriously was abroad in the
world; that fired not only four Yankees on an imperiled frontier but
also inspired a tall, red-haired fiddle-playing Virginian and his radical
associates. The cautious quartet in the Grants, Thomas Jefferson and
his colleagues in Philadelphia, moved independently toward the same
end.

The Grants conspirators had no clear idea how their dream was to
become actual; how the word was to be made flesh. The materializa-
tion must be deliberate, foresighted, immensely vigilant toward events.
Only their purpose—independence—was wholly clear to the four men.
How it was to be accomplished none of them yet knew. Fulfillment
must wait on time. It must be brought about by skill and enduring
patience, for the resolution of this quartet ran far ahead of even the
most radical faction in the Grants.

On the ever-turbulent Eastside, already there had been vague talk
of forming the valley land on either bank of the Connecticut into a
separate commonwealth. That had been only the loose speech of
insurgents who asked for more than they hoped to get. The intentions
of "the four leading men of the Grants" were earnestly realistic and
reached further.

The Grants were to be free—with the consent of the Continental
Congress if possible, otherwise, without it. Eastside and Westside,
ignoring their differences in politics and beliefs, oblivious to the barrier

ridge between them, were to unite and form a single nation. The odds against the establishment of such a union were fantastic; the difficulties, internal and external, between the vision and its realization seemed completely overwhelming. It may be that some of the secrecy in which the quartet held their meetings was due to a Yankee aversion to being laughed at.

Yet self-possession was their purpose, and the dislocations already wrought by war, their opportunity. When the dream would come true, no man might say, but the aspiring four determined to do all they might to bring it to life. Their obvious first task was to preach this startlingly heretical gospel to the high and the low.

"Great care," Ira Allen relates, "was taken to prepare the·minds of the people for such an event."

He was always an excellent preparer.

This was the end purpose that Heman Allen carried, carefully concealed, when he arrived in Philadelphia, May 8, and presented his petition. It was read before Congress and referred to a committee whose members all were delegates from southern states, far removed from association with the Grants-New York controversy or the real-estate deals which had fathered it.

While Allen lingered, waiting audience with Congress, John Adams inadvertently supplied the quartet's still-hidden cause with armor and a sword. He had no idea he was making this contribution. In the stormy years ahead, when Vermont was opposing both a new and an old nation on the strength of Adams's words, he must have regretted their utterance. On May 15, he proposed the following resolution, which Congress adopted:

> That it be recommended to the respective assemblies and conventions of the United Colonies, where no government sufficient to the exigencies of their affairs hath been hitherto established: to adopt such government, as shall, in the opinion of the representatives of the people, best conduce to the happiness and safety of their constituents in particular, and America in general.

Which merely meant that Mr. Adams urged the people of all unorganized territory to pick the sort of government they wanted. The leaders of the Grants subsequently followed his prescription, though with more consideration for the happiness of their constituents than for the well-being of America in general.

Eventually, the wary Heman Allen appeared before Congress in person. Already the committee that had considered his petition had reported its recommendations. These bade the Grants submit loyally to New York authority until the war was over, with the understanding that all land quarrels should remain in abeyance till then.

To one who secretly hoped for no more relief than the petition asked, this might have seemed a satisfactory temporary answer to the whole problem. It did not suit Heman Allen. It alarmed him intensely.

Such a resolution was not at all what he and his three secret associates wanted. If it should be adopted by Congress, it would mean that the body had declared itself for New York and had prohibited, as well as its dim authority might, any more resistance in the Grants to New York's claim of ownership. And Congress obviously intended to adopt the resolution.

Here was a crisis in which a man must think quickly and move fast if he hoped to get out of it with his cause undamaged. Heman Allen did both. Before Congress could act, he revisited it with every evidence of penitence and embarrassment to announce that he was obliged to withdraw the petition.

Not for long. Just temporarily. Through a lamentable oversight he had failed to bring along to Philadelphia a number of vital documents pertinent to the petition. These he asked Congress's permission to assemble before he presented his plea again. His request was granted. Heman emerged from Independence Hall with his secret cause intact and, if the Allen inheritance was constant, hastened in his relief to the nearest tavern for a flowing bowl.

He had blocked any immediate decision in favor of New York. He had averted official instructions from Congress to the Grants by an audacious appearance of guilelessness.

Heman Allen admitted later that he was aided in his predicament by "sundry gentlemen of distinction." These were not impossibly land gamblers who possessed New Hampshire rights. The early American hunger for real estate kept bobbing up in the most unexpected places. These same distinguished gentlemen, Allen said further, urged him not to accept New York jurisdiction under any circumstances, but "to associate and unite the whole of the inhabitants of said Grants together."

It may have been, in retailing this counsel, that Heman Allen was adopting the puppeteer method of Ira and putting in the mouths of

other persons ideas and ambitions that were his own. Before Mr.
Jefferson had dipped his quill into the ink and had carefully inscribed:
"When in the course of human events—" the New Hampshire Grants
were moving, or being surreptitiously pushed, in the direction his
famous document was to point, an eternal signboard.

x   Design Plus Accident

THE FORCES that actually cleared the Grants' way to freedom were external and unpredictable. The original four Westside leaders and the others who joined them used these fortuitous powers with cool agility. The year 1776 was a time of earthquake and tempest. Such violences were to be equally frequent in the years immediately to come. They were the motive impulses that, harnessed, moved a people toward a goal.

Each calamity that passed over the physically weak frontier settlements left their inhabitants more purposeful. Each threatening peril revealed, on subsidence, a more nearly integrated nation. No men ever found in cloud linings more negotiable bullion than these nasal leaders, these shabby whirlwind-riders with fresh loam on their boots and a solid intention in their minds. No chieftains ever better understood the democratic art of unobtrusively, with soft persistence, pushing a people toward an end which, at last, the people come to believe has been their own purpose from the first.

Exterior violences were not these leaders' only steeds. The population of the Grants, snorting, wild-eyed, hard of mouth and head, also must be subdued—cautiously, for no people ever delighted more in bucking off the timorous or the peremptory rider.

The travail out of which Vermont was born was unlike most revolutions, including that which surrounded it on three sides. Here was no explosive revolt, no uprising against intolerable tyranny. The Vermont revolution began with the leaders themselves, and worked downward. Most of the dramatic elements of insurrection were lacking. Sublime persistence, resourceful obstinacy, replaced them. It could not have been a particularly exciting upheaval to watch, but it moved more efficiently for its lack of spectacle—as Vermonters still constitutionally prefer to move.

The decayed remnants of the Canadian expedition had reached Ticonderoga and Crown Point. They tarried there chiefly because they lacked strength to retreat further. The northwest frontier of the

Grants, where farms were being cleared along the Otter and the Onion rivers, had been left bare, and at any moment the British might come.

A cry went up from these settlements for aid—a desperate cry from farmers who knew that if they deserted their crops now, they were merely postponing possible immediate death at Indian hands for a surer, slower extinction by starvation in the coming winter. Sullivan spared one hundred and fifty of his troops to garrison the blockhouse on Onion River and uttered cries of his own for more soldiers. General Gates supplanted him in July and began to strengthen Ticonderoga. Carleton's army, the rumor ran, was on its way, and Crown Point was to be abandoned. The fears of the frontier farmers grew more swiftly than their corn.

There was irresolution, too, on the Eastside, though it had a different source. The region that so recently had pledged its loyalty to the New York convention was beginning to take it back. The old hatred was stronger than the new fealty. The convention had authorized the enlistment of a ranger force of two hundred and fifty men in the Grants under the command of Major Joab Hoisington to protect the Eastside's frontier against Indian raids. Now New York was displaying a pardonable suspicion that the rangers were something less than faithful to the province that supported them. Pay for the battalion was held up, pending investigation, and Eastside antipathy automatically increased.

Massachusetts, apparently, was doing nothing to reinforce New York's hold on the Grants. Massachusetts had not forgotten the boundary decision of 1740 whereby she had been deprived of twenty-eight surveyed towns and much other territory. The present distressful time might offer an opportunity to recover that which had been lost, at least in part. Bay Province missionaries were whispering plausible promises in the ears of Eastsiders.

The meeting held at Westminster, June 21, 1776, indicated that the gospel according to Massachusetts was gaining converts. The committees of safety of the Eastside towns assembled at the instance of New York to elect delegates to another New York convention to be held in August. They chose the delegates but stipulated that the voters reserved the right to repudiate whatever these delegates might do while under nefarious alien influence. They also announced that maybe they didn't care to be governed by New York any longer and might prefer an alliance with "that ever-respectable and most patriotic government of the Massachusetts Bay Province."

Matters on the Eastside were growing scrambled again with the prospect of worse confusion still to come.

On the Westside, there was comparative solidarity. The people there had the more competent leaders; and these had gone to work, not with orations and inflammatory maneuverings—no people took fire less easily—but with slow, sure intention. The progress of the Grants toward independence had no explosive movement. It was marked by the cautious deliberation of an elephant crossing a dubious bridge—a tentative step, a pause to estimate its consequences, another step.

The convention held in Dorset, July 24, was the first of these purposeful, yet still hesitant, advances. Ostensibly the committees of safety gathered at Cephas Kent's tavern to hear Heman Allen's report on his mission to Congress. What actually happened was brought about by the Westside leaders' firm seizure of the appropriate moment. There was a new, external force abroad. They applied it to their purpose.

Tidings of Mr. Jefferson's document and of how it had been received by Congress had reached the Grants, turning the minds of men toward the way in which their leaders had planned they should move. Sheer good luck was their ally, then and later, as always it is of astute and patient men.

The farmers in Kent's tavern heard Heman Allen's report and endorsed his conduct. Their further actions were an echo of the Declaration of Independence. Resolutions proclaimed their country's loyalty to the new United States of America in general but expressed continued hostility to New York in particular "which renders it inconvenient in many respects to associate with that province or state."

Thereafter, the meeting took the first hesitant, testing step. They voted, with only one dissenting voice, that the Grants should be proclaimed "a separate district"—something that might mean much or little, depending on the attitude of the already established states. This was a position from which the Grants could retreat, if necessary, with scant humiliation.

A committee of evangelists was appointed to go up and down the land, Eastside and Westside alike, preaching to the dwellers therein the new, still only half-revealed gospel that another committee would supply. This second group was composed of four men—probably the "four of the leading men" of whom Ira Allen later wrote—Ira and Heman Allen, Dr. Jonas Fay, and Colonel Thomas Chittenden.

The first three already had served the Grants well in strife and negotiation. The last was to be the Vermont Republic's chief executive through all its years, save one.

In stature, Thomas Chittenden was the counterpart of Ethan Allen, whose neighbor he had been in Salisbury, Connecticut. A remarkable number of Vermont's early leaders were unusually big men. In nature, the future state's chief was the opposite of his blundering, overwhelming friend. Allen vehemently advertised his virtues; Chittenden concealed his own under a pretense of ignorance. He kept his mind perpetually in ambush.

His pose was intensely rural. He used a bucolic appearance, an artless manner to win the sympathy or the disdain of his adversaries, who later learned at sore cost how thoroughly he had induced them to underestimate him. Behind a deceptively guileless face, with its high forehead running up to a bald skull peak, with small whiskers curving forward from either ear like parentheses, with bland eyes, one of them sightless, was a keen and crafty brain. No one ever saw clearly the workings of that alert organ. Its apparently wholly intuitive deftness astonished even his intimates.

Ira Allen wrote later of Chittenden, almost ruefully, that he had never known a man who could be so unvaryingly right in all his decisions on even the most complex questions, without ever being able to tell why. It probably was not that Chittenden couldn't; he wouldn't. He had chosen for himself the role of farmer—a particularly artless pioneer farmer—and he stuck to it.

He liked the pose. He also relished the life of a pioneer, for he had sold a good farm in Salisbury during 1774 to settle on wilderness land he had bought from the Allens in the Onion River country. He took great zest in matching his big body against undisciplined nature; and, besides, that occupation fortified his impersonation, which yielded much profit and saved him a deal of argument and persuasion.

Chittenden avoided dispute and, instead, asked questions with a disarming innocence. By these he converted many, and few of them ever appreciated that those innocent queries gently had prodded them into exactly the state of mind for which the giant had aimed. Folk believed they were instructing him when, actually, he was converting them. No one ever hid his abilities more thriftily.

These abilities had won him distinction before he moved to the Grants. He was a farmer and a farmer's son, but he had followed the sea in his youth, had been captured by the French, and had had some personal acquaintance with a world that lay beyond provincial Connecticut. During his residence in Salisbury, he had been six times a representative in the legislature, had been justice of the peace and a colonel in the militia.

Chittenden's shambling, clownish demeanor woke an amused tolerance in his associates. It enabled him to cut corners and get things· done by swift, unconventional means. His legislative experience must have grounded him thoroughly in parliamentary law, yet he professed an extreme ignorance and would violate all statutes of procedure, while governor, to barge in upon legislative debate, harangue the debaters without warrant, and get the vital measure adopted with a minimum of fuss.

An acquaintance remembered him as "a shrewd, cunning man, skilled in human nature and agriculture," which are more closely related than most persons suppose.

"One-eyed Tom," his enemies called him. He had many foes, but he was dismayingly immune to them all. He kept his actual self so well hidden that it was almost impossible to reach and wound it. Once the Yorkers of the Eastside actually irked him into open expression of a wish to hang them all, but these had unusual abilities to enrage men. Normally, the Vermont Republic's almost perpetual governor accepted rare defeat with the outward indifference with which he welcomed success. He shrugged off these infrequent humiliations with wry Yankee humor.

Daniel Stannard, of Jericho, a man Chittenden detested, was chosen justice of the peace over the Governor's objections. He said when he heard of it:

"Well, well—I really believe he will make a better justice of the peace than I think he will."

No more potent ally than this purblind, canny giant could have been engaged by men who moved with caution and still half-hidden purpose toward the establishment of the Vermont Republic. Chittenden knew an angular and obdurate people thoroughly; he let them think they knew him, yet kept his actuality hidden from all mankind.

Something of his own masked nature got into the Articles of Association that he, Fay, and the Allens prepared at the Dorset convention for endorsement by town meetings throughout the Grants. The delegates approved these before they adjourned and resolved that any persons circulating documents contrary to the Articles' sentiments should be deemed "enemies of the common cause."

The Articles of Association were a façade of resounding patriotism behind which was visible the ancient hostility to New York; behind which, too, the determination of the Grants to be free was almost wholly concealed. It was not a structure that any but the most violent Tory or Yorker would dare disapprove, so ardent was its enthusiasm for a righteous cause.

> We the subscribers, inhabitants of the Districk of Land commonly called and known by the name of The New Hampshire Grants do voluntarily and solemnly engage under all the ties held sacred amongst mankind, at the risque of our lives and fortunes to defend by arms the United American States against the hostile attempts of the British fleets and armies until the present unhappy controversy between the two countries shall be settled.

So it valiantly began. The ostensibly minor provisions—opposition to incorporation in New York, determination to make the Grants into a separate district, had the appearance of inconsiderable afterthoughts. The committees of safety, the men who unobtrusively had guided them, departed from Kent's tavern with the consciousness of praise-worthy work accomplished.

Thereafter, the leaders waited. They had taken the first significant step. The length and time of the second would depend upon the consequences of the first, which had been tentative, and could be, at need, easily withdrawn. They had merely got the meeting to say that it would prefer not to associate with New York and would like to set up a separate government in the Grants. No irrevocable statement had been made, other than that vociferous pledge of loyalty to the cause of the brand-new United States.

From their post of command in Fay's Bennington tavern, the leaders listened intently for sound of internal dissent, which was less than they had expected; for thunderous external objection from New York or Philadelphia, which never came at all. Again fortune favored the Grants. Congress, and New York as well, had their hands too full of calamitous problems to pay any attention to the real significance of a farmers' meeting on a faraway frontier.

On Champlain, frantic efforts were being made to repair the rotten fortifications of Ticonderoga, and Gates was appealing in every possible direction for more men. Seth Warner, his Green Mountain Rangers disbanded and spreading through the Grants the dysentery that was epidemic in the land all this summer, had received a colonel's commission from Congress and was raising a new regiment for the

Continental service to join as soon as might be the army at the forts, where pestilence was still working for the British cause; where Colonel Samuel Wigglesworth was writing to the New Hampshire Committee of Safety:

> There are no medicines of any avail in the Continental chest; such as there are in their native state unprepared; no emetick nor cathartick; no mercurial nor antimonial Remedy; no opiate or elixir, tincture or even capital medicine. It would make a heart of stone melt to hear the moans and see the distresses of the dying.

There was little time to spend in heart-melting. Carleton was bringing ships, piecemeal, up the Richelieu Rapids to assemble them on Champlain and sweep the lake clear. Gates was mobilizing anything that would float to meet him.

In New York's lower harbor, Howe was landing his army on Staten Island while Washington watched from Manhattan, weak, fuming, and helpless to prevent him. The first attempt to cut the revolution in half along the Hudson and lake waterways was about to be launched. Fortune seemed to have turned her back upon the American cause, but she smiled upon the Grants.

Here, the Articles of Association were being approved without dissent by the Westside town meetings and with a minimum of protest by similar gatherings on the Eastside. A few towns in the land's southeast corner objected to the lightly inserted joker severing relations with New York, but the general response was favorable. The York cause was not appreciably advanced when from Harlem, whither it had retired behind Washington's retreating army, the New York convention declared that all land rents heretofore paid to the royal government were now due the new state and asked the Grants please to remit.

Events were fitting nicely into the Grants leaders' purposes. Clearly, the time was ripe for a second and bolder forward step, and luck decreed that this should be taken at a most propitious moment.

Representatives of forty-four towns met at Kent's tavern in Dorset, September 25. For the first time, Eastside and Westside assembled in concert. Delegates reported from eleven communities in the Connecticut Valley. The convention said in essence merely what the July meeting had uttered, but it spoke louder and more emphatically, endorsing unanimously the creation of the Grants into a separate district and nailing down that decision with supplementary measures.

These abolished whatever New York laws might, through some

oversight, still be in force, placed the militia under the convention's command, and authorized the preparation of a covenant to be signed by all males of sixteen years and upward resident in the Grants.

That covenant, published September 27, recited all over again the people's grievances against New York—a task that Grants publicists must have been able to accomplish practically automatically by now—and pledged its signers to obey all decrees of this and subsequent conventions so long as they were not contrary to "the Resolves of the Honorable Continental Congress Relative to the General Cause of America."

The reiterated reverence for the dictates of Congress expressed by the Republic throughout its entire life, the lighthearted way these were ignored when it was inconvenient to obey, were not the least noteworthy characteristics of a remarkable commonwealth.

The convention then flung itself into a fury of committee-appointing: A committee to obtain signatures to the covenant, a committee to petition Congress for admission to the union, a committee of war for the Westside, even a committee to ask New York if it had any objections to the establishment of the Grants as a separate state! There is no record that this last ever functioned.

Thereafter, the meeting adjourned, to assemble again January 15. Members journeyed through the land acquiring signatures to the covenant and, once more, the leaders sat attentive and listening. They heard, not squalls of outrage from robbed New York nor the awesome voice of Congress, but only the distant speech of guns—guns to the south, where Howe deliberately thrust Washington off Manhattan Island; guns nearer at hand and more ominous, thundering across Lake Champlain, where Benedict Arnold's fleet of tubs fought Carleton's armada with an American loss of twelve out of fifteen craft engaged.

Once more fortune had supplied distracting catastrophe to attend the Republic's birth. Even the New York convention was too busy wondering where it might sit down without being chased away by the British to pay its revolted territory much immediate heed. Its sole comment on the current state of affairs in the Grants seems to have been a reproof administered to certain members of the Cumberland County Committee of Safety who, elated by the prevalent spirit of independence, had taken to writing the convention gratuitously insulting letters.

This and other evidences of disloyalty determined New York to hold up any further pay to Hoisington's Rangers. These stalwart defenders of the frontier were yelling again for prompt remuneration, an occupation to which they seem to have been chiefly dedicated, for Colonel J. Bedell wrote General Schuyler in early 1777 that they had not done three days' soldiering since their enlistment.

There was dismay in the land this fall and a looming peril that drew. factions closer together and fortified their faith in an independent government. Crown Point was abandoned before Carleton's advance, and more of the Grants' frontier thereby was exposed. Ticonderoga was threatened, but the mauling dealt by Arnold to the British fleet made the invaders wary of direct assault. Howe, with the irresponsibility of most of His Majesty's generals, had not advanced up the Hudson but was chasing Washington across New Jersey.

The first attempt to divide the United States had failed. Carleton tapped and fumbled about Ticonderoga's defenses. Settlers relaxed when in early November he withdrew to Canada, having inflicted no · harm, save a few minor Indian raids, upon the Grants, which began a new year by formally declaring their independence.

The convention that assembled January 15, 1777, in Westminster took another and still bolder elephantine forward step. Its proceedings merely magnified and emphasized the voices of its preceding gatherings. It was small in size and may not have been wholly representative, for delegates from only seven Westside and fourteen Eastside towns were present.

Endorsements of the Covenant indicated that the Westside approval was practically unanimous. It was reported on less sure warrant that three-fourths of the Eastside's man power had approved it. The leaders had more confidence now. Their followers were certain. The convention's actions were smooth and swift; and, if there was a single dissenting voice raised, its protest was not entered in the records.

With apparent unanimity the convention resolved: "That the district of land commonly called and known by the name of the New Hampshire Grants be a new and separate state and for the future conduct themselves as such"; and a committee consisting of Nathan Clark, Ebenezer Hoisington, John Burnham, Jacob Burton, and Thomas Chittenden was appointed to draw up a declaration of independence.

That document paralleled the Federal declaration in form and frequently in phraseology, but it chose as the villain against whom insupportable outrages were charged, not His Britannic Majesty, but that ancient and riddled target, the State of New York.

The Grants' declaration propounded: "That whenever protection is withheld, no allegiance is due nor can of right be demanded," skimmed briefly through New York's offenses, and quoted as justification for this final separation from that state John Adams's resolution adopted in Congress, May 15, 1775. This proclamation that unorganized territory should be permitted to form its own government had lodged in Yankee minds and was destined to stay there.

The document then proclaimed: "That the district or territory comprehending and usually known by the name and description of the New Hampshire Grants of right ought to be and hereby is declared forever and hereafter to be considered a separate, free, and independent jurisdiction or state; by the name and to be forever hereafter called and known and distinguished by the name of New Connecticut."

The amputation, after preliminary probings and testings, had been deftly accomplished; and New Connecticut—a name of brief duration —had been established where New York's unruly territory once had stood. The die had been cast, defiance had been hurled; but the world at large displayed only a humiliating indifference.

There still was no protest from the emancipated land's deprived proprietor; and Congress, which had scuttled off to Baltimore when Howe had advanced toward Philadelphia, was too far away and too completely occupied to heed the state that had just formed itself and was about to apply for admission to the Union.

If there were squalls of outrage and insurrectory meetings on the Eastside, these could be ignored in the elation of a purpose accomplished. The time would come when the uproar of the indignant Eastsiders no longer could be overlooked. Even now, they are crying "fraud" and wondering at the tops of their voices why Ebenezer Hoisington of Windsor, who had certified that three-fourths of the Eastside people favored independence, had not already suffered Ananias's uncomfortable fate. If dissenting noise was any criterion, Hoisington had overestimated the total considerably.

Center of the protestant tumult were the towns in the self-constituted state's southeast corner—Halifax, Guilford, Vernon, Brattleboro— where the enthusiasm for New York now burned bright for no clearer reason than the fact that Yankee obstinacy feeds on opposition. Of this there was plenty, for a majority elsewhere on the Eastside seemed to approve, with varying warmth, the establishment of independence, and, local partisanship being what it was, the subject stopped being a cause for argument and became a provocation for brawls.

In April, New York, which seemed determined to ignore the Grants' secession and certainly did nothing to pacify the insurgent citizenry, adopted a new state constitution. This converted a number of the dubious, whom the secessionists called "neuters," to the gospel of state independence. The New York Constitution confirmed all the patents issued by royal governors, thereby technically nullifying the land titles . of many Grants inhabitants.

Under this document, Cumberland County got three assemblymen, Gloucester two, and each a senator. Paul Spooner was chosen sheriff for Cumberland and ordered to prepare for the first New York State election. His course from the outset was beset with numerous difficulties and obstacles and even a larger amount of obloquy. The people of the Eastside were in the throes of getting mad all over again.

The progress of their ire can be traced by the earliest of the unnumbered appeals that Yorkers in the years to come were to address to the sympathetic but not specially co-operative state of their choice. · On April 25, Brattleboro petitioned New York for aid and counsel.

The Brattleborovians, it appeared, were having an extremely unpleasant time. They found it dangerous even to speak slightingly of the so-called State of New Connecticut, and they wished New York would defend the faithful. Furthermore, they confided, the York Committee of Safety for Cumberland County could not act without a quorum, and there wasn't any quorum in these parlous times. What should be done about that?

In reply, the New York convention urged them to persevere. This was to become a favorite word of that state but an extremely difficult prescription in the face of surrounding difficulties for the Yorkers to fill. The convention also said that the Committee of Safety might still act even if there were only a minority present.

The parent state, mistakenly believing that the Grants' declaration of independence was merely a squall that soon would blow over, had been trying to ignore the growing turmoil, which in itself had been no small job and rapidly was becoming an impossible.

New York now passed the waxing problem on to Congress, which had more than enough of its own already, asking that body to intervene and still the Eastside anarchy. Congress obligingly launched a mild thunderbolt. It resolved to refuse the Vermont secessionists "countenance or justification." The missile seemed to miss fire, for the brawling went on without either.

The surviving remnant of the Committee of Safety met in Brattleboro, June 26, and once more lifted a plaintive, petitionary voice. In the first place, it told New York, nobody paid any attention to the Committee if it did act; and, in the second place, how could it act when Sheriff Spooner, its enforcement officer, had resigned and the insurgents were in possession of the jail? Perseverance was the only suggestion New York could make at the moment, and she offered that rather snappishly. She had more serious and immediate matters on her mind.

Summer was bringing a new army out of Canada to sweep the lakes clear, to follow the waterways to Albany, and there, uniting with Howe, who was to move up the Hudson, to split the rebellion in two. It was a magnificently equipped army, officered by the best generals Britain owned or could buy, and in late June it was on the move.

So impenetrable was the screen of Indian scouts the host threw out before it, that no one knew when it would strike or how far it had advanced, yet its shadow already lay on Ticonderoga and, lengthening, spread across New Connecticut. There was more of dread than pride in the hearts of the men who, on July 2, 1777, met in Windsor to frame a constitution for the infant state. If it had not been for that dread, the task might not have been done so swiftly. If it had not been for a thunderstorm, it might not have been accomplished at all.

Looming military disaster hushed contention and hurried along the work that meteorological violence was to bring to completion. The sermon the Rev. Aaron Hutchinson preached to the delegates before they convened at Elijah West's tavern was probably the most lengthy part of the entire proceedings, for the Reverend Aaron covered a deal of ground—religious, economical, and historical—before he finally ceased. Thereafter, the sweating delegates sought the L-shaped house of Landlord West with a thirst not entirely for righteousness.

The sessions began deliberately enough, but on July 3 a letter from Colonel Seth Warner quickened their pace. The British army, the Colonel's hasty scrawl proclaimed, had been sighted and its destination learned. Its flotilla was coming up the lake, with troops on either shore, and its obvious goal was Ticonderoga. All available militia units should be sent to the fort at once.

It was not merely concern for their country that made the delegates hurry thereafter. More personal anxiety drove many to clamor for more haste. These urgent men were folk from the Westside whose families were in the possible paths of invasion should Ticonderoga fall. Earlier bickering was abandoned, faltering motions to adjourn were ignored, and the convention bent purposefully to its task.

It had been stung by Warner's letter. Now it turned to another missive as a possible short cut to its purpose. This was one of the more recent of the communications with which Dr. Thomas Young, Ethan Allen's friend, had been bombarding the new Republic's leaders for some time. It was filled, like its predecessors, with aphorisms and exhortations that must have seemed faintly secondhand and moldy even in that day, but it enclosed a copy of the constitution of Pennsylvania as a suggested model for the infant state.

The industrious Dr. Young seems to have taken as much present interest in establishing the young commonwealth as he had formerly in disestablishing Jehovah with Allen's aid. He had addressed this particular letter, dated April 11, 1777:

"To the INHABITANTS of VERMONT a Free and Independent State, bounding on the River CONNECTICUT and LAKE CHAMPLAIN."

Dr. Young is generally accepted as the originator of the name "Vermont," which at some time between the state's declaration of independence and the constitutional convention had been substituted for the earlier "New Connecticut." The latter title, it had been discovered, already had been adopted by a region in northwest Pennsylvania, and the substitution had been made, apparently entirely informally.

Young is said to have accomplished his invention by the unholy alliance of the Gallic words for "green" and "mountain." If this be so, his French was more dubious than his orthodoxy.

The Rev. Dr. Samuel A. Peters, a clergyman of Connecticut, is rival claimant to this ungrammatical christening. Peters possessed something less than normal ecclesiastical veracity. He holds that the event took place in 1763 while he was preaching in the Grants to "the thirty thousand settlers in that country." The population at that time could not have been more than a sixth of his estimate.

The christening, according to the minister's claim, was performed in October, when he climbed a peak in the Rutland region which he called "Mount Pisgah" and with the aid of a bottle of rum—used only ceremonially—baptized the land "Verd Mont, in token that her mountains and hills shall be ever green and shall never die."

The contradiction of the name to its present form irked the reverend doctor, who wrote in 1807:

> Since Verd Mont became a state, its General Assembly have seen proper to change the spelling of Verdmont, Green Mountain, to that of Vermont, Mountain of Maggots.

Other authorities hold that the word is actually of Latin derivation. Whatever its origin, it came into general use between January and July, 1777.

The Pennsylvania constitution submitted by Dr. Young seemed a life preserver to the worried and floundering convention, but even in the delegates' haste, their independence and the sundry purposes of that independence kept them from entirely duplicating the model document. They did accept its general framework and in many passages its entire phraseology.

The preamble was a strictly Vermont creation. With the British on their doorstep and their land imperiled by the host of George III, the pattern of Vermonters' hatred remained unaltered. One paragraph sufficed for expression of grievances against Britain's king. Fourteen were required to list the reasons for detestation of New York.

The obdurate passion for freedom radically amended certain parts of the Pennsylvania constitution. Through this alteration, Vermont became the first American state to abolish slavery. It provided that no person—slave, apprentice, or servant—should be held in bondage after the age of eighteen, if female, and twenty-one, if male. The Republic was also the first American state to establish universal manhood suffrage.

Vermont's constitutionally expressed attitude on religion was conservative and definitely out of character. It may be that consciousness of imminent danger which oppressed the delegates at their labors moved skeptical souls uneasily to propitiate a possible—and Protestant —Lord of Hosts.

In any event, the constitution provided that no man could be deprived of his civil rights because of his membership in any Protestant communion. It also implicitly barred Ethan Allen and his fellow scoffers from public office by forbidding such posts to men who did not declare under oath their belief in God, Protestantism, and the divine inspiration of New and Old Testaments. Vermont's early years are filled with just such rigidly conventional and empty gestures.

The constitution provided for a governor, deputy governor, a council of twelve men, and a house of representatives composed of one man from each town—all to be elected at the first Freemen's Meeting Day to be held in December. Later, due to the disorganizing turmoil that swept the land that summer and the consequent delay in getting the constitution printed, Meeting Day was postponed to the first Tuesday in March, 1778.

Pending establishment of a constitutional government, the Republic was to be guided by a council of safety. Thomas Chittenden, Heman and Ira Allen, Joseph and Jonas Fay, Moses Robinson, Jacob Bayley, Paul Spooner were among its membership of twelve. The names of the others have been lost. The wind of panic that blew through the convention on July 8 has whirled them out of history.

Word came that day that Ticonderoga had fallen, that the frontier defenses had caved in, that a British host—vast, terrible, ruthless—was marching into Vermont as irresistibly as, even then, swollen, black clouds were piling up behind Ascutney's ridges.

There was no immediate outcry after the disheveled rider had bawled his tidings. Silence, magnified by a distant rumbling, lay on the convention hall, and delegates, peering about, saw only the white, stricken faces of other men. The great fortress had been captured. The citadel in which had lain all Vermont's strained hope for protection from invasion had been taken with incredible ease.

The palsied moment passed. Feet scuffled, chairs clattered as the meeting rose. Voices babbled for immediate adjournment and then were smothered beneath explosive flashings as the storm broke. Windows were slammed against the roaring downpour that lashed the tavern and turned the highway into a brown river.

The storm went by like an advancing army, and men who would march with the last militia companies and men whose families were on the now-defenseless frontier were forced to linger, waiting for its passage. One cleared his throat and addressed Joseph Bowker, the presiding officer, in a wry tone more self-possessed than earlier outcries.

Since time was precious now and should not be frittered away, might it not be better if the convention, instead of just sitting here on its behind, occupied itself until the storm was over in approving the Constitution of the State of Vermont, just in case Johnny Burgoyne left anything to apply it to later?

That constitution had been adopted before the tempest had moved along the Connecticut Valley. Muskets were to echo its thunder, imitative cannon were to rock the West in the weeks immediately ahead.

XI Invasion

TICONDEROGA'S NAME in revolutionary America held a power and a glory that its physical self always lacked. It was the fort's destiny to fall to Americans, to British, and, later, to Americans again in an atmosphere thick with anticlimax.

Burgoyne's magnificent army of nine thousand regulars, German hirelings, Tories, Canadians, and Indians captured the strengthened post in 1777 almost as easily as Ethan Allen had taken its ruin in 1775.

Ticonderoga stood on the west shore, where the long, crooked handle of lower Champlain becomes a two-tined fork. The eastern and lesser water prong is the lake's riverlike upper reach, running south to Whitehall, then called Skenesboro. The longer and thicker western prong is Lake George, whose outlet washed the fort's feet.

Misfortune and dissension forever hung over Ticonderoga, along with the malaria and other ailments that attended its garrison. The post recently had been subject of an enduring squabble between the American generals, Gates and Schuyler, and, at the moment of Burgoyne's advance, Schuyler temporarily had won. He had received command of the northern department and had appointed as commandant of the fort General Arthur St. Clair, a Scotch immigrant, grandson of the Earl of Roslyn, a veteran of the French and Indian War, and a chronically unlucky man.

Even the strengthening of the post, at which the Americans had been working desperately for a year, had not been wholly wise. The engineers, who included Thaddeus Kosciusko, the Polish patriot, had been too much under the spell of Ticonderoga's great name. They had welded the ancient French works, the later British, and new American into a fortress it would have required ten thousand troops adequately to man. St. Clair had about twenty-five hundred Continentals and, before Burgoyne actually invested the fort, received a reinforcement of some nine hundred militia.

The engineers had been not only overenthusiastic but also under-intelligent. That latter defect seems to have been constant in Ticonderoga's history.

From the east shore opposite the fort, a knoll with the oversize name of Mount Independence juts out, pinching the lake into half its normal width. Kosciusko and his associates had fortified the hill and had linked it with the parent fort by a pontoon bridge and a boom across the narrows. They had wholly ignored a higher hill near by.

Mount Defiance is a lumpy and steep-sided eminence, lifting its rock and scrubby trees six hundred feet above Mount Independence's peak, almost eight hundred feet above the level of Ticonderoga itself. It stands at the top of the narrow strip of land enclosed by the tines of the watery fork and commands both Ticonderoga and Mount Defiance. Guns placed on the crest would batter to pieces fortifications and garrisons of both.

This was an obvious fact of geography and ballistics that the engineers and Gates and Schuyler and Congress all refused to admit. Cannon, they insisted, could not be dragged up the hill's steep flanks. They let it go at that, though Colonel John Trumbull had proved that Mount Defiance's crest lay within easy cannon shot of the fort, and he and Arnold and Anthony Wayne had reported the eminence's perilous importance to all available authorities.

Burgoyne, when he arrived, was able to see at once a point to which the American command had remained resolutely blind.

He came up the lake in this summer of alternating heat and downpour with his great flotilla of sailing craft, bateaux, and barges; with his strong train of artillery and his war-wise generals—Phillips, Fraser, Powell, and the Brunswicker, Riedesel; with his splendidly equipped regiments and his mistress and his traveling wine cellar and his resounding proclamations.

Scouts, red and white, so perfectly screened his advance that St. Clair was not certain of his purpose or his strength until all at once he was landing his troops just below the fort. Bands crashed, flags blazed languidly in the hot sunlight, and water cast back broken flashes of color—the British scarlet, the dark blue of German infantry and lighter of dragoons, the green of a *Jäger* company—as the troops disembarked on either shore and, July 2, invested the fort.

On July 5, Phillips, the artillerist, had dragged cannon to the top of Mount Defiance, and St. Clair, marking their brazen blinking, knew that Ticonderoga must be abandoned before Riedesel, who had been held back from advance along the east shore by the guns of Mount

Independence, worked his way around an intervening swamp to strad-
dle the Castleton road and completely close the trap.

John Adams was to say, when the news of Ticonderoga's fall was
rocking the young nation: "We shall never be able to defend a post
until we have shot a general," a statement which was just another increment of St. Clair's perennial bad luck. He was cursed and charged
with treason because he did the only thing possible under the circumstances.

Men were all that he could save out of looming defeat, and Continental troops such as his were precious. In the whole northern department there were barely three thousand, and twenty-five hundred were
in St. Clair's command. If these were destroyed or captured, there
would be almost no seasoned soldiers to stiffen the militia army that
eventually must fight it out with Burgoyne.

The unfortunate St. Clair had to get as many of his Continentals as
possible back to Schuyler. On the night of July 6, Ticonderoga was
abandoned.

Even though St. Clair had been perfecting his plan of retreat for
twenty-four hours, the idiocy of subordinates, which is part of a general's bad luck, almost ruined the withdrawl at its outset. The ill and
as much of the supplies and artillery as could be loaded were placed in
bateaux and sent off up the lake toward Skenesboro. The garrison,
minus the men detailed to guard the boats, prepared to abandon the
fort and take the still-open road to Castleton. Their purpose was to
meet the flotilla at Skenesboro.

The moon was full, and feet rang loud and hollow upon the bridge
across to Mount Independence. If any other disturbance were needed
to rouse the British, Roche de Fermoy, a dim-witted French adven-
turer commanding at Mount Independence, immediately supplied it.
Before he led his men out of the works to join the retreating column,
he set the dwelling that had been his headquarters afire, illuminating
the marching troops and advertising the abandonment to all persons
within twenty miles.

The flames painted the laden bridge and shook across the still water.
They roused Fraser, commanding the advanced corps of Burgoyne's
army. Bugles sounded in his camp on the lake's west shore. Bugles in
Riedesel's bivouac on the east bank caught up their echoes. By the
time the fire had died down, the pursuit had been organized and
Fraser's grenadiers and light infantry were crossing the causeway.

St. Clair's bad luck held constant. When his rearguard regiments—

Seth Warner's Vermonters, the 11th Massachusetts Line, and the 2nd New Hampshire Line—had crossed and had passed out of the lurid glow into darkness beyond, the General posted grape-loaded cannon at the bridge's end to sweep the structure when the British tried to follow. Four gunners were detailed for this forlorn hope, and in the haste of the moment no one marked that they had added to their armament a keg of Madeira. When Fraser led out his troops, they bumped into the cannon muzzles. Beside the guns' trails, with lighted linstocks still in hand, slumbered the valiant four, and the Madeira keg was empty.

It was almost dawn when Fraser and seven hundred and fifty men took the rutted and trampled trail that was the Castleton Road. Behind his swiftly moving column, Riedesel's eleven hundred grenadiers, light infantry, and *Jägers* marched more ponderously. The Germans, heavily equipped, drilled to a mechanical precision that the atrocious road dislocated, fell behind despite their general's bellowings; and he, increasingly frantic, took the *Jäger* company and eighty of his swiftest marchers and hurried on ahead of the plodding column to overtake the British.

Fraser's own grenadiers and light infantry, the companies which contained the strongest and most active men of each British regiment, themselves were having trouble with the road. The wretched track wound up and down, over hills that elbowed each other, through the dankness of virgin forest that began to steam as the sun rose higher. Sweat and shortness of breath and the everlasting leg-drag of the uneven way were not the troops' only afflictions. About their heads hung swarms of flies that sang and stung. Not even the castaway clothing and equipment which told of the haste of St. Clair's flight or the occasional weak-bodied or faint-hearted straggler they caught could spur the men on.

By one o'clock they were wholly spent, and Fraser called a halt. The files dropped by the roadside and lay there, gasping and feebly batting at the persistent flies. They were still there when Riedesel's advance guard came up.

The road that St. Clair fled along does not exist today. It went past the present town of Orwell, around the north end of Lake Bomoseen, across the site of Hubbardton, and by a taxing upgrade through the pass in the increasingly high hills down to what is now the little village of East Hubbardton.

St. Clair was heading for Castleton and outfooting his pursuers, though the retreating column had stretched, as the slower marching units lagged, until the rearguard was some miles behind the main body. All regimental commanders had orders to press on to Castleton, where the bulk of the army paused for the night, but the leaders of the rearguard chose to ignore these instructions.

Colonels Warner of Vermont, Francis of Massachusetts, and Hale of New Hampshire halted near what is now East Hubbardton. Future settlers had cut a few clearings and girdled some trees, but the rest of the region still was virgin forest. The militia regiments of Colonels Bellows and Olcott camped in the woods beside the road, midway between the rearguard and Castleton. St. Clair's bad luck still was holding.

When Riedesel's blown advance guard had joined Fraser's exhausted column, it had been clear to both commanders that their men could not be forced much further. The rigid German main force still was struggling far behind on this most unmilitary road. Fraser was determined to march for another hour and then bivouac. Riedesel promised to get his column as far up as possible before nightfall. Both generals agreed to move again at 3 A.M., July 7. The trail was too hot for delay.

The insubordinate colonels of the American rearguard had halted their men in a hollow through which ran the road they had followed all day toward the southeast. Behind them, as they faced northwest to bivouac, the woods marched steeply upward to the secondary ridges of the Green Mountains. Before them was a jumbled hilly forest with small, crowding peaks through which the road snaked its way.

Warner's regiment, some of whom at least wore brown uniforms faced with blue, lay with its left on the slope of Zion Hill, a crumbling, rocky eminence. On Warner's right camped Colonel Francis's 11th Massachusetts and, beyond that regiment, the 2nd New Hampshire, Colonel Hale, settled for the night along the swift little stream called Sucker Brook. The leaders compounded the military sin they already had committed, by placing no outposts. Thus, when Fraser struck at them at sunrise, they had no warning until he was actually among them.

The British general had moved before the east had lightened. His purpose was to attack the rearguard and hold it until Riedesel's ponderous column could come up. A former Vermonter led Fraser's advance.

John Peters had been an original settler of Moorestown, later Bradford, clerk of Cumberland County, and justice of the peace. His loyalty had been too forthright for his neighbors to endure, and he had fled to Nova Scotia, where he had become lieutenant colonel of a battalion of Tory irregulars. Peters and his men led the way, this morning of July 7, up the steep trail, through the pass in the hills, and down again into the woods where night still was entangled with the trees.

Behind Fraser, Riedesel's command was on the move, too, while their general swore strange Teutonic oaths at their heavy pace and, at last, too impatient to match his gait to theirs, hurried forward again with the *Jägers* and the eighty more who had accompanied him yesterday.

The east was golden now, and the smoke of the American rearguard's breakfast fires drifted across it. Hale's men were splashing beside Sucker Brook when Fraser came down upon them.

A volley gushed from the woods, and on the heels of the tearing crash came cheering and the flicker of red coats among the tree trunks as the grenadiers and light infantry ran in and the 2nd New Hampshire, led by its colonel, ran out. One-third of the rearguard had been dislodged by that first attack. It was to be harder to shake the remainder.

Before Fraser could reload, the Vermont and Massachusetts men had turned from breakfast to battle. Muskets banged, singly and then with a swelling roar. Smoke that was pink in the sunrise blanketed the American front, and through it the bearskins of the grenadiers, the brass and leather caps of the light infantry moved forward and paused and, as the bullets swarmed, went down or else retreated.

Twenty-one men were dropped by that first American fire. Major Grant of the 24th Foot was dead. Major the Earl of Balcarres, commanding the light infantry, was wounded. Fraser sent a runner back along the road to hurry Riedesel and then turned to the problem before him that had grown tougher than he had expected. It appeared that the rest of the Yankees had no intention of following the fleet Colonel Hale and his men.

Almost none of the Americans could be seen now. Warner's and Francis's troops had settled among the fallen trees, had hidden behind the standing, as naturally as a quail covey vanishes. In the quickening light, scarlet coats were fair targets as the British in their ignorance of bush fighting re-formed their ranks as though this wilderness forest were a Flanders plain and began to blast away with unaimed volleys at no better marks than fire that darted and smoke that spurted from logs and tree trunks.

The noise of quarreling musketry went through the sultry morning to Riedesel, urging his advance guard up the road toward the pass. His curses stung his men's ears along with the swarming flies. St. Clair, forming his army at Castleton to continue the retreat, also heard the far tumult, not of skirmish, but of indubitable battle, and sent two aides back to find the lagging militia of Bellows and Olcott and order them into the fight with the assurance that the entire army would follow.

Meanwhile, in the smoking hollow among the hills the little conflict continued stubbornly. Part of the best corps in Burgoyne's army was being held by no more than its own number. Fraser now withdrew grenadiers from his left and sent them to his right and over Zion Hill, a brutal climb, to fall on the American left flank, which Warner held.

When the bruised and panting redcoats attacked from this new angle, the Vermonters did not run. They withdrew their threatened flank, faced about, and by their keen shooting broke the grenadiers' advance, knocking over Major Acland and a number of his men. The weight of the British upon Warner gave the 11th Massachusetts its chance. It attacked the enemy's weakened left wing and thrust it back.

There was a burst of rapid shooting in the woods and much wild yelling as the British gave ground. Then through the tumult came a sane and baffling sound—the hoarse cadence of drums, the piercing fifes, the silvery music of the *Jägers'* bugles, and above all these the breathless voices of men, chanting in German a marching song.

Riedesel, advancing, was making up in noise for what he lacked in numbers. He spoke briefly with Fraser, then threw his little force into the still-wavering scales of the battle. The *Jägers,* in green and red, were played in by their drum corps as they advanced against Massachusetts. The eighty German light infantry and grenadiers swung wide to the left to roll up the American right flank. Rifle fire crackled. Colonel Francis and many of his men were killed. The rest, as the flank attack drove home with a deep hurrahing, broke and ran.

The panic swept along the line and infected the Vermonters. White-faced men came dodging out of the smoke, past the bellowing Warner, whom they paid no heed. The big colonel could not check the rout; and, seeing the battle fall to pieces before him, he hurled himself down on a log, beating it with his fists and screeching curses at the vanishing backs of his regiment and then, when the fugitives only quickened their pace, recovered sanity, shouted, "Meet me at Manchester," and ran, too.

There was breathless cheering as the fire slackened and died. The smoke cloud thinned, and in the forest the wounded wailed. Fraser's mauled command began to number its losses. From the woods in which they had hidden, Colonel Hale and some of his men came timorously to surrender. St. Clair's aides, advancing, met the first of the Massachusetts and Vermont retreat and wheeled about, knowing that nothing now could be done.

The aides had hoped to lead the militiamen of Olcott and Bellows into the fight, but these had run at the first distant burst of gunfire and still were running. Their panic, the fugitives from the actual battle who soon began to reach Castleton, shook the morale of St. Clair's own command. Word came, too, from the flotilla which had started for Skenesboro. Burgoyne had overtaken and almost completely destroyed it. St. Clair resumed his march, no longer heading for Skenesboro, but Dorset and Manchester.

The rearguard had atoned for its disobedience by stopping permanently Fraser's and Riedesel's pursuit, but the unlucky fight had robbed St. Clair of sorely needed regiments. Some eighty Continentals had been killed or so sorely wounded that they had fallen into British hands. Two hundred and seventy-four more had been taken prisoner. The British lost in the needless little battle of Hubbardton—the only one ever fought on Vermont soil—thirty-five dead and one hundred and forty-eight wounded. A large proportion of their casualties were officers. The New England men had spent their bullets thriftily.

Of the more than three thousand troops who had evacuated Ticonderoga, only seventeen hundred still marched through the rain with St. Clair, the unlucky, when he joined Schuyler at Fort Edward on July 12. Warner had been left at Manchester with the ninety men of his regiment who already had rallied. He was to patrol roads to the north lest Burgoyne be only feinting toward the Hudson and his real intention be to pour his army into the Connecticut Valley and overwhelm New England. This was the dread that continually haunted all Vermont that thundery July.

Already, it seemed to most men that the war disastrously was over, so great a place had Ticonderoga held in popular imagination, so dire had been its swift capture. The wavering saw in the fall of the great fortress a portent straight from Jeremiah. God, it appeared, had endorsed the British cause. The less faint-hearted laid the surrender, not to divine intervention, but to treason.

One of the fatherless tales that minds believe in times of panic ran up and down the land. St. Clair, this proclaimed, had sold out to Burgoyne and had been paid for his perfidy by silver bullets fired into the fort. Neither this rumor nor the belief that the deity had had a hand in the disaster did much to elevate Vermont morale.

The thing the settlers so long had dreaded now actually had come to pass. The west and north frontier had been stripped bare, and St. Clair's army, the land's sole defense, had scuttled through a corner of the Republic and vanished, leaving Warner's handful at Manchester the only Contintental contribution to Vermont's protection.

Men were facing a brutal fact that hitherto had been only a vague trouble in their minds. If they kept to their farms, tilling the ripening crops which were their life insurance, whatever disaster Burgoyne chose to loose would roll over them. If they fled, they abandoned their own, their women's and children's, sole source of livelihood. Even those who would choose to stand and fight had not enough lead and powder for a half-hour skirmish.

The bewilderment, the mounting terror, filled the land with the babble of anguished voices. These, spoken from the Eastside where the convention at Windsor before it adjourned empowered a committee to pledge the newborn state's credit for ammunition. There were shriller cries from the Westside's Bennington, where Joseph Farnsworth, Continental quartermaster, was assembling supplies, not for Vermont, but for Schuyler's army.

Bennington's appeal to Connecticut and Massachusetts for immediate aid was filled with the frenzy of folk whose terror-smitten imaginations already saw Burgoyne advancing, "killing, robbing the inhabitants, driving off the cattle." There was a threat in their prevision of disaster. They warned their sister commonwealths that Vermont's forces in their present state could do nothing but "retreat down into the New England states, which will soon reduce the country to the Cleanness of Teeth."

The awful Burgoyne, meanwhile, was not planning the annihilation of Vermont. He was quartered in the fine stone house of Colonel Philip Skene, who had accompanied the army from Canada. The General was devoting himself to the traditional solaces of victorious warriors. When he moved, by proxy, on July 12, it seemed to Vermont that the day of wrath actually had dawned. The feint that Riedesel and a

German column made toward the Connecticut looked like invasion. The blue and yellow infantry—Riedesel's own regiment and Breymann's grenadiers with their ridiculous brass-plated and tasseled dunce caps—plodded to Castleton on a threefold mission. They were to forage, they were to terrify New England by threat of attack, and they were to receive the submission of all who were willing to acknowledge the error of their recent ways and swear allegiance.

Burgoyne's proclamation, which Riedesel published, the counter manifesto immediately issued by Schuyler, if taken with complete credence, sentenced all Vermonters to death either at British or Continental hands.

The Burgoyne broadside called upon settlers in the whole region to report to Colonel Skene at Castleton, July 15, and take the oath of loyalty. All men who refused were threatened "with military execution."

Schuyler's counterblast held that submission by Vermonters not only would subject their state to a duplication of the church burnings, child murders, and wholesale rapes which, he charged, had distinguished British occupation of New Jersey, but also would cause such backsliders to be "considered and dealt with as traitors" to the United States.

The unprofitable choice confronting Vermonters routed many of them from their homes. The trails along which the hopeful had marched into the wilderness bore a backwash of that migration now, as distracted families hurried south toward Bennington. Those whom the land already held too tightly for them to leave it appeared at Castleton on the appointed day. Riedesel was not impressed with the sincerity of their oath-taking. "A large number of these persons," he reported "were not in earnest."

The lot of those who deemed their farms worth a little perjury was not wholly happy thereafter. Many of them were gathered in by Warner, on orders from Schuyler, and were sent to Bennington to be dealt with there by the Council of Safety. This body was embarrassed by so large an influx of supposed traitors. The Council took a less vindictive attitude toward the culprits than Schuyler had prescribed, and merely swore them back again into patriots, many of whom later fought at Bennington.

Riedesel's foraging enterprise was hardly more successful than his attempt to obtain submission. Warner's men swept the country clean of horses, cattle, and vehicles before the blundering German columns. The supplies of livestock, wagons, and food continually increased at

Bennington. The store of ammunition throughout Vermont remained dishearteningly low.

The war that had not been of the young Republic's choosing, the war in which it had joined with a dedicated disregard of its own best interests, now stood on its defenseless doorsteps; and the states of the Union were displaying an almost complete indifference to their neighbor's appeal for aid.

New York, in particular, immediately moved to shatter the region's feeble protection. On July 14, the Eastside Rangers that this state had equipped and supported were ordered to leave at once for Kingston. That organization increased its already considerable record for recalcitrance by refusing to go. New York immediately cut off, not only their pay, but the slender supply of ball and powder it had been furnishing.

Without arms, without ammunition, without money to pay for either, with an increasing store of foodstuffs at Bennington to attract the attention of Burgoyne, the Vermont Council of Safety led a wretched and harried existence, bedeviled on all sides by appeals for protection, harried by Warner's requests and Schuyler's peremptory demands for troops.

To these last, the Council for the moment remained persistently deaf. Schuyler, a New Yorker, was unpopular in Vermont, which already had a partial invasion on its hands and no ammunition or organized troops with which to meet it. In the hope that a New Englander might succeed where Schuyler was failing, Major General Benjamin Lincoln presently was sent to Manchester to co-operate there with Colonel Warner in raising militia for the Continental Army.

Meanwhile, the Council of Safety was debating with the acerbity of helpless men the possibility of enlisting a new ranger force for Vermont's frontier defense. Equipment for such an organization was lacking, and money for its purchase and the troops' pay, even more conspicuously absent. There was a quarrel in the council over the project. Tempers flared, and Ira Allen, an advocate of the plan, was challenged to find cash for its accomplishment.

The youngest of the Allens blinked his large brown eyes at the scorn and skepticism on his elders' faces, asked for a few hours to consider the matter, and on the morrow presented the stunned council with a wholly practical solution which it immediately followed.

All property of British loyalists in Vermont was to be declared confiscated by the state. Enough of it was to be sold at public auction to finance the regiment, which was raised swiftly.

Samuel Herrick, Ethan Allen's old comrade at the taking of Ticonderoga, was chosen colonel of the rangers. The thoughtful Ira Allen not only had solved an immediate problem, but also had supplied his state with a sure source of income in the years immediately ahead.

Herrick's Rangers may have worn green uniforms faced with red. Such is the legend. Part of the banner Vermont's own troops bore still exists and is in the Bennington Museum. Thirteen white stars shone in a blue canton on a field of solid green. This was the flag the rangers followed into the Bennington battle.

Vermont was helping herself to the best of her ability and ingenuity. She had received, until now, no aid from her neighbors, to whom the movement of Riedesel to Castleton was a less immediate threat. The German column remained, but Warner had swept the land so clear that there was small inducement for it to embark on extensive foraging raids.

Burgoyne, biding his time at Skenesboro, had determined to advance, not by the obvious Lake George waterway, but through the wilderness of Colonel Skene's domain. A single narrow road ran to the Hudson, and Schuyler's axmen had been hard at work ruining it by dropping trees across it and breaking down bridges. Skene is said to have persuaded his exalted guest to take the overland route. Nothing short of massed effort by royal engineers could ever clear up the mess in which Schuyler had left the Colonel's land.

Meanwhile, the threat of Riedesel's presence in Castleton endured, though it still hung fire. Warner was writing to New Hampshire for aid against an enemy three thousand strong—almost a treble overestimate. Massachusetts had heeded an earlier appeal and had sent him some Berkshire County militia. Ira Allen, on behalf of the Committee of Safety, already had forwarded to New Hampshire an earnest and significant plea for troops, which pointed out:

Our good disposition to defend ourselves and make a frontier for your state with our own cannot be carried into execution without your assistance.

It was an eloquent letter, and it had a significant termination, for it urged that succor be sent before hard-pressed Vermont should "be put to the necessity of taking protection."

If the ominous ring of that predicate were intended to stir hitherto indifferent ears by its hint of the state's possible submission to Britain, it was not a vain endeavor. This suggestion, or some more informal that may have preceded it, caused a number of recently oblivious persons and powers to react as though they had been severely jabbed with a pin.

Schuyler forwarded a thousand pounds of gunpowder to Bennington. Charles Phelps on the Eastside wrote another of his profuse letters to the Massachusetts authorities, who responded with three hundred muskets, a hundred and fifty pounds of powder, three hundred pounds of lead, and four hundred and fifty flints. New Hampshire belatedly yet hurriedly began to assemble a force to send to her neighbor's aid.

The success of the implied threat may have opened Ira Allen's alert eyes to the possibilities of a strategy that, later, he and his associates were to exploit to the full. With the startled and hearty response of her associates, Vermont's actual peril abated. Burgoyne moved, July 24, marching south through Colonel Skene's recently disheveled land that His Majesty's engineers had satisfactorily policed, replacing in the course of their task forty ruined bridges.

Riedesel, turning to follow him, led his threatening column out of Vermont. This was respite, and relief was on the way. New Hampshire had lured her foremost military man out of his angry, self-imposed retirement and had forced leadership of her expedition upon John Stark.

With this hard-bitten and vindictive soldier moving to her defense, Vermont had no need to fear that her reinforcement would be diverted into Schuyler's army, which was falling back from Fort Edward to Stillwater. Against the whole Continental host and, more particularly, against the Congress, to whose whims it was subservient, Stark carried a cherished grudge.

This spare, dry man, with sharp, light blue eyes and a tight mouth below jutting cheekbones, had learned his soldiering the hard way. He had been a keen scout, resourceful Indian fighter, an able captain in Rogers' Rangers. As colonel of a New Hampshire regiment, he had served with distinction at Bunker Hill, in the Canadian expedition, and in Washington's early New Jersey Campaign.

In March, 1777, Congress issued the list of promotions that sowed the seed of treason in Arnold's spirit. Both he and Stark were ignored, while men of lesser ability and accomplishment were promoted over them. Arnold, after threatening to resign, remained in the army on Washington's earnest plea. Stark was deaf to persuasion. He threw up his commission and stormed back to New Hampshire to let the war run its course with no more help from him.

He still was galled by the memory of injustice and must have stipulated that he be allowed a free hand before he accepted the command of the New Hampshire force with the state rank of brigadier general. The state's legislature, by an act passed July 19, exempted Stark from obedience to Congress or officers of the Continental Army. He was to co-operate with the Vermont Council of Safety in whatever way he deemed best, but otherwise his was a wholly independent force, responsible only to the state that fathered it.

Events were moving more swiftly now, foreshadowing in their passage the patterns of many things to come, immediate or remote.

On July 29, Burgoyne's army came out of the wilderness and paused at the recently evacuated Fort Edward. Bands played and cheering ran along the red and blue columns. Before the exultant regiments lay the Hudson's broad valley, splashed with sunlight and cloud shadow in the thundery summer weather. The army's task had been almost accomplished, with incredible ease and infinitesimal loss.

The triumphant end almost was in sight. Ahead lay Albany; and there Howe, working up the Hudson, was to join hands with Burgoyne and strangle the rebellion. This had been the whole campaign's purpose, and Howe's co-operation been expressly stipulated in Burgoyne's own orders.

But Howe never had received equivalent orders. Lord George Germaine, Colonial Secretary, in his haste to get away for a holiday week end, had pigeonholed them and then permanently had forgotten them. The lightheaded British general, though he knew of Burgoyne's advance and its intention, was moving, not to his aid, but toward the strategically purposeless capture of Philadelphia.

No gloom of this inexcusable blunder lay on the army that had reached the Hudson's shore. There were, though, annoying but infinitely minor problems to be solved. The British lines of communication, stretching back through the lakes to Canada, were far extended, and provisions came through slowly.

The forest was behind the column now, and open country lay ahead in which cavalry could be employed. Burgoyne had a horse outfit with him, the Dragoon Regiment von Riedesel, hitherto a ponderous nuisance but now an actual aid in the campaign if mounts could be obtained. Horses and carts as well were needed for transport. Already there were rumors afloat of an undefended Continental depot in a town called Bennington, off to the east, that might supply all the army's lacks.

Other patterns were forming, too. On July 30, by an inauguration generally ignored throughout distracted Vermont, George Clinton became governor of New York. The time was not far off when most Vermonters were to consider him a more detested adversary than any or all of Burgoyne's mercenaries. The strife Clinton helped to sponsor was to endure far longer and more stubbornly than the savage little battle that flared on August 16 about a squat hill in the valley of the Walloomsac River, a few miles from Bennington.

xii   They Keep Their Farms

THE BATTLE OF BENNINGTON was an unpremeditated and extremely personal fight. It was less an ordinary conflict between British and American forces than the punishment by angry farmers of folk who had broken in to steal.

The clash was no part of the strategy of the opposing armies. Neither Schuyler nor Burgoyne ordained or even expected it. Actually, it was a magnified, almost spontaneous brawl, wherein larger loyalties were remembered dimly, if at all, and the opponents fought each other for immediate and intimate reasons—the Yankee militiamen to keep their land from invasion and their property from confiscation, the German mercenaries to save their hides.

There are other oddities. The Bennington battle was not fought in that town but some six miles to the northwest in what, by modern boundaries, is New York's territory. It is one of Vermont's moments in history and a state holiday, but the general who won the victory and more than half of the troops he commanded were not Vermonters, but Massachusetts and New Hampshire men. Furthermore, the victor was so little engaged by the Continental cause that only a few days earlier he had defied the ranking American army officer in the region by bidding him go jump in the lake, or its equivalent.

It was a singular battle, this fight that roared and smoked one sweltering afternoon in the Walloomsac Valley, but its impromptu and amateur nature did not detract from its deadliness. Few defeated forces ever have been more completely vanquished. Rarely in history has a hastily gathered militia so decisively overwhelmed splendidly trained and equipped regulars.

Bennington was peculiarly the farmers of North New England's battle. Some days before it was fought Brigadier General John Stark of New Hampshire had made it bitterly plain to Major General Benjamin Lincoln of the Continental Army that whatever Stark's men did would be New Hampshire's and Vermont's private business—not Lincoln's, or Schuyler's, or Congress's.

Stark, tarrying at Charlestown to organize his troops, had sent some two hundred and fifty of these on to Manchester, through the Green Mountain pass in the present town of Peru, before he himself followed with the main body of more than a thousand.

Fortune was kind to the General and his cherished grievance. When he marched off the mountains into the little village, he found there an opportunity for which, in his retirement, his affronted spirit increasingly had yearned. There was fat General Lincoln, who had been promoted for no clear cause over Stark's head, and Lincoln blandly had assumed command of the New Hampshire advance guard.

While Riedesel had lingered at Castleton and the actual course of Burgoyne's further invasion still was hidden from the Americans, Lincoln, with Warner's fragment of a regiment and what militia they could obtain, had waited at Manchester, fearing a thrust toward the Connecticut. Now that Riedesel had rejoined Burgoyne and the entire British army was lumbering down the Hudson Valley, the well-meaning Lincoln had appropriated Stark's first installment of his force and was going to send it to Schuyler.

Schuyler's, and Congress's, representative was about to lay profane hands on troops that the New Hampshire legislature had reserved for their own general's exclusive use. This was an opportunity for which Stark would gladly have paid a couple of teeth. This was his chance to get back a little of his own again, along with a piece of Lincoln's extensive hide.

The New Hampshire men actually were forming on Manchester Green when their own commander rode into town. General Stark galloped up to General Lincoln. Their greeting was not cordial. Less so was the manner in which the former drew forth his New Hampshire commission, absolving him of subordination to anyone, and shook it under Lincoln's nose, meanwhile inviting the shocked General to keep his hands off Stark's men, now and hereafter.

It was a pleasant moment for the man whose sense of outrage done himself had been long in pickle. It was a less agreeable for the plump and placid Lincoln, who, had his own character been more peppery, might have had a fight of almost any dimensions on his hands. He relinquished command of Stark's men with what dignity he could and voiced only mild objections when the New Hampshire brigadier, after conferring with members of the Vermont Council of Safety who had come to Manchester to meet him, marched all his farmer-soldiers on to Bennington. Seth Warner rode with him, leaving his own troops under the command of Lieutenant Colonel Samuel Safford. Stark, Lincoln wrote to Schuyler, seemed "exceedingly soured."

With drums battering and fifes squealing, the dusty column made a Roman entrance into Bennington, where new clapboarded houses, built with the singular symmetry that Yankee carpenters seemed to absorb from the air about them, shouldered older log cabins, and refugees from the north stood with the townsfolk and cheered. Respite from fear, security for the stores in the Continental depot, marched in with the grinning New Hampshire men who followed their mounted general and, ironically enough, the flag of the nation whose authority he had rejected.

This flag was a homemade banner of thirteen stripes, red and white, and in its blue canton were thirteen stars, eleven of them set archwise above the numerals "76" and one in each of the canton's upper corners. It is cherished today in the Bennington Museum.

Stark's purpose apparently was twofold—to protect New Hampshire by defending its buffer state, Vermont, against invasion; if this did not come, to strike at Burgoyne's over-extended supply line. He had explained his intentions to the placating Lincoln before the New Hampshire column marched from Manchester, and Lincoln had hurried off to Schuyler to enlist his co-operation.

After camping five days at Bennington, Stark was tired of waiting and had resolved to move out independently against Burgoyne when tidings from a breathless farmer on a lathered horse changed the General's mind. The first in one of the series of accidents that bring about most battles already had taken place, and Stark was made aware that he need not seek an enemy, for invaders already were marching on Bennington.

The rumors of the rich Continental depot in the little Vermont town that had told enticing tales of horse and cattle herds, of vast stores of flour and other provender, to Burgoyne's pinched and transport-lacking army, gradually had taken form and substance. Tories from Bennington had confirmed the presence there of large and almost entirely unprotected supplies. These informants had left the town before Stark had arrived. Their partisanship also had led them to picture the region as overwhelmingly loyal to the Crown and waiting deliverance.

Already Burgoyne had found his supply line an elastic tether that he had stretched almost to its limit. Looming privation had decided him to launch another foraging raid into Vermont. His original plan provided for a descent on Manchester and a subsequent advance across the mountains to Rockingham and Brattleboro. The purposes of this expedition as Burgoyne outlined them were:

> To try the affections of the country, to disconcert the councils of the enemy, to mount the Riedesel dragoons, to compleat Peter's [the Vermont loyalist's] corps, and to obtain large supplies of cattle, horses and carriages.

The men to be mounted, about two hundred dragoons, were to be the core of this raiding force. A hundred Brunswick infantry, two three-pound cannon of the Hesse-Hanau artillery, fifty British sharpshooters under Captain Fraser, a nephew of General Fraser, and about three hundred Canadians, Indians, and Tories also were included.

At the last minute, the alluring tidings from Bennington made Burgoyne change his mind. He set the column in motion toward that profitable and supposedly undefended objective instead of Manchester. Colonel Philip Skene, the General's late host, went with the expedition to organize the horde of Tories that, it was expected, would flock to its banners. Just before the raiders marched, Burgoyne added fifty Brunswick *Jägers* to their strength. This made a rank-and-file force of some seven hundred men, to which officers, servants, musicians, and camp followers, including several women, gave a total strength of about eight hundred.

Lieutenant Colonel Friedrich Baum, commanding the dragoons, was the expedition's chief. He marched on August 13 from where the Battenkill River joins the Hudson and followed the road along the valley of the lesser stream, toiled up the punishing grades over a line of hills, and came down again into Cambridge, New York, where he camped for the night.

The pace of the march was tormentingly slow, for it was governed by the column's most deliberate element, the Dragoon Regiment von Riedesel, whose uniforms and equipment were almost as unfitted as divers' suits for the duty assigned them. Ahorse, the dragoons might have been redoubtable. On foot, they were an everlasting handicap.

While the Indians looked on in amazement and the more mobile British, Canadian, and Tory elements fretted and swore, the dragoons, whose sweating and puffing was the only flaw in their cherished Brunswick precision, plodded forward and halted to reorder their ranks, and plodded again. They wore for this frontier foray vast cocked hats, with towering white plumes, voluminous light-blue coats, faced with yellow, bright yellow waistcoats, leather gauntlets reaching almost to the elbow, buff leather breeches, and tremendous jack boots.

About these dismaying uniforms was hung a hampering amount of hardware. Brass spurs, heavy and straight, insured frequent stumbling on the miry roads. Immense straight swords dragged along or malevolently thrust themselves between their wearer's legs. Carbines, stubby and heavy, additionally weighted down the wheezing men, and the road they followed made their pace tortuously slow. It had become, in this summer of recurrent rain, according to a surviving German officer's memory, "one prodigious swamp." The wonder is not that Baum moved so deliberately. It was a miracle that, encumbered by his outrageous dragoons, he was able to advance at all.

The march to Cambridge gave the Indians who scouted on Baum's front opportunity for a little burning and cattle-killing. They were fired upon by pardonably indignant folk of the region, and five of these were captured. From them, and from a few Tories who joined the column, Baum first learned of Stark's presence in Bennington.

The news did not disturb him, but he sent it back to Burgoyne in a confident letter. On the morrow, he slogged forward again. The miles clung to the great boots of the dragoons, whose presence in the expedition gave Stark ample time to meet it.

Tidings babbled by the first excited messenger to reach Bennington described the advance as an Indian raid, and Stark ordered forward two hundred New Hampshiremen under Colonel Gregg. Another horseman, galloping in later, reported that the Indians were screening a column of regular troops with cannon.

Drums beat the long roll in the New Hampshire camp, where Stark, with the gravely concerned Warner beside him, barked instructions to his couriers. One spurred his mount up the valley toward Manchester with orders from Warner, bidding his regiment come on. Others rode through Vermont and near-by Massachusetts farms summoning the militia. The drums' cadence changed. With Stark at its head, the New Hampshire brigade moved out, following the road that led past the blunt-peaked hills that crowd in upon the Walloomsac's flow.

It was a sultry day with a hot and ashen sky. Along the narrow valley of the lower Walloomsac, from the trees that crowded its shore and the shouldering hills above the river, muskets banged flatly in the shimmering air. There was breathless shouting and the shrill howling of Indians, then silence, broken again by the reviving quarrel of gunfire. Gregg was making Baum's dragoon-clogged advance more deliberate still.

His two hundred had struck the invading column first at Van Schaik's mill, near the present town of North Hoosick. After a single volley, New Hampshire's men had fallen back, reloaded, fired, and fallen back again. They crossed the bridge over Little White Creek, running into the Walloomsac from the north, and set it ablaze before they retired further. It was an hour before Baum could extinguish and repair the structure and take up the pursuit once more.

He moved on again at last and found in battle array across the valley before him, not Gregg's pestiferous two hundred, but Stark's drab farmer regiments. Baum halted, and a windy sigh of relief ran through the dragoon regiment. Fighting was far preferable to further marching.

Baum was not equally comforted. These deployed men were only militia, but they were disquietingly self-contained. The figures on the road beyond them, the distant groups scuttling in and out of the clearings on the further hills, were not faint-hearted fugitives. They were hurrying forward, musket in hand, to join that brown line.

A whole countryside was up and moving. To Baum it appeared that already there were eighteen hundred men opposing his eight hundred. He made no further advance, but deployed on a hillside above a bridge that carried the road across the river, and waited attack. Meanwhile, he scribbled a second dispatch to Burgoyne, asking for reinforcements.

For a space, the two little armies waited beyond musket range, watching each other. The sky was darker now, and the breeze that cooled sweating faces carried a flavor of rain. Stark, when he saw that Baum would not attack, deliberately withdrew a mile nearer Bennington and camped on a slope overlooking the valley. Each hour increased his strength. Horns were blaring in farmyards, and armed men were hurrying along the roads and across the fields, screaming the tidings to neighbors as they went.

"Goddam Dutchmen. An Almighty lot of 'em. Come to take our land, hev they? Wal, by Jees, we'll teach 'em better. Git your firelock, Obed, an' come along. Ain't goin' to let 'em hev your farm, be ye?"

In Bennington, the Council of Safety was issuing muskets and ammunition to the weaponless, and presently Heman Allen told his fellow members good-by and, gun in hand, went out through the lowering afternoon to the hillside where Stark waited.

The gusty wind was bringing raindrops now. Stark's men swore heartily and began to build themselves hasty and inadequate leantos. Baum's less resourceful and tentless troops endured the waxing downpour unprotected. Their officers had appropriated the few deserted log huts along the road near where the column had halted. Rain drenched the couriers, riding back to the Battenkill's mouth, where Burgoyne and part of his army now was camped. The storm grew, quenching in wet and miserable men all desire, all ability to fight.

At seven that night, Baum's first courier, with the Lieutenant Colonel's letter telling of Stark's reported presence in Bennington, reached Burgoyne, who wrote an immediate answer. This bade:

> Should you find the enemy too strongly posted at Bennington, and maintaining such a countenance as may make an attack imprudent, I wish you to take a post where you can maintain yourself till you receive an answer from me: and I will either support you in force or withdraw you.

On the rain-lashed morrow, August 15, Baum received his orders and tried to obey them insofar as the storm and his own mentality, which had been schooled in European methods of war, would permit. The soil, recurrently soaked all summer and flooded afresh now, could not be trenched. The sodden soldiers slopped about, building redoubts. Logs from the huts, tree branches and trunks, even hay from near-by stacks, were used in the makeshift fortifications. The shivering Indians watched these preparations doubtfully. Loot, slaughter, and arson seemed remote joys in this rainswept world. The simple children of the wilderness found an omen in the enduring storm and, one by one, began to slip away. The tempest may have also scattered Baum's military senses.

He chose to defend the hill below which he had halted. This is a squat and flat-topped knoll rising some three hundred feet above the Walloomsac that washes its southern base. North, east, and west of it crowded similar blunt eminences, many with bare slopes now, but in that time thickly wooded. Baum chose the summit for his post of command and built his chief redoubt there, which his dragoons garrisoned. Half of Fraser's fifty sharpshooters and what Indians still remained were placed on the hilltop, too, with one of the brass three-pounders.

The Walloomsac, running brown and bank-full in the storm, flowed in a deep, irregular curve, west, north, and west again at the hillock's foot. Along its arc, on the stream's banks or on the knoll's south slope, Baum scattered his remaining men.

The *Jägers* held a barricade at the eastern end of his dislocated defenses. Downstream from their position stood the bridge, and Baum took special pains to hold this, evidently expecting to advance across it when reinforcements arrived.

The Canadian contingent were in the dismantled log cabins at the bridge's either end; and on the hillslope above, holding a breastworks, were the rest of Fraser's marksmen, half the German infantry, and the other field piece. Across the stream from the knoll and midway between *Jägers* and the force holding the bridgehead, Baum, for no clear reason, built another redoubt, which he garrisoned with part of his Tories. More Tories and the remaining fifty German infantry were posted on the river's hillside bank, downstream from the bridge.

The small force thus was split into six isolated units. From his post of command on the hilltop their commander could not even see most of them. The soaked troops squelched to their positions and waited. The rain went on all day while Baum peered westward through its grayness for reinforcements. None arrived from Burgoyne, but Colonel Francis Pfister, a retired British officer living near what is now Hoosick Corners, brought ninety Tories in through the storm.

More help was coming, but it still was a long way off and traveling even more slowly than the dripping moments passed for the watchers on the hill. Baum's second dispatch of August 14, telling that he was opposed by Stark with eighteen hundred men, reached Burgoyne early on the morning of the fifteenth. By 8 A.M. Lieutenant Colonel Breymann, with the German grenadiers and light infantry and two six-pounder cannon—about six hundred men in all—had started along the road Baum had taken on August 12. If it was a swamp then, it was a running river now.

Mud sucked at the feet of the toiling Germans, clotted and clung to gun and caisson wheels. The storm tormented straining men and horses. Inevitable delay was enormous. Breymann, the martinet, incredibly increased it. If his men were to relieve his beleaguered brother officer, they would do it after the best and most precise traditions of the Brunswick army, or not at all. The fact that this was a wilderness trail and not a parade ground wrought no relaxation of discipline.

Ten times hourly the troops in their rain-blackened, mire-daubed uniforms were halted. Ranks were dressed, intervals corrected by bawling officers before the sloshing march went forward for another brief space. All day this fantastic ritual was observed. When twilight fell, with the rain still enduring, the relieving column had not reached

Baum. It had not even reached Cambridge. It had made only eight miles.

The rain still fell, enveloping Breymann's wet camp, Baum's men in their redoubts, Stark's army squatting in their leantos, in common misery. In his worn campaigning tent, New Hampshire's general was far from happy. His soldier's sense appraised time at its proper waxing value. He knew that Burgoyne already must be moving to extricate Baum. Undoubtedly, reinforcements were on the way. At the moment, the odds were in Stark's favor. If this hellish storm endured another day, they might swing against him. Certainly, Baum would be reinforced before the morrow ended.

The downpour drummed on the canvas roof. To Stark, it was not a soothing sound. His pestered mind re-estimated probabilities for the hundredth time. It was true that the enforced delay was strengthening him. Tomorrow, Warner's regiment should be up. It had not marched from Manchester until companies away on scout had returned, but Safford was leading it south now through the rain. Stark needed Warner's hundred and fifty regulars to stiffen his own untempered men.

Sam Herrick's rangers, Vermont's sole professional troops, should be here in the morning, too, and the Massachusetts militia already were coming in, dripping and surly farmers who nursed a common grievance. They had brought along their chaplain, Parson Thomas Allen of Pittsfield, who had bounced into camp in his one-horse shay. Stark prayed for fair weather and went to bed.

Slumber did not come to him immediately. The Massachusetts men had huddled together and, after the fashion of their breed, had aired their grievance at a meeting. Parson Allen, their deputy, invaded Stark's tent, and his words were bitter.

The Berkshire militia were tired of wild-goose chases. They had been called out times without number by this, that, and the other authority. Always they had marched willingly. Always they had marched back home again without the chance to fire a shot. They were sick of running after their own tails. If this expedition ended, like all its forerunners, without a fight, folks needn't yell for Berkshire troops after this because they'd decided they weren't going to turn out any more.

The Rev. Thomas Allen had completed his report. Stark sat up in his camp bed and looked at him.

"Wal," he asked, "want we should start a fight right naow?"

The wind ballooned the tent's side; the rain fell heavily. The minister flinched.

"Wal, no," he demurred. "Not at just this minute."

"Parson," Stark promised, "if the good Lord should once more give us sunshine and I don't give you a bellyful of fighting, I'll never ask you to turn out again."

Parson Allen looked at the bright blue eyes above the jutting cheekbones and went away, well satisfied.

In the morning the rain had ceased. In Stark's camp, men moved stiffly and ill-temperedly about reluctant breakfast fires whose pine smoke scented the fog. This filled the Walloomsac Valley and immersed the low hills, but beyond it the sun was at work. You already could feel his heat through the intervening cloud.

At Stark's tent, officers came and went—Colonel Symonds of the Berkshire men, Colonel Herrick in the green and red regimentals of the Vermont Rangers, Captains Samuel Robinson and Elijah Dewey of Vermont's farmer levies, Colonels Gregg, Nichols, Hubbard, and Stickney of Stark's own New Hampshire brigade. There were Indians, too, wooden and guttural men from Stockbridge who had come with the Massachusetts troops, and who presently trotted down the hill and into the fog that now had brightened to moonstone hue.

Warner sat with Stark. His regiment had arrived at North Bennington, sodden and spent by its night march. When uniforms had dried and men had been fed and powder and ball to increase their scanty supply had been obtained from the Council of Safety, the Continentals would be up. Stark's voice crackled as he railed against the delay, but Warner shook his head gravely and persevered. Nothing could be done, anyway, until the fog lifted. Out of its depths came thin howling and thump of guns. The Stockbridge Indians had struck Baum's pickets.

On the hill and about the riverside redoubts where the dank cloud lay thickest, the British force torpidly had roused. Confidence had returned with the increasing warmth. Colonel Pfister boasted to Baum of the unnumbered Tories who today would follow his ninety into camp. Colonel Skene was not so sanguine. Presently, with Baum's permission, he mounted and rode back toward Cambridge to find and hurry along reinforcements.

The sun was breaking the mist. Clammy bodies felt his heat and were grateful. The brief exchange of musket fire between the pickets and Stark's scouts amused Baum's men. Clodhopping Yankee farmers could not oppose regular troops. The idea was laughable. On the knoll's height the British Indians did not laugh. Yesterday's uneasiness had increased among them. This was not the sort of warfare they understood or approved. More of them vanished in the fog and never reappeared.

That fog was lifting now, a fraying cloud that let hot sunshine through. It would be a stifling day. Baum, on the height, peered through his field glass at Stark's distant camp. It seemed larger than it had on Friday. The Brunswicker turned and looked long at the road to the west. Beyond the furthest redoubt where Tories and German infantry waited, the way was empty.

It was after noon before Stark moved. Warner's men had not come up, but he would wait no longer. With Warner, he rode along his army's uneven front, calling the orders his officers already knew by heart. The heat had grown with the day. Men sweated, breathing hard, before a file stirred. They had placed distinguishing green badges in their hats—a sprig of leaves, a husk of corn. It was their sole uniform.

Then, at the bawled commands of their colonels, either wing of the army wheeled and moved out. Nichols' regiment clumsily shouldered firelocks and marched off to the right. A hill soon screened them from Baum's puzzled regard. He believed, so ragged was their alignment, that they were deserters quitting the field. Out of his sight, Nichols led his men on a long detour to strike the hilltop redoubt from the northwest.

With their star-spangled green banner flapping before them, Herrick's rangers swung away to the left. They were to come down at the end of their semicircular maneuver upon Baum's westermost redoubt that Tories and half the German infantry held. Thereafter, the remainder of Stark's host waited an almost unendurable time for the flanking columns to get into position.

You waited and the day grew hotter, and yet your hands and your feet were cold. You stood there in the stiffly dried clothes you'd slept in wet last night, and your militiaman's equipment hung so heavily on you, you wondered however you'd move if Cap Robinson told you to.

You had your hatchet—some of the boys had swords instead—your gun worm and priming wire, your powder horn and bullet pouch, your pound of powder and four pounds of bullets, your six good flints. You leaned on your musket, "a well-fixed firelock, the barrel not less than three and a half feet long," as the regulations said. That barrel, as you moved, was hot in your clammy palm.

The sunlight, striking Walloomsac's water, bounced back into your eyes and made you squint. Nothing had happened since Nichols and Sam Herrick had marched away. The bright specks on the hill and about the breastworks along the river hadn't stirred. In the heat-shaken air they looked like bugs, not damned Dutchmen who wanted to kill you and take your farm. You wished this waiting was over. You wished you were back home. You wondered if you weren't going to be sick.

You glanced at Sam Whipple on your right and Obed Clark on your left. They looked sick, too, and you started to speak to Sam about it, but Cap Robinson hollered, "Silence in the ranks," in a voice that made you know he hoped General Stark would hear him.

Stark and that big beef, Seth Warner, trotted their horses forward. You thought it was going to start now, and you wondered whether, when the order came, you'd go the wrong way. It wasn't the thought of the Dutchmen's muskets that put a stone in your stomach. They said the fools never aimed but just let fly and all you had to do was keep low and pick them off. Those cannon worried you. A cannon ball could cut a man clean in half. Uncle Peleg had seen it in the French and Indian War. If the cannon opened up, you didn't know what you'd do.

Over there on the hilltop there was a puff of smoke and then a sound like a barn door slamming. You heard Sam Whipple grunt beside you, and you knew you'd grunted too. All along the line you saw Vermonters and New Hampshiremen alike looking over their shoulders. There was a sort of moaning sound in the ranks.

Stark and Warner came bucketing back up the hill. They both were laughing, and Stark hollered in that sharp voice of his:

"Those rascals know we're officers. They honor us with a big gun salute."

You felt better then. You found that you were laughing, too. The gun fired again, and again nothing happened. Jerushy, what were cannon to be afraid of! All they did was waste good powder and ball.

It was hotter than Tophet. Sweat ran down out of your hat with the cornhusk in its band and stung your eyes. If this was all there was to war, you wondered why you'd come. You thought of Martha alone on the farm and of the Sukey cow due to freshen any day and the south mowing fence you'd meant to mend. You felt lonesome, here away from your farm. Were you just going to fry on a hill all day long?

Down the valley, something said "Wop" and "Wop" again, and

small voices began to holler above a sound like corn popping. Stark and Warner came galloping back. They stopped to stare toward the Walloomsac, and you heard the General say to Seth in a pleased sort of voice:

"It's just three o'clock to the minute."

He wheeled his horse, and you thought his bright blue eyes were looking at you as he stowed his watch away and drew his sword. He looked twice his regular size in his shabby blue coat and buff pants as he shouted, "Forward march!" and after that something you couldn't hear because your heart had turned all the way over and there was a roaring in your ears. Later, they told you that Stark had cried:

"Boys, we win today or tonight Molly Stark sleeps a widow." Which wasn't too sensible when you recalled that Mrs. Stark's name was Elizabeth. You couldn't have remembered your own name, though, while Cap Robinson was bawling and shoving you into your place in the column and the whole tarnal army was moving downhill into the valley where there was smoke enough for a dozen brush fires and the hollering and the corn popping was growing louder and the cannon had begun banging again. You kept thinking of that south mowing fence and of how you ought to be fixing it, and all the while your legs somehow were carrying you along.

Cap Robinson's face was as red as a Britisher's coat as he ran down the line yelling for you all to look to your flints and freshen primings. You were down close to the river now, and the column stopped so sharply that you bumped into Hosea Miller. You could smell burned powder, and above a screeching that had gone on, it seemed like forever, muskets were banging like a hundred muster days at once. Stark galloped by, waving his sword and yelling: "Colonel Stickney, ford the river and drive 'em from that bridge!" and someone said that Herrick and his rangers had captured the Tory redoubt downstream and that the Dutchmen on the hilltop had mistaken Nichols' regiment for more Tories coming to help them, and the New Hampshiremen had got right in among them.

You found yourself cheering as Stickney's men swung off to the left down the bank and into the water and then you were running with all the rest of them uphill, keeping low, moving from tree to tree. There was a breastworks ahead of you and men in green behind it. All about you, firelocks went off and you felt yours kick your shoulder and were ashamed because you'd shot without aiming.

BATTLE'S AFTERMATH—THE PRISONERS' COLUMN ARRIVES IN BENNINGTON

From the Painting by Leroy Williams (Courtesy, Bennington Historical Museum and Art Gallery)

Your hands shook as you stood behind a pine and rammed the military load into your piece—a half-palmful of powder and three buckshot and a musket ball on top of that. The woods were full of smoke, and you forgot to be afraid. You forgot everything except that you owned a farm, and that you and Martha were free folks and that that was what you were fighting for.

Something blew bark into your face when you peeked out from behind your tree, and when you looked again New Hampshiremen were swarming up over the breastworks and the noise was a caution and a man in a green uniform went running across the slope in front of you in big jumps like a deer and, like he had been a deer, you lined your sights and held in front of him and let go and when the powder blew away, he wasn't running any more and you felt a little sick again, and figured you'd never been so hot.

The smoke stung your throat and your head seemed swollen and your shirt bound your chest. The powder when you poured it stuck to your hand. You were ramming down the buck and ball when Cap Robinson bawled in your ear to come on, and you and Obed and some others started to follow him when a noise louder than any thunderclap nigh knocked you all over and Obed squalled, "Goddlemighty, what was that?" and Cap Robinson, who generally is a godly man, hollered: "The bastards' goddam caisson's blown up. Come on, boys."

You ran up the hill, though each step made you feel you couldn't take another, and you got over the breastworks somehow and dropped into the most tarnal mess of men worrying each other and screeching and whaling away with hatchets and swords and musket butts, in a big cloud of smoke. It was like the hell Parson Dewey preached about in Bennington meetinghouse, only a mite overstocked with devils. You couldn't shoot because you couldn't tell who'd be hit.

Then, through the dogfight, tearing it apart like a plow through fallow, maybe forty men came running. They were heavy men in blue and yellow, and some of them wore cocked hats with stringy plumes above staring red faces, and some of them were bareheaded with their pigtails bobbing and all of them had high shiny boots and laid about them with long straight swords.

You dodged them, and they got clear of the redoubt and started clumping off downhill to the west, all together, but the shooting began again and some of them fell, and the rest couldn't run far or fast in that outlandish rig. You laid your firelock across the breastwork's top log and aimed, but somehow you couldn't pull trigger until Cap Robinson hollered, "Fire, ye fool." You shot then, and another runner went down, and the rest of the Dutchmen threw away their swords and began to bawl "Quarter" in queer voices. Some of them knelt right where they were, squealing, and those of the enemy who were still alive in the redoubt called "Quarter" too.

You tried to cheer but your voice stuck and Sam Whipple pounded you on the back and yelled in your ear: "Come on, spile the Egyptians!" You remembered then that Stark had promised his army all the plunder if they beat the British, but you didn't care for any now.

There on the hilltop, where the powder haze thinned and the wounded lurched past and hooting men were beginning to herd the prisoners, you stood against the hot little cannon and looked out to the Green Mountain wall, bright in the slanting sunlight, and Mount Anthony, standing alone to the southeast, and all you could hold in your mind was that the Dutchmen would never have this, and then you thought of Martha and wondered whether Sukey had calved and knew that it would be you who mended the south mowing fence after all.

Men who ranged the hill for plunder, men who already had begun to urge the prisoners on toward Bennington, jeered Warner's Continentals for their tardiness when the regiment marched into view just after the last gunshot had died away. Their scorn was brief, but while it endured it held the late arrivals together. Elsewhere units broke apart and fell earnestly to looting. Stark had guaranteed them this privilege and, though the thought of a possible relieving column still dwelt uneasily in his mind, he could not restrain his men.

The finality with which raw militia units had stamped out the invaders supplied some warrant for disregard of the future. Baum's force had been practically abolished. The Brunswicker himself and the Tory, Colonel Pfister, both had been mortally wounded. They were borne to David Mathew's farmhouse in Shaftsbury, where they died.

Stark's helpless wrath over the dissolution of his command found some outlet when he saw one Samuel Ely, formerly of Conway, Massachusetts, carting an inordinate amount of plunder from the field. Him, since he confessed that he belonged to no accredited unit in the fight, Stark ordered arrested.

Later, before a court-martial, Ely proved that he had fought throughout the battle. Therefore he held that, by Stark's own promise, he was entitled to share in its spoils. As for the charge that he belonged to none of the organizations engaged in the fight, Ely put forward the plea that he had served with an exclusive outfit whose field, company, and noncommissioned officers as well as the rank and file were composed of Samuel Ely. This one-man regiment was acquitted by the court-martial and permitted to keep its loot.

Meanwhile, Colonel Skene had urged his horse westward along the swampy road until in mid-afternoon he encountered Breymann's command, halted and dressing its ranks for the five-hundredth time near Van Schaik's mill. Not even Skene's earnest appeal could induce the Lieutenant Colonel to abandon precision for speed. The column crawled forward with the customary maddening corrective halts.

Armed farmers had gathered behind a stone wall, and when Skene, believing they were Tories, rode forward and hailed them, they made their sympathies known by shooting his horse from under him. A volley from Breymann's foremost ranks drove them off, but beyond a turn in the road more men with wilted green in their hats had gathered. These, too, legged it after the first discharge. The column moved on with an unsteady swarm of farmers firing and retreating before it. Breymann was still seeking to unite with Baum, but he never reached the knoll where his associate had fallen and some two hundred lay dead.

There had been panic in Stark's scattered force when firing began in the west and rolled nearer. Warner's tardy regiment was the sole unit still under complete control. Led by its colonel, it marched toward the sound of the guns and, establishing itself on a hillock overlooking the road, formed a rallying point for the retreating skirmishers and for the men who at Stark's insistence abandoned their plundering and went forward in an increasing stream.

Gunfire quickened, swelled into a roar spaced by the even crashes of precisely executed and unaimed volleys, as Breymann deployed his command with its backs to the sunset.

The six-pounders thundered, but Stark's men had lost their early respect for cannon. Some of the more ambitious even trundled forward one of the captured Baum fieldpieces and, after Stark had shown them how to fire it, banged away at the Germans.

The New England line went back no more. Presently, with Warner's regulars in its center, it began to move forward, driving Breymann, surrounding and capturing his guns, hustling him and the two-thirds of his force he was able to bring off, into headlong retreat during which no halts were made to reorder ranks. Twilight was closing in now, and, for fear that his own men slaughter each other in the gloom, Stark abandoned the chase.

Twilight was gathering in Bennington, too, when women who had prayed all afternoon in the meetinghouse while gunfire roared along the northwest hills came out in the sudden silence and saw the first files of prisoners come plodding in through the dusk.

Powder-blackened farmers guarded them. Captors and captives alike moved at a sleep-walking pace. They were spent, not only by strife, but also by the day's terrific heat. Many, now that the battle fury had burned away, were physically ill. Stark, Warner, and Heman Allen suffered heat prostrations from which only the first wholly recovered.

There was no room in Bennington's little village for seven hundred unwilling visitors. The prisoners were packed into the meetinghouse that closely resembled, architecturally, Captain Dewey's barn, in which the overflow was jailed. Townspeople were kind to the uniformed captives, British, German, and Canadian. Toward Bennington's own neighbors, the Tories who had joined Baum, the town displayed that peculiar rancor which always distinguishes a family fight. Legend holds that the housewives of Bennington surrendered their bedcords so that the unhappy loyalists might be paraded through the village, tied together, two by two, with a Negro horseman leading them.

The soldier prisoners soon were sent into Massachusetts, where housing was more adequate. Some of the Tories were banished from Vermont, others were sentenced to the prison mine at Simsbury, Massachusetts, and a few of the lesser or more popular sinners were allowed to return to their farms with the assurance that they would be shot if they ventured off.

Stark's brigade camped at Bennington for almost a month after the battle. If its general believed that the British might come that way again, he was wrong. The price the New Englanders had set on Bennington's stores was too high for Burgoyne to negotiate further.

The British general had no stomach for further action against Vermont. He seems to have felt only an earnest hope that, thereafter, its people would leave him alone, for he wrote, about this time, to Lord Germaine:

The New Hampshire Grants in particular, a country unpeopled and almost unknown in the last war, now abounds in the most active and most rebellious race on the continent and hangs like a gathering storm on my left.

Yankee farmers with scant war experience and only a smattering of drill had smashed and more than half-eliminated some fifteen hundred of Europe's best disciplined and equipped troops. They had killed more than two hundred, wounded many, and had captured seven hundred prisoners, four cannon, seven hundred muskets, and a deal of other material, not counting the spoils Stark's men had been permitted to take for their own use. All this they had done at a cost of thirty dead and forty wounded.

Stark lingered in Bennington, basking in a fame that was a soothing warmth on his recently galled spirit, returning evasive answers to the pleas of Gates, who had supplanted Schuyler, that he join the American Army with his brigade. Men who had ignored Stark hitherto, now were full-throated in their praise. His most cherished encomium came from the Massachusetts legislature, which voted the General "a complete suit of clothes becoming his rank, together with a piece of linen."

Stark marched at last to join Gates, but he moved, inexplicably, at the time when the service of his men, who had enlisted only for two months, practically was completed. The New Hampshire brigade tramped into the American camp on the morning of September 18, looked around, and then, apparently disliking the view and the accommodations, marched out that afternoon for home, leaving Stark himself as the sole reinforcement he had brought Gates.

The war which had beaten against Vermont's door had subsided to indistinct mutterings along the old waterways of conflict. There was tumult in the north, half-battle, half-raid, where Herrick's Rangers and a militia force from Massachusetts, painfully assembled by Lincoln, tried to break Burgoyne's supply line and retake Ticonderoga.

Captain Ebenezer of the Allen clan, a man of Ethan's own stripe, led a company of rangers up Mount Defiance and chased its garrison away. Colonel John Brown, whom Ethan Allen accused of having failed him before Montreal, moved up Lake George, taking prisoners, releasing a hundred Americans captured at Hubbardton, and burning boats. General Powell, holding Ticonderoga for Burgoyne, was summoned to surrender, just on the chance that possibly he would. He refused indignantly, and the expedition withdrew.

There was thunder in the west, where Arnold and Gates and their regulars, together with a horde of militia who swarmed in for the kill, at last brought Burgoyne to bay. On October 17, he surrendered in an atmosphere heavy with protocol and ponderously courteous interchanges between men who, the day before, had been bent on shooting each other.

The summer-long danger, the ever-present threat, had passed at last. The garrison at Ticonderoga retreated into Canada, and peril no longer hung over the Vermont frontier.

The dire time had not been spent wholly without profit to the infant Republic. Events once again had served Vermont's leaders obscurely but well. Dread and violence and their attendant distractions had made a contentious people forget all about the Republic's constitution that had been submitted to them in early July for endorsement or amendment.

The leaders were quite willing that they go right on forgetting. If each town meeting were to start altering the document after its own particular bent, the instrument never would be established. It were better not to call attention to the omission and go ahead.

Thus, exterior violence—invasion and the threat of conquest—obliquely had favored Vermont. War's peril had withdrawn now. The bronze and crystal tranquillity of late autumn lay upon the land—a serenity marred only by the revived impact of faction upon faction, the resurgent flurries of accusations and counter-charges, of name-calling and general bad language that was the Republic's normal internal response to an external equivalent of peace.

PART THREE

REPUBLIC

Come York or come Hampshire, come traitors or knaves,
If ye rule o'er our land, ye shall rule o'er our graves;
Our vow is recorded—our banner unfurled,
In the name of Vermont we defy all the world!
                    —JOHN GREENLEAF WHITTIER

XIII Tumult and Shouting

VERMONT'S CALAMITY-ATTENDED birth throes appear, when compared to her subsequent chaotic infancy, a serene and pastoral interlude. No young creature or country ever took its first independent steps amid more disheveling varieties of suspicion, abuse, opposition, conspiracy, and general hostility, internal and external, and still survived.

The Republic's childhood was a continual nerve-taxing rumpus, a hurly-burly of shaken fists and half-drawn swords, of outraged yells and threatening bellows, of contusions and lacerations which should have turned any young thing, including the infant Hercules, into a jittering neurasthenic, a depraved bully, or a corpse.

All this bedlam immersed a newborn state ,whose original constitution was not too rugged. While trying to keep alive in an environment overstocked with menaces, Vermont continually and additionally was afflicted with stomach aches.

The Republic was a chronic sufferer from pangs and spasms, chiefly in its Eastside, that it would have required all the most noteworthy qualities of Aesculapius and Job to allay. These traits Vermont's leaders partially acquired, along with an opportune quickness of wit and stark audacity which belonged to neither of the above celebrities, but was the leaders' own unique possession.

The founders of Vermont do not lend themselves appropriately to perpetuation in such inert materials as bronze or marble. They would have been more easily and accurately immortalized on the film of a high-speed camera. They were not deliberate personages, given to august poses and ponderous oratory. In their activity, their desperately swift changes of objective, they did not resemble Websterian statesmen. They moved, in the Republic's more stirring days, like the hapless base-runner who has been trapped between second and third.

Vermont's leaders were not Olympian. They were fleet, agile, persistently daring. They had to be.

Exterior dignity was beyond them. Austerity could be no attribute of persons who were obliged to jump so fast and in so many directions.

If, in their frantic darting about, they had slipped and fallen flat, the consequent tragedy might have ennobled them. They never more than stumbled, and the peril which they continually thwarted so dexterously wears at this distance a surface aspect of comedy. Men galloping from hither to yon and always avoiding by a hair's diameter apparently inevitable disaster are sure to seem funny to everyone but themselves.

The founders of Vermont and that part of its population who followed them already had proved that they had a crafty skill which may have been an intensification of the New England bargaining ability, and a courage that was, perhaps, part of their Old England heritage.

The serial riot, the complicating dangers that began to afflict the young Republic immediately after Bennington had been fought and the internal truce imposed by external war had abated, sharpened and burnished Vermont skill and courage into the redoubtable immaterial weapons which were to be the state's chief defense against multiple attack. The tiny nation's leaders learned their statecraft in necessity's school. That brutal master never had more apt pupils.

The humor of the frantic expedients these men were forced to employ does not quite hide the patriotism which underlay it. The laughter that is quickened by the contemplation in long perspective of their manifold woes and the fashions in which these were abolished or evaded need not blind later and lesser men to the audacity of these solutions. The person whose house and breeches are ablaze, who yet manages to extinguish both with small harm to either, has qualities beyond the mirth his plight has quickened.

By the enduring skill and resolution and bravery, by the long-delayed but eventually complete triumph of these singular pioneer leaders, all Vermont's early inhabitants themselves are dignified. None but men of their own breed and mind could have held so turbulent a folk together. None but statesmen who voiced the majority's intention could have survived the explosive years that now confronted the Republic.

The purpose of these men was so plain and simple that all, both enemies and adherents, completely understood it. They had resolved that Vermont should be an independent state—within the Union of states if possible; otherwise, still a republic of freemen equal in voice, each secure in the possession of his own, whether that own were the Allens' wide acreage or the humblest and northermost cabin standing in its patch of clearing.

Necessity taught Vermont's duly chosen officials to meet bullying with resolution, to play force against force, to feint and duck and shift, and eventually wear enmity away. Necessity compelled these men in clear-eyed, unheated determination to risk their individual necks to save the Republic. Always they were hard-pressed, frequently almost defeated, perpetually distracted by insurgent upheavals; but when the strife at last ended it was their opponents' weariness and slackening resolution—not their own—that brought it to its close.

Victory, complete and uncontested, stood at the end of this serial war whose first seed George Clinton, royal governor of New York Province, had sown, whose full growth another George Clinton, republican governor of New York State, bitterly reaped. In that conflict, all of North America save Mexico and Louisiana, at one time or another and sometimes in concert, assailed a republic that was only a small wedge of wilderness where a few thousand pioneers dwelt.

When the dust of conflict had settled and the smoke of anger had blown away, Vermont stood precisely where, from the day of its declaration of independence, it had purposed to stand; and everything for which it had struggled was completely in its hands.

While the gunfire of the 1777 campaign still endured, various elements in the tempest that was to buffet the state and screech in her leaders' ears for years to come already had raised their individual voices, not yet mingled in an abiding dissonance.

From Albany, where he governed what portions of New York the British had not occupied, George Clinton spoke, summoning Vermont's militia to the aid of the commonwealth of which he deemed the new republic still a part. This utterance was completely ignored in the confusion and dread immediately preceding the Bennington fight. Vermont was to hear that peremptory voice frequently from now on, reproving her, threatening her, heartening her enemies.

George Clinton, a distant cousin and namesake of New York's royalist governor, was a patient and stubborn man. His devotion to his state was great, and his vigilance in protecting her authority unremitting. He would have saved himself a deal of trouble if each of these had been a little less.

Patriot, soldier, statesman, Clinton was destined to be chief obstacle in every road by which Vermont strove to attain inclusion in the Union. Merely physically, he could afford no inconsiderable obstruction. He was a burly, ruddy man with heavy nose and mouth, deep-set eyes overshadowed by thick brows, and a wide forehead beneath grizzled hair which Vermont was to be an agent in turning snow-white.

New York's new governor neither forgot his friends nor easily forgave his enemies. He could hold a grudge with Indian tenacity, and Vermont shortly was to furnish him with an infinite number of causes for acute dislike. In the turmoil of that battle summer, the Republic's disregard of his summons seems to have gone unreproved; but Clinton did not forget it and bided his time.

Another voice, already drearily familiar, was raised this fall of 1777 from the northern frontier, temporarily swept clear of invaders, but almost wholly defenseless. There, farmers who dared remain in that region of peril began to cry for protection to the Council of Safety, which gave them what small aid it might.

Blockhouses were built, and a few larger forts constructed and garrisoned. Strongest of these was Fort Ranger, a ditched and palisaded post built in 1778 at Rutland, which served as headquarters for troops on frontier service. Vermont's strength in men and money never was sufficient adequately to protect her northern border. Always that weakness, that wholly vulnerable exposure to British inroad, was in the minds of the state's leaders. An army could have blown all the forts away. Raiding Indians had no difficulty in slipping through their barriers.

A party of hostiles marauded as far south as Pittsford in September 1777. The wife of Felix Powell, at home with only her fourteen-months-old child, saw them coming and hid in the brush, stifling her baby's cries while the Indians plundered and burned the homestead. On the morrow, neighbors found the woman, still cowering in the thicket, with two babies in her arms.

New York's continued attempt at domination, the plight of border farmers, the weakness of the frontier against British attack—these were three problems that Vermont's leaders continually were called to face. Other protestant and accusatory voices now supplied additional perplexities. These disturbing utterances issued as usual from the Eastside that, freed from the threat of immediate invasion, had resumed its normal output of domestic discord.

Time had not simplified the Eastside's political organization. It had only more intricately tangled it. Factions had multiplied, and the hearty dislike of each for all others materially had increased. The customary brawling, which had been suspended by the war, revived now with accrued energy and went noisily on with enough fresh grievances

and strong-headed, intolerant convictions to supply disorder for years
to come. Those who deem Vermonters a stony and emotionless race
never have considered the early history of the upper Connecticut Valley, its hysterias, rages, rebellions.

By the fall of 1777, the Eastside had split itself into no less than five
easily identified and strongly antipathetic groups, each with an abiding
faith in the justice of its own particular cause and a great willingness
to fight all or any of the other factions in that cause's defense.

Foremost among the embattled were the republican Vermonters,
who acknowledged the new state government and were heartily eager
to beat the head of anyone who traduced it. This probably was the
largest group, but its adherents were scattered up and down the
whole Eastside.

The York party, on the other hand, was compact. The majority of
the residents in the state's extreme southeast towns had espoused it.
They looked upon Governor Clinton as their deliverer, and in time
he must have come to regard them as unmitigated pests.

Opposed to and despising both the Vermont and York factions, who
reciprocated by looking upon them with extreme detestation, were
the adherents of New Hampshire, who cried for union with that
commonwealth and were encouraged in their clamor by Meshech
Weare, president of the state and a stable, if ambitious, intellectual.

The Massachusetts group's purposes were more circumscribed, but
its dislike of the New Hampshire, New York, and Vermont adherents
was unlimited. The exponents of this cause demanded that the Bay
State receive again the territory of which it had been deprived by
George II's boundary ruling in 1740. Temporarily, for no clear reason
save innate perversity, the mountainous and garrulous Charles Phelps
of Marlboro, six feet three, with a peaked bald head, snub nose, a little
mouth—an inadequate orifice for the amount of speech with which
his fat body seemed crammed—had chosen himself leader of this
faction.

The fifth, most recently established and most vociferous of the
cliques, was what rival groups called, usually with a number of uncomplimentary qualifying phrases, the "College Party." This owed
allegiance neither to New York, Massachusetts, New Hampshire, nor
Vermont. It was headed by persons associated with Dartmouth College—John Wheelock, son of Eleazar, that very pious man, and Professor Bezaleel Woodward. The gospel they preached held that western
New Hampshire and eastern Vermont should be wrested away from

their current and detestable governments and made into a brand-new, wholly independent state. This revelation had been proclaimed at a convention held in Dartmouth the previous year and already had gained many converts on both banks of the Connecticut.

There were, besides these main bodies, many persons of opinions so individualistic that they did not fit in any established party. Furthermore, in moments of emotional stress, the divergent factions were prone to join each other, for no more obvious reason than that, so combined, they could make just twice as much trouble. The Eastside was, in 1777 and subsequently, an explosive region whose inhabitants dearly loved a fight, or else soon moved to some more placid clime. The disputants now were tuning up and preparing to bellow their convictions or yell for help as their case might be.

Charles Phelps, in the fall of this year, prepared one of his monumental memorials, which he sent to Massachusetts. This justified the Bay State's claim to its lost property and urged the commonwealth to come and get it.

As the new year dawned, the Yorkers assembled in Brattleboro to do some earnest wailing in Governor Clinton's ear. Their appeal charged the Vermonters with numerous crimes against the sovereign state of New York and begged Clinton to punish the offenders. In his reply, the Governor used an incautious vigor that time was to teach him to restrain. He promised protection to all loyal Yorkers and also proclaimed that Vermonters would be forced by New York "to yield that obedience and allegiance which by law and of right they owe to this state." This was sheer bluff, which, the Governor was to learn, never awed such expert bluffers as the Republic's governor and council.

Clinton's valiant words heartened the Yorkers and made everyone else pretty mad. They were printed as handbills, distributed through the Connecticut Valley, and burned with much reprehensible language by most of their recipients. The Eastside already had its tail over the reins and the bit in its teeth before the constitutional government of the Republic was organized.

The first Freemen's Meeting Day was held March 3, 1778. On March 12, the members of the legislature assembled in Windsor to poll the returns and inaugurate the state officers. On that same day, the deadliest danger to the continued existence of the Republic was emphasized in Shelburne on the frontier, where Moses Pierson's house was attacked by a mixed force of British and Indians.

Captain Thomas Sawyer and sixteen militiamen temporarily were garrisoning Pierson's farm when the raiders struck. The assault failed, but not before three of the defenders had been killed and the farmhouse roof twice set afire. The second blaze was quenched, water having been exhausted, by dousing it with the Pierson family's supply of beer.

Vermont's first legislature convened with howls for aid from dwellers on the frontier and the waxing tumult of the Eastside dinning in its ears. These were to be almost continual sounds from now on.

Tally of the state votes showed that Thomas Chittenden had been elected governor; Joseph Marsh of Hartford, lieutenant governor. There had been no majority for treasurer or secretary of state, and the legislature elected Ira Allen for the first and Thomas Chandler for the second office.

Thereafter, the duly chosen representatives of the people went briskly and hopefully to work. The self-confidence that was sublimely theirs speaks in their postponement of the task of making a law code for the commonwealth. It was voted that Vermont should be governed by the laws of God and Connecticut "until we have time to frame better."

The Republic was divided into two counties, Bennington west of the mountains; Unity, east. Soon thereafter, possibly because of the name's ironic implications, the old title of Cumberland was restored. It was Cumberland County that furnished the trouble into which, almost at the outset of its session, the General Assembly ran, head on.

Through one of the kaleidoscopic shifts of policy that were prevalent on the Eastside, many members of the New Hampshire party and the College party had become allies and had acquired a new objective. This startling union presented to the assembly a petition from sixteen New Hampshire river towns, asking for inclusion in the new state of Vermont.

The petition disparaged New Hampshire's claim to the towns and argued that the Federal Declaration of Independence had left all the inhabitants of royal grants "in a state of nature," free to do as they pleased. By its presentation, the harmony in which the Vermont General Assembly had begun its work was irretrievably shattered.

The Westside leaders—Ira Allen, the Fays, Chittenden, and others—were startled, then suspicious, then flatly hostile. Vermont already had a war with Britain on its hands. By Clinton's own promise it soon would be obliged to resist New York as well. The petition, if approved by the assembly, would bring New Hampshire actively into the Republic's already more than adequate list of foes.

The Westside leaders opposed this raid on the territory of a friendly neighboring state, only to find, while angry Yankee voices squalled at each other, that the assembly was determined to welcome the petitioning towns into union.

The Vermont river settlements were solidly behind the petition. They announced wrathfully that, if it were rejected, they themselves immediately would secede from the Republic, and, with their brethren from across the river, establish the new state that originally had been advocated by the College party.

Clinging to time as their only apparent ally, the Westside leaders fought off immediate decision and managed to jam through an act referring the petition to Vermont town meetings for their endorsement or rejection. The leaders' reluctance to offend New Hampshire's government could not keep the legislature from taking Dartmouth College "under the patronage of this state" or from making President Eleazer Wheelock an honorary Vermont justice of the peace. Adjournment was brought about before any more harm was done, but not before Yorkers had managed to trumpet their own defiance in the ears of bewildered and inexperienced statesmen.

A mass meeting attended in Brattleboro by delegates from that town, Guilford, Putney, Vernon, Newfane, and Rockingham forwarded its defiance to "the gentlemen convened in Windsor under the style of the General Assembly of the state of Vermont." The Yorkers protested against the formation of the state of Vermont and announced their firm intention not to be governed by its laws.

The proclaimed mutiny had no immediate consequences other than to enlighten the Westside leaders concerning the Eastside's whimsical and perpetual uproar, though the mass meeting's defiance may have been in part responsible for the sad experience of Hubbell Wells, Vermont justice of the peace in Halifax, when he had John Kirkley and Hannah, his wife, summoned into court on David Williams's complaint.

Mr. and Mrs. Kirkley, devout Yorkers, had met the complainant, a Vermont partisan, on the highway, and for reasons obscure yet probably political had fallen upon him and had beaten him with scrupulous thoroughness. Williams got no relief in court, for a mob of Yorkers, bludgeons in hand, invaded the premises and took the Kirkleys out of custody.

Such internecine tumult, such schisms and heresies, seditions and insurgencies, such hearty willingness of neighbors to assault one another, were bewildering to the men of the Westside, where a uniformly vindictive folk were united in a great enmity to New York. On the Eastside, it was clear that New York had many and noisy adherents. These had embarked on a campaign of letter writing to Clinton which was to become an unbreakable habit.

Wherever two or three Yorkers were gathered together, they straightway composed an appealing epistle to New York's governor, and he scrupulously replied to these, counseling with an odd choice of adjectives "a firm and prudent" resistance. It was a comfort to most of Vermont's officials to remember that the General Assembly was to hold its next session in the comparatively peaceful precincts of Bennington.

That session, when its members gathered on June 4, was greatly enlivened by two nonlegislative events. A traitor was about to be hanged, and Ethan Allen had returned to his own people from his English captivity.

The prospect of viewing these spectacles—Colonel Allen in the fine new clothes presented him by Dublin admirers, and the execution of David Redding for holding communication with the enemy and stealing muskets from the arsenal—brought a large and enthusiastic crowd to Bennington.

As many as possible jammed their way into Landlord Fay's tavern, where the emancipated hero showed that his skill in tossing about the flowing bowl had not been impaired by imprisonment. The rest of the spectators gathered around the gallows, where presently Colonel Allen and his admirers joined them.

At the crucial moment, someone announced that Redding's hanging would have to be postponed. It appeared that the culprit had been convicted by a jury of only six men instead of the twelve required by "the laws of God and Connecticut" and for the repute of Vermont justice would have to be tried all over again.

Disappointment was so intense that a riot of Eastside dimensions and a possible lynching seemed imminent, but Ethan Allen quelled the disturbance at its outset by bawling in that tremendous voice of his: "Attention, the whole!"

That old, familiar, long-silent bellow beat down the tumult, and there was silence while the hero explained the delay and promised that the hanging had only been postponed a week. If the audience would return then, "You shall see somebody hung at all events, for if Redding is not then hung, I will be hung myself."

This pledge satisfied the crowd, which dispersed with cheers and laughter. Allen was appointed prosecutor by the Vermont authorities, the trial was held again with twelve jurors, and Redding was hanged at the appointed time.

Meanwhile, the General Assembly seemed determined to supply the already trouble-beset government of Vermont with a fresh increment of distress. Despite the arguments and the pleas and the warnings of Bennington leaders, who saw how clearly disaster stood at the end of the course the legislature had chosen, that body was resolved to admit New Hampshire's unruly river settlements into the Republic. The referendum had only postponed but had not altered the event. Town meetings had endorsed the union, thirty-seven to twelve.

Governor Chittenden, the Allens, the Fays protested; Lieutenant Governor Marsh, Timothy Bedell, Elisha Payne of the Eastside defended the union. The measure was adopted, and Vermont announced to the world—to a scandalized Congress, an outraged New Hampshire, and a secretly delighted New York—that she had wrested Cornish, Lebanon, Dresden (later Hanover), Lyme, Orford, Piermont, Haverhill, Bath, Lyman, Apthorp (Littleton and Dalton), Enfield, Canaan, Cardigan (Orange), Landaff, Gunthwaite (Lisbon), and Morristown (Franconia) away from her sister commonwealth.

The usurpation roused as much joy on the Eastside as this contentious region possibly could harbor. By the union, Cumberland County had been tremendously strengthened and Bennington consequently weakened. Hereafter, in the legislature, the Eastside would be supreme, if it could keep its delegates from fighting each other and could concentrate instead on the subjugation of the Westside.

Bennington was not equally pleased; and its leaders, looking beyond the immediate event, were profoundly alarmed. They went with their heads low and their shoulders hunched up, knowing full well that missiles which might herald the collapse of the whole Republic's structure soon would begin to drop all around them.

Chittenden, the Allens and Fays, and their colleagues did not have to wait long. A furious letter to the seceding towns arrived from President Weare of New Hampshire denouncing Vermont's action, insisting that not more than half of the river people approved the union, and threatening to bring the presumptuous communities back into their parent commonwealth by force if necessary. On the heels of this first letter came a second, addressed to Chittenden and containing a number of things the wrathful President had forgotten to say in his first.

Weare's common sense had not been blurred by his anger. He warned Chittenden that Vermont was "merely supplying its enemies with arguments." He termed the union "an idle phantom, a mere chimera, without the least shadow of reason for its support." The Bennington leaders flinched while they read. This also was their own belief.

New Hampshire was not going to sit and merely make protest while her towns were kidnaped. Its legislature immediately petitioned Congress, asking that Vermont be forced to rescind her action and grimly predicting otherwise "an effusion of blood."

This appeal to higher authority muffled even the Eastside's triumph. Chittenden convened his council in an emergency meeting. Someone hastened to Fay's tavern, where Ethan Allen was found enjoying what he termed "rural felicity sweetened with friendship," and routed him out. The council sent him off immediately to Philadelphia. He got there just in time.

Delegates from New Hampshire already had called the attention of Congress to the outrage committed by Vermont. Delegates from New York, grinning into their sleeves, were endorsing the protest and adding more of their own, quoting from the bale of letters and petitions that Eastside Yorkers already had sent to Clinton. Colonel Allen worked fast and with no small skill. He persuaded an indignant Congress to suspend judgment until after the October meeting of the Vermont legislature, at which he promised to try to get that body to rescind its calamitous action.

Allen attended the fall session of the General Assembly at Windsor, not only as the Republic's ambassador to Philadelphia, but also as a representative duly elected by Arlington. There, while Westside men glared at Eastside and Eastside men glared at West, and sometimes at each other, the Colonel made his report as resounding as possible. Either, he announced, Vermont would put New Hampshire's stolen towns back where it had found them or else "the whole powers of the Confederacy of the United States will join to annihilate the state of Vermont."

These were dire tidings to folk who, in general, were looking forward to eventual union with that confederacy, but from the Cumberland County representation there came a number of irreverent suggestions as to what the United States could do with its whole powers.

With New Hampshire's late towns as allies, the Eastside was in the ascendant. Allen had frightened the legislature less than he had hoped. It appointed a committee to consider the matter, naming thereon only two Westside men, Chittenden and Jonas Fay, and three Eastside members of the College party—Lieutenant Governor Marsh, Elisha Payne, and Bezaleel Woodward. This committee reported, three to two, its determination to hold onto the kidnaped towns, but offered to arbitrate the matter.

Where Vermont at the moment, with Congress offended, with Massachusetts, New York, and New Hampshire all itching for part or all of her territory, with the British even then planning another raid into the Republic, was to find unprejudiced judges, the committee omitted to say.

The committee reported October 21. Between then and the morrow, when the legislature met again, something happened. It may have been that Ira Allen wheedled. It may have been that Ethan blustered or that Chittenden exerted his own artless powers of persuasion. Possibly all three of them worked, each according to his own method.

Whatever took place during the recess, the legislature returned to its toil in a singularly altered state of mind and ready to execute as graceful and tactful an about-face as possible. It did not throw the New Hampshire towns out of the Republic; it merely left them out.

A motion that the two counties of the state remain as already established was adopted thirty-five to twenty-six. A motion that Cumberland County be extended to include the seceding New Hampshire towns was defeated thirty-three to twenty-eight. A final motion that the New Hampshire towns be formed into a new county was lost by the same majority. The legislature left the recently absorbed communities nowhere to go but back home.

They did not depart peacefully. There were yells, accusations, threats, terrific verbal explosions, while Ethan Allen grinned and Ira Allen dreamily watched the ceiling and Thomas Chittenden blinked and seemed genuinely bewildered by all this uproar.

That uproar was immense, but the protest was not wholly verbal. Squalling farewells, uncordial and unrestrained, a large minority rose and stormed from the assembly chamber. In the departing group were Lieutenant Governor Marsh, Peter Olcott and Thomas Murdock of the Governor's council, and twenty-four members of the legislature, ten Vermont men, and fourteen whose towns, having seceded from

New Hampshire already, were now being abandoned by Vermont.

All the departing were too thoroughly angry to hold any further communion with the assembly. They denounced its vote as unconstitutional, resolved that they all would remain aloof until it was withdrawn, and meanwhile issued a call for a convention of the disaffected to be held at Cornish, New Hampshire, on December 9.

Vermont, in striving to pacify New Hampshire, had created for itself a new and vehement enemy. Ira Allen was sent to soothe President Weare's wrath. He bore a letter from Ethan announcing that the temporary union had been dissolved and apologizing for "the imbecility of Vermont."

That awkward young nation was heir to enough troubles to unsettle a more adult mentality. In November, a British force came up Champlain in several vessels and raided the Vermont lake settlements as far south as Orwell. At the new village of Middlebury, all buildings save one barn of green timber were burned.

In December, the folk who had walked out of the last legislature assembled at Cornish, still furious, and voted that any three New England states—there were no three unprejudiced—be called upon to adjust the dispute. The self-exiled Lieutenant Governor Marsh was made head of an executive committee which chose as its motto, "Trust in God and defend ourselves."

Winter's recurrent truce, halting interior and exterior strife, came down from the young Republic's freshly charred north frontier. Vermont had moved with youthful incaution and a waxing accumulation of trouble throughout the year. It had time now to consider where it stood and what it faced. The eyes of the United States were diverted by the new French alliance and the friction between that nation's expeditionary force and the Continental command. They would not be always turned away from a small, unsponsored, unwelcome, and upstart commonwealth.

During the year, Vermont had added New Hampshire to her list of enemies and had incurred the disapproval of the American Congress. It had roused a portion of its own people to open revolt and had seen how disaffected were others who had not yet seceded. There were rumors abroad that New Hampshire and New York might move to divide the Republic between them. Massachusetts, urged on by Phelps, was fretting over the injustice of the 1740 boundary decision and beginning to mutter about redress.

Wrapped about these various menaces was the all-inclusive peril of the war itself, which, it was clear, Vermont must fight hereafter with only her own meager resources, unexpectant of further hearty aid even from New Hampshire, the recently affronted.

Such was the Republic's plight after eighteen months' existence. She was the object of universal suspicion and of many intense and acquisitive hostilities from Great Britain's down to her own Lieutenant Governor's rebellious committee. She was friendless, weak, with her shins barked and her elbows skinned by the headlong flounderings of the previous summer. These were matters that the unseasoned statesmen considered wryly in the council chamber of Fay's hostelry while the winds blew and the drifts swelled and the bowls of flip went round.

They were learning by their own errors. Their past experience was teaching them, too. They considered their republic's current state with the sour and unscrupulous humor of folk who have been bested in a horse trade. This was no time for vain lamentation. The problem was how one might get out of this mess without loss of face or property.

The method to be employed was still dim. It must evolve itself out of the shocks and stresses ahead. The course to be taken, however, was clear. It must be, not backward, not sidewise, but brazenly forward. There was no other possible way. All roads but this must lead, soon or late, to surrender.

No one can tell who prescribed that inevitable strategy, but its substance is of Ethan Allen himself. He and his handful of young rebels had fought New York to a standstill—well, maybe not exactly "fought," but they had bluffed and bedeviled her dizzy. The tactics of the Green Mountain Boys might be transformed and transferred to the needs of statecraft.

Soldiers were few in Vermont. Ammunition was scarcer still. The Republic must depend upon its own strength if it were to survive. This was almost entirely mental and consisted of a canny comprehension of human nature, a devotion to the land out of all proportion to its size and wealth, and some experience in and a gift for extreme pestiferousness.

Ethan Allen already had shown how unbearable an annoyance a small but determined number of persons could be. He had demonstrated that the meek may inherit the earth and the belligerents win victories, but that the ingeniously vexatious, if they persist in their course, are likely to get what they want, slowly, but in the end most cheaply.

The beginnings of a plan and a purpose came to the frequenters of the council chamber that winter. They must hold the already crumbling Republic together by internal firmness. They must defend it against the universally hostile world by exploiting their land's nuisance value to the utmost.

That intention and that method were to be tested while the year 1779 still was young.

xiv   Chittenden Hits Back

The provocations that brought about the Great Cow War were pardonable, even logical. That campaign was the direct outcome of action by the Vermont General Assembly when it met in Bennington, February, 1779. The legislature's action was part of the government's resolution to strengthen itself against all enemies, inside and out.

The lawmakers themselves had become aware of the extreme peril in which the Republic stood, and therefore worked at last with a minimum of turbulence and a maximum of resolution on internal and external repairs. Time now being available in which to improve on the laws of God and Connecticut, a legal code for Vermont was compiled and adopted.

Effort was also made to appease the still not unreasonably resentful state of New Hampshire. A committee headed by Jonas Fay presented resolutions proclaiming that the insurgent towns on the Connecticut's east bank "are of right included within the jurisdiction of New Hampshire." The assembly unanimously adopted these and passed a further act, February 13, declaring the recent unfortunate union "totally void, null, and extinct." These placations were duly carried to President Weare of New Hampshire by Ira Allen, ambassador extraordinary.

This complete renunciation did not awe the rebellious towns in New Hampshire or their Eastside allies in Vermont. They preserved an attitude of defiance so extreme and affronting that Ethan Allen, no mean defier himself, wrote to Weare about it, urging him to discipline his own rebellious communities who had been incited into this "schism" by "a petulant, pettifogging, scribbling sort of gentry that will keep any government in hot water."

The blackened frontier was a reminder to the legislature of what had happened last fall and might occur again at any time if more troops were not raised for its protection. Toward this end the militia law was revised. It needed revision, for hitherto it had worked with extreme ineffectiveness, particularly on the Eastside, where officers were

Yorkers and more intent on preserving Vermont for Governor Clinton than against its enemies.

The new militia act, as adopted by the General Assembly, provided for the drafting of troops for frontier service. The men of each militia district were to be divided into groups, and each of them was expected to furnish a soldier in time of need. If the group refused to supply its man, it was to be fined £18. If it refused to pay, property to that amount was to be confiscated and sold at auction.

The howl of dissent which this legislation wrung from the Eastside was a warning of trouble ahead, but the lawmakers ignored it and provided further disciplinary measures. They declared forfeit to the state all property of enemies of Vermont and made defamation of a state official a crime—which hampered considerably the Eastside's most popular pastime.

Further, if more devious, attempts to strengthen Vermont may be discerned in the application made at this session by Ethan Allen for the grant of eight townships north of Onion River. Only three Vermonters were among the aspiring proprietors. The others were members of the Continental Congress and officers of the Continental Army—Horatio Gates, Roger Sherman, Oliver Wolcott, and ten more. Military and political authorities were likely to support a state wherein they held property. The Republic was throwing up fortifications with whatever trenching tools it might reach.

The militia law was deemed an outrage by the rebellious Eastsiders, but they regarded the measures to suppress enemies of the Republic as a deliberate insult. Persons devoted to insurgence and slander thought up a number of new things to call Vermont's government and predicted as loudly as possible that it would not dare to attempt to enforce its decrees.

The defense committee of the towns on either bank of the Connecticut went further with a sublime disregard for consistency. These persons, who recently had been New Hampshire's bitter enemies, now switched completely around and on March 17 asked the legislature of that state to absorb the entire Vermont Republic.

When the New Hampshire lawmakers recovered breath, they voted to table the matter for the present, but urged that the petitioners poll Vermont's inhabitants to determine their willingness to become part of their neighbor.

It was now the turn of the Westside to screech with indignation, to become intemperate in its language and violent in action. Ambassador

Ira Allen went back, post haste, to confer again with President Weare. The poll was held, but it was only partial and inconclusive. Its sponsors charged that Vermonters burned up most of the ballots. There was much indignation on the part of everyone, and before this had had a chance to subside, the Cow War began.

Governor Chittenden ordered a militia draft to reinforce the frontier garrisons. That frontier, so great was the fear of further British and Indian attack, had retreated this year as far south as Pittsford, leaving the upper three-fifths of the Republic empty of settlers.

In accordance with the new militia law, Sergeant William McWain in Captain David Jewett's Company of the 1st Regiment of Vermont Militia demanded of James Clay, Benjamin Wilson, and one Cummings, all of Putney, that they furnish a soldier for service. They refused, with embellishments. Thereupon, Sergeant McWain notified the sheriff, who confiscated one of Clay's and one of Wilson's cows and announced they would be sold, April 28, in accordance with the law.

There was a large crowd at the sale, and it was led by Colonel Eleazar Patterson, who held under New York a commission in the militia. When the cows were led out, he and his followers closed about them, pushed the protesting sheriff aside, and escorted the cattle, with cheering and defiance, back to their original owners.

Immediately, the Eastside's perpetually simmering pot once more came to full boil. Few cows, since Europa's day, have been productive of more trouble. Their abduction had roused Yorkers to a high pitch of fury. Their reconfiscation made Vermont's adherents equally irate. Dark hints of terrible vengeance and some nose punchings were exchanged by the more ardent partisans and filled Cumberland County with dissonance which was audible even in Bennington.

The tumult sapped the courage of Colonel Patterson, who had exhausted all his martial ardor in the cows' rescue. The Vermont party demanded a punitive force to discipline the Yorkers, and Patterson followed the system invariably employed by all Yorkers when anything happened. He wrote to Clinton, saying that he had heard that an army was being mustered to recapture the cows and begging the Governor to send at once another host to capture the army.

New York's governor must have groaned when he got this appeal. He had enough trouble on his hands without it. There was an earthly hell in the Mohawk Valley, where erstwhile neighbors were doing their bloody best to exterminate each other. Furthermore, there were signs that the British in New York City were contemplating a thrust up the Hudson Valley. Clinton's faithful letter-writing adherents in Vermont had a genius for sending him petitions at the worst possible times.

Nevertheless, the governor scrupulously answered Patterson. He predicted with hollow optimism that Congress soon would decide the conflicting claims of jurisdiction over Vermont. Meanwhile, he counseled his militia colonel to display "firmness and prudence," though how these were to be exercised in the then-seething state of the Eastside, the Governor did not say.

Before Clinton had received Patterson's appeal, another and even more urgent had followed it. The rumors of a punitive force to be launched against the cow-rescuing Yorkers were taking definite and dire shape. It even was whispered that the awful Ethan Allen, uniform, sword, and all, would lead the invasion. Chills coursed so violently up and down Yorker spines that another petition to Clinton was inevitable.

This frantic appeal was formulated at a mass meeting in Brattleboro, May 4. Yorkers from that town, from Dummerston, Guilford, Putney, Rockingham, Westminster, and Springfield were present. Marlboro does not appear to have been represented. Its chief citizen and Vermont's supreme interior trouble maker, Charles Phelps, still was flirting verbosely with Massachusetts.

The petition, which was rushed to Albany, proclaimed that conditions in Cumberland County had become unendurable. Anarchy raged; York property, chiefly cows, was being confiscated. The more unpopular Yorkers were getting free horseback rides from their unadmiring neighbors. Perched on bareback steeds with specially sharp ridge poles, these unfortunates then had a heavy weight tied to each foot and thereafter were trotted about until their enthusiasm for New York had been jolted out of them. Clinton's loyal servants were being oppressed with considerable ingenuity, and something would have to be done about it at once.

Patterson's increasing unpopularity among his non-Yorkist fellow citizens wrung another letter from him on the following day, May 5. It was brief and final. Either, he wrote, Clinton would support his faithful colonel in this crisis, or that colonel would quit, resigning both his commission and his allegiance. A man had a right to expect a little peace from existence.

With a British force on his doorstep and about to capture Stony Point on the Hudson, Clinton still made time to reply to the epistolary clamor from Vermont. He promised, with no very clear idea where he would get it, an army to defend the Yorkers if the Vermonters marched against them, and he concluded with a plaintive aspiration that went wholly unheeded in Cumberland County's turmoil:

> I could ardently wish [the frantic governor wrote] that the inhabitants of Vermont could conduct themselves in such a manner as to avoid the necessity of bringing matters to a crisis ruinous to them and very injurious to individuals among us.

Clinton did not limit his attempts to clarify matters merely to a scrupulous answering of letters. New York's delegates in Congress introduced a resolution that the boundaries of the thirteen states should conform in every detail to the boundaries of the thirteen colonies, and that no portion of any state could separate itself from the parent body "without the express consent and approbation of such state."

This did not straighten out things materially, for at about the same time, Massachusetts presented Congress with a claim to southeast Vermont. The national legislators made at the moment no attempt to disentangle the snarl. They only sat and held their heads.

Meanwhile, the crisis was rocketing toward apogee. When the new Vermont militia law had been defied by Patterson and his cow-catchers, Chittenden had summoned his council and considered the mutiny. This, they decided, could not be overlooked. If the interior structure of the Vermont Republic were not immediately propped and strengthened, the whole edifice would crumble of its own weight. Ethan Allen was summoned. A hundred men were placed under his command. Colonels Joseph Marsh and Samuel Fletcher, Vermont militia leaders on the Eastside, were ordered to co-operate with him.

On May 24, Ethan Allen and his cavalry rode over the mountain wall from Bennington and descended into the Connecticut Valley with terror running wild-eyed before them. Allen carried writs which he would aid the Cumberland sheriff to serve, sworn out by Sergeant McWain, signed by Ira Allen, and charging no fewer than forty-four persons, implicated in the cow rescue, with "enemical conduct."

Out of forty-four objectives, the Allen expeditionary force captured thirty-six. The only resistance his invasion met was verbal, and even that was not up to Eastside standards. The giant, bellowing horseman with his enormous sword, his tarnished gilt lace, and his towering, amazingly plumed military hat palsied resistance and filled men's souls with unholy dread. Apollyon himself had come down upon them. One

Yorker, Samuel Minott, in writing the customary appeal to Clinton for aid, confided:

> Otherwise our persons and property must be at the disposal of Ethan Allen, who is more to be dreaded than death with all its terrors.

In tumult and shouting, supplied chiefly by Colonel Allen, Patterson was arrested, his lieutenant colonel, John Sergeants, was arrested, and most of the Yorkist militia officers in Brattleboro, Putney, and Westminster were taken too. They all were prisoned in the Westminster jail, where militiamen of Fletcher's and Marsh's regiments guarded them. Ethan Allen, that tall and glittering pillar, had held up the sagging authority of the Republic.

Clinton raged. He promised the abased Yorkers an army of one thousand men if Congress did not immediately act, and he revenged himself for the innumerable letters written him by forwarding all the Yorker petitions to Philadelphia with an urgent covering letter of his own.

While Congress clucked and shook its head deploringly, while Yorkers tried vainly to induce New Hampshire's militia to invade Vermont and rescue the captives, these prisoners were tried under Vermont's new law. This prescribed for the crimes of rioting and disregarding constituted authority, with which the miscreants were charged, fines covering all costs and damages, plus a hundred lashes.

Court was held at Westminster, May 26, with Moses Robinson as chief judge, Noah Smith as prosecutor, Stephen R. Bradley as counsel for the defense.

Bradley, with his long, clever face and his Yale degree, had come this year to Vermont from Connecticut, where he had been a militia officer in the early days of the Revolution and an aide to General Wooster at the time of his death in the Battle of Danbury. He was building himself a great square house in Westminster and had just been admitted to the Vermont bar. His keen and loyal mind was to serve the Republic well. His current, unpopular role had been assigned to him by the court.

The defense attorney moved efficiently and with a disappointing absence of spectacle. The crowd that filled the courtroom, expecting a Roman holiday, was vaguely disappointed. Colonel Allen was elsewhere on affairs of state, and the preliminary proceedings were drab. Bradley obtained the discharge of three prisoners on the plea that they were minors. Smith, the prosecutor, at Bradley's instance, dismissed the indictments against three more. To the audience, this was all very formal and disappointing. The Eastside was accustomed to fireworks at its gatherings. These, though tardily arriving, were on the way.

Great military boots pounded on the courthouse stair. A sword clanked loudly, and towering plumes brushed the door lintel as Colonel Allen entered, immense, magnificent, red-faced, and filled to bursting point with indignant speech.

The glowering apparition caused Noah Smith, a small, precise man, to falter in his opening address to the jury. He stared at Allen for an instant and then lamely picked up the thread of his argument, reinforcing it, as though to amend for his momentary discomposure, with erudite quotations from Blackstone. This was more than the pent indignation of Colonel Allen could endure. His great voice overwhelmed Smith's.

"I would have the jury to know," he bellowed, "that in the observations I am about to make, I shall not deal in quibbles."

He transfixed the quailing Smith with a terrible glare and then pursued, even more thunderously:

"I would have the young gentleman to know that with my logic and reasoning from the eternal fitness of things, I can upset his Blackstones, his whitestones, his gravestones, and his brimstones."

The audience sat straighter. Its members grinned and nodded at each other. This was something like. This was what they'd come to hear.

Judge Robinson was less pleased. Ethan Allen was his friend. His Honor was familiar with such explosive outbursts and their most common source, but nevertheless the dignity of the court must be preserved. While the Colonel drew breath for another blast, Robinson spoke gravely:

He would be glad to hear anything Colonel Allen had to say that applied to the present situation, but he objected to this invasion of the civil authority by a person in military attire.

Colonel Allen thereupon demilitarized himself. He slapped his remarkable hat down upon the bar table, unbuckled his sword and flung it, crashing, beside his headgear. Thereafter he appeared to search his possibly roiled mind for retort and dredged up a not particularly apposite quotation from Pope's "Essay on Man." He thundered:

> *For forms of government let fools contest;*
> *What'er is best administered, is best.*

The judges were pardonably bewildered. They whispered together, uncertain whether this were a tribute or a contempt of court. The Colonel marked their perturbation.

"Fools," he cried, "I said fools might contest for forms of government—not your Honors; nor your Honors!"

Thus having spread oil on troubled judicial minds, Colonel Allen supplied himself with a deep breath and launched resonantly into his grievance. He was not exactly a Daniel come to judgment; he more resembled one of the prophet's noisiest lions as he roared:

"Fifty miles have I come through the woods with my brave men to support the civil with the military arm; to quell any disturbances should they arise and to aid the sheriff and the court in prosecuting these Yorkers—the enemies of our noble state.

"I see, however, that some of them by the quirks of this artful lawyer Bradley are escaping from the punishment they so richly deserve, and I find also that this little Noah Smith is far from understanding his business since at one moment he moves for a prosecution and in the next wishes to withdraw it.

"Let me warn your Honors to be on your guard lest these delinquents should slip through your fingers and thus escape the rewards so justly due their crimes."

Emptied of his indignation and breathing hard, the mighty warrior put on his hat again, buckled his sword about him, tramped out through the enraptured crowd, and clanked away downstairs. There was one thing about Ethan Allen: you could always depend on him for a good show.

In his absence, the subsequent proceedings must have seemed trite and inconsequential even to the prisoners. Their sentences also were anticlimax. They were spared the hundred lashes and heavy financial penalties. All of them were let off with admonitions or small fines. When dealing with its own, Vermont persisted in clothing the savage justice set forth in her statutes with whatever garments of mercy were available.

The government always was extravagantly lenient with citizens arrested for political crimes and, also, extremely wise. The person who has risked his head for a cause and is then fined eight shillings for his insurgency is bound to feel that his rebellion and the purpose that fathered it have been definitely cheapened. Vermonters had lived long enough in the midst of violence to have learned how avidly it feeds upon itself.

The government's tolerance was also good statesmanship since it snatched out of the hands of the Republic's enemies a bludgeon they were eager to wield. When the culprits who had been brought to trial had been released, Chittenden issued a blanket pardon to all who had revolted against the state.

Thus it came about that when, on June 16, Congress, egged on by the New York delegation, who had been incited by Clinton, who still was being excessively pestered by petitions from Vermont, bluntly ordered that the unrecognized state immediately release from jail all political offenders, the order fell flat. Vermont replied with an air of wide-eyed bewilderment that there were no such prisoners.

Congress, meanwhile, was having great difficulty in keeping its mind on the war, thanks to tumult which was astoundingly large for the amount of territory involved, that continued to issue from Vermont.

New York delegates were shouting their claims in other members' ears. Massachusetts was demanding her rights. New Hampshire was hinting that hers superseded all others.

Behind these protagonists' clamor, there was a confused, irascible sound. Yorkers were crying to Clinton that, if he did not rescue them immediately, they would desert his cause and join the Republic; and the hard-pressed Governor was urging these resentful insurgents to "continue firm in the cause in which you are engaged and conduct yourselves with prudence." The rebellious river towns also were making their own variety of racket.

Deafened and a little dizzy, Congress appointed a committee to determine where all this noise came from and why. Only two of its five members—John Witherspoon of New Jersey and Samuel Atlee of Pennsylvania—made any real attempt to find out. They actually journeyed to Bennington and conferred with Chittenden there.

Vermont, while exploiting its nuisance value to the utmost, was preparing as well as it might for more serious trouble. It still was drafting men into its army, of which Ethan Allen had been chosen brigadier general, which must have caused him to make some brilliant additions to his uniform. It still was summoning Yorkers to serve and selling their cows when they wouldn't. The Republic was moving forward to the best of its ability.

Even on this course, it continued to be assailed by claim and counterclaim. On July 23, the Cumberland County Yorkers, despairing of any further aid from Clinton than more exhortations to firmness and prudence, appealed directly to Congress. Their petition pictured themselves as enduring "the greatest anarchy possible," begged Congress to uphold New York's claim to her seceded territory, and declared that Vermont's admission as a state would be the worst imaginable misfortune.

The next day, the New Hampshire legislature mixed up matters still further by voting to incorporate all of Vermont within its own state.

The government of the young Republic was growing accustomed to living in an atmosphere of chronic earthquake. It was beginning to see with anxious but observant eyes that this very turbulence was a protection. As long as Vermont was afflicted by so many enemies wanting so many different things, the state was comparatively immune. Harmony among the Republic's adversaries was the thing to be dreaded. If they were once to agree on how the state was to be divided, Vermont's extinction would be close at hand. The government did its best to prevent such harmony.

Toward this end, Chittenden dealt with Congress's emissaries, Atlee and Witherspoon, like a bucolic Machiavelli. He was hospitable, he was artless; but the envoys, departing, carried away the impression that he was a determined person, maybe a little smarter than he looked, and one thing he said rankled in their minds.

Vermont's governor, Witherspoon and Atlee found when they thought things over, actually had yielded on no single point. He had promised to stop persecuting Yorkers in the state, but only when these Yorkers condescended to obey Vermont law. He had refused promptly and stonily to acknowledge New York's jurisdiction, saying that his state would submit to Clinton no sooner than America would surrender to Great Britain.

He had assured his visitors that Vermont had no intention of hampering the union, but only wanted to be included therein, and none of joining the enemy.

That last assertion worried Atlee and Witherspoon a little. They wondered whether Chittenden really meant it. There were rumors abroad that made thoughtful men question whether it would be wise to push Vermont too far.

The Republic did nothing to mitigate this doubt. In the fell clutch of a number of increasingly painful circumstances, its government made no gesture toward appeasement or negotiation. It moved so fast and with such determination that it gave its slightly uneasy enemies the impression that it was truculently facing them all. There must, these antagonists began to think, be some still-hidden force behind such valiant leaders of so obviously weak a country.

There was no hint of contrition in Jonas Fay's and Paul Spooner's mission to Philadelphia. These representatives of the sovereign state of Vermont informed the Congress that, since their nation had been thrust into the attitude of defendant in the current dispute, they had been sent to demand copies of all papers relating to it. Their audacity served. They got all the copies, but how they carried home so vast an accumulation, history does not say.

Chittenden, too, uttered gratuitous defiance. He sent a letter, probably written by Ethan Allen, to John Jay, President of Congress. Ostensibly, it was an answer to the petition forwarded to that body by the Yorkers of Cumberland County. Actually, it was part of the new Vermont system of annoyance—and bluff.

The Governor charged that the protestant Yorkers were spineless shirkers who hid behind another state's authority "to screen themselves from service." The letter also took notice of Clinton's threat to send his militia into Vermont and notified Jay that, whenever the Governor felt inclined to make that invasion, Vermont's troops would be ready to greet him.

This was not the talk of a doubtful, or even a disturbed, man—though Chittenden must have been both—but the speech of one serenely certain of himself. People wondered anew just what secret surety the so-called governor of a self-appointed and feeble state cherished that made him dare to speak so defiantly.

While this haze of uncertainty thickened, while the poker-faced leaders of Vermont may have been congratulating each other cautiously out of the corners of their tight mouths, Congress suddenly and calamitously gathered itself together and prepared to act. There was a determination on the part of that august body to settle this unending squabble for good and all. This awed the Republic for a moment, and delighted its enemies.

Congress proclaimed that the brawl in what it still considered the New Hampshire Grants had "risen so high as to endanger the internal peace of the United States," which in itself was a tribute to Vermont's resourcefulness. To abate this growing menace, Congress asked the contesting commonwealths—New Hampshire, New York, Massachusetts—immediately to pass laws empowering the United States to settle all claims of jurisdiction over the contested land, permanently.

February 1, 1780, was set as the day for final judgment. It was then September 24, 1779.

This, of itself, was enough to overthrow the hopes of ordinary men, but Congress did not stop there. It forbade the Vermont government to issue more land grants, pending decision, or sell any confiscated Tory property. Thereby, not only the Republic's future was threatened, but its chief source of current income also was ordered abolished.

Clearly, Vermont enemies told each other, the brash little nation had overstepped itself and was about to collapse. Subordinate disasters, loosened by Congress's decision, now fell upon it. New York's and New Hampshire's legislatures immediately empowered the United States to sit as judge on their claims. Massachusetts was a shade more reluctant. She hesitated but notified Congress of her "clear and indisputable right" to southeast Vermont. Doomsday apparently was about to dawn.

Yet there were matters that might, incredibly, delay daybreak. Foremost was the resolution of Vermont itself. She, of all the parties involved, had not yet acknowledged the authority of Congress that had just announced its intention of trying her. More than this, Vermont was appealing over the august heads of that body to the people of America, whose constitutional sympathy for the underdog was, in the years to come, to lead them into acts of great nobility and an inordinate amount of expense and suffering. That sympathy was astir now, and Vermont, the outnumbered, the desperate, the much-defamed, was its object.

Bluff and subterfuge, momentarily at least, could no longer serve the small Republic. The sword of General Ethan Allen was a spectacular but a comparatively weak weapon. There remained his pen. Powder and ball were scant, but there still was plenty of paper and ink. Propaganda might win where battle was sure to fail.

General Allen's pamphlet, resoundingly entitled "A Vindication of the Opposition of the Inhabitants of Vermont to the Government of New York and their Right to Form an Independent State," still was damp from the presses. It was being circulated widely. He resharpened his quill and began another: "A Concise Refutation of the Claims of New Hampshire and Massachusetts Bay to the Territory of Vermont." Jonas Fay assisted him in preparing this, which, with its forerunner, completely shattered—to Allen's satisfaction at least—the pretensions of Vermont's external American enemies.

Stephen Bradley and Ira Allen meanwhile were collaborating on still another literary counterblast, to be known as "Vermont's Appeal to the Candid and Impartial World." The state's war department was feeble, but its public relations department was unsurpassed.

The propaganda, though it perceptibly was swaying the general American mind, had not wholly solidified Vermont's internal opinion when the legislature met at Manchester in October. Awed and worried men attended. The thunderclap from Congress had shattered their resolution.

Congress was not merely a more authoritative gathering of folk like themselves. The gentlemen who sat in Philadelphia, with their powdered wigs and dress swords and finely woven raiment, with their education and cultured background and polished manners, with their snuff boxes and their Madeira, their carriages and their blooded horses, seemed only distant and superior relatives of those who had assembled in a Manchester tavern.

To the village, sitting in frontier squalor at the foot of Mount Equinox in its Joseph's coat of October colors, had come rough men, hard men, deplorably costumed in homespun and home-dyed fustian, linsey-woolsey, tow cloth. There were sprucer representatives from the longer-settled towns. There were hairy, grimed, and untempered persons from the log hovels in the north. For many of them, it was a far simpler chore to fell a hundred-and-fifty-foot pine at any point of the compass than to scrawl their own names. Their language and their manners were uncouth, their pastimes largely alcoholic and belligerent, their reverence for authority extremely slight; yet the stern voice that had come to them from Philadelphia had cast them all down.

Congress, to the Vermont pioneers, was the substance of something new and glowing in a world of subserviencies, the fountainhead of liberty, the very voice of freedom. Toward that body of largely imaginary splendor, the Vermonter's mind had turned when he had thrown away his last fealty to the British king.

Now, this Olympian tribunal had spoken fell words which promised defeat for lank, horn-handed men in their long struggle to conquer and hold land of their own. The utterance had been too blasting for immediate resentment. The assemblage at Manchester had none of its earlier headstrong willfulness. It was meek, bewildered, yet not immune to the fire its leaders already had determined to quicken.

The gaunt, unhappy delegates kindled slowly. It was the Bennington leaders who resolutely nursed the flame. Ira Allen pointed out that Congress's disapproval of further land sales was simply an attempt to starve the government of Vermont into submission. General Allen and others held that, since Congress had not yet admitted the new state into the Union, it had no authority whatever over it.

These were valiant words, but the legislature warmed only gradually. The problem was referred at last to a committee consisting of four members of the council and four members of the assembly, one of them Ethan Allen. On October 20, council and assembly in joint session received the committee's report.

The document set forth "that this state ought to support their right to independence at Congress and to the world in the character of a free and independent state." It also voiced the belief that Vermont should go right on selling land grants.

It is difficult, as all who know the breed will testify, to rouse Vermonters. It is still sorer trial, as a number of concerned powers soon were to learn, to check a Green Mountaineer, once he actually has laid his course and has started upon it.

The General Assembly, which had met in such perturbation and awe of Congress, now resolutely hitched up its pants, spat on its hands, and proceeded to establish Vermont as one of the wholly free nations of earth by adopting the committee's resolution.

It also voted to go on granting land and, to emphasize its purpose, bestowed upon Ethan Allen, Samuel Herrick, and others twin islands at the north end of Lake Champlain, which the warriors named, with accustomed modesty, after themselves. To this day they are known as the Two Heroes.

It seemed more certain now that implacable New York and the more recently aggrieved New Hampshire were working together to bring about Vermont's downfall, with the understanding that thereafter the two states were to split the booty between them along the geographical dividing line established by the Green Mountains ridge. More warmly personal propaganda than even Ethan Allen could pack into a pamphlet was needed to offset this probable plot.

Ira Allen was sent southward to preach the new nation's cause in New Jersey, Pennsylvania, Delaware, and Maryland. Ethan Allen rode furiously off to Massachusetts to block if possible whatever predatory intentions might be hers.

The General appeared before the General Court in Boston and made his plea, reciting at length the reason why Vermont should be permitted to be a separate state, and begging Massachusetts to endorse rather than oppose her cause. As an oration it pleased General Allen, and it might have had effect if Charles Phelps had not been called immediately thereafter.

While Allen was forced to sit and turn from red to mulberry and finally to a rich plum color, Phelps contradicted everything his predecessor had said and ended by begging Massachusetts to assert her claims and save an unhappy land from anarchy. Emotion had unsettled the General so that he could not catch his opponent when the session ended, but he swore at length and vividly to kill him at their next meeting. Phelps left hastily for Marlboro. There is no record that the two men thereafter met.

The conflicting testimony apparently weakened whatever purposes Massachusetts had cherished against Vermont. The commonwealth did not place its claims in Congress's hands, as New Hampshire and New York had done, but added further complication to the situation by informing the United States Government that by charter Massachusetts was entitled not only to southeastern Vermont but also to central and western New York, as well as all the land from there to the Pacific.

Dismay caused by this modest assertion may have had some effect in blunting Congress's intention to clear up the strife of which Vermont was center quickly and finally. Vermont's own action must have slackened decision too. It was plain, in the face of that republic's flat rejection of any responsibility to Congress, that the only obvious way in which to suppress the gallingly independent precinct would be by open war; and the American statesmen at the moment had more war already in their laps than they could conveniently handle.

Once again large events were aiding the leaders of Vermont. Under the blows dealt by the British, the southern part of the confederacy seemed about to fall to pieces. Savannah had been taken, Charleston was about to be invested, and South Carolina was talking of a separate peace.

These matters served to temper Congress's boldly expressed intention to deal with the upstart Republic and have done with her. Members of that recently so-resolute body were beginning to look forward to the stipulated day of doom, February 1, 1780, with more apprehension than Vermont displayed. Why, they asked each other, stir up trouble when there already was more than enough to go round?

In this changing attitude, the pamphlets Vermont had so lavishly circulated through the states, the efforts of her personal missionaries—the fulminations of General Allen, the quieter persuasions of Ira—had played their part. Propaganda, the untutored Green Mountain statesmen were beginning to believe, had an important place in any nation's policy.

The dire day came around, and Congress tried to ignore the calendar and called neither Vermont nor the complaining states to the bar of justice. That august body seemed willing to forget the whole thing. That was a more difficult feat than it seemed on the surface. Vermont, in its current, uproarious state, was no easier to overlook than an aching tooth.

Congress's pose of forgetfulness was shaken early in the spring, when Cumberland County's Yorkers tried to hold an election. In Guilford the ballots were actually cast. In Putney they were destroyed, and a number of persons were beaten up in a riot of respectable proportions. Elsewhere, the notification posters were torn down and would-be voters were threatened with a mixed retribution of which skinning alive was the mildest feature.

The Yorkers, as was customary, immediately wrote to Clinton, who replied, counseling as usual "prudence and firmness." He then once more complained to Congress, which already had had its air of determined obliviousness marred by a frantic appeal from the still-insurgent Connecticut river towns.

This petition recited the atrocities committed by Vermonters and urged that the whole matter be settled by incorporation of the entire state into New Hampshire. It was impossible for the gentlemen in Philadelphia to pretend to be deaf and blind any longer. Congress on June 2 gathered itself together and adopted slightly anticlimactic resolutions proclaiming that Vermont's conduct, manners, and general behavior were "highly unwarrantable and subversive to the peace and welfare of the United States."

Thereafter, conscious that it had made very much the same pronouncement before and that no good had come of it, Congress named the second Tuesday in September as the day when the positively decisive hearing on Vermont's case would be held.

Something again postponed that final judgment. It may have been the disastrous tidings from the south. Gates, with no Arnold to extricate him from his blunders, had been ignominiously defeated at Camden, where Tarleton's and Webster's cavalry had plowed with wet sabers through the screaming fugitive militia. Whatever the cause, the hearing date was postponed again to September 19. On September 12, Ira Allen and Stephen Bradley arrived in Philadelphia and presented

Congress with a remarkable letter from Chittenden. The farmer-governor had been pushed around long enough. Now he struck. It was a desperate but a beautifully timed blow.

In his letter all the old Vermont arguments were rehearsed with all the old Vermont truculence. Thereafter, a new and explosive contention—it was more like a threat when you came to think of it—was introduced with a bewilderingly light and glib air.

Since, Chittenden's letter said, it was evident that Vermont was to be refused the right to become one of the United States, then certainly the Republic "was at liberty to offer or accept terms for cessation of hostilities with Great Britain without the approbation of any other man or body of men."

This was the lighted bomb that the Governor placed, ever so gently, in Congress's lap. Just in case he had been misunderstood the first time, he repeated his argument. The words were different, but the intention was unaltered.

If Congress, Chittenden pointed out, persisted in its refusal to recognize the statehood of Vermont and still attempted to thrust the Republic into New York's arms, Vermont, which, after all, had been fighting for the United States and not primarily for itself, had no longer "the most distant motive to continue hostilities with Great Britain and maintain an important frontier for the benefit of the United States and for no other reward than an ungrateful one of being enslaved by them." Governor Chittenden had the honor to be, etc., etc.

To the consternation displayed by Congress, Allen and Bradley presented guilelessly impassive visages. This bald confirmation of an uneasy rumor shocked the honorable gentlemen profoundly. The southern front of the Revolution seemed to have broken in irreparably. One did not need to be a military expert to understand what would happen if Vermont, the keystone of the northern frontier, were to quit the war.

On the day Chittenden's dire letter was presented, Congress also received another from Professor Bezaleel Woodward, a leader of the still-mutinous river settlements. This urged that New Hampshire be permitted to absorb Vermont and scoffed at the idea that Vermont had any chance of making a separate peace. It was easy to jeer if you hadn't already seen Chittenden's missive.

The long-delayed proceedings actually did begin on September 19. They were to have been definite and decisive. They appear to have been conducted in a fog of irresolution that the peremptory conduct of Allen and Bradley did nothing to dispel. These gentlemen had been told they might attend the hearings but only as spectators, since they were not the representatives of an acknowledged state.

Vermont's emissaries, thereupon, assumed what seemed to Congress an air of extraordinary high dudgeon. They announced that under such circumstances they did not care to be present at all. Furthermore, they followed their formal remonstrance of September 22 with a further announcement two days later. On that date, Allen and Bradley told Congress that their commissions had expired and that they were going home, hinting also that it might be well if all the other disputants followed their example.

Why not, the departing emissaries asked as though they did not care a whoop, let the whole matter rest until the war was over?

Such calm audacity took Congress's breath. It recalled to fearful minds the reiterated threat in Chittenden's letter. Just what, uneasy members asked each other, did Vermont have up its sleeve?

Once more the luck of the little Republic's statesmen held. Once more events beyond their control or apprehension obligingly harnessed themselves to the purposes of Vermont's leaders. When Bradley and Allen turned their backs upon an amazed Congress and rode out of Philadelphia, expresses were galloping toward the city with tidings that added the final disaster to a year of calamity.

Benedict Arnold, the dispatches ran, had turned traitor. Arnold, the army's great fighting general, had sold out on September 23 to the British. The emissaries who were returning to Vermont after their impudent treatment of Congress could not have known of the treachery that so appositely served their purposes, yet infinite planning and the closest timing would not have arranged matters better for their state's interests. On September 27, Congress, which had pledged itself to decide Vermont's fate, resolved "that further consideration of the subject be postponed."

All this was hidden from Allen and Bradley as they rode along, yet it is probable that, once Philadelphia was behind them, they regarded each other and grinned with the Yankee's silent relish of a joke.

Allen was certainly, Bradley may have been, a participant in a game that could have amused only men of that tough substance which was the building material of pioneer Vermonters. For the moment, the venture seemed a colossal jest, yet it might at any instant become a terrific flareback that would blow them and their associates—more properly, their accomplices—into Kingdom Come. There never was a second in the two and a half years ahead when that explosion was not imminent.

xv The Men on the Flying Trapeze

How AND WHEN the plot actually began, no one surely knows. Why it was furthered is more certain, and the fashion in which it was advanced is reasonably clear. The Vermont conspirators, being canny men on whom the peril of the intrigue rested, left few records. They appreciated from the outset the great unwisdom of implicating themselves on paper, of signing anything.

The British agents, on the other hand, were officers accomplishing their superiors' bidding. They made reports that still survive.

As for the true purposes, the inmost intentions of the Vermont plotters, we have only their own explanations, which may or may not be candid, plus the trite witness-bearing of events and the vaguer testimony offered by probability.

Out of these not wholly satisfactory substances may be built an empirical narrative of how hard-pressed leaders desperately dabbled in treason to the United States and ostensible betrayal of their own people, in order—according to their subsequent explanations—that this people, and the farms that were theirs and the Republic which was the sum of farms and men might be preserved.

The paradox seems more comprehensible when it is placed against its own background. The calm skill of the men who, quite literally, put their lives in jeopardy for the sake of a cause is not so easily rationalized. Their audacity is understandable. That was part of the forming Vermont character. No one endured long in that persistently imperiled, constitutionally riotous region unless his original fiber were tough and had the ability to toughen further under stress.

Mere bravery is not the marvel; but the deftness, the delicate agility, that untrained backwoodsmen employed is miracle's close relation.

Chittenden was a pioneer farmer; Ira Allen, a backwoods surveyor; Joseph Fay, a frontier tavern-keeper's son. Ethan Allen was the only one of the leading Vermont plotters who had had any experience with the erudite sphere in which such intricate negotiations customarily are conducted, and Ethan had only an early and dwindling part in the conspiracy. Intrigue seems to have been one game that was too strenuous for Vermont's blustering champion. He started out boldly, but he quit soon, leaving the taut ordeal to less transparent men.

Where these wilderness dwellers acquired their·accomplishments is mystery. This plot was not just another bartering or horse-trading. It became a tense enterprise requiring special skills, a game demanding extreme caution and immense co-ordination, a contest in which, if one should slip, he would have, in all probability, only a brief time to mourn his blunder.

The men with whom the Vermont plotters dealt were not of their own breed. They were trained, polished, and exalted personages of the British Empire, who, though they commonly spoke through deputies, directed the conspiracy.

George Germaine, Viscount Sackville and the then British Colonial Secretary, was a skilled diplomat, unscrupulous and slippery even when judged by the standards of his time and place.

General Sir Henry Clinton, son of the George who had been New York's early governor, was an able soldier, Commander of the British Army in America, an experienced and intelligent administrator.

General Sir Frederick Haldimand, a Swiss-born, Prussian-trained officer, possessed not only military but statesmanly qualities that recently had won him the post of governor general of Canada.

These were the British instigators of the plot. These were the personages whom a handful of bumpkins exasperated and bewildered and at last completely hoodwinked. Vermont farmers of today soaring gracefully back and forth with trained acrobats on a flying trapeze would present no more astonishing a spectacle.

Whatever the real intention of the Vermont statesmen who juggled so deftly with treason, the opportunity was offered them; they did not seek it. It was Lord Germaine who went shopping for bargains among American leaders and eventually succeeded in buying Arnold for more than he subsequently was worth. It was Germaine who, March 3, 1779, wrote Clinton bidding him find out what the Vermont authorities would charge to make a separate peace.

Lord George was something of a scoundrel, but he was no fool. He saw that the small Republic stood, neglected and distracted, on the doorstep of the United States with no immediate prospect of admission. He also knew that possession of Vermont would be of immense strategic value to Britain. It would mean a clear road to the Connecticut, a knife driven hilt-deep into New England's back.

Germaine liked the idea of drawing Vermont into treason. Bribery always was a pleasanter enterprise to him than battle. He wrote to Haldimand in Canada, too, urging the scheme:

> The drawing over the inhabitants of the country they call Vermont to the British Crown appears a matter of such vast importance for the safety of Canada, and as affording a means of annoying the northern revolted provinces that I think it right to repeat to you the King's wishes that you may be able to effect it, though it should be attended with considerable expense.

His enthusiasm did not infect Haldimand, who had served long in America. The General promised to do what he could but held out no great hope of converting Vermonters, who, he informed Germaine, were "a profligate banditti." He was to think of a number of even harder names for them before the conspiracy ended.

When it actually began, no one can tell. Whispers of it must have got about when in June Chittenden assured his visitors from Congress, Atlee and Witherspoon, that Vermont had no intention of selling out to the common enemy. There is no clear reason, even now, to doubt his then assertion or to believe that he, or his associates, even when elbow-deep in conspiracy, purposed actual treason.

The simplest and most plausible explanation of the whole thing is that Vermont was in desperate straits; that she needed most sorely at the moment a lever and a shield—the first to move Congress into admitting her to the Union, the second to protect her temporarily from Canadian invasion.

The Republic was beset by ills within, without. On the Eastside, loyal Vermonters, disloyal Yorkers, and the insurgent river towns were still keeping their Witches' Sabbath.

Congress deliberately was making plans to dissect the state and distribute the pieces among a number of claimants.

The British in Canada already had proved how open the northern frontier lay to invasion. They would come again and soon.

Vermont, though its government strove with a grave frenzy to hold it together, was spinning rapidly and threatening to fly into fragments. At any minute—and her statesmen knew it—dissolution might come. The Republic was defenseless, increasingly detested, gravely imperiled.

Furthermore, the United States seemed heartily willing to let the state go from bad to worse, with the probable idea of encouraging a nuisance to eliminate itself.

To expedite that desirable demise, none of the munitions of war taken at Ticonderoga, none of the cannon captured at Bennington were left in Vermont's hands. Warner's regiment had been marched elsewhere, though its colonel still remained, ailing, at Bennington. New York had withdrawn its garrison from Skenesboro. The lake forts had been abandoned. Defense of her long-threatened frontier was wholly in Vermont's hands, and those hands were empty.

The Republic's putative allies in the war against Britain seemed eager to turn the screw further. Early in 1780, Chittenden was informed by Isaac Tichenor, in charge of the Continental supply depot at Bennington, that the commissary general had refused to permit the issuing of any more rations, arms, or ammunition to Vermont troops.

The state was almost prostrate, but still not abject. Its government responded to this rebuff, February 29, by slapping an embargo on the exportation of any foodstuffs from Vermont. The Republic's neighbors, observing her with general animosity, hoped that this vindictive and painful kick might be part of her death throes. It couldn't, they told each other hopefully, be long now.

While her neighbors watched expectantly and the government of the sick state hung on with nothing but stubbornness to sustain it, Lord George Germaine's relayed enticement at last reached the persons for whom it was intended. It is not remarkable that this seemed less like an insult than a reprieve to harried men. When your craft is foundering you do not inspect too closely what calking material comes to hand.

The miracle lies in the fact that the British, who planned to use Vermont for their own ends, found when the negotiations had ended that they had been adeptly, persistently exploited themselves; that farmer folk playing an unfamiliar and exquisitely dangerous role had excelled in skill men of the world like Arnold and André.

It was one of the corruptors of Arnold—a loyalist colonel, Beverly Robinson—who made the first recorded move toward seduction. Germaine had ordered Clinton to get into contact with the Vermont authorities, and Clinton has passed the task on to Robinson, who addressed his letter to the Republic's best-known citizen, Ethan Allen, entrusted it to a soldier disguised as a farmer, and sent him north.

In July a stranger shambled up to Allen on the street of Arlington and thrust a missive into his hand. The general of Vermont's army opened and read it. Robinson informed his involuntary correspondent that he had heard that Vermont was sick of "the wild and chimerical scheme of the Americans in attempting to separate the Continent from

Great Britain." He added that, if Allen would aid in bringing about a reunion of his state and the mother country, it would be distinctly worth his while.

General Allen later insisted he told the messenger he would think the matter over and at once laid the letter before Governor Chittenden and the council. He did not admit what other facts bear out—that he waded immediately deep into the plot and presently found himself in danger of going over his head. Dissimulation, conspiracy, were beyond Ethan Allen. He had no more subtlety than a sneeze.

His progress is indicated only by the comments of the British negotiators themselves. He must have got in touch with Haldimand, if not Clinton, for the former wrote bitterly to the latter, August 13: "No dependence can be placed in Ethan Allen or those associated with him in Vermont."

Whatever hidden course the General and his colleagues took, it fortified and stimulated them, gave them elbow room, abolished the pressure of their shoulders upon a wall, and offered a weapon against their thronging adversaries.

It is doubtful whether any of Vermont's statesmen ever intended actually to travel the dark passageway of treason that suddenly had been opened for them. It was a relief to them, though, to know that it was there.

Furthermore, if the rest of America could be made aware of that sinister exit, its mere presence would be valuable. Finally, negotiation with Britain might be used in defense of a frontier that, otherwise, was virtually without protection. The game was worth the danger involved. Vermont's leaders never lacked confidence in themselves.

Whatever native reluctance the Republic's government may have had to embark on correspondence with America's common enemy was weakened by an intensification of Vermont's old ailments this fall.

The Eastside was in rebellion once more. Dissenters who had boasted to their Vermont loyalist neighbors of the upstart Republic's impending doom when Congress finally began hearings on her case, were humiliated and then enraged by that body's failure to decide anything. Mounting wrath caused another kaleidoscopic shift in Eastside sentiment. The insurgent river towns, some of the supporters of New York —once extremely distasteful to each other—suddenly became allies. They were not certain, so far, exactly what demands they would make, but they were ready to screech for them.

External menace became critical, too. In October the British again came up Lake Champlain, a thousand troops and Indians in eight vessels under Major Carleton. Their prime military intention was to create a diversion for Sir John Johnson's raid into the Mohawk Valley; their secondary, to sear the Vermont frontier.

Panic swelled as the lightly held Forts George and Anne fell before the British advance. General Ethan Allen mobilized his army—it was less than three hundred men—and hurried north. Carleton's regulars kept to the west side of the lake, but a strong force of British-led Indians went up the Onion River Valley like a grass fire in a high wind.

The frontier people made small attempt at resistance. Their resolution had been sapped by previous raids. They fled headlong, after concealing their chief household treasures. Mrs. Ebenezer Eaton of Newbury, which the attack never reached, hid her silver spoons and her husband's shoe buckles so thoroughly that in all her long life she never found them again.

The raiders moved with a gathering herd of prisoners and horses in their center and a smoke-soiled horizon behind them. Houses were burned in Tunbridge and Randolph. Royalton was almost abolished. Twenty-one dwellings and sixteen barns went up in fire there. A hundred and fifty cattle were slaughtered with many sheep and hogs. Twenty-six persons and thirty horses were captured. The enemy were pursued with such deliberation by Colonel John House of Hanover that they escaped scot free, leaving the frontier blasted and all Vermont shaken by the heaviest attack—so far.

Knowledge that more and severer might follow that same fire-blackened way; realization—emphasized by this latest raid—that America had left Vermont in the forefront of the battle to bear alone the first shock of whatever British thrust might be launched, turned the government's attention to Generals Clinton and Haldimand's blandishments. The reeling little state's starkest need was time to recover its balance, temporary immunity from further British invasion.

Already, on September 27, Chittenden had written Haldimand, proposing a truce between the Republic and Canada for the exchange of prisoners. It is certain that negotiations proceeded thereafter with Ethan Allen as Vermont's chief representative, for on October 13 Carleton wrote Haldimand that a messenger to General Allen had been pursued and had been obliged to destroy his dispatches.

On October 29, Captain Sam Herrick, on outpost duty near Allen's headquarters at Castleton, notified his superior that Carleton, still lingering at Crown Point, had sent an officer under a flag of truce to arrange with the General a cartel for the exchange of prisoners. This officer, when he arrived at the farmhouse of Isaac Clark, where General Allen lodged, turned out to be Justus Sherwood, now an officer of Peter's loyalist rangers who had fought at Bennington, and a neighbor and friend of the Allens in the old Grants days.

The commander of Vermont's army had all ten of his field officers with him when Sherwood entered. Later, as one perhaps might with an old friend, General Allen and the British officer went for a walk together. During this, and a subsequent conference on the morrow, preliminary plans were made for the exchange of prisoners and for a truce, to be declared immediately.

Allen insisted that the New York territory along Lakes Champlain and George should be as immune as Vermont from attack. Sherwood sent a letter to Carleton at Crown Point by Isaac Clark. The commander of the British force agreed to the terms, and the war between the Republic of Vermont and Great Britain momentarily was over.

It was established by Allen and Sherwood that negotiations for the prisoners' exchange should be used as cover for further discussion of Vermont's possible return to the Crown. General Allen snorted a good deal and advanced numerous objections, but he was not wholly discouraging. When Sherwood had left, Allen disbanded Vermont's army and rode south to Bennington, to report openly to the legislature and more privately to Chittenden and his associates. He did not accomplish the first half of his task with noteworthy skill.

The General Assembly was relieved to learn of the end of what had promised to be an extinguishing invasion, but there were some of their number who harbored suspicions. Allen's report was not wholly convincing. He seemed to be holding back something. The whole thing smelled funny, and William Hutchins presented a remonstrance to the assembly demanding further inquiry.

Allen, with a fine show of indignation, resigned his general's commission and stormed from the meeting. Chief consequence of this display of rage was a supporting remonstrance presented by Simeon Hathaway. The legislature quashed both and soothed ex-General Allen's injured sensibilities by granting him and his associates the town of East Haven.

Vermonters, even then, had minds that, once they had been made up, were extremely difficult to unmake again. This fact weakens the theory that the state's leaders in their negotiations with Haldimand's representatives had any intention whatever of turning their land over to Britain. Those leaders themselves had led the people toward independence. By keeping just ahead of popular thought, they had made Vermont a republic.

Being Vermonters themselves, who understood their constituency, they must have known how fantastic it would have been to hope that they might be able to face these self-owning mountain folk about and return them to their old and never highly esteemed dependence on the Crown. The best cause for believing they knew such a feat was impossible is that they never tried it.

There was none of that propaganda in which Vermont was adept, urging the people toward such an end. There was, to be sure, a deal of sober-faced discussion with British agents concerning the steps that must be taken "to prepare the people" for reunion, but not one such step was attempted.

The furtive negotiations were essential to the safety of the Republic, and the more deliberately these could be conducted, the better. The longer the Vermont plotters could make Britain believe that they were yielding gradually to persuasion, the more time the state gained to set its internal affairs in order. Safety, while the conspiracy endured, was guaranteed the frontier. Finally, rumors of Vermont's intention to declare a separate peace disturbed and disorganized her enemies. These seem to be the chief reasons that the Republic's leaders dabbled so dexterously in treachery.

Already that dabbling had begun to pay dividends. Carleton's invading force still lingered at Ticonderoga and Crown Point, as inoffensively as a picnic party. It observed the terms of the truce which exempted the New York as well as the Vermont frontier from attack, but its placid deportment, the fact that the Vermont army had disbanded in the face of peril and had gone home to do its fall plowing, alarmed and bewildered General Schuyler, once more in command of the northern department. He wrote Governor Clinton of his fears. Vermont's conduct, the General said, was "alarming and mysterious."

General Ethan Allen, resigned, had been supplanted in the plot by less noisy, not to say less clumsy, men. Chittenden, with the legislature's sanction, appointed the persuasive Ira Allen and the quietly reliable Joseph Fay commissioners to deal with the British. Conscious, perhaps, of his own inadequacies as a conspirator, the erstwhile General withdrew for a space from the world and began to work over the agnostic script he and Dr. Young had half completed in their youth. Plotting against Jehovah had comforting securities that the current conspiracy did not afford. Allen was quite willing to leave that in the hands of his brother and Fay.

These journeyed to East Bay and there, on November 9, met the British agents, Sherwood and Dr. George Smyth, a Tory physician who had fled from Albany. The details of the cartel were established in an atmosphere of extreme wariness. Haldimand had warned his representatives to be careful "in view of the sad fate of Major André," and the Vermonters made no advances. They were quite willing to protract the negotiations and agreed to come to Canada during the winter and confer directly with Haldimand.

The conference ended in mutual distrust. Sherwood and Smyth went back to Carleton, who sailed down the lake with his whole command just before the ice of an early and unusually bitter winter closed the waterways. The Vermont agents went home, well satisfied. They had bought their state, at no expense except half-promises, immunity until next spring.

The agents did not go to Canada. From the first, they probably had had no intention of going. Chittenden wrote Haldimand explaining that their failure to attend him at once was caused by the early ice. Even the weather, it seemed, worked to aid Vermont.

Interior conditions, however, were not favorable to the Republic; and the services of Ira Allen, the trouble-shooter of the Vermont government, were needed at home in a variety of crises. On the Eastside, the river towns with their new allies who recently had been Yorkers, had found themselves a new and surprising objective.

These whimsical but vociferous persons now had decided that they wanted neither a New York nor a New Hampshire alliance, but a new state all their own, composed of Vermont east of the Green Mountains and as much of New Hampshire as they could bite off and digest.

A convention was to assemble at Charlestown early in January, 1781, to vote on this project or any better cause for disturbance that could be thought up in the meantime. Vermont's government was worried by the new insurgence, but it did not immediately interfere, having learned how much of the Eastside's sedition boiled itself away if left alone.

The trouble still threatening Vermont from so many quarters would have kept lesser men on the defensive. The Republic's government followed another strategy. With its hand already more than adequately full of problems, it moved now to create more—to remind a nation, which for the present would have been quite willing to overlook the fact, that Vermont still was truculently and provocatively defending its claims.

Chittenden wrote with bland presumption to governors of the New England states, suggesting that they unite with Vermont in the common defense and also proposing that New Hampshire and Massachusetts relinquish their pretentions to Vermont territory. New Hampshire ignored this barefaced plea, but it had its effect in Massachusetts. The General Court voted to abandon claim to land within the Republic when and if Congress granted Vermont statehood.

Chittenden also wrote to Governor Clinton, with less respect and more vigor, making "a positive demand" that New York "give up and fully relinquish their claim to jurisdiction over this state." As a reward for this, the letter offered "solid union" to protect the northern frontier, beyond which Haldimand still waited patiently for the envoys who did not come. When Clinton got his breath back again, he turned the peremptory missive over to the New York legislature with the comment that it was "insolent in its nature and derogatory to the honor of this state."

The trapeze was swinging high, wide, and free, and the inexperienced performers were accomplishing the most daring feats thereon. Chittenden, who seems to have spent much of this winter at his desk, wrote again to Haldimand, attributing the nonappearance of the Vermont agents to heavy snows. The Republic's government was so busy at the engaging task of pestering its neighbors that it turned its attention to the convention of the Eastside's disaffected barely in time.

Delegates from forty-three towns east of the Green Mountains and west of interior New Hampshire met at Charlestown on January 16. It was a larger group than Vermont had dreamed would assemble, and the Republic's leaders were caught napping. Ira Allen was sent off hastily from Bennington to attend, but by the time he arrived, the harm already had been done.

The convention had turned from the purpose of establishing a separate state, for which originally it had been called. Before the Vermont government's agent, frosted and weary, reached Charlestown, the delegates had voted by a heavy majority to join the entire Eastside to New Hampshire.

The thing was done; the fat was in the fire. To an ambassador less resourceful, to an official with less understanding of his own people's minds, to a man with smaller courage than Ira Allen, the situation would have seemed hopeless. At the least, the convention's action would mean civil war on the Eastside; at most, it might wreak the downfall of the Vermont Republic.

Enemies grinned at the stocky little man and told him he had come too late. Stub Allen's large brown eyes blinked beneath their derision, but his firm mouth tightened. No one knows precisely what he did. He vanished like a diving seal. All night he worked, hand on elbow and mouth to ear, wheedling, persuading, promising. If his enemies had esteemed him at his true worth, they might have watched him more carefully, and the details of his activity might not now be so wholly hidden.

Only their consequence is plain. Ira Allen attended the session of the convention on the morrow. His face was haggard, and his eyes seemed still larger for the darkness about them; but his mouth, recently so tight, was softened by a half-smile.

When the convention completely reversed itself, when the delegates who had voted half of Vermont into New Hampshire the day before, swapped ends and voted it back into Vermont again, thirty-two to twelve, the small, half-smiling mouth stretched itself into a grin. Ira Allen had done the impossible again, but to this day no one knows how he did it.

To perform his miracle, he had had to make some concessions. He had had to promise the delegates from the New Hampshire river towns that Vermont, which had accepted them once only to cast them out at Congress's order, would take them back permanently into the Republic now.

He had no illusions concerning the consequences of this pledge. New Hampshire, he knew, would rage over the deprivation; Congress would threaten. Ira Allen and the government he represented doubted whether either protestant would do more. If the Canadian conspiracy could be made to endure, it would not dare.

The inexperienced trapeze acrobats were floating through the air with the greatest of ease behind which lay clear purpose. Vermont, if it was to survive, must use its only available weapons—the threat of a separate peace; its native gift for creating infinite disturbances.

By one or both of these it must enrage, then frighten, and at last weary its enemies, wearing them down to the point of acquiescence at which they might say: "For God's sake, let her be a state, and then maybe we'll get some peace." No other course was apparent to resourceful and uninhibited statesmen. They prepared to follow it more vigorously henceforth.

Already this policy of apparently suicidal recklessness showed signs of bearing surprisingly precocious fruit. New York the implacable, New York the ancient and obstinate enemy, suddenly indicated that she had had enough, that she was weary of the whole enduring mess and willing to quit.

Clinton had presented Chittenden's "insolent" letter to the February, 1781, session of the New York legislature, apparently believing this body would echo his own scorn and indignation. Amazingly, the New York Senate was of a wholly different mind. Talk of a Vermont alliance with Canada was disturbing all the nation, and no other state quite as much as New York, which would be a chief sufferer from such a separate peace.

The Senate resolved, with but one dissenting vote, that commissioners be appointed to confer with representatives of Vermont to effect a relinquishment of all New York's claims upon the Republic's territory. It is questionable whether tidings of this action surprised Chittenden or Clinton more, but the New York governor's astonishment was no whit agreeable. The grudge he had acquired against Vermont had grown steadily. He had no intention of relinquishing it, unappeased.

Clinton recovered from his shocked amazement in time to check the assembly, which was beginning favorable consideration of the Senate resolution. He demanded that the project immediately be dropped. Otherwise, he swore, he would prorogue the legislature. It was to be ten more years, thanks to Clinton, before the settlement move could be revived and accomplished.

Already events were marching that would cause New York's governor, secretly, to doubt his own good judgment. Vermont, having offended New Hampshire as much as possible, now turned her attention to the possibility of wreaking similar indignity and deprivation on New York.

The towns beyond the Republic's vague western boundary had no reason to be loyal to their parent state. They had been scared stiff by Carleton's advance and New York's failure to defend them. Only the truce that Vermont had established with Haldimand protected them now from Canadian attack. Their militia were unpaid, unfed. The disaffected settlements had more cause to be grateful to their eastern neighbor than to New York. Vermont prepared to absorb them, too.

There was a twofold purpose behind this intention. Usurpation of New York territory would produce another of the national spasms to the creation of which Vermont's leaders had dedicated themselves. Furthermore, the New York towns were needed to re-establish equilibrium within the Republic. The admission of the New Hampshire towns would fortify the Eastside. The Westside needed additions to keep the balance of power more level, so Vermont prepared to get them. If the United States should move to punish these larcenies, spring was coming and the secret weapon of the conspiracy would again be in the Republic's hand.

Tidings of that conspiracy had buzzed in many ears all this winter. If Ethan Allen had not been originally concerned therein, the plot might not have been so widely advertised. The Philosopher, as he had begun to call himself, was not geared to deal unostentatiously with anything, particularly so delicate and devious a matter.

Philosopher Allen must have talked too much—it was one of his failings—and reports of what he had said reached the ears of Seth Warner, still ailing in Bennington, who shook off his illness sufficiently to pay Cousin Ethan an unheralded visit at Sunderland.

Warner was still an officer in the Continental Army with a soldier's creed of loyalty, and his fondness for his kinsman never had been overwhelming. He spoke forcefully of treason and gallows and other uncomfortable matters and left his cousin half-converted and wholly uneasy.

Allen's anxiety was the more extreme because, just before Cousin Seth's visit, he had received a second letter from Beverly Robinson, Clinton's agent, enclosing a copy of his first communication and urging an immediate and favorable answer. Since all of the Philosopher's negotiations had been with Haldimand's and not Clinton's emissary, he could feel half innocent, and he proceeded to display this unsullied portion of himself to the world in general and Congress in particular.

Both Robinson letters were sent to Samuel Huntington, President of Congress, with a covering missive in Allen's best style. In this he atoned for the defensiveness of his action by the extreme offensiveness of his periods.

Philosopher Allen inveighed scathingly against the refusal of Congress to give Vermont her due, assailed the "exorbitant claims and avaricious designs" of the hostile states, and, having worked himself quite thoroughly into a frenzy of self-righteousness and indignation, upheld the authority of the Republic to make a separate peace with Great Britain if it so chose. He ended:

I am as resolutely determined to defend the independence of Vermont as Congress is that of the United States and rather than fail will retire with hardy Green Mountain Boys into the desolate caverns of the mountains and wage war with humanity at large.

This resonant self-absolution no doubt pleased its author, and probably Vermont as well, which wished a certain amount of publicity to accompany its plotting. It can have had small influence in abating Congress's suspicions toward Allen, and it wholly disqualified him from any further share in the conspiracy, the British thereafter not unnaturally regarding him in the light of a squealer.

Allen presented copies of Robinson's and his own letters to the April session of the Vermont legislature, which voted him confidence and wanted to make him a brigadier general all over again. He refused the appointment, and Chittenden sent him into eastern New York, feeling that his peculiar talents would be of more use in that disaffected district than nearer at hand with the conspiracy about to get under way again.

This same session of the legislature admitted thirty-four recently New Hampshire towns into the Republic and received several petitions for inclusion from New York settlements. These were advised to hold a convention and make preparations for incorporation in Vermont. The Republic would need the threat of an alliance with Britain if she was going to accomplish her purposes, but the negotiations for which she hoped seemed slow in starting.

Ethan Allen's defiant confession had not expedited matters. His was not the only disclosure. No conspiracy ever was more fully supplied with leaks. On February 11, Germaine, who had made the plot his hobby, wrote to General Clinton, speaking as though the Vermont alliance practically had been accomplished and discussing a plan of campaign with Haldimand, Clinton, and the Vermont forces in association. The ship bearing a copy of this letter to Haldimand was captured by a French frigate.

Germaine's missive was forwarded to Paris, where it was handed over to the American Minister, Benjamin Franklin, who sent it to the American Congress, thereby unwittingly advancing Vermont's cause.

Haldimand, at this time, appears to have become disgusted with the whole affair, for he wrote to Germaine, "Ethan Allen is endeavoring to deceive both the Congress and us," a statement that confirms the intelligence of Canada's governor general. He might have pursued the conspiracy no further if the colonial secretary had not kept prodding him with urgent letters. As it was, the British and Vermont commissioners, assembling ostensibly to perfect plans for the interchange of prisoners, did not meet until May 9.

Isaac Clark, Chittenden's son-in-law, and Ira Allen had been appointed Vermont's agents; but Clark pled, either sincerely or out of the wish to establish an alibi, that his family was ill. His colleague went in state to the trysting place, escorted by Lieutenant Simeon Lyman, two sergeants, and sixteen privates of the Vermont army.

British boats rowed them to Isle aux Noix, just beyond Lake Champlain's outlet in the Richelieu River, where the British commissioners—Major Dundas, the post commandant, and Justus Sherwood—greeted Commissioner Allen and the solemn, rawboned men of his escort.

This was to be a dauntingly unfamiliar task for the sturdy and suave little man. Treason itself is hard enough successfully to accomplish. To pretend to yield to treachery and at the same time to hoodwink the would-be seducers is still more difficult. These agents were not the men whom Ira Allen best understood, not the angular mountain folk whose hard-headedness he so persuasively could soften.

Sherwood and Major Dundas were intelligent, world-wise, and extremely suspicious—thanks to Ethan Allen's disclosure—in the bargain. They would be hard to deceive. Ira Allen set about the job with a guileless air. By instinct or intellect, he had resolved on his course. He could best disarm his accomplices by being as reluctant as possible about the whole affair.

This he proceeded to be, but there must have been many moments on the pleasant island, with Champlain's overflow sliding by on either hand, when Commissioner Allen felt that the foundations of the Vermont Republic were likewise slipping away; when he must have endured the uncomfortable sensation of a hempen band about his neck and a knot pressing just behind his ear.

Progress of the negotiations is told only in the letters Sherwood sent back to Captain Mathews, General Haldimand's military secretary.

For the sake of appearances and to satisfy the overintrusive curiosity of Lieutenant Simeon Lyman, debate on the exchange of the prisoners was held in public, but between sessions Sherwood and Allen took long walks together during which the actual business of the conference was discussed and the patience of the British agent endured much wear and tear. He discovered at once that here was no eager plotter but a most exasperating person, wary, sinuously evasive, ingenuous of eye, but tough of mind.

Haldimand's and Sherwood's suspicions had been thoroughly roused. They had prepared to drive a hard bargain with the brother of the perfidious Ethan Allen. Now Sherwood found to his dismay that he must abandon his disdainful pose. Instead he must beg and plead with a most irritatingly unwilling person. He had to sell the idea of treason all over again to Vermont's representative, and in the ardor of his salesmanship he forgot his qualms.

Sherwood's letters trace the course of the indirect conversion which Ira Allen gradually accomplished. Their recurrent theme is complaint at a delay almost unendurably protracted by endless quibbling.

From the first, Sherwood found Allen "very cautious and intricate." At times he also could be truculent, for when they discussed the terms under which Vermont might return to the Crown, Sherwood reported that Allen said they would have a free state, without any royal governor, or else "they would return to the mountains, turn savages, and fight the devil, hell and all human nature at large"—an admiring brother's variation of Ethan's own defiance to Congress.

Sherwood complained that all his efforts to bring about an immediate alliance were thwarted by his antagonist's insistence on delay, "the people not being ready for such a change." Before the obstinate verbal struggle hoodwinked the British agent, he had at least one flash of insight.

> My opinion [he wrote on May 11] corroborates with the Major's [Dundas's] that Mr. Allen's errand here is to prolong the time and if possible to alarm Congress into a compliance with their demands.

It might have been better for his own reputation and Britain's cause if he had ended the negotiations with that most accurate statement. Later, Sherwood wailed:

> He gives reasons which he refuses to sign and then writes them himself but still refuses to sign.

He reported, a little distractedly, that he accused Allen of dawdling deliberately and that the other's reply was "of a defiant character." Vermont's representative "sometimes induces contempt and always suspicion" and was turning the negotiations into "a shuffling business."

Allen's evasiveness was not the only burden Sherwood had to bear.

The perpetually inquisitive Lieutenant Lyman was a sore trial, "a downright, illiterate, zealous-pated yanky," who "has just enough breeding to listen or look over a man's shoulder when he is writing," which Lieutenant Lyman may have been doing when Sherwood set down that scathing line.

Allen, apparently grown weary of pestering and confusing the earnest Sherwood, now demanded that he have a personal interview with Haldimand himself. When this was refused him, he wrote the Governor General in what the letter's recipient thought were "abstruse terms." Haldimand's reply was sent by his adjutant, Major Lernoult, who told Allen that Vermont must either rejoin Great Britain "or continue at enmity with it." Lernoult also brought the Governor General's ironic apology for answering Allen's letter orally. He explained that Haldimand did not care to have his communications read aloud in Congress.

Perhaps in reprisal for that slap, Allen let the British commissioner suffer a little longer. May 20, Sherwood wrote that his opponent was still pursuing "the same equivocal and tedious line" and "says many plausible things but nothing to the point."

Five days then intervened, and at some time in the course of these the British agent must have felt a thrill of triumph and the Vermont a hidden spasm of amusement. Ira Allen abandoned his objections and doubts—they must have begun to irk even himself—and agreed, incredibly, with Sherwood. In the exaltation of this achievement, Haldimand's deputy seems to have cast his last suspicion away.

> From every appearance [he informed his chief] I believe Allen would gladly bring back the people to Government if he could.

Now that this conviction had been established in Sherwood's mind, final agreement was made. It had to be verbal. Allen still refused to sign anything.

Hostilities were to be suspended until after the next meeting of the legislature—longer than that if Haldimand deemed it wise. At this imminent session, an attempt would be made to appoint commissioners who would conclude a formal alliance between Vermont and Great Britain.

The Vermont authorities were to make every effort "to prepare the people" for reunion. Messages to the conspirators—Chittenden, the Allens, Timothy Brownson, Jonas Fay, John Fassett, and Matthew Lyon were named—were to be forwarded from Haldimand by a trustworthy messenger and in a form for immediate swallowing if necessary.

The long contest of wits was over. Ira Allen had obtained essentials for the government of Vermont—time, immunity from British attack, a weapon with which to threaten American aggressors—and had paid for them with only more empty promises. He had completely overcome the original hostilities and suspicions of an extremely intelligent man.

Sherwood's keenness had not wholly deserted him even now. He wrote to Captain Mathews his belief that the Vermont leaders would work for reunion "from interest, not from loyalty." This much insight remained, but Allen had blinded him to the more important fact that those leaders actually had no intention of working for Great Britain at all.

Ira Allen, Lieutenant Lyman the zealous-pated, and the rest of the escort left Isle aux Noix, May 25, well supplied for the return journey by Major Dundas. The Vermont commissioner, working alone, had deftly misled Haldimand and all his subordinates. Now he faced the task of hiding the pretended treason from his fellow countrymen at large and shortly was to learn—if he already did not know—that this would be the most difficult part of his mission. The level-eyed, straight-thinking mountain men were not easily bewildered even by the complex acrobatics of their republic's most daring young man on the flying trapeze.

XVI "Turbulent Sons of Freedom"

HILLS WERE a dozen shades of green; the unlocked brooks ran full; suns were kind and ox-drawn plows spread ridged brown rugs across the new-made fields as Ira Allen rode back from Isle aux Noix. Something more than springtime's spell elated him. He was never a man who found it hard to please himself, and he now had great warrant for complacency. He might have been a shade less satisfied had he known that a spy, detailed by Sherwood and Dundas, followed him at a distance to watch and report his actions.

Farmers hailed Stub Allen. They begged for news from the north, and the Commissioner told them importantly that they need have no fear. Though Vermont's army might not guard the frontier this summer, there would be no war out of Canada. Not disbelief but doubt troubled cool eyes that watched the horsemen through the clearings and into the forest again. No war, eh? Haow'd he git to be so plagued sartin? Heered he was cookin' up somethin' with the goddam British. Mebby 'twas true, b' God. Seem's 'if, anyways.

The mixed relief and perturbation Allen left behind him was parcel of the bewilderment that troubled the whole Republic that May. Men were aware that there had been communication with the Canadian authorities. Questioners had been told that it was merely a negotiation for the exchange of prisoners. Hmm! Mebby!

None of this general uneasiness affected Ira Allen's spirit. He was riding home in triumph from victory. He was bringing to hard-pressed Vermont what she needed most sorely—the pledge of temporary immunity from attack by Britain, a promise of time in which she might deal with her domestic enemies.

The republic to which he bore these essentials was larger than when Allen had left it, if still less stable. A shock, a spark—and Vermont's environment was profusely supplied with both—might set off detonation that would blow the state and its government into fragments too small for identification.

With its high resolution to be as offensive as possible under all circumstances, the little nation had embarked on fresh affront. Surrounded by earnest ill-wishers, it had done its best to increase their malevolence. Hitherto, it had tramped joyously on New Hampshire's toes and appropriated her river towns. Since Allen had ridden north to Isle aux Noix, Vermont had faced about, heedless of New Hampshire's yells of deprivation, had kicked New York severely in the shins, and now was about to kidnap a number of her communities.

On May 9, the day Ira Allen had arrived at Isle aux Noix, infatuated New York towns had assembled in convention at Cambridge and had voted that the district they represented—the land lying between the Republic's present west frontier on one side and the Hudson River and the lakes on the other—should be considered thereafter part of Vermont and that application immediately should be made for inclusion.

Already the protests of New York and New Hampshire were tremendous, but so far entirely vocal. Reports of their nefarious neighbor's intrigue with Canada postponed physical reprisal. It would be better to wait; it would be wiser to find out just what Vermont was up to before resisting by arms her current whim for larceny.

Such doubts and perturbations drew more than the ordinary number of spectators to Bennington when the legislature began its June session there. Vermont not only was to answer the New York insurgents' request for union; it also was to hear Ira Allen's report on the Canadian prisoner-exchanging negotiations. The Commissioner was gratified to note on opening day that the gallery of the meetinghouse where the sessions were to be held was packed with "gentlemen of discernment" from other states. He also was aware that among these attentive strangers were several British agents, sent by the not too wholly trustful Haldimand.

New York's seceding towns were voted into the Republic of Vermont, and thereafter the assembly formed itself into a committee of the whole to learn of Allen's mission. Tough-minded representatives listened warily while Governor Chittenden with his most guileless expression drawled through a preliminary explanation.

When the governor ended there was less of approval than suspicion on the faces of his auditors. Someone asked in a dry voice whether the British had made a like arrangement for exchange of prisoners with any other state, and Chittenden admitted that they had not, as far as he knew.

Hmm! Toil-hardened, tanned men cleared their throats and looked at nothing in particular, narrow-eyed. Something was wrong. They could sense it but they couldn't point a finger at it. They watched Ira Allen, when he rose to report, rather as though he were a prisoner at the bar instead of a triumphantly returning ambassador.

The weathered faces of his audience were not wholly cordial. They belonged to plain men with a plain purpose. These folk had caught hold of an ideal and they were clinging to it with Vermont pertinacity, beside which the bulldog's or the snapping turtle's application seems frivolous.

Freedom, to these hard-bitten folk, was a word of blinding intensity, hiding from its addicts whatever material benefit might lie in compromise. They cherished it even more ardently than they clove to the land of their winning. Freedom forbade freemen even to consider alliance with the British. Subterfuge, evasion, pretense, belonged to more accomplished persons. They were no part of the ordinary Vermonter's equipment.

The legislature was, in its native tongue, "all haired up." The British invitation to treason still was to most of its members only the vaguest and wildest of rumors, but they were determined to smoke out whatever sinister thing might be in hiding and then to stamp upon it.

Commissioner Allen, facing his carefully observant fellow countrymen, was not wholly at ease. An audience, and the larger the better, inspired Brother Ethan. Ira was most effective with only two or three close beside him. Now, with many hard eyes watching and spies from Canada taking notes, he merely elaborated, tritely, on Chittenden's statement. When he had ended, questions boxed his ears.

Didn't he have no papers to show what was done at Isle aux Noix? Wal, whar was they, then? What did he leave 'em home for? Couldn't he git 'em? Would he bring 'em tomorrow and read 'em aout to the meetin'?

Allen promised, appeared next day with what documents it seemed fitting that the legislature should hear, read them, and asked for questions. His bland manner, the easy brevity of his responses dispelled the lurking hostility. On the face of things, it appeared that Vermont had won a diplomatic victory. Allen wrote, long afterward, probably with a shadow of the smug smile his mouth must have borne that day:

All seemed satisfied that nothing had been done inconsistent to the interest of the States and those who were in the interest of the

United States paid their compliments to Colonel Allen for his open and candid conduct. In the evening he had a conference with the Canadian spectators on the business of the day and they appeared to be as well satisfied as those from the neighboring states and Vermont. It is not curious to see opposing parties perfectly satisfied with one statement, and each believing what they wished to believe and thereby deceiving themselves.

Again, he was thoroughly pleased with himself. He was granted that privilege more often and more deservedly than most men.

The legislature emphasized its restored trust by naming Allen with Jonas Fay and Bezaleel Woodward ambassadors to the United States. They were to appear before Congress and artlessly request the admission into the Union of a predatory republic considerably enlarged on either side by territory lately wrested from its neighboring states.

The ordeal of his appearance before the vigilant legislators, or perhaps a concern for the safety of his own neck, or even a not unnatural dread that eventually he might hang in solitary state, impelled Ira Allen to acquire from his accomplices an odd declaration absolving him of everything save merely technical treason.

This document, which was signed by Chittenden, Joseph and Jonas Fay, Samuel Safford, Samuel and Moses Robinson, Timothy Brownson, and John Fassett, set forth that Allen "had used his best policy by feigning or endeavoring to make them [the British] believe that the State of Vermont had a desire to negotiate a treaty of peace with Great Britain—thereby to prevent the immediate invasion or incursion upon the frontiers of this state."

It concluded: "We are of the opinion that the critical circumstances this State is in, being out of the Union with the United States and thereby unable to make that vigorous defense we could wish for—think it to be a necessary political maneuver to save the frontiers of this state."

In other words, no matter what Ira Allen agreed to in his negotiations with the British, his associates insisted he didn't mean a single syllable.

Nevertheless, he was in constant communication with Canada. At his and Ethan's house in Sunderland, messengers came and went all summer long. Haldimand was prosecuting the plot with German thoroughness. His persistence interfered with whatever rest Allen might have taken after his arduous mission. There always were fresh letters to write, urging delay, sparring for time, swearing that the people were being prepared, predicting a large separate peace delegation in the next legislature.

This reiteration of pledges never quite stilled Haldimand's worthy suspicions, but they nearly addled at times his methodical mind. On July 27, Captain Mathews, his military secretary, sent one of Allen's dispatches to Sherwood with the following harried plea:

His Excellency desires that you and Dr. Smyth will peruse Allen's letter with the utmost attention and compare its extraordinary composition of perhaps Truth, Falsehood, Candour and Deceit with the different intelligence you have received, it is perfectly honest or perfectly Jesuitical and His Excellency is at a loss what to think of it.

Absolution for this correspondence also was issued in another document, signed by all those who had endorsed Allen's previous exculpation, save Safford and Moses Robinson, who felt that this batting back and forth of communications with the enemy might be leading them all, step by step, toward the gallows.

There were other matters besides this progress to distract the minds of Vermont's government. Foremost of these was a shortage of British prisoners within the Republic. How were negotiations for exchange to be consummated without an adequate supply of captives? Actually, Vermont had taken four times the number of her own men now held in Canada, but these had been turned over to the Continental authorities, and Washington, when appealed to now, wouldn't give them back. He and the United States were regarding the Canadian flirtation with anxiety and disapproval.

So intense did Washington's worry grow, since the movement of his army toward Yorktown already was in his mind, that he appointed John Stark to the command of all the militia forces in northern New York, hoping that memory of the Bennington battle would lead Vermonters to co-operate with their old leader. The Father of His Country was no more than just barely hopeful, and Stark, who knew the mountain people better than he, was downright pessimistic. He wrote Washington:

Not having seen or been acquainted with these turbulent sons of freedom for several years, I am at a loss to determine my reception.

It turned out something less than cordial.

Meanwhile, the deal with Canada was at a standstill, where Vermont was far more willing than Haldimand to let it remain. None of the promises made at the Isle aux Noix conference had been fulfilled, and Ira Allen waded deeper and deeper into pseudo-treasonable correspondence in explanation of the Republic's inertia. He could not abolish the suspicions of the British authorities, but he did succeed in keeping these from overflowing into action. Pen, paper, and a bottle of ink, plus the plausibility of Commissioner Allen, defended the Vermont border from attack that summer.

There were a number of things that Allen had to rationalize as glibly and convincingly as possible. Vermont's British prisoners—what there were of them—were being exchanged with immense deliberation. The legislature had adjourned without even mentioning a treaty with Canada. No perceptible effort was being made to "prepare the people" for an alliance with Great Britain.

Haldimand, so far, had gained nothing whatever by negotiation save a heavy increase in his correspondence. There was no actual evidence, save Allen's assurances, that the conspiracy was progressing at all.

"Things must be kept under the rose," one of the plausible Commissioner's letters warned, "until after the new election when in all probability a large majority of the officers of the Government will be well disposed."

Haldimand had to content himself with this promise, plus Allen's agreement to meet the British agents under a flag of truce not later than July 20. When he did not appear on that day but merely sent a letter, pleading that he was unavoidably detained, Haldimand still kept his temper. He was a most patient and persevering man. Concerning Allen's excuse, he wrote to General Clinton:

> It is fraught with much sincerity or much duplicity, the latter I fear is the real sense of it, which I am more inclined to think from his not coming with the flag.

Meanwhile, on the undisturbed frontier farms, hay barns were full. Corn stood high and wheat was ripening. Cattle grazed unthreatened. Men who otherwise might have been serving with the militia worked all day long in their fields.

To atone for Allen's absence, to explain the increasingly tardy exchange of prisoners, and to keep Haldimand's indignation below the bursting point, Joseph Fay went late in July to meet the British commissioners. He was received on H. M. S. *Royal George*, which lay off

Dutchman's Point in Champlain, with no discernible heartiness and more than a hint of suspicion.

Fay, notwithstanding the inhospitable atmosphere, stayed a long while. It took him two whole weeks to explain to his own and his chilly hosts' satisfaction why all the British prisoners were not immediately forthcoming, and even then he was not wholly convincing, for Captain Chambers, one of the British commissioners, wrote Haldimand his belief that all this delay by Vermont was deliberate and was employed so that farmers might "get in their harvest in peace while we reap no kind of benefit."

Before Fay exhausted procrastination and started back home, he promised that Vermont's agents would meet with the British immediately after the state election—at which Allen had predicted there would be a swing of sentiment toward a separate peace—and draw up final plans for reunion with Britain. Resourceful as the Republic's plotters were, they were being worked gradually into a corner from which there seemed no escape.

Despite the irksome length of his visit, Fay appears to have assuaged some of the suspicion which he had sensed on arrival, for after his departure Sherwood wrote to Haldimand:

> Major Fay took his leave with as much apparent satisfaction and sincerity as Colonel Allen had done before him and left us as much in the dark.

If Sherwood was bewildered, General Sir Frederick Haldimand, who knew less about Vermonters, was even more at sea. None of the British negotiators, small or great, ever fathomed the mountaineer plotters' tactics. It was beyond European comprehension that backwoods farmers should have such great devotion to their republic and a calm audacity that would inspire them to shove their heads through a noose so that their spent nation might gain a breathing space and a weapon to use, however briefly, against its other enemies.

Canada's governor general continually wavered between skepticism inspired by Vermont's dawdling, and credulity born of an underestimate of Vermonters' acting ability. He informed Germaine: "The real intention of these people is to get better terms from Congress, but there may yet be hope of success," and at almost the same time wrote Clinton: "Considering the uniformity of Ira Allen's conduct, he must be the most accomplished villain living if he means to deceive us."

Deception was only one of the useful qualities the Vermont Republic trouble-shooter was called upon to display this summer. He not only had to go on bewildering Haldimand, but he had also to deal with Congress, which again was uttering sounds of hollow menace.

Chittenden, on July 18, formally admitted the New York towns into the Republic. Governor Clinton's roars of outrage were dutifully echoed by the deprived state's delegates at Philadelphia. They blended with the bereaved utterances of New Hampshire and together composed such a racket that Congress no longer could pretend to pay no attention.

Whatever weak determination that body may have cherished for adjudicating the continually more scrambled mess was blighted at this time by tidings from overseas. For the unnumbered time, fortune once more served Vermont.

While Congress was swelling portentously with what wrath it could muster, a dispatch came from Dr. Franklin in Paris. This enclosed the letter that had been captured by the French, wherein Germaine had written to Sir Henry Clinton of the favorable prospect for an alliance with Vermont. Lord George's screed was read aloud in Philadelphia, July 31.

There were, of course, cries of "Treason!" and demands that the perfidious Republic be punished, but sober second thought questioned the wisdom of stern action. If a punitive hand were to be raised against the miscreants, would not the gesture throw Vermont into an open union with Britain? Then bang would go the northern frontier. Quite possibly, with a louder detonation, bang would go the United States.

Congress took thought. Congress discovered that it was in reality occupying no lofty judgment seat. More accurately, the small Republic, so long despised and rejected, had Congress over a barrel. There was only one thing to do while these Canadian negotiations still hung fire —temporize, compromise with Vermont.

"There is no question," James Madison wrote to Edmund Pendleton at this time, "but that they will soon be established into a separate and Federal state."

Congress, its austere judicial air somewhat marred by revulsive gulps and shudderings, appointed a committee to confer with the representatives of Vermont—Ira Allen, Bezaleel Woodward, Jonas Fay—"respecting their claims to be an independent state."

Since, however, it was unbefitting the dignity of the Government of the United States to appear as an accessory after the fact, it also was resolved that Vermont must give back the purloined precincts of New Hampshire and New York before she could even be considered an applicant for admission to the Union.

Thereby, and unwittingly, Congress placed Vermont's emissaries on a most uncomfortable and dangerous spot. No one was sooner aware of it than Ira Allen and Jonas Fay, who were both ambassadors and conspirators. They had a bear by the tail, and they knew it.

Submission, relinquishment of the New York and New Hampshire territory for nothing more substantial than a Congressional promise, would weaken and imperil Vermont and bring down Haldimand's wrath and his army as well. Retention of the disputed towns would bar the Republic from statehood. The situation was even more tangled than that. If Vermont let go of New Hampshire's and New York's property before she became a state, she relinquished the lever with which she might pry her way into the Union, and implicitly terminated, by her obedience to American authority, the British conspiracy.

Not even so patient a man as Haldimand would continue to extend a truce after such submission. Allen and Fay, backed by the uncomprehending Woodward, who had no wish to see the New Hampshire towns surrendered, wriggled away from both horns of the dilemma by assuming a high and mighty air. They sounded warlike, but actually their purpose was to hold fast, by further delay, to immunity from British attack.

Wherefore, they professed a possibly not wholly unjustifiable suspicion of Congress's sincerity and announced themselves reluctant to let go of the new territory Vermont had absorbed until after the Republic had become the fourteenth state. They professed a great Yankee unwillingness to give something for nothing. Thereafter, they went home with a fine display of indignation, leaving Congress blinking and irresolute.

Their defiance supported Haldimand's dwindling belief in the conspirators' candor, but his durable patience was wearing out. The better part of a year had elapsed, during which the Canadian authorities and the British army in Canada had observed a truce that had won for them so far only an enormous number of letters and a few returned prisoners. If diplomacy could not hasten the reluctant Republic into an alliance, Haldimand was going to see what an invasion might do.

Ira Allen, arriving home from his defiance of Congress, was teamed with Joseph Fay, and both were hurried off to Skenesboro to try by further talk to wring more delay from the British commissioners, Sherwood and Smyth. A mere six weeks would be enough. By then winter would have closed in, and the attack from Canada would have to wait until another spring.

There was a sense of crisis in the air. Washington's army was marching south toward the Chesapeake, and Haldimand was at last demanding action from Vermont, not just another set of promises and explanations. His representatives were brisk and blunt.

The British conspirators, from Lord George Germaine down, had been most considerate and patient. Henceforth, they would be neither. They had waited for Vermont's leaders "to prepare the people"; for peace commissioners who never had been appointed; for the election which was to fill the legislature with pro-Britishers; for this, that, and the other event; and so far nothing had happened.

The dilatory Republic now had a final choice. When the General Assembly met in October, it could transform itself into a separate Crown colony, with its own legislature and a governor appointed by the King, or else it immediately would be considered an enemy to His Most Gracious Majesty and his Canadian army.

To hurry on a decision, Colonel Barry St. Leger with a fleet and two thousand troops was to come up the lake at the time the General Assembly met. If the Vermont authorities issued a proclamation adhering to Great Britain, St. Leger's guns would thunder for that happy event; if they didn't, it would not be salutes the Colonel would fire.

That, Smyth and Sherwood told the Vermont agents, was the situation; and they hoped it satisfied Messrs. Allen and Fay. If the British commissioners expected dismay, they were disappointed. Ira's impressive eyes were clouded by thought, but his face otherwise was impassive. He had just one suggestion to make. No, no indeed; it had nothing to do with further delay. He simply wanted to propose that General Haldimand himself issue the proclamation. It would have better effect.

Here, Allen told his wary antagonists, was the point: The legislature immediately after it convened would consider Congress's demand that the New York and New Hampshire territory be surrendered. The body would reject this with indignation and then, while that indignation was high, let Canada's governor general proclaim that a welcome awaited Vermont in the British fold. That would be bound to have a most favorable reception.

Ira Allen was lying, and he and Fay knew it; but Sherwood and

Smyth did not. Vermont's agents were still scrabbling for time. It was just remotely possible that answer to a proclamation by Haldimand might be delayed long enough for some yet-undiscerned event to rescue the Republic. Furthermore, if the proposal came from the Governor General, there was less prospect of Allen and Fay and all their associates hanging than if they had issued it themselves.

The British agents conferred and agreed, pending Haldimand's approval. Fay and Allen were most helpful. They even outlined the form they thought the proclamation should take, the better to impress the people. Their hearty co-operation, which must have been supplied while they themselves were faintly nauseated by the prospect of imminent disaster, completely abolished Smyth's and Sherwood's suspicions. The latter wrote Haldimand:

> I am fully of the opinion that Messrs. Chittenden, Allen and Fay with a number of the leading men of Vermont are making every exertion in their power to endeavor to bring about a reunion with Government.

This endorsement reassured the Governor General, and he consented to Allen's amendment and promised to issue the proclamation himself at the appointed time. He had no intention, though, of canceling St. Leger's expedition.

Allen and Fay rode back from Skenesboro through kindling hills in the bright September weather, past the shocked encampments of the corn, and orange and green heaps of pumpkins and squashes. Such peace had not blessed the little frontier farms for years. It did not invade the spirits of Fay and Allen. They were beaten, and they knew it.

By pretense and procrastination they had kept war away from the Republic, only to fatten these farms for slaughter.

Even now, invasion stood in the doorstep. It would be the peculiarly vindictive invasion of recently deluded men, and nothing could be done to stop it.

The Vermont conspirators had exhausted their last resource, spent their final subterfuge, and the General Assembly was gathering at Charlestown for what, quite probably, would be its last meeting. The final delay the plotters had obtained was the last they could expect, and it could only briefly postpone, not avert, disaster. The nausea that had first oppressed Allen and Fay at Skenesboro was heavier upon them as they rode drearily through the lovely countryside.

Charlestown, they found, was a brawl of vigor and excitement. Representatives from the newly absorbed towns hailed Allen joyously. Chittenden, clumping along gawkily, was acclaimed, too. Though one of Washington's own aides, Captain Ezra Heacock, had visited the Governor, he had refused to surrender the New York and New Hampshire towns until Federal union actually had been accomplished for Vermont.

It was clear that the temper of the legislators was against surrender, though emissaries of the deprived states were present with arguments and persuasions. New Hampshire had reinforced its missionaries with two hundred militia, sent ostensibly to keep order, under a Major Runnals.

Tidings that British sail had been sighted coming up Champlain and that Vermont's armed forces under General Roger Enos were marching to protect the frontier sent patriotism higher. The general elation must have seemed flat and ironic to Ira Allen.

In its present mood, the legislature considered only briefly Congress's demand that it surrender the purloined territories. It voted to retain them, tempering its defiance by expressing a willingness to arbitrate the matter. New Hampshire and New York agents indicated that their states were in no mood to argue.

Meanwhile, St. Leger's force had reached Ticonderoga. It lingered there, and Sherwood waited the word from the conspirators that would mean publication of Haldimand's proclamation. This word did not come.

Vermont's plotters were stretching the already overextended delay to the breaking point. Their silence began to worry Sherwood, and he persuaded St. Leger to send a patrol across the lake in the hope of capturing a Vermonter who might be employed as a messenger to Ira Allen or Chittenden.

General Enos, whose militia watched St. Leger's army across Champlain, was aware of the plot. He had not told his troops about it, though. A British officer and twelve men, scouring the woods to find a live Vermonter for Sherwood, ran into a patrol of six who had the illusion that a war was still on. Before the Vermonters could be subdued, their leader, Sergeant Archelaus Tupper, had got himself killed, selling his life cheaply and unnecessarily. He was just a plain non-com, save for his remarkable name; but major generals have been shot with less consequent agitation.

Sherwood, who had asked for a prisoner, St. Leger, who had ordered one, were dismayed when their expedition returned to Ticonderoga with five captives and a corpse. The British agent emphasized to the British colonel the enormity of the offense. At this pregnant and delicate moment, the truce had been shattered. Dead men had an inconvenient way of causing trouble.

St. Leger was an impressionable person, and he sought at once and with disruptive clumsiness to make amends. The clothing and equipment of the late lamented Archelaus were sent to General Enos with a letter of profound apology.

The British colonel hoped that Enos would overlook this unfortunate error and assured him that the sergeant would be buried with full military honors. If Governor Chittenden or his representative cared to attend the funeral, he would be most welcome.

This Gilbert and Sullivan situation was a little beyond Enos's matter-of-fact mind. He sent an express to Chittenden at Charlestown with news of the British army's arrival and St. Leger's contrition over Sergeant Tupper's untimely end. Fate's practical joke ordained this express should be the Simeon Hathaway who, when the plot had been hatched, had voiced his suspicions of Ethan Allen to the General Assembly and, since then, never had abandoned them.

The recent implausible goings-on rankled in Hathaway's mind as he spurred his horse along the military road from the lake to Charlestown. The more he thought them over, the greater became his distrust and indignation. He was full to the brim with apocalyptical surmises and a great desire to share them when he reached his journey's end.

The legislature was recessing. Hathaway delivered his dispatches and then went abroad to cry his tidings and his presumptions to all and sundry in the streets with the rancor of one who belatedly has found confirmation for long-held suspicion.

Hard men gathered about him to gape, then scowl and mutter. The tale, as they passed it further, lost nothing. Waxing anger was in the voices that relayed it.

What call had a goddam redcoat colonel to take on so just because he shot a sergeant? Hell, milishy sergeants wa'n't wuth sixpence a dozen. They said St. Leger couldn't have raised more fuss if he'd killed Haldimand himself. This was a war, wa'n't it? Then what was all this folderol about? B'God, it didn't smell right. St. Leger had even asked One-eyed Tom to the funeral. A pretty kettle of fish. Wal, b'God, there wa'n't no place in Vermont for another Benedict Arnold.

"Come on, boys; lets get to the bottom of this."

The mutter in the streets was becoming a louder, more unpleasant sound. Hathaway was quickening it to the best of his ability, and Major Runnals of the New Hampshire militia was abetting him. Anything that would embarrass Vermont was praiseworthy in the eyes of her sister state's soldiers. Runnals led the angry crowd that clumped into the legislative chamber where Ira Allen was talking in a low voice to lingering members of the assembly.

The solid little man looked at the intruders in amazement. Undoubtedly, his admirable mind already had been considering how best, in Vermont's desperate plight, the death of Sergeant Tupper could be employed. He had had no idea that the tidings had spread so quickly until he looked upon the harsh faces that thronged about him. He found himself the object of a raucous babble of questions and accusations. He never was at his best when dealing with men in mass.

Charges of treason, demands for explanation were bawled at Allen. He shrugged. He knew nothing about the matter save what the dispatches said. Read them now? How could he? Governor Chittenden had them and would communicate them, doubtless, to the assembly in his own good time. His self-possession did not reassure the New Hampshire major. Runnals pointed a finger and shouted:

"Why should Colonel St. Leger apologize for the death of a sergeant in Vermont's army? Answer me that."

The invaders snarled indorsement. Allen shrugged again. His eyes were narrowing; his tight mouth was more compressed than usual. For the only recorded time in his career, his temper was getting away from him, and appreciation of the inanity of his retort to Runnals must have quickened it.

"I don't know," said Allen. "It may be because all good men sorrow when good men die."

He lost his usually perfect self-control at the uncomplimentary sound the New Hampshire major uttered.

"If you wish to find out," Allen cried to Runnals, "take your men and go and ask St. Leger instead of tarrying safely here at the public's expense."

It was the best he could do, and momentarily his answer amused and quieted the mob. He stalked with dignity from the hall and then hurried off to find Chittenden, who was considering the compromising dispatches with his council. It was clear that the documents could not be submitted to the legislature, since they referred openly to the plot. Publication would mean the end of the conspirators, of the truce, quite possibly of Vermont itself. Men who had dabbled in treason so long could not shrink now from a salutary bit of forgery.

Nathaniel Chipman, a young lawyer in the conspiracy, hastily prepared another and far less implicating set of dispatches. These, Chittenden, with his usual guileless air, submitted to the assembly. That body was appeased and reassured. It blamed the manifest exaggeration of the facts on the spiteful mind of Simeon Hathaway. Once more the sorely threatened conspirators had gained a grudging dole of time.

Presumably, they used the death of Sergeant Tupper, the unfavorable effect it had on the public mind, the breach of trust it had constituted, for every ounce of their worth. St. Leger soon afterward moved his force from Ticonderoga further down the lake to Crown Point, where it would not be regarded as a menace to Vermonters at so critical a time in the conspiracy.

The Colonel was eager to be as obliging as possible, but he would not go back home where Allen and accomplices most earnestly wished him. St. Leger lingered, a threat to the Republic, while October and the patience of the British commissioners waned together and the brief respite the plotters had won for themselves dwindled away.

Then, when the tension drew toward the snapping point once more; when any but the most stubborn pretenders would have abandoned their simulation and have sought refuge from disaster in flight; when protracted, breathless maneuvering seemed wholly thrown away, Fortune, the incredibly constant, once more intervened. Still again, an external event which Vermont neither had inspired nor furthered came to the rescue of the Republic in its extreme need.

It was only a whisper at first, blowing with no accompanying warrant from the south. It was a rumor so splendid, so fraught with relief, that tormented men could not believe it. Cornwallis, the whisper ran, had surrendered. Yorktown had fallen.

Before the tidings were confirmed, Ira Allen had them in a drowning man's grip. They were the basis of a sorrowful letter he wrote to the waiting British commissioners from Charlestown. He himself, he informed them, could not tell whether the rumor was true or false, but its mere circulation had dislocated all the conspirators' cherished plans. It would be worse than useless, he informed Haldimand's agents, to publish the proclamation in the present moment of popular exultation.

Similar rumors of Yorktown's surrender had reached the army on the lake. For once, the British commissioners and Allen were wholly in accord. November 1, St. Leger's host embarked.

The white sails went northward, bearing the invasion back to Canada, away from the Republic, whose only defense for a year had been the deft, the daring, the magnificently unscrupulous wits of a handful of wilderness Yankees.

Vermont had held the British at bay for a twelvemonth with no more deadly weapons than correspondence and conversation. Her only casualty in this intricate campaign had been the elaborately lamented Sergeant Archelaus Tupper.

Chittenden stressed this next-to-bloodless victory in a letter he wrote to Washington that fall. The missive, which was inspired by the visit of the commander-in-chief's aide, Captain Heacock, reviewed at length the Republic's plight, skipped over the more implicating details of the Canadian negotiations, but called particular attention to St. Leger's empty excursion.

The enemy, the Governor proclaimed, "were maneuvered out of their expedition and are returned to their winter quarters in Canada that it might be fulfilled which was spoken by the prophet, 'I will put my hook in their nose and turn them back by the way which they came, and they shall not come into this city [alias Vermont], saith the Lord.' "

Chittenden's sonorous quotation of Scripture—which sounds more like Ethan Allen than the Governor—and his celebration of the nose-hooked St. Leger's retirement may have had a faint flavor of red herring. Perhaps he hoped that his magnificat would keep General Washington's attention away from happenings in the territory recently appropriated by Vermont at New York's expense.

There, events were marching toward what promised to be a lively civil war.

XVII Problem Child

THERE WAS TROUBLE in the recently appropriated portion of New York that Vermonters called "the West Union." There was marching and counter-marching of militia and numerous incidents, any one of which might bring about open battle.

There was trouble in "the East Union," too—the precinct wrested from New Hampshire—and the lively promise of more to follow.

The Republic's own interior also was about to be afflicted with spasms of rebellion induced by Charles Phelps, the fat mullah of Marlboro, who had seen a vision and turned his coat and now was preaching revolt in New York's name even more earnestly than recently he had been advocating the cause of Massachusetts.

Apparently there was to be no rest for the transgressor; and Vermont, having extricated herself by luck and dexterity from the frying pan of the Canadian conspiracy, found she was falling into the fires of several waxing hostilities.

Hitherto the threat of an alliance between the Republic and Britain had kept these fires low. Now Yorktown had fallen, and relief had made men valiant. Furthermore, St. Leger's army had gone back home; and, with winter on the threshold, the heartiest treason by Vermont could claim no aid from Canada before the next spring.

That peril, if not eliminated, was at least suspended. It seemed a propitious time for New York, New Hampshire, and the Yorkers of Vermont to display resentment over grievances too long and meekly cherished. The fires were unbanked and fuel piled on.

The war, which New York launched to recover her land newly incorporated into Vermont, was not impressive, but it was the best that could be waged with the materials at hand, which were all low-spirited militia whose most distinctive qualities were their fleetness of foot and their long-thwarted appetites. The Mohawk Valley, New York's granary, was charred and smoking, and all the State troops were short of rations.

When it became clear that anyone who moved against Vermont

would not be required to fight St. Leger's army as well, Brigadier General Peter Gansevoort marshaled militia units under Colonels Yates, Van Vechten, and Henry K. Van Rensselaer at Albany and ordered them to advance and reclaim New York's lost province where, for some time now, the most scandalous behavior had been prevalent.

A slight Vermont army of occupation had been quartered in the West Union. To this organization most of the neglected native militia had deserted, inspired by a love of freedom and the prospect of regular rations. A number of their officers, who also were hungry, had accompanied them, much to the wrath of Colonel John Van Rensselaer, in command of New York's dwindling local armed forces.

The Colonel did not have enough troops remaining to start a battle, but he gathered a handful of loyalists about him and did what he could. Lieutenant Colonel Samuel Fairbanks and other back-sliding New York militia lived in Lansingburg. Van Rensselaer raided the town at night, broke into the culprits' houses, and took them prisoners.

This employment by aliens of an old Vermont custom enraged the Republic. Chittenden wrote, demanding the prisoners' release. Colonel Samuel Robinson of the Vermont troops informed General Stark, commanding all northern New York's militia:

> If your honor cannot find the militia of Albany some other employment, I shall march my regiment to that quarter and try powder and ball with them, which I have as well as they.

The war, however, remained chiefly verbal. There was a mild skirmish along the Walloomsac, in which some powder was burned and three New Yorkers were slightly wounded. Thereafter, the host sent by Gansevoort from Albany settled down on one side of the stream, the Vermonters on the other, and from these positions conducted the martial enterprise of yelling insults at each other.

The troops maintained their lines under heavy slander, and while the contest endured Colonel Abbott of the Vermont forces wiped out the disgrace of the Fairbanks abduction by kidnaping Colonel John Van Rensselaer at North Hoosick. The captive was taken to Bennington where, a letter from him informed Gansevoort, he was treated "like a gentleman." Honor being satisfied, Van Rensselaer then was released.

The Battle of the Walloomsac now had reached such a high pitch of invective that someone was likely to be shot if it continued. There was disaffection in the New York reinforcements of Colonels Henry Van Rensselaer and Yates. These troops, having marched as far as North Hoosick and having learned there that food was plentiful in the encampment of their enemies, were deserting in droves, leaving the invaders with not enough men to attack a blockhouse that barred their way.

The profusely abandoned colonels appealed to Gansevoort for more men and cannon; Gansevoort appealed to Stark; Stark appealed to General Heath, his superior, who apparently lost the dispatch, for no troops were forthcoming. Gansevoort himself then went to the front to lead what remained of New York's host.

Meanwhile, the Vermont government had sent Ira Allen to the West Union to estimate and report on the situation. Peace, Allen told Chittenden, would best be served by sending an overwhelming force into the combat zone. This would impress the fragment of New York's army who had valued their duty more than the prospect of three square meals daily, with the vanity of resistance.

Colonel Ebenezer Walbridge and five hundred militia were ordered forward with an old unreliable cannon and Ethan Allen, who, though he no longer had military command, still had his uniform. He appeared the most awesome portion of Walbridge's column to a Mrs. Bleecker of Albany, who saw him in all his glory and immediately thereafter wrote: "General Allen was bound up in gold lace and felt himself grand as the Great Mogul."

The arrival of Ethan Allen and the less conspicuous five hundred completely disorganized the remnant of the New York expeditionary force. Gansevoort, advancing to place himself at the head of the loyal troops, was almost run over by the retreating army which now numbered barely eighty men. In Colonel Van Vechten's regiment only one private remained.

Gansevoort formally disbanded the faithful eighty and accompanied them back to Albany.

Vermont had won another victory most economically, but her government had scant time or breath to celebrate it. Trouble in the West Union had been abated, temporarily at least; but it was gathering in New Hampshire's late river towns. The strife that ensued here was less martial than the New York war. It resembled more a vindictive and vehement tag game.

Sam Davis, constable under the Vermont government in the erstwhile New Hampshire town of Chesterfield, was attacked while serving a writ by two New Hampshire supporters. He arrested them and marched them off to Charlestown, where they were jailed, much to the indignation of Enoch Hale, New Hampshire sheriff of Cheshire County.

Hale stormed down upon Charlestown, demanded the immediate release of Davis's prisoners, and found himself in jail beside them. This was more indignity in a short time than the Granite State felt it could possibly bear. Its authorities talked angrily of marching troops to the rescue of its imprisoned citizens. Chittenden replied to the threat by commanding Lieutenant Governor Elisha Payne to mobilize the Eastside militia.

By way of reprisal for her nationals' arrest, New Hampshire took into custody on a dim complaint Samuel King, member of the Vermont legislature. King was imprisoned in Keene, but not for long. A mob surrounded the jail, rescued the captive, and abused his captors in what they reported was "a shameful and barbarous manner."

At this point, New Hampshire's long-controlled indignation showed definite signs of boiling over completely. Its legislature voted to raise a thousand men to invade and reclaim its rebellious territory, and President Weare issued an ultimatum. Vermont had forty days to get off, and stay off, the disputed soil. Otherwise, there would be war.

In her plight, the Republic, as usual, took to judgment-beclouding propaganda, as instinctively as a threatened deer dives into brush. The government issued a new pamphlet with a no more than commonly brief title.

"The Present State of the Controversy Between the States of New York and New Hampshire on the One Part and the State of Vermont on the Other" was supposed to be the product of a committee of which Ethan Allen was a member. The voice—and the spelling—are his. It concluded:

> Vermont does not mean to be so overrighteous as by that means to die before her time; but for the states of New York and New Hampshire to stand griping their respective claims fast hold of Vermont and at the same time make such a hedious outcry against the grip of Vermont upon them is altogether romantic and laughable.

The reviving and drearily familiar dissension that was immersing Vermont must have made her authorities think wistfully of the late summer's truce and yearn for the tranquillizing influence of conspiracy. To complicate matters still further, the Eastside Yorkers were beginning to display a determination to start a good old-fashioned rebellion once more, with Charles Phelps and his son Timothy whooping them on.

In January, 1782, Brattleboro and Guilford Yorkers framed another of their practically continuous petitions and sent copies to Clinton and Congress. This document begged for the return of Vermont to New York, asserted that most of the Eastsiders longed for it, clucked deploringly over the Republic's intrigue with Canada, and viewed with alarm the increasing violences committed upon Yorkers by their neighbors.

In January, too, a grave and tempered voice spoke, hushing momentarily the increasingly shrill sounds of strife. George Washington wrote Chittenden neither a denunciatory nor a reproving, but a calmly counseling, letter.

Washington accepted the Vermont governor's explanation of the intrigue with Britain that Chittenden had written him, but pointed out its dangers. He supported Vermont's claim to independence, within that state's original limits. There could be no question of the Republic's right to statehood. Indeed, Congress already tacitly had affirmed it.

The only point now in dispute, according to Washington's belief, was the matter of boundaries. He was sure that if Vermont were to relinquish the New York and New Hampshire territory she had appropriated, she would receive recognition by Congress. As it was, all this turmoil the state persistently had encouraged was a bad example to other commonwealths. Further misbehavior might lead to coercion.

The calm and friendly speech penetrated deeper than Weare's outraged expostulations, Congress's threats, or Clinton's blusterings ever had driven. The quiet advice from one whose greatness the subsequent celebration of lesser men has half-obscured awed and convinced the normally irreverent Republic.

George Washington, of all mankind, actually reduced Vermont to earnest, though brief, contrition. He had shown her the error of her ways. Now, unbelievably, she sought swiftly to mend them. Reform would bring her statehood, goal of seven years' uproar and struggle. Washington had said so.

He offered his counsel in January. The February session of the legislature, at Bennington, listened to the letter from the Commander in Chief, to another from the equally friendly and admonishing Oliver Wolcott of Connecticut. There seems to have been little debate and none of the verbal fireworks and slanderous explosions which generally accompanied Vermont's frequent shifts in policy.

With the zeal and trust of new converts, the General Assembly obeyed Washington. It let go of the New York territory it had held; it relinquished New Hampshire's towns; it divested itself of the bargaining points it had stubbornly maintained so that, as its counselor had promised, it might be immediately admitted to the Union.

The renunciation took place by coincidence or design on February 22, Washington's own birthday.

Moses Robinson, Jonas Fay, Paul Spooner, Isaac Tichenor were appointed, optimistically, ministers plenipotentiary to arrange with Congress details of Vermont's inclusion in the United States. Only one trace of characteristic foresight and thrift is discernible in their instructions. They were bidden to assume for Vermont as small a share of the national debt as possible.

Absolved, disarmed, the suddenly reformed character that had been, until Washington had spoken, America's terrible infant, waited expectantly for admission to statehood.

Congress, with only its normal tardiness, endorsed the hope. On March 1, 1782, this body resolved that if, within one month after notification, Vermont had returned to New York and New Hampshire their territorial belongings, she would be welcomed forthwith into the Union. This measure was adopted one week after Vermont had conformed to the stipulation.

The way was clear at last. Elation ran high. Chittenden wrote to Washington that his counsel had been followed, that Vermont obediently had shrunk itself to its original proportions, and that henceforth:

The glory of America is our glory and with our country we mean to live or die as our fate may be.

Drifts were grimed and granulated, mud was deepening; but the spring seemed filled with promise. Not even the persistent discord supplied by Yorkers of the Eastside discernibly marred the brave new harmony. The prospect of living and dying as Vermonters was abhorrent to these permanent dissenters. They held another mass meeting which resulted in the usual petition to Clinton. This begged New York's governor not to let his embarrassingly faithful adherents be sold downriver, and Samuel Avery bore it to Albany.

Yorkers, though, were only a minor flaw in an otherwise radiantly tranquil scene. The effulgence endured while Vermont's ambassadors journeyed to Philadelphia; while they notified Congress, March 31, that its orders had been obeyed and that no obstacle now remained to bar the Republic from transformation into the fourteenth state.

Congress, assured that New York and New Hampshire had received their stolen property, became vague and absent-minded. It did not consider resolutions for the incorporation of Vermont into the Union until April 17, and it tabled them then.

There was no need now for haste. The war was dwindling. It soon would end. Their territory had been restored to the Republic's aggrieved neighbor states.

Vermont had fulfilled its part of the agreement, and Congress had what it had wanted. As for that body's reciprocal duty, that could wait. Vermont could wait, too. A little discipline would be good for that commonwealth. It could do nothing particularly offensive now. Its hands had been thoroughly tied by its own eager compliance with Washington's advice.

Vermont's no longer hopeful ministers left Philadelphia as empty as they had come. They rode home, that late April, through a spring that suddenly had lost its effulgence. There is no record of what actually was said by Chittenden and his council when the indifference of Congress was made known to them, whereby the annals of imprecation have lost some glowing passages.

There is no record, either, of what George Washington thought of the congressional double-crossing, whereby he had led a trusting people into a hostile wilderness and left them there.

There are grounds for belief that Congress's procrastination was something more than just that. On either side of the small Republic, suddenly left completely alone in the world, were avaricious and justifiably angry commonwealths.

New York and New Hampshire had never wholly abandoned the hope that, eventually, they might split Vermont between them. The former was the active, the latter the passive, conspirator in this plot.

That aspiration now seemed reasonably close to fulfillment. Implicitly barred from the Union, deprived of recent territory and population, with threat of a Canadian alliance no longer a potent weapon, due to the flagging war, with a thoroughly well-earned bad reputation, and with only clumsy farmers to guide her feeble government, Vermont obviously was close to the end of her stormy career. Inevitably, the Republic must soon fall apart. Then New York and New Hampshire would pick up and appropriate the pieces.

To expectant eyes there already seemed to be evidences of this disintegration. An enterprising Fishkill, New York, newspaper had got hold, in some fashion, of the correspondence between Haldimand and Sir Henry Clinton concerning the Vermont intrigue and had published it all. The details scandalized a number of persons hitherto sympathetic to the Republic, and New York's Clinton snorted triumphantly over "the traitorous correspondence between the leaders of the New Hampshire Grants and the enemy."

The Governor also did his best to hasten Vermont's disintegration. The New York legislature, April 14, passed an act pardoning all residents of Vermont their "treasons, felonies and conspiracies" against New York and recognizing, without payment of additional fees, all grants of land originally made by New Hampshire and all territory granted by Vermont itself.

Thereby the original causes of rebellion against New York authority were completely abolished. There could be, in all common sense, no further reason for Vermont to retain its identity. This magnanimity by its ancient enemy must bring the little state's whole structure crashing down.

So New York believed, and there were fresh signs that this collapse was imminent—significant creakings and saggings that quickened panicky or exultant voices. The Eastside Yorkers were speaking more boldly. The egregious Charles Phelps had prepared another petition for Clinton's already bulging file. This asked, in the name of Brattleboro, Halifax, and Guilford, that New York government be re-established in Cumberland County and that civil and militia officers be appointed. Vermont's weakness was the Yorkers' opportunity.

In May, 1782, four Vermont towns—Newbury, Bradford, Hartford, and Norwich—petitioned New Hampshire for inclusion in that state. The inevitable break-up was under way.

One cohesive, intense force the complacent watchers completely overlooked. It had remained uncelebrated by a people who commonly did not—and do not—publicize their deepest emotions; yet it had existed among them for more than a decade now, rooting deep, growing steadily on a diet of adversity. The surface misbehavior of determined folk long had hidden it. Most of the expectant onlookers did not perceive it, even now, though at last it had been bared.

It was an immaterial need, and Freedom was its name. That abstract was all plain men could gain by further resistance. Possession of their land, immunity to further fees, absolution for their insurgent offenses—

all had been guaranteed by the recent and lenient New York law. Sustenance for a still passion was the sole advantage a reeling state could offer its people that they could not get more easily by surrender. Vermont, the lately deluded and abused, the weakening and distracted Republic, held itself together by no other bond.

The spirit may have been Spartan. The tactics inspired by this obstinate patriotism were peculiarly Vermont's own. There was no dignified talk of Thermopylae among the soured and obstinate statesmen, most of whom had never heard the word. There was no windy exhortation concerning backs against walls and resistance to the last man. Vermont had a better system than that. It had been tried, and the Republic had seen it work.

The rejected state, America's dismaying problem child, resolutely prepared after brief reform to make itself as objectionable as possible to the neighbors once more. It got ready to lie on the floor and kick and scream and in this dire hour looked hopefully for something to yell about.

Some of the less crafty leaders considered a revival of the Canadian conspiracy, but the longer-headed knew that this threat was losing potency daily. Peace was in the air, though the actual cessation of hostilities was still a year away. The danger of further plotting was greater than its promise.

Communications to and from Canada had continued all through the previous winter with no great enthusiasm on the defrauded Haldimand's side and only mild cordiality on Vermont's. The conspiracy had become so dubious an ace that the Republic doubted the use of keeping it any longer up its sleeve.

Ethan Allen made the only vigorous attempt to revive the plot now, and it was clear from his method that the Philosopher was guided more by his anger toward Congress and its snide treatment of over-trusting Vermont than by his ordinary good common sense.

Philosopher Allen, in a most unphilosophic mood, wrote to Haldimand proposing what amounted to an alliance between the British nation and Ethan Allen. He spent a large portion of his letter in blackguarding Congress:

It is Liberty they are after but they will not extend it to Vermont; therefore Vermont does not belong to the confederacy or the controversy but are a neutral republic.

Haldimand was invited to meet the Philosopher at any point he should select on Lake Champlain, and Allen informed him:

> There is a majority in Congress and a number of principal officers of the Continental army continually planning against me. I shall do everything in my power to render this State a British province.

Canada's governor general does not seem to have looked favorably on the invitation or the proposition, and the Allen wrath gradually steamed itself away.

Less volatile statesmen were seeking some other means whereby Vermont might make itself especially offensive to its neighbors and induce them to bombard Congress once more with a whole new set of pestering complaints. Before questing eyes loomed the new insurgency of the Eastside Yorkers that Charles Phelps so industriously was inflating.

Here was a situation that, if cannily employed, could stir up endless turmoil and stench. The leaders of the Republic drew deep breaths, grinned hardily at each other, and prepared to employ it.

XVIII Nuisance Value

No CLEARER EXPLANATION can be found for the protracted Second
Yorker War and the fantastic events which adorned it than the hazard
that it was deliberately planned and nurtured by Vermont's statesmen,
who had determined to exploit an internal disaffection for the sake of
its obvious external nuisance value.

The yells of rage, the screeches of woe, the alarums, the excursions,
the kidnapings, the jailings, the comic battles and bizarre trials, the
anguished petitions to Congress and reiterant appeals to Governor
Clinton that this so-called conflict sponsored supplied enough com-
motion for an empire in the throes of dissolution.

The vast output of disturbance appears incredible when one considers
the meager number of its sponsors. New York's supporters in Vermont
were comparatively few, and the entire population of the Republic
was small. The active rebels never could have numbered more than a
couple of hundred men, but each of them was an expert in voice
production.

Vermont for a time did everything possible to stimulate and amplify
their tumult. It indulged in no suppressing reprisals; it only prodded
and spurred. When it captured men who had been charged with
high treason, the Republic did not hang them, as it had promised, but
imposed punishments it neglected to enforce. The armed expeditions
launched against the insurgents might have been led by Falstaff
himself. By persistently provocative tactics, Vermont nursed along for
more than two years a revolt it might have quashed in a month.

When the uproar seemed to have fulfilled its purposes, the Republic
abolished it. Before then, all witnesses to the revolt had earnestly
wished that it were over. Congress had grown immensely tired of the
whole mess and, foiled in its attempts to order it, had conspicuously
and exasperatedly washed its hands of all responsibility, leaving the
seething state to stew in its own broth.

New York and New Hampshire, that once had looked forward
with eager eyes and predatory intentions to the partition of Vermont,

had, ere the racket died away, disavowed any such purpose. Both
were suffering from sick headaches. They had been avaricious, then
bewildered, then aghast, and, finally, profoundly thankful that they
had not performed the dissection. It was intolerable even to think of
taking such addicts of uproar into their own commonwealths. It was
bad enough to have them as next-door neighbors. New Hampshire
had made no effort to aid the rebels. She could not, without fortifying
Yorkers' claim to land she herself hoped to acquire. New York by
openly assisting them would have offended New Hampshire, her ac-
complice. The unflattering distrust of the conspirators in each other
was sign of weakness the Republic artfully exploited. The York insurgents implicitly were rebels against New Hampshire rule as well
as the explicit foes of Chittenden's regime. Furthermore, they occupied
territory New York secretly had agreed to relinquish to its co-plotter.
It was an intricate situation. The Republic did not try to simplify it.
Its best defense lay in keeping the Yorkers offensive.

Vermonters themselves emerged from the Yorker War a more
unified and solidified people. The artificial threat to the Republic had
closed the ranks of its citizenry.

All, in due time and to the accompaniment of tremendous hubbub,
had worked out just as, from the first, the statesmen of the Republic
of Vermont had planned.

That happy conclusion was far away on April 30, 1782, when
Charles Phelps petitioned Clinton for the establishment of a New
York government in Cumberland County.

Clinton, replying May 6, no longer was in his "firmness and prudence" mood. He, with most of the rest of the country, believed that
the Republic was about to fall in upon itself, and his answer had
unusual vigor.

The Governor pledged his "best endeavors" to give the petitioner
his demanded aid and added that if Vermont, in the throes of its
dissolution, dared to bother Yorkers, "you will perceive that resistance
by force is, in every point of view, justifiable."

He must have wished, during that long subsequent resistance, that
his pen hand had dropped off before it had written such counsel.

The Governor's heartening letter was read to a meeting of Yorkers
in Guilford, informal capital of the gathering rebellion. That town
of rolling hills and small quick streams was then the largest community
in the state and had cherished with a disconcerting and long-term
fidelity a passion for New York; why, no one knows, since its popula-

tion was largely Yankee and it was almost as far removed from the state of its inexplicable choice as any town in its particular region could be.

Nevertheless, Guilford had long since disavowed allegiance to New Hampshire, had refused to pledge its fealty to Vermont, and had continued to live by its own laws and under its own elected town officials, a miniature republic with unappeasable yearnings for New York which it was to pursue through a great deal of thick and much thin as well.

Even in Guilford, there was a Vermont minority, and Clinton's endorsement of direct action against the Republic caused a lamentable split in what once had been a mutually tolerant population. The York majority straightway elected town officers responsible to New York. The Vermont faction, not to be outdone, immediately chose town officers pledged to the Republic. Thereafter the community was governed by two antagonistic groups with no less friction than might have been expected under the circumstances.

Records of Guilford's internal strife are incomplete, for, at some time in the course of her administration by two opposing town governments, one of the contesting parties stole the public records and buried them, away from the reach of its rivals, in the town pound. Years passed before they were recovered, for the thief forgot or else never would admit the exact site of their interment. When at last the records were dug up, protracted burial had ruined many of them.

While the York fervor aroused by Clinton's message still was high and Yorkers were pledging themselves to resist Vermont with "our lives and fortunes," the opportunity for such opposition suddenly was presented. The Republic declared a militia levy, and the Vermont officers of Guilford were bidden to supply the men required from that town. They complied with extreme heartiness and satisfaction. The men they summoned all were leading Yorkers.

The chosen declined to serve, and the sheriff of Cumberland County was ordered, in the face of their further refusal to pay the customary fine, to confiscate and sell cows to supply it.

Barzillai Rice, deputy sheriff, invaded Guilford, kidnaped Joel Bigelow's cow, and started to lead her to Brattleboro. A York mob pursued Barzillai, took the cow away from him, and marched her back in triumph to Bigelow's pasture.

The die thus was cast. The cattle of Yorkers thereafter were to live in constant peril of abduction, and their owners as well as persons from Brattleboro, Halifax, and Marlboro sent another appeal to Clinton by the hand of Charles Phelps in person, on May 17.

This petition asked Clinton to take over Cumberland County immediately, establishing courts and appointing civil and military officers. The Governor did not gag over this actual invasion, or else Phelps, who had been known to address a jury for two hours without ever getting as far along as his client's cause, talked Clinton into issuing the commissions.

These, borne back in triumph to the rebellious towns by Phelp's own hand, gave him, not strangely, chief honors. New York commissioned him justice of the peace, justice of the court of oyer and terminer, justice of the quorum. Timothy Phelps, Charles's son, was appointed sheriff of Cumberland County, and Timothy Church, colonel of the New York militia. The resistance against Vermont authority that Clinton had prescribed now was organized.

This was a sturdy beginning of rebellion, and Vermont replied at once. The June session of the legislature passed an act "for the punishment of conspiracies against the peace, liberty and independence" of the Republic which promised conspirators confiscation of their property, banishment for life, and execution if they returned from exile. The lawmakers also empowered Chittenden to send troops to the aid of any sheriff who found it difficult to perform his duties otherwise.

Action as drastic as this was more than the embattled Yorkers could endure without uttering another petition. This latest in the series of appeals that were to keep flopping down on Clinton's desk with a panicky sound for another couple of years dwelt as usual with the perils and anguishes Yorkers and their cows were enduring and begged the Governor to be sure and send New York's militia when and if the Vermonters attacked his faithful servants.

With a laudable desire to keep the record straight and to evade all responsibility possible, the plea asked definite instructions from Clinton "to stand and fight" if the worst should happen.

Things were moving too fast. This was a more bellicose order than New York's governor was willing to issue. He replied: "Your own prudence and virtue will dictate the mode and measure of your opposition." He had no wish to offend New Hampshire by fomenting actual warfare in territory secretly allotted to her.

Yorkers chose to regard this cautious and equivocal reply as an urgent summons to arms. Thereafter, their conduct, which had never been distinguished for its meekness, grew downright provocative. Its consequences were innumerable petty squabbles and minor skirmishes with their republican neighbors—clashes that were distinguished for a' maximum of noise and a minimum of bloodshed. Ensanguined noses, trivial lacerations and abrasions were all the physical damage wrought, but the scandalous deportment of the Yorkers graveled patriotic Vermonters.

Isaac Tichenor and, later, Ira Allen, the pacifier, were sent by Chittenden into the uproarious corner of the Republic to see if the refractory citizenry could not be prevailed upon to hush their tumult and behave themselves. Both missions were futile.

The current, unwonted tolerance of the Government was encouraging the insurgents, who swaggered and ruffled and spoke darkly of resistance "even to blood" and "the terrible times" that were in store for Vermont if it dared to interfere. The Yorkers had not enjoyed so untrammeled a rebellion since Guilford had been founded. They were getting out of hand with every apparent intention of going further. Meanwhile, the Vermont government watched, and heard, and did nothing.

There were ample causes for intervention if Chittenden and his council had sought them. From brawls with the neighbors, Yorkers now were turning to open resistance of constituted authority. Sheriff Jonathan Hunt of Cumberland County emerged from an attempt to arrest for debt Timothy Church, colonel of the Yorker militia, considerably mussed up and without his man.

Hunt and his posse had invaded the home of Church and had laid hold upon the prisoner, who had been unco-operative. Friends of Church attached themselves to the Colonel also, and after an animated tug-of-war obtained full possession of their somewhat strained intimate and chased Hunt away.

A Vermont constable and several assistants appeared at the farm of Timothy Phelps, the swarthy, wild-eyed and explosive York sheriff of Cumberland, and attempted to confiscate his oxen for nonpayment of taxes. Phelps's response was direct and uncompromising. He whacked the constable over the head with a pitchfork handle and felled him. The assistants ran away when threatened with the other end of the fork, and after a time the constable got to his feet and followed them, oxenless.

These and similar acts of violence were increasing and gave Vermont authorities thought. They also supplied Clinton with additional correspondence, for Yorkers never did anything without sitting down promply thereafter to write the Governor about it. He forwarded their versions of these affrays to Congress, which, already confused by the clashing claims of the thirteen states to the newly opened lands in the West, wished heartily that it would not have to hear of Vermont again for at least another ten years.

By the summer's end, the embattled Yorkers had become so stridently defiant, so brimming over with pugnacity, that the spectacularly long-suffering Vermont authorities at last moved. If the rebellion was to be mitigated as bloodlessly as possible, there obviously was only one man for the job.

Ethan Allen, soldier and philosopher, was summoned from his literary labors. These currently consisted of a lively correspondence with the Canadian authorities and intervening work on the book with which he purposed to abolish New England's God. He was ordered by Chittenden, who seems to have regarded the Yorker revolt more ill-temperedly than did his associates, to enlist two hundred and fifty troops, mobilize them secretly, and move by stealth against the rebels.

Thus it came about that, on September 9, dwellers on the marches of the disaffected territory looked up and saw a column of armed men on weary horses and at their head a giant rider in a direly familiar uniform. The observers looked just once and then started running.

In Marlboro, Ethan Allen detached Ira Allen and twenty men from his force with orders to round up Timothy Phelps. The main army moved on toward Guilford. The searchers for Phelps, in attempting to enter his house, found the way barred by a doughtier antagonist than the pitchfork-wielding York sheriff himself. This was Mrs. Phelps, who, in order to give her husband time to escape, snatched up a fire shovel, stood in the doorway, and promised with evident sincerity to brain the first man who entered.

The crisis endured for several moments and was abolished at last by Yankee appreciation of the ridiculous. Someone said something wryly amusing. Mrs. Phelps tittered, and the impasse broke down in hearty guffaws. By then Sheriff Phelps had vanished, but they caught him before the day was over, and he was one of the few stout-hearted who dared defy Ethan Allen to his face.

Guilford tradition holds that the prisoner, when brought before the expedition's commander, proclaimed himself high sheriff of Cumberland County, charged his opponent with riotous conduct, and bade him disperse his men. Allen, the tale runs, gaped in amazement, then leaned from his horse, slapped his defier's hat from his head, bawled to a subordinate: "Take that damned rascal away," and galloped off.

The column came down off the hills into Guilford and rode through, the terror-palsied town, gathering in those leading Yorkers who had not already fled. Foremost among the prudent fugitives was the portly Charles Phelps, who doubtless remembered Allen's promise to kill him when next they met and still believed it.

All Guilford men were not stronger of leg than heart. The valiant of the town, forty-six in number, had assembled and laid ambush on the Brattleboro road where a mound with Broad Brook coursing along its base made a natural fortification. Pride impelled them to resist, outnumbered though they were, but the thought of conflict with the terrible Ethan Allen dampened martial fervor.

Local tradition holds that the warriors purposed to make only technical resistance and loaded their muskets with blank charges. In any event, when the head of the column approached, Guilford's army fired a volley at nothing and made a perfect score. Their astonishment at the result must have been intense.

General Allen's army yelped, wheeled about, and ran. In the rear of the headlong retreat rode the soldier-philosopher himself, bellowing noteworthy imprecations.

The flight did not halt until it had reached Guilford village once more. There the fugitives' raging leader overtook them and got them in hand again. Allen's fiery face disparaged the brilliance of his uniform as he turned from telling his troops what he thought of them to address the delighted villagers. These, as the apocalyptical voice rose, felt elation ebb. Their hair stirred and chills coursed their spines as the awful General trumpeted:

"I, Ethan Allen, do declare that I will give no quarter to the man, woman, or child who shall oppose me; and unless the inhabitants of Guilford peacefully submit to the authority of Vermont, I will lay it as desolate as Sodom and Gomorrah, by God!"

Thereafter, he led his abashed column out once more. Guilford's resistance had been knocked as prostrate by his proclamation as Jericho's walls after similar brazen blaring. Unopposed, the troops and their prisoners moved on to Brattleboro, but Guilford holds to this day that they went by another road than that on which the harmless ambush had been laid. Nevertheless, for the moment at least, rebellion had been squashed flat. When Allen led a detail of troops to Guilford some days later and levied wholesale on the property of Yorkers to satisfy unpaid Vermont taxes, there was no sign of resistance.

On the day after the Broad Brook ambush, Allen, after bellowing that he would give quarter to no man who contested his advance, led his column and his twenty captives to Westminster, where the prisoners were jailed.

The trouble with the Yorkers' opposition, one of Clinton's many Guilford correspondents informed him ruefully, was that none of them dared stand against Ethan Allen, "whom they fear more than the Devil."

Satan also was named an accessory before the fact in the trial of the five most important prisoners—Colonel Church, William Shattuck, Timothy Phelps, Henry Evans in person, and the fugitive Charles Phelps *in absentia*. The indictment charged that this quintet, "not having God before their eyes but being moved and seduced by the instigation of the Devil," had rebelled against Vermont and had urged New York to invade it.

Until the moment of their sentence, the prisoners maintained a lighthearted belief that they would be rescued before the trial was over by New York's governor. Memory of the inconsiderable penalties meted out to captives in the earlier York revolt may have buoyed them, too. The offended Republic was not so temperate now, ostensibly at least. As in the previous York trial, Moses Robinson sat as chief judge, but Ethan Allen took no volunteer part in the prosecution. That was handled deftly by Stephen Bradley, while the brass-bound giant stayed out of the courtroom, displaying his uniform to a delighted multitude about the courthouse steps and giving a thorough goddaming to Clinton and all his works.

"Had I but orders," he shouted to his admirers, "I could go to Albany and be head monarch in three weeks, and I have a good idea to do it."

Within the court, proceedings moved more rapidly for Allen's absence. They were expedited still further by the prisoners' refusal to offer any defense, pending rescue. The trial concluded with no intervention by Clinton. Evans, Shattuck, Church, and the Phelpses, absent and present, were sentenced by Judge Robinson.

The criminals were to be held in Westminster jail until October 4. They were then to be escorted across the Connecticut to New Hampshire, their decree of permanent banishment to be read to them there, their property to be confiscated to the uses of the state, and they to be hanged if ever they returned to Vermont. That was the sentence the new law prescribed, and that was what they got.

No hint of Christian compassion impelled Ethan Allen to visit later the no longer defiant Timothy Phelps in prison.

"You have called," Allen jeered, "on your god, Clinton, till you are tired. Call now on your god, Congress, and they will answer you as Clinton has done."

The sixteen minor miscreants were dealt with even more speedily than the York leaders had been. They were fined and released. On September 17, escorted by Allen's troopers, the court moved to Marl-boro and there tried all remaining persons who had taken commissions, civil or military, under New York and still could be found. Among the prisoners was Samuel Ely, the one-man regiment of the Bennington battle, whose military record could not save him from eighteen months' banishment as penalty for his intense and extremely inclusive defama-tion of Vermont's government. Ely's indictment quoted him as saying:

> The state of Vermont is a damned state and the act for the pur-pose of raising ten shillings on every hundred acres of land is a cursed act and they that made it are a cursed body of men. The general court are a pack of villains and if no other person will undertake to destroy the government of Vermont I will do it and I have that in my pocket that will overset them. Damn the state of Vermont and all its officers and damn the laws passed by the General Assembly.

While Vermont's soldiers and juries were bringing the recently bellicose Yorkers into a mood of temporary respect for the Republic's power and authority, Charles Phelps and Joel Bigelow—he of the confiscated but rescued cow—were hastening to Albany with their tidings of calamity; and Bigelow, being built for more speed than his fat rival, got to Clinton first.

The volunteer messenger must have been dismayed when the Gov-ernor, after hearing what had happened to the rebellion he had been encouraging, did not leap up and gird his sword about him but, instead, reached thoughtfully for a pen. Association with the letter-writing Yorkers had affected Clinton, for he now wrote three letters himself.

One, enclosing Bigelow's deposition, went to New York's delegates in Congress, urging them to try once more to rouse that body to action against Vermont.

The second was sent back by Bigelow to the faithful of Guilford and environs. It encouraged a resistance which Clinton went no further than this to aid and suggested that the Yorkers take as many prisoners as Allen's men had captured and send them to New York "as hostages."

The last missive was in the Governor's best threatening vein and was addressed to Jonathan Hunt, Vermont sheriff of Cumberland. This dwelt with such solemnity on the gravity of the offenses Hunt had condoned that the sheriff, being a mild man, was scared into resigning his office forthwith.

By the time the Governor had completed this installment of his interminable correspondence with the Yorkers, Charles Phelps had arrived in Albany, filled with more dire speech than he had breath remaining to utter.

Clinton, before the interview ended, appreciated in full the advantages of doing business by letter. Phelps was embarrassingly co-operative. He assured the already slightly deafened Governor that he was quite willing to tell his story to Congress; and when New York's chief executive, mindful of the dampening effect such verbosity might cause, tried to dissuade him, rejected counsel and went to Philadelphia.

Even among experts, Phelps found no one who could surpass him. His version of the Guilford affair, recited before Congress, made it sound like a hideous as well as an unduly dreary and long-drawn-out massacre. When he had ended, James Duane wrote to Clinton: "He overflows with the plenitude of his communicative powers," which was probably the longest possible way of putting it.

Indifferent to the wrath of New York's governor and the deliberately gathering disapproval of Congress, to both of which they were reasonably well acclimated by now, the Vermont authorities proceeded with the finalities of the Guilford campaign.

Timothy Phelps, Church, Evans, and Shattuck, on October 4, were marched across the river into Walpole, New Hampshire, and permanently banished from the Republic. Enough of their confiscated property was ordered sold to pay the expenses of Ethan Allen's army. The Yorkers prepared and sent a petition to Clinton forthwith.

The four exiles for life, who had supposedly trod Vermont soil for the last time on their one-way trip from Westminster jail to New Hampshire, who had been bidden by their homeland a stern and final farewell, all were back on their farms within four months.

Just possibly, it might have been longing for their own soil that
·conquered the dread of the hangings so solemnly promised them if
ever they returned. More probably, they believed the intention of their
sentence was less fell than its text. They had grounds for such a
belief. Vermont, after girding her loins, rising in wrath, and smiting
the offender hip and thigh, usually found that she had used up all
her vindictive resolution. Instead of hurling the sinner into merited
doom, the Republic was more likely to try thereafter to overlook his
past iniquity. ·

Vermont had been cast permanently in the role of miscreant during all her independent existence and therefore had an unscrupulous
sympathy for all other miscreants. That perverse and sentimental
prejudice may have been one of the factors that drew the state into
the Revolutionary War. It was also one reason she welcomed as settlers hordes of deserters from the Continental Army.

There is no clearer explanation why Evans, Shattuck, Phelps, and
Church, the temeritous neck-riskers, were not hanged. All save the
discreet Evans, who evaded half-hearted efforts to recapture him,
flagrantly called attention to their return by immediately engaging in
further subversive activities. Each of them was rearrested, reimprisoned,
then pardoned. After being thus absolved, each of them took up
again seditious enterprises.

Sentimentality does not wholly explain the Republic's leniency. The
Government actually wished the Yorker brawl to endure, within
limits. It deemed this continual burden to Clinton, this persistent irrita-
tion to Congress, the best possible way of wearing out the hostility of
both.

Congress, prodded on by Clinton, adopted another of its ostensibly
blasting resolutions, December 5. Once more it viewed with alarm and
disapproval the perpetually riotous behavior in Vermont. Myopically, it
laid the entire blame for the Guilford disturbance upon the Republic's
government, brusquely demanded that it make immediate restitution
to the abused Yorkers and threatened, if Vermont went right on ignoring everything Congress said, "immediate and decided interposition."
This was something that might mean much or little, depending on
interpretation.

To Robert R. Livingston of New York, it seemed an ultimatum, and
he wrote gleefully to General Schuyler, dragging out into clear daylight
a long-hidden intention:

·· If terms are not accepted within one month of receiving the resolution, the Green Mountains are to be the division between us and New Hampshire.

To George Washington's straightforward mind, the resolution seemed an outright promise of coercion if Vermont did not yield. It worried him, not only because he must have remembered how trustfully the Republic had followed him up a blind alley, but also because he knew better than most how many of his own erstwhile soldiers had found refuge in the state.

The Commander in Chief wrote to Joseph Jones, delegate from Virginia, his fears lest Congress had gone too far. Coercion might split the Union; it might drive Vermont into the arms of Canada. Furthermore:

> The country is very mountainous [Washington wrote], full of defiles and extremely strong. The inhabitants, for the most part, are a hardy race, composed of that kind of people who are best calculated for soldiers, in truth who are soldiers for many, many hundreds of them are deserters from this army who, having acquired property there, would be desperate in defense of it, well knowing they were fighting with halters about their necks.

Governor Clinton, on the other hand, had small assurance that the national government at last was going to step in and solve a problem the mere contemplation of which was occupying an inordinate and ever-increasing amount of his time. The New York congressional delegates, William Floyd and Alexander Hamilton, warned him that Congress's boding attitude was largely bluff and urged him to make whatever compromise with Vermont he could obtain. Clinton shook off the advice and stubbornly persevered.

The least impressed auditor to Congress's solemn warning was the Republic of Vermont itself. It had become weathered to threats. It may be that it detected the hollowness of this. There was neither awe nor any hint of placation in the responsive letter Chittenden wrote.

The Governor pointed out that the difficulty with the Yorkers was Vermont's own internal business and none of Congress's. He also called attention to the fact that, once again, the national government had passed judgment in a dispute after hearing only the plaintiff's testimony. He pursued:

> That Congress at the special instance of Charles Phelps (a notorious cheat and nuisance to mankind as far as his acquaintance and

dealings have been extended) should come to the decision of so important a matter, *ex parte,* is illegal and contrary to the law of nature and nations.

The legislature, when it next convened, elaborated on that theme in a formal reply to Congress which James Madison found "indecent and tart." Copies were distributed, as propaganda, throughout the Continental Army.

The "immediate and decided interposition" remained only a phrase. Having portentously uttered it, the national government tried its best to forget all about Vermont, which, considering the loud and increasingly sprightly events on the Republic's lower Eastside, demanded a high degree of disregard.

Following the invasion of their capital and the punishment of their leaders, the Yorkers had turned over a new leaf and had begun to inscribe on this fresh page violences precisely similar to those which had adorned its predecessor. Their misbehavior was tentative at first. They had no wish to see Ethan Allen storming in upon them again.

As time went on and the Vermont government showed a desire to slap back only mildly when it was offended and an odd reluctance again to visit widespread retribution on the offenders, insurgency increased in tempo and force. Violence begat violence in a genealogy of biblical length, and the Yorkers wrote their troubles to Clinton and he forwarded them to Congress, and the leaders of the Republic showed a singular willingness to allow strife to continue.

Blow and counterblow in the reviving York war were dealt with considerable sportsmanship and a gratifying absence of bloodshed. When Vermont took the exiled-for-life Colonel Church away from rustication on his farm, where he was heartily encouraging sedition, and thrust him into Bennington jail, the Yorkers embarked on immediate reprisal. They captured John Bridgman, a Vermont judge, and marched him in triumph to Guilford. Remembering on arrival that they had no jail in which to put him, they released the Judge "on parole."

Shattuck, it was reported to the Vermont militia authorities, was celebrating his homecoming after a lifetime sentence of banishment by raising a Yorker army. Colonel John Sergeants marshaled troops of the Republic at Brattleboro and on the night of December 23 marched them out to invade Guilford and disperse the hostile force. Shattuck learned of this—the intelligence systems of both parties were excellent—and laid an ambush for the invaders, who were not, however, commanded by another Ethan Allen.

It was dark on the Brattleboro-Guilford road, and the advance guard which Sergeants had sent out began to feel lonely and chilly. Accordingly, it faced about to rejoin the column, whose nervous members, seeing dim figures approaching, deemed the enemy were upon them. They wheeled and fled by the way they had come, with outcry; and the advance guard, observing the sudden and noisy flight, presumed that some peril unseen by them had scattered Sergeants's army. Wherefore, the guard ran too, but it was not until Brattleboro had been regained that it caught up with the column.

Shattuck, for whom with scant justice Yorkers claimed this victory, was permitted to flourish like the green bay tree for another full year. Then Vermont officials took him into custody, jailed, pardoned, and released him. It was hard to avoid arresting these returned exiles. No gentlemen with halters about their necks were ever more obtrusive.

Timothy Phelps had barely got back home before he practically put himself into prison. When the Vermont Superior Court, Judge Moses Robinson presiding, met at Marlboro, February 4, 1783, Phelps attended, uninvited and with the maximum of ostentation, clanking into the courtroom with his sword of office as New York sheriff of Cumberland at his side.

Fired by zeal, or no one knows what else, he presented himself at the bar, challenged the authority of the court, and began in a loud voice to read the threatening resolution of Congress. Judge Robinson, who may have been getting a little tired of having eccentric swordsmen breaking in upon his court's sessions, thundered as soon as he could get his breath:

"What supercilious arrogance have we here? Sheriff, take that disorderly man into custody. We are not subject to the authority of Congress."

The sheriff, Dr. Elkanah Day, hesitated and looked doubtfully from his rival's flashing eyes to his oversize weapon.

"In the name and by the authority of the state of New York," Phelps bellowed, "I demand that this unlawful assemblage forthwith disperse."

"Sheriff," Robinson cried to the still dubious Day, "do your duty. Arrest that convicted traitor."

Day, with a martyred look, drew his own official sword and advanced. To his relief, Phelps mildly surrendered his own weapon, crying:

"Fellow citizens of Cumberland County, your sheriff is deserted; his lawful authority is disobeyed. I yield to brute force."

With this for his valedictory, he was taken to Bennington to be a cellmate for Colonel Church. Both men were pardoned out, both professed future abiding loyalty to the Republic, and both immediately entered into correspondence with Clinton again.

Vermont, this same February, with a straight face and a calm voice, again requested admission to the union, which Congress with natural snappishness declined to grant. The national government preserved at least a pose of neutrality by refusing Clinton's demand for troops to coerce the uproarious Republic into decorum. Congress was getting almost as tired of Vermont as Clinton was becoming of his continually petitioning Yorkers.

Patriotic Vermonters hailed the capture of Timothy Phelps, which had been contrived almost entirely by Phelps himself, as a victory offsetting the rout of Colonel Sergeants's army by no one at all. The summer which saw the peace treaty between Britain and the United States signed in Paris brought a similitude of tranquillity to Guilford.

Farm work during the growing season cut down the recreations of Yorkers and republicans alike, but they eagerly employed what spare moments they could snatch in the popular pastimes of fighting each other.

Clinton continued to be snowed under by complaints, petitions, requests for counsel. His faithful but overconfiding followers in Vermont kept on ignoring state law, refused to pay Vermont taxes, brawled with their republican neighbors whenever they could afford the time, and became so vehemently revolutionary in general that few Vermont officials dared enter that region without military escort.

When autumn came, and harvests at last were in, when barns and granaries were full and Thanksgiving loomed, rich with promise, the local citizenry of both political faiths looked forward to a hearteningly vigorous winter of assault in all degrees and an occasional mayhem.

The insurgency season really began that year on November 16, when Yorkers led by Francis Prouty invaded Newfane and for no clear reason kidnaped Luke Knowlton. Where they had intended to take him is equally obscure, for a rescuing party, after pursuing the abductors into Massachusetts, met the released Knowlton coming back home, pardonably indignant but unharmed.

Deputy Sheriff Barzillai Rice shortly thereafter attempted to arrest Prouty, who had no intention of being a prisoner. He came at the deputy with a hayfork, loudly promising, "I'll let out your guts, b'God"; and Rice, esteeming intestinal integrity above intestinal fortitude, fled. Yorkers immediately thereafter kidnaped Benjamin Carpenter merely to show that they had not been awed a bit. They let him go, too.

There were Vermont officials of more substance than Rice, however; and Oliver Waters, constable of Brattleboro, soon thereafter became the Republic's champion. He wiped out the stain of the Carpenter abduction by arresting the exiled-for-life William Shattuck, nor did he weakly release his prisoner afterward, but jailed him in Bennington. The Yorkers petitioned Governor Clinton at once.

This triumph was followed on January 3, 1784, by Waters's arrest of Charles Phelps, the Yorkers exiled chieftain, who, having worn out all available listeners elsewhere, had returned to Vermont, inexplicably enough, on a safe conduct.

Why the Eastside's chief trouble maker should have been permitted to come back is obscure, unless one accepts the theory that the Vermont government deliberately was encouraging the York party in the hope that Clinton eventually would find the situation intolerable.

Phelps rewarded Vermont's magnanimity by immediately dabbling in seditious enterprises. He was imprisoned, and his followers sent another plea to Clinton, post haste.

The activity of Constable Waters was becoming extremely offensive to Guilford. There was, Yorkers held, such a thing as being too devoted to your job, and when Waters with others scored again by taking Francis Prouty, from whose guts-seeking pitchfork Barzillai Rice had fled, Guilford determined on drastic reprisal.

Accordingly, on the night of January 16, 1784, an armed host of Yorkers surrounded Josiah Arms's tavern in Brattleboro, where Waters lodged, and demanded the surrender of the Republic's champion, emphasizing their request by industriously shooting out the window lights of the establishment, wounding Major Boyden in the leg, and hitting a traveler who up till then had taken no side in the controversy. At the earnest request of the landlord and other occupants of the riddled tavern, Waters surrendered and was hurried away toward Massachusetts.

There were faint-hearted who were not sorry to see so persistently disturbing an influence withdrawn from circulation, but Joseph Tucker and a dozen followers were not among these. They mounted and followed the abductors, found Waters in Northampton, rescued him, and on the way home, having overcelebrated their victory, raided the home of Charles Phelps, Jr., in Hadley, for good measure.

There they found Timothy Phelps, who recently had sworn allegiance to the Republic and now was on his way to Clinton with two more Yorker petitions. Tucker's expedition gathered him in and rode on, but thirst overcame them, and they halted at an inn near Deerfield.

Sheriff Elisha Porter of Hampshire County, Massachusetts, with his posse overtook the raiders there. Timothy Phelps was liberated. His abductors were arraigned in Hadley and fined £21, for which, long afterward, Joseph Tucker still was plaintively petitioning the Vermont General Assembly.

The Yorker War was getting too rough again. Assaults, kidnapings, shootings were overstepping that golden mean which the Vermont government considered seemly. It appeared time for another military invasion of Guilford.

Three hundred loyal militia under Colonel Stephen Bradley assembled in Brattleboro on Sunday, January 15. A ricketty cannon, more dangerous to its attendants, Ebenezer Haven and Isaac Miller, than anyone else, was trundled in from Dummerston. It was snowing hard next day, but the column marched; and York scouts, seeing only dark movement through the swarming flakes, carried back word to Guilford that a host of at least a thousand was on its way.

In the York citadel bells were rung. Guilford's armed manhood assembled at the sound or else went galloping off over the hills, depending on individual dispositions. Even the valiant made no attempt to oppose the snow-magnified invaders at the town's borders, but fell back into the interior and resolved to do or die at the Stowell farm. There they spent the night, while the Republic's forces bivouacked peaceably enough in Guilford village.

On the morrow, it still was snowing, but the army plodded forward through the storm's uneasy white to the Stowell farm. The invaders captured a few late sleepers here, but the bulk of the defenders had retired to the homestead of Mrs. Lucretia Holton, a widow, which they deemed a better place to stand or perish. On the enemy's approach, neither alternative seemed momentarily desirable. The invading column made prisoners of some of the slower-footed here, too, and quartered itself for the night at the Stowell and Holton places.

In the morning, the snow still was coming down, but the ponderous game of hide and seek was continued. In the two-day battle no one yet had been hurt, and the proceedings were resumed in the best spirit of fair play. The advancing column was considerably retarded by drifts, but it pressed on with such vigor that it interrupted the York army while it was having dinner at the home of Justice of the Peace James Packer, on a hill a mile and a half from the Massachusetts line.

The disturbed diners fled as their opponents toiled up the slope, and Squire Packer himself appeared in the door as the panting, snow-plastered pursuers reached his dwelling and warned them to desist. War was war, the squire admitted, but the boys weren't too good-tempered at having their dinner busted up, and if the battle endured any longer someone was bound to regret it.

Deaf to well-meant advice, the army pressed forward with Sergeant Sylvanus Fisk leading the advance. The only-half-fed enemy proclaimed their justifiable resentment by firing two volleys from the woods. Some careless marksman grazed Joel Knight's arm with a bullet, but Fisk continued to lead his men forward. At the clap of a single musket, the sergeant pitched into the snow, shot through the belly.

An instant of stricken silence followed this flagrantly foul play. Both sides waited aghast. Then Theophilus Crawford bent over Fisk.

"Syl," he quavered, "are ye hurt bad?" And the excusably indignant sergeant, raising himself on his elbow, squalled:

"God damn you, don't ask questions. Push on. Kill the bastards."

Fisk was mortally wounded, though he lived till spring. The ire of his associates, the shame of the Yorkers on discovering that they had a professional in their ranks, practically terminated the battle. Guilford's army abandoned strategic retreat and ran, pell-mell, over the border into Massachusetts. From this neutral ground they sent back a flag of truce to Vermont's authorities and promised earnestly to behave if they were permitted to return home. When this appeal was ignored, they sent off another petition to Clinton.

A garrison was left in Guilford to abate any Yorkers' reviving appetite for trouble, and the main army marched back to Brattleboro and thence to Westminster, where it jailed its prisoners.

Vermont's second invasion of the insurgents' citadel had an air of determined finality about it which, when coupled with the universally deplored accident to Sergeant Fisk, awed the revolutionaries. The effect was not immediately apparent. Rebellion continued, but it dwindled steadily. By the vigor with which the Republic had pushed the last mild battle in the southeast, it had served notice on the perpetually seditious Yorkers that it was growing almost as weary of continual disorder as Congress and the unhappy Clinton already had become.

No trace of this impatience was apparent when the Yorkers captured in the invasion were brought to trial. Most of them were released with light fines, and many of these afterward were remitted.

Vermont's unique sympathy for the erring among its own people lightened the lot even of Charles Phelps and obscured his iniquities. Though, under the law, he faced a death sentence when he was brought to trial, he was punished only by sixty days in jail, most of which term he already had served, and confiscation of his property, which already had been confiscated at the time of his banishment.

This tolerance apparently moved Phelps to immense contrition. He took a deep oath "of allegiance and fidelity to the State of Vermont," and the legislature by special act released him from all further punishment and restored his property to him. After this love feast was over, Phelps immediately returned to a cautious advocacy of New York's cause. His last will was headed: "Marlboro in the County of Cumberland and the State of New York." The Eastside, through his death, became a quieter place.

There was momentary uproar in Guilford during March, 1784, that actually was part of the throes of a failing cause. David Greenough, a member of the scattered York army and now lingering in Bernardston, Massachusetts, tried to steal back to his home in Guilford on the night of March 4, taking Daniel Spicer, a young man of Bernardston, along for company. They fled when they encountered a patrol from the garrison, and Spicer was shot and killed.

This accident formed the basis of still another petition to Clinton, one of the last in a monumental series and one of the most remarkable. It ended:

> Thus fell the innocent.
> Our young men fell by the sword and no one layeth it to heart.
> Traveller, can you refrain from shedding a tear?

It is probable that Clinton had more difficulty in suppressing a yawn. Only innate obstinacy kept him from surrender in what he must have known had become a lost cause. He sent his accumulation of York petitions and letters to Congress with an air of abandoning the whole business. The national legislature did not vote him thanks for his gift. Now that turmoil in Vermont was ebbing, Congress was beginning to realize what a peaceful place the world could be.

Clinton's ordeal, however, was not entirely over. Early in 1786, in the businesslike fashion of receivers closing up a dead enterprise, leading Yorkers in Cumberland County presented him with a bill. It represented claims against New York of one hundred and twenty-five persons, who, in the statement's language, "sacrificed their all; suffered such exquisite tortures, banishments, imprisonments in loathsome gaols, half starved and threatened with being put to ignominious deaths."

These unpleasantnesses, Clinton's debtors carefully had figured, were worth exactly £16,663, 13s. 8d. They would be glad if the Governor would remit promptly.

Fomenting of insurgency obviously came high. No payment was made in cash, but an eight-mile-square plot of land in western New York was set aside for the faithful hundred and twenty-five as payment in full for their woes. Many to whom the government of the Republic remained offensive, moved thither. The town of Clinton, Chenango County, New York, now is situated on part of the property.

With this transaction the revolt of the Yorkers that had afflicted the Republic almost since its foundation finally was ended. It had been not only an ailment; it had also been useful. Vermont, by the serial convulsions she had tolerated, perhaps even had induced within herself, had kept outstretched and greedy hands from her territory. She had emerged from the ordeal a tacitly recognized republic within her own original limits.

Seldom in history has a civil war been employed as a defense against avaricious external enemies. Never has any nation, large or small, emerged so serenely whole from so long a series and so large a variety of hatreds, covert attacks, and candid assaults.

xix Panorama

In Vermont's southernmost, oldest settlements—though all the Republic's towns in 1786 still were young—strife with the wilderness was subsiding. Leantos had become log huts, and these had been succeeded by clapboarded small farmhouses. It may have been the influence of the land itself that held the craftsmen of the Republic to so sure a sense of seemliness.

The dwellings Vermonters built were not mansions. They were sturdy, oblong, expedient structures, painted an economical red or else left for the weather to stain its own harmonious hue. Most of them fathered, as their occupants prospered, ells, sheds, and barns—a string of architectural afterthoughts attached to the parent dwelling.

The little houses fitted with singular, unobstrusive propriety into new and tranquil landscapes their occupants had wrought. Where the stump-filled first clearings had lain, were now fenced meadows and pastures. These clothed with their pleasant patchwork a recently disciplined land. Only vestigial woodlots stood where, twenty years earlier, virgin forest had towered.

On these settled farms, the sons of those who had matched their bodies and axes against the wilderness lived in the moderate ease of which their fathers had dreamed, with glass replacing oiled paper in the dwellings' windows, tallow candles instead of pine torches, cattle in pastures, sheep in the folds, and a still-fertile forest loam that each year gave abundant crops. Labor now yielded generous reward in the southern settlements.

Northward, men still were pioneers. Farms that had been abandoned at the first British advance had become jungles of second growth when their fugitive owners returned. Beyond these tangles stood the giant woodland. More than half Vermont was still primeval.

The ring of axes was the most prevalent sound in the Republic's upper settlements. In those further south, mills talked all day long. An ingenious and ambitious race had harnessed water power to its purposes. No stream of any size in Vermont today lacks dim traces of mill dams, though the ancient factories that companioned them crumbled long ago.

There were saw mills and grist mills, turning, cider, tanning, carding, linseed oil, potash, and iron mills. The mills sang with a cheerful, industrious sound, but in the natures of the cheerful, industrious people who had contrived them there still was little of their mechanical stricture and rigidity. Vermont character still cherished more of the animating brooks' irreverent freedom.

The citizenry of the Republic were warm and untrammeled folk for New England to maintain, but racially an extremely homogeneous. Of some seventy-odd thousand persons in Vermont at this time, 98 per cent were of English or lowland Scottish stock. Their resemblance to their ancestors was chiefly physical, and a free life in a still half-wild land was at work even on obdurate bodies, foreshadowing the eventual type—the angular, bent-shouldered, deliberate, and durable Green Mountaineer.

These were outwardly harder, inwardly mellower, men than the rest of New England commonly bred. Resentment toward the stark propriety of conduct imposed in the older provinces had been one of the impulses that had thrust them northward. Hostilities that completely had immersed them had quickened not only their physical resistance but an emotional responsiveness.

By heritage they were New Englanders, ostensibly echoing Yankee culture and standards. Innately they were a lustier, rowdier, merrier, and more merciful people. To chill Puritan eyes they were scandalous, licentious, and affrontingly satisfied with a reprehensible existence.

It was not a life of sinful luxury. Men drove their bodies with less compunction than they showed their horses and oxen. Women worked from sleep to sleep at the manifold tasks that made of each small farm an almost wholly self-supporting unit. Agriculture, lumbering, carpentry, tool and furniture making, cobbling, blacksmithing were male occupations. Over and beyond the normal duties of house tending, wives and daughters accomplished wool carding, yarn spinning, cloth weaving. They made garments, soap, candles, chairbottoms, baskets, carpets, quilts and coverlets.

Everyone worked, yet unremitting toil does not seem to have oppressed or even muted the spirit of the people. Children, as well as their elders, labored according to their abilities. Girls, in the time not required by the immediate tasks of the household, added to the items in their "hope chests." A bride, to be regarded with approval by the nuptial assemblage, had to be clothed from the skin out in garments of her own spinning, weaving, tailoring.

Boys customarily received, on reaching the age of twenty-one, a "freedom suit." This was the region's version of formal attire, and was vigorously carpentered out of material as stout, resistant, and almost as unyielding as a pine plank. Not infrequently, men were buried in the freedom suits that they had worn on Sabbaths and other occasions of state for fifty years.

There was more of substance than splendor to the costumes of the citizens of the Republic. Women possessed one calico dress for formal wear. This, with a cloak, usually red, and a muff and tippet of home-trapped fur, composed a ceremonial costume that often lasted a lifetime.

These people, whose waking hours were so thoroughly earmarked for toil, were not overwhelmed nor even downcast. Vermonters were working for themselves in a new republic where men were free and land was cheap and rewarded the industrious. The soil of the river bottoms produced mighty crops. Forty bushels of wheat per acre was a not uncommon harvest. The forest mold of the cleared hillsides was amazingly fertile until its substance was exhausted by the blind farming of the era. This, their own country that they had won, was a responsive land, and those who had married it were a happy race.

By modern standards, many of the people were squalid and privation-hounded. Their physical existence was scarcely easier than the lives of mountaineers in the Appalachian hinterland today. These are a static, the early Vermonters were an eager, kinetic folk. They were a joyously unregenerate, not a degenerate, race.

Their daily toil would have ruined, their pastimes and relaxations would have crippled, the average present-day mortal. Dickering, swapping, sparring for advantage in trade was the chief intellectual exercise of the wilderness people. Little other was available, and minds grew strong on this strenuous diet.

Churches, to which the elder New England had turned from the first for intellectual and emotional comfort, were few in the senior settlements, and in the newer frequently did not exist at all. The modest white building with square tower adorned at each corner of its summit by an upright wooden spike was a later addition to the Vermont landscape.

Even where congregations did gather, it was found necessary to enforce reverence by a constant display of authority. "Tithing men" sat during the services directly below the pulpit, and each of them was armed with a five-foot stave with which to abate the too-vigorous dissenter or rouse the raucous snorer.

Church music was wholly vocal. Each hymn was "lined out" after a pitch pipe had set the key.

Besides the tithing men, who kept order not only in church but also at all public assemblies, there were other officers in the Republic's town governments whose posts had been created by the era's needs. The "hog reeve," or "pig constable," already was becoming a subject for jest at town meetings. Before the land was wholly settled, the hog reeve was employed to round up wandering swine and protect crops against their ravages. Pigs commonly were penned now, but the office endured and frequently was bestowed by the citizenry with distinctly uncomplimentary intent.

The Reverend Leonard Worcester of Peacham had a disagreement with his congregation, which sought to revenge itself upon its pastor on Town Meeting Day by nominating him for pig constable. The Reverend Mr. Worcester blandly accepted in this wise:

"I came among you to be a shepherd of a flock, but it is clear that henceforth I can serve you better in another capacity."

The nomination hurriedly was withdrawn.

The Anglo-Saxon yearning for education provided a school for every town, one or more academies of secondary instruction for every county. Ira Allen already was dreaming of the state university of which he eventually became the founder, but in republican Vermont there was little opportunity for men to gain much enjoyment from book learning.

A newspaper was founded at Westminster in 1781. Its proprietors entitled it "The Vermont Gazette or Green Mountain Postboy: Pliant as Reeds where Streams of Freedom Glide; Firm as the Hills to Stem Oppression's Tide," but most of its energy seems to have gone into its name. It endured for two years and then perished.

Strength of body still was a standard of excellence for Green Mountain men. They had an Indian, a Spartan, respect for physical stamina. They wrestled, felled trees for wagers, vied with one another in the weights they could lift, in the miles they could run through the forest. Deftness with gun and ax were distinguishing talents.

All their enterprises and amusements were steeped in a daunting variety of liquors. Each town had its distillery and at least one tavern. Thomas Chittenden, the chief of the Republic, had a bar in his Arlington home at which he did not deem it beneath him to serve the traveler.

Captain Charles Church of Westminster mixed toddy twice a day in a vast bowl and served it at breakfast and supper to his household, from the youngest weanling upward.

While each drank, the Captain stood behind him, toddy stick in hand, until he judged the draught had been sufficient. Then he cried, "Cut!" and brought the stick down on the drinker's pate if obedience was not prompt.

As crops increased, new and horrendous liquors were added to the rum that had been the frontier's staple beverage—cider brandy, potato whisky, maple rum. Women brewed beer as regularly as they baked bread. No store was complete without a liquor barrel on the counter with a free-lunch tray of salt codfish beside it to stimulate infrequently lagging thirsts.

They were profoundly intemperate but not dissolute people. Indulgence did not abate their natural forces. Something of the soil's own fecundity seems to have got into them. Children swarmed about the farms in breath-taking plenitude. John Taplin of Berlin and Samuel Wood of Halifax each had twenty-one offspring. Two hundred and nine descendants mourned Abiah Edgerton of Pawlet when he died at eighty-five. Josiah White of Rockingham, when he was cut off in his flower at ninety-six, left three hundred and eighty-six children, grandchildren, and great-grandchildren. Eight families of Clarendon Springs supplied that town with one hundred and thirteen children, ninety-nine of whom were attending school at once.

Travelers venturing into Vermont from more moderate and ordered parts of the world were at once shocked and bewildered. They sighed over the grimly primitive lives of its people and deemed that their privations served them right for the harum-scarum disregard of New England's mores. Ministers were supremely puzzled by the fact that these unfortunates who were suffering Jehovah's well-merited disapproval seemed jovially unaware of their sorry plight. Instead, they all appeared to be enjoying their punishment heartily.

The Reverend Nathan Perkins, a leading divine of West Hartford, Connecticut, was driven by missionary zeal to tour western Vermont in the summer of 1789. He did not enjoy his trip, and he returned from those profane precincts a confused and dejected man.

Few Vermonters were saved by his preachments from obviously destined burnings, but the Reverend Nathan was unable to denounce their obduracy as heartily as he could have wished. He found himself, incredibly, envying them a little.

The Reverend Nathan, who hitherto had led the pampered life of West Hartford's foremost preacher, suffered sundry afflictions of the body and the spirit during his crusade. He traveled a full hundred miles without seeing a single church. He learned that the food was terrible, that the only liquid offered him which a pampered digestive tract could endure was brook water, that the hospitality of the benighted dwellers in a godforsaken land, though given eagerly, was marred by "bedbuggs" and that he was "eat up with flees."

With pious conscientiousness, he reported the inhabitants of this savage land "miserable," "loose," "dirty," "nasty," "poor, indelicate and miserable cooks," "dress coarse and mean, nasty and ragged." He discovered that at least a quarter of them were nothing better than deists, and many of the remainder had no religion in particular. All this the Reverend Nathan complacently could denounce. Obviously, their miserable lives were their own fault.

There were difficulties, though. The parson was an honest man. He could bewail the fact that in the northern settlements there was no cheese or butter and that moosemeat took the place of beef. He had to admit also that the friendliness, the untempered kindness of the benighted heathen daunted him. They were a disconcertingly contented and joyous folk—"many profane yet cheerful and much more contented than in Hartford and the women more contented than the men."

The Reverend Nathan may have exaggerated their squalor, their flees and bedbuggs, as ills deservedly afflicting the unorthodox. He had no reason save a reluctant adherence to fact to picture unbelievers as enjoying thoroughly their depraved state, yet he wrote:

"Some very clever men and women, serious and sensible"—"The women quiet, serene, peaceable, contented"—"Tough are they, brawny their limbs, their young girls unpolished and will bear work as well as mules."

"Woods," the bewildered parson hazards, groping for an explanation, "make people love one another and kind and obliging and good-natured. They set much more store by one another than in the old settlements."

This was the raw, the undominated and glad-of-it material out of which Vermont fashioned its peculiar citizenry. In its own time, by imperceptible, unslackening pressure, the sternly lovely land molded its possessors, softening angles, fitting convexities into receptive concavities, gradually by environment's and selection's laws establishing a type.

Its hills, after the fashion of hills, intensified Vermonters' resentment of arbitrary power that became almost at once an odd, still passion for freedom. Liberty, in the Vermont creed, was—and still is—the right of each man to own himself and the land of his winning. Slavery was intolerable. The Republic's first act was to cast it out. The oath it made by which the voter qualified was not the citizen's, not the subject's, it was the Freeman's Oath. Election day was Freeman's Meeting Day.

Out of this hill-quickened passion for freedom grew tolerance. No statute decreed it. No law ever captured it. Men whom their neighbors with some justification regarded as "banditti" and worse, inherited much of their distress during the Republic's formative years because of that singular aversion to interfere with the beliefs of others.

Only when the clamor of dissenters, insurgents, became so great that the safety of the state actually was threatened, did Vermont move to suppress it, and even then her action was ponderously deliberate and the penalty visited upon the citizen evil-doer brought to justice was comically light.

This reluctance to punish was not cowardice or slothfulness. The men who stood against invasion at Hubbardton and Bennington were tainted with neither. It was rather the unwillingness of the person who sets great store by his own independence to interfere with the rights of other freemen.

Out of this tolerance came mercy. Ostensibly, the government of Vermont resembled the government of the other New England states. Its code of statutes was a savage blending of Mosaic and Connecticut laws. The hair-raising penalties it prescribed were replete with blood-lettings and mayhems.

By Vermont law, crimes for which death was the stipulated penalty included murder, high treason, conspiracy, blasphemy, false witness, malicious maiming, arson. Adultery was to be punished by thirty-nine lashes and branding with an A. The counterfeiter was to be branded with a C, have his right ear hacked off, and then be imprisoned for life. Petty larceny was to merit ninety-nine lashes; Sabbath-breaking from five to ten. Drunkenness, lying, profanity were to be expiated by sessions of varying duration in the stocks.

Vermont proclaimed its savage statutes and probably felt the better for it. Some of them it never employed. Criminals were rarely thrashed. Threat of mutilation and branding gave the law a gratifyingly horrendous flavor that hurt no one. Even the persistently annoying, the treasonable and pledge-breaking leaders of the York party received ridiculously light sentences and had these remitted if they said they were sorry and would not do it any more.

Vermont rigidity, Vermont austerity, Vermont's implacably savage code of laws were merely a surface conformity to the New England way. They were nothing more than a misleading label on a bottle of particularly high-proof spirits. No one could have been a more gifted blasphemer than Ethan Allen, who died a natural death.

No other state ever dealt so gently with internal enemies. No people, to this day, are more liberal, more philosophical in their attitude toward the wrong-doer. It may be that because in her formative years Vermont and all her works were so thoroughly denounced by propriety, she cherished then and still maintains in her heart a sympathy for the erring.

The land also taught its people democracy. By brutal labor, by flood and freezing and famine, by foes red and white, internal and external, Vermonters established an almost casteless society based on rigors commonly endured.

Men called—still call—that implicit brotherhood "neighborliness." There is no better word for the level they laid upon which all folk were to move. It was born of a time when community aid was the only insurance of survival. In rural Vermont it maintains today.

The social life of the Republic was meshed in this spirit of neighborliness. The most frequent festivals were concerned with the supplying of aid to a neighbor. Corn huskings became regional frolics. There were apple-paring bees, quilting bees, and numerous similar occupations. Barn and house raisings were high-spirited and alcoholic community enterprises.

Frames or "bents" of the new building's walls were constructed while they lay horizontal. Then, on the appointed day, the neighborhood gathered and set them upright, pinning them in place, usually with wooden pegs, to the accompaniment of heavy libations, much excitement, and the occasional toppling of some unaccountably dizzy person from the upright frame, to his considerable detriment.

Sense of equality is the foundation of neighborliness. This acceptance of the level on which all men stand is at the opposite end of the spectrum from mass surrender to one man's will. By 1786, Vermont's leaders already had learned that theirs was a people to whom a way might be shown but who would never, for an instant, consent to be pushed along it. The state still clings to the right of every citizen to his opinion and his voice.

The town meeting where each person with a grievance or a cause has an equal right to air it, the implicit recognition that there is something above material success which permits the richest man in the town and the most no-account payer of the poll tax the identical privilege to yell his head off over what he believes to be injustice—these are free and tolerant and democratic standards that the land and its people bore, and still preserve.

Wealth, in the Republic, fathered small ostentation and had no great influence. Men seem to have been judged by some finer unit of measurement. Chittenden, Vermont's almost perpetual early governor, was a plain and ungainly farmer. Roswell Hopkins, secretary of state, lived on the frontier in what a traveler called "a wretched log cabin." There were few stately mansions in republican Vermont. There are few today that natives occupy.

The travail and the turmoil, the brawlings and battles and bewilderments, that attended the birth of the Republic of Vermont planted a special and intense patriotism in the minds of its people. This rough, original ardor the land also mellowed. Season by season, Vermont held its beauty up to unsentimental eyes. Little by little, human hearts found possessive delight in the loveliness they had suffered so much of violence to hold.

State pride is a growth more common in America's south and west. It lives sturdily but modestly in Vermont. Men saw the circling years reiterate the fairness of their land and, as all men will toward the difficultly obtained and beloved thing, grew proud of the beauty they had won and jealous for it.

The land imposed its peculiar discipline upon its people. No other lines of its impress cut so deeply. New England's privation-enforced frugality was intensified here, first by necessity, later by habit, later still by necessity again.

From the first, Vermont was a nation of small capitalisms in which each man was his own employer and employee. No great industrialization has transformed that original pattern, and out of this careful way of life came abiding thrift and thrift's salutary attendant virtues—suspicion of ostentation, hatred of extravagance, a firm belief in arithmetic's stark laws. To these a people clung a hundred years ago. To them they even now hold.

Those who yearned for splendors—the restless, the ambitious—went from Vermont. The names of these impatient are on monuments from New York to the Pacific. Their brethren stayed and tilled their land and raised their stock and were content with the returns, negotiable or otherwise, of small, self-contained enterprises—which, possibly, is as close to actual freedom as mortals may ever approach.

The stability of the stay-at-homes was not inertia. The subsequent history of the state refutes that hazard. What detractors term "stagnation" is simply the calm adherence of a people to a region and a doctrine they have proved and found good. The breed is constant and, by American standards, more than ordinarily enduring. Almost all the Vermont surnames mentioned in this book still are borne by Green Mountain natives in the writer's neighborhood.

This union of men and their land, this submission of a difficult soil to its possessor and the reciprocal molding of human natures to fit the soil's peculiar needs, had been consummated by the time the Yorker revolt deliberately had expired and Vermont, ignored by the United States and no longer coveted but thoroughly detested by its immediate neighbors, calmly took its small place among the independent nations of earth.

Its place was in neither chair on which her statesmen had indicated her willingness to sit. Congress repeatedly had rebuffed Vermont. Canada had angrily and ostentatiously washed her hands of a profitless negotiation. The Republic had fallen between two stools and now was discovering that her inadvertent site was not at all calamitous. It was even enviable.

Of all the Western Hemisphere's participants in the Revolution, Vermont had emerged from the ordeal in a better, more solvent, more prosperous condition than had been hers on entering the strife.

Thanks to the real-estate transactions of the Republic's government, which had confiscated and auctioned holdings of Tories and other insurgents and had found additional income in the sale of new land grants, the small nation's financial health was enviable. The thirteen United States were reeling about under the colossal cost of the war. Vermont watched them stagger with a dryly humorous eye. Since she had been refused admission to the confederation, she was not obliged to assume any share in its war debt.

The Republic calmly turned its back upon the distresses of the thirteen snobbish sisters and went about the comparatively insignificant task of setting its own house in order. There was peace at last within its borders and what promised to be a long truce outside them.

Vermont had bought independence with the least possible blood and the most possible noise. From the first, it had exploited to the utmost the profitable enterprise of being an unmitigated annoyance and nuisance.

Already the state was exercising most of the prerogatives of a free nation. It was issuing its own coinage, though only copper pieces were struck off. The mint was a small building in Rupert, owned and operated by Reuben Harmon, Jr.

The earliest coins displayed on the obverse a rising sun and a plow; on the reverse, thirteen stars radiating from a single glaring eye—probably the deity's, possibly Vermont's indignant own. A later design was a not too radical revision of Britain's own coinage. The obverse displayed the profile bust of a fat person who bore an unwelcome resemblance to George III, though his crown had been turned into a laurel wreath. The reverse was stamped with the image of a seated figure which was supposed to be Liberty, but certainly was Britannia's twin.

Despite the Republic's prosperity, all cash, domestic or imported, was extremely scarce. Business was transacted almost entirely by notes or simple barter. A bushel of wheat took the place of a monetary unit.

Under Anthony Haswell, postmaster general, a mail system had been established. Post riders traveled weekly routes that included Bennington, Rutland, Windsor, Newbury, and Brattleboro.

The Republic also assumed the right to make honorary citizens of its benefactors. Most enthusiastic and industrious of these recipients of the freedom of the state was Hector St. John de Crevecoeur, French consul at New York and friend of Ethan Allen. Just what De Crevecoeur did to merit this honor is dim, but he took his citizenship dismayingly hard and continually presented the Vermont legislature with French names which he wished to have bestowed upon the Republic's towns.

Most of the consul's suggestions the lawmakers ignored; but they did, at his earnest instance, name St. Johnsbury for him, Vergennes for the then French minister of foreign affairs, and Danville for Rochefoucauld, Duc d'Anville.

Vermont also attempted to exercise the prerogatives of a nation and conclude a trade treaty with Canada. This never was consummated since the British authorities had a perhaps warranted reluctance to enter into further negotiations with the Republic's statesmen. Commerce with Canada nevertheless was brisk. Vast rafts of logs went yearly down the lake and piecemeal through the Richelieu River to the St. Lawrence. A growing amount of agricultural produce also was exported, and "pearl ash," refined potash salts, was the state's profitable manufactured commodity.

Three-fourths of the Republic's citizenry still were living in the lower half of the land. Despite the mills on every stream, the people were overwhelmingly farmer folk, and townships were sparsely populated and actual villages much smaller. Guilford, with some twenty-four hundred citizens, was still Vermont's metropolis. Burlington, now the state's largest city, was not among the first twenty in 1786.

The population was increasing rapidly, not only through the prodigious accomplishments of Vermont's fathers, but also through a steady stream of immigrants, eager to settle in a land of small taxes where soil was cheap and the yield spectacular. Between the close of the Revolution and 1791, when the Republic resolved itself into the fourteenth state, first settlements were made in sixty towns, and sixty-seven more had acquired enough people to warrant the establishment of town governments.

Hasty granting of these towns, the vagueness with which their limits were defined in the books of record, caused innumerable conflicts over titles between indignant landholders and increased the work of the courts as well as the prosperity and unpopularity of attorneys.

Prevalence of lawsuits and the lack of currency, when added, brought the same old total of discontent, roused the identical spirit of revolt that had overset New York's authority years before, and brought about the final, swiftly stifled rebellion with which the Republic was forced to deal.

xx Fulfillment

VERMONT'S REGULATOR RIOTS were a mild consequence of the strong disillusion and resentment that follows all wars. They voiced the ordinary man's belief that he had been betrayed again and foreshadowed the rebellion headed by Daniel Shays, which was the most violent expression of an epidemic discontent.

The millennium, hailed so certainly at the Revolution's dawn, unaccountably had failed to fulfill most of its daybreak promises. When the conflict ended, few men were richer, many were poorer, and existence that was to have been so glowingly transfigured was resuming its normal drab appearance.

Folk still must labor if they would live. Taxes still had to be paid, and a government had to be obeyed painfully. The penniless still were hailed to court. Money was bitterly scarce, and the unfortunate saw their property wrested from them to satisfy legal judgments. In Vermont, earlier than elsewhere, a people trained in and accustomed to insurgency rose against the courts.

The Republic's manner of dealing with this revolt bore little resemblance to the slipshod, semiprovocative fashion in which it had handled the Yorker rebellion. Then, Vermont had striven to wear out all its opponents by tolerating, even encouraging, disorder. Now, with domestic tranquillity infinitely to be desired, the lately so-dilatory government did not temporize for a minute. It fell upon the astonished insurgents and violently shook the sedition out of them. They never had the opportunity to indulge in one wholly satisfactory riot.

Mutterings that had endured for a long while against the injustice and rapacity of the courts grew louder in the fall of 1786. Men with a common sense of oppression were banding themselves into groups called "Regulators," and on October 31 they transformed their resentment into action.

Thirty armed Regulators, led by Robert Morrison, a Hartland blacksmith, and Benjamin Stebbins, a farmer of Barnard, marched to Windsor with the loud intention of preventing the court from sitting.

These Eastsiders were disconcerted to find that Vermont's own law officers were more difficult to frighten than the earlier New York had been.

Benjamin Wait, sheriff of Windsor County, went out to meet the invaders. He was uncordial and definitely prickly of manner, and the sincere fashion in which he read the riot act did not encourage them. Stephen Jacob, state's attorney, was even more severe. He warned Regulators of a number of unpleasant things that inevitably would happen to them if they strove to break up the court and advised them so solemnly to go home that, after some apprehensive conversation among themselves, they dispersed.

That did not end matters. The Republic had been enjoying the first complete peace in its entire national life and did not look kindly upon disturbers of such serenity. The recently threatened court issued warrants for the mild dissenters. The ringleader, Robert Morrison, and some of his followers were arrested. He was immensely penitent, and the judges tempered their wrath toward their erring lamb. Morrison had to pay £10 and serve a month in jail. His associates were let off with lighter fines.

Meanwhile, though, the remaining and unrepentant Regulators had assembled at Captain Lull's house in Hartland and were talking too loudly about rescue of their associates. Sheriff Wait, who also was colonel of the 3rd Vermont militia, surrounded Lull's dwelling with a detail of his regiment, attacked, beat up the dissenters thoroughly, and arrested twenty-seven.

The battered twenty-seven were "very humble and penitent" when arraigned and "were treated with great tenderness by the court." The remnant of the Regulators briefly considered massing for another rescue, but they learned that six hundred troops were assembled in Windsor and more were coming in. The Eastside's rebellion ended then and there, at a cost of a few bruises and scalp wounds.

An outbreak on the Westside was even more swiftly smothered. Here an armed mob that had tried to break up the session of the Rutland County Court found itself caught between two militia forces and tamely surrendered. The leader of these Regulators, Jonathan Fassett, who was serving his fourth term as a member of the legislature, was fined £25 and at the next meeting of the General Assembly permanently was expelled from that body by a unanimous vote. Vermont at last seemed to have had her fill of disorder. She was growing dismayingly respectable.

So thoroughly had the last insurgency been stamped out that Shays' rebellion quickened no responsive tumult in the Republic. When the muskets of General Lincoln's troops, banging dully through the falling snow at Petersham, Massachusetts, February 3, 1787, had broken up the last considerable fragment of the revolt, Shays and a few of his followers fled into Vermont.

Lincoln's aide, Major Royall Tyler, who was destined to become Vermont's chief justice, brought Chittenden a letter, asking his aid in capturing the fugitives. This assistance Vermont's governor withheld, not through any vast sympathy for the rebels, but because the missive addressed him as "Thomas Chittenden, Esq." and not by his proper rank and title.

One-eyed Tom's sudden assumption of dignity must have been a startling spectacle to those who had dwelt in the Republic during its catch-as-catch-can and riotous youth. Times were changing, and men were altering with them or else were giving place to younger, sprucer folk to whom the Green Mountain Boys were only a yawn-inducing tradition and who never had sat through a taxing session in the Council Chamber of Landlord Fay's Bennington tavern.

Influence was slipping from the hands of the founders of the Republic. Peace, which still was a novelty to Vermont, demanded suaver, more conventional leadership than theirs had been. Impatient, more youthful men were fretting over the state's continued absence from the Union. In Congress, even in New York, sentiment for admission was growing. What had promised to be perpetual storm was at last subsiding.

These were new days. New ways accompanied them, and Ira Allen, the deft, the smoothly ingenious, was in trouble. The intolerant younger men were finding the Allens, whom youth once had so eagerly followed, tiresome, outdated folk. Ethan, in retirement, was a stuffy legend. Ira, after so many years in office, had been defeated in the 1786 election for state treasurer. That downfall did not completely satisfy his enemies. Now, they charged him with corruption in the administration of the Vermont land office.

The transaction, which had to do with the acquisition of a land patent by Allen in lieu of salary owed him, was complex, and the unscrupulous bayings of accusers did nothing to simplify it. There was a brawl in the legislature that the one-time reliable troubleshooter of the Republic could not still. Chittenden defended his old friend so stoutly that he drew animosity upon himself and was defeated for governor at the next election in consequence. Moses Robinson took his place for one year. Subsequent calmer investigation cleared Allen of fraud.

The stalwart old days were only memories now. In these punier times, strange sights were visible. There was a movement, initiated by Assemblyman Alexander Hamilton in the New York legislature, to surrender the state's stubbornly held pretensions to jurisdiction over Vermont. The measure Hamilton proposed passed the lower house. It was defeated in the Senate by the influence of the still-implacable Clinton.

Unfamiliar forces were abroad in a tame world, forming new patterns, establishing fresh alliances, disparaging old heroes. Now he who most ruggedly exemplified a stirring past vanished and left a daunting emptiness in Vermont's existence. Ethan Allen died February 13, 1789.

He had moved from Sunderland to the new house he had reared on fertile land by the shore of Burlington Bay. Peace, in some strange fashion, had entered his own uproarious spirit. Farming was his profession, and his young wife his great satisfaction. The glittering uniform that was to be his shroud had been laid away.

The needs of his stock, and perhaps a craving for more robust companionship than his tranquil home afforded him, sent him across the ice, February 12, to Ebenezer Allen's home on South Hero Island to bring back a sled-load of hay. A Negro drove the ox-team.

Cousin Ebenezer made his kinsman welcome with all the ancient rites of hospitality. Others who had marched with Ethan Allen lived on the island. They gathered about Ebenezer's hearth, tossing the flowing bowl, reliving in these piping times the splendors of more spacious years. None spoke oftener, laughed louder, drank deeper than he who had been chief hero of those old adventures. It was past midnight when Ethan Allen climbed back into the sled.

The cold was piercing. The plodding oxen breathed out gusts of steam. The sled runners creaked. Hay, piled high behind him, spread a warm and pleasant smell about the great captain, the protector of the Republic, who now was bringing home fodder for his cows.

Wrapped in his cloak, Allen leaned against the fragrant cushion. The familiar, glowing ease that was liquor's benison immersed him. The voice of the Negro, urging on the oxen, came from a long way off. The strong punch ran through Allen's veins, soothing him, adorning old memories that the evening's revel had revived.

He had had good times, all his days; gallant and valiant times. Perhaps now, while he lingered on the illogical borderland of slumber, half-forgotten revels, adventures, triumphs, defeats rose up before him, vivid and sharp of line. It may have been that the warm tingling coursing through his great body abolished time and space, reviving old enemies, recalling old friends.

He could almost feel the galloping horse between his knees. He could actually see that hellion, Robert Cochran, racing him down into the Otter River clearing to chase away the terrified Scottish loons who had dared to trespass on New Hampshire-granted land. He could hear the hoots of the Green Mountain Boys, the dull tumult of hoofs behind him.

Plain as it had been that long-ago day, the unbreeched Lieutenant Feltman stood in the dawnlight washing Ticonderoga's stair. Other memories crowded in—the ghastly face of the Indian who almost had murdered him on the St. Lawrence's shore, Prescott's empurpled visage, Arnold's disdainful smile, the grave and kindly features of George Washington as he welcomed the liberated captive, Moses Robinson's affronted stare when Allen addressed the court at Westminster, fat Charles Phelps and his presumptuous son. They all swam before him, a host from the past.

Out of the old years they came thronging, the great and the small, the heroes and the scoundrels, that had been part of his lusty life. Their faces flared and faded like the moon behind scudding clouds. At last they all dwindled, save two. These marched beside the sled, substantial, comfortingly real. He could see each trudging movement, could hear their feet on the snow-covered ice.

Tough Remember Baker swung along, firelock on shoulder and cap askew on his sandy hair. Beside him solidly strode the hulking figure of Seth Warner in faded regimentals. The starlight slid along Remember's musket barrel. There was a trace of frost on Seth's thick shoulders. Warner smiled, catching Allen's eye, and Ethan smiled too. Jealousy and suspicion were spent. Wounds healed and left no scars as one grew old. The cousins had turned from Ebenezer's fireside to see their kinsman home. There was tremulous warmth about Ethan Allen's heart.

He sat up suddenly and drew so deep a gasp of the bitter air that he coughed. Seth and Remember had not been in the gathering on South Hero. They who just now so plainly had walked beside him were long dead. Baker's bones moldered beside Lake Champlain.

Warner had died, five years before, from the ailment that had smitten him first just after Bennington's battle.

Only the snow's dim emptiness lay about the trudging oxen and the creaking sled. Only Ethan Allen and the Negro were abroad on the lake in the night's chill silence. It was strange that a dream could seem so real. He no longer could see his escorting kinsmen, yet sense of their presence still was strong upon him. It was moonshine, nothing more. No one but the oxen and the men and the load they hauled were stirring in this black hour before the tardy February dawn.

There was one light ahead. It shone like a fallen, brighter star where pale shore met dark sky. The astonishment that was Ethan Allen's substitute for fear was passing. A warm serenity replaced it. Fanny had set that light to guide her husband home. Ebenezer's punch had been plaguy strong. It made you see things. It sent strange pricklings through your body. Your breath, too, came difficultly out here in the cold.

The oxen lurched on in gusts of steam. The runners squealed. Ethan Allen watched the light his wife had kindled.

> *Dear Fanny wife, the beautiful and young*
> *The partner of my joys, my dearest self,*
> *My love, pride of my life—*

The great body sat still beside the Negro. After a little the man spoke. Ethan Allen neither answered nor stirred.

Ezra Stiles, president of Yale College, noted in his diary for February 13, 1789: "Ethan Allen died this day and went to hell."

If this be so, the infernal confinement is not too close. The Original Something that once was he still walks the land to which he gave his own peculiar devotion.

The old order faded, and the bright young men held sway. The rumpus raisers of another time who had found continually uproarious Vermont their element felt control of the state slipping from their grasp into softer, more temperate hands. Voices that had bawled defiance to all the world were dwindling. More plausible, ingratiating speech, more subtle expedients, held sway.

The successors of the Republic's blustering founders softly were working Vermont into the Union, easing her way with political pledges. Politics had become a powerful lever. The young men laid hold upon and plied it.

A group of Vermont's new statesmen met July, 1788, at Tinmouth in the home of Judge Nathaniel Chipman and considered the forming of political parties in the United States. Thereafter, Chipman, with the counsel of his fellows, wrote a letter to Alexander Hamilton, already a chieftain among the Federalists. The Republic, this missive pointed out, was heartily in favor of the Federal gospel. Vermont, if admitted to the Union, would be loyal to Hamilton's party.

For a year thereafter, the burden of that suggestion clung in Hamilton's mind. Vermont, by her indifference to the United States, was gaining more than her earlier more earnest attempts at inclusion had been able to acquire. When the first Congress to assemble under the new Constitution met in New York, March 4, 1789, it was inclined to look upon the hitherto disparaged Republic with warmth, almost with hospitality.

The thirteen states, it appeared, could not maintain permanently their exclusive little society. Kentucky was clamoring for admission, with Southern endorsement. The North opposed the acceptance of another slave state, unless a balancing free commonwealth was included also in the Union. The line of cleavage along which the nation seventy years later was to break in two already was discernible.

Vermont had been waiting for years. Mr. Hamilton, who clearly was to be a power in the new national government, was urging her cause. Congress turned toward the frequently rejected Republic. There was an expression on Congress's face that Vermonters did not at once recognize. It was a smile of welcome.

The big man with ill-fitting false teeth and a delivery as bad as his words were profound, who stood, April 30, 1789, on a Wall Street balcony and was inaugurated first President of the United States, was Vermont's advocate. George Washington remembered his earlier wholly involuntary deception and was eager to make amends.

These influences, working together, cleared the way. The eternal New York dispute must finally be settled before Vermont received statehood, but even Clinton's obstinacy broke beneath the forces raised against him. He was a politician himself.

On July 14, 1789, New York's legislature authorized the appointment of commissioners to meet with Vermont representatives and settle for all time the quarter-century dispute. The notification sent to Chittenden hailed him for the first time in all New York's correspondence with him as "Your Excellency." This may have salved pride which had been bruised by the election of Moses Robinson as the Republic's next governor.

IRA ALLEN

From a Miniature Painted in His Forties
(Courtesy, University of Vermont)

While Chittenden was in eclipse and Robinson governed in his stead, the Vermont-New York negotiations went on, with halts, stumblings, and disagreements; yet they progressed. On October 7, the commissioners, meeting in New York City, agreed on the establishment of Vermont's present western boundary. The Republic consented to pay land claimants under New York patents a total of $30,000. New York, in return, withdrew all opposition to Vermont's admission to the Union.

Vermont held a convention in Bennington, January 6, 1791, to ratify the Constitution of the United States and make formal petition for statehood. The proceedings were not as smooth as the Republic's new statesmen had intended. Dissent almost at once lifted a raucous voice. There were, it appeared, a number of Vermonters among the delegates who were quite satisfied with matters as they stood. They were unfortunately forthright folk with long memories.

They recalled, with rancor that the years had not appreciably diminished, the number of times a hoity-toity Congress had slammed the door right in Vermont's supplicating face. Wal, no call for us to supplicate naow, is they? We're gittin' 'long smooth as ile as 'tis. Thirty thousand dollars to them cussed Yorkers? Ain't three thousand dollars wuth of Yorkers in the hull world. Want us in naow, don't they? Kin use us, hey? We'll bring that damn slave-holding Kentucky along behind us. Let 'em wait, I say. Made us wait long enough, b'God. Vermont suits me, just the way she is.

Such lamentable protests were impossible to ignore. They did not prevail. Chittenden, who had been re-elected governor, had presided at the convention, soothed some of the dissenters. Others, the new statesmen talked into a stupor. Oratory had begun to replace slanderous personal attacks in Vermont debates, and the advocates of Union turned it on full. By the time they ran out of wind, most of the insurgents had been subdued. Only four held out grimly for a continuation of the Republic. The hundred and five other delegates ratified the Constitution.

George Washington presented Vermont's petition for statehood to Congress, February 9, 1791. On February 18, Washington signed the act that made Vermont the fourteenth of the United States.

Vermont's long-deferred admission to the Union was celebrated in Rutland, March 8, 1791. The wintry sunrise and a small, shivering, but patriotic group of the town's 1400 inhabitants saw the Federal ensign creep up the flagpole in the village square. It was not until afternoon that the festivities advanced further. Then the justices of the Vermont Supreme Court, the state's attorney general, and lesser dignitaries slopped through the slush to Williams' Inn. Here what a scrupulous contemporary account terms "an economical collation" was served.

The collation, however sparse, could not have left the partakers with more than adequate room for the toasts drunk thereafter. Their number was daunting; their context, under the influence of pledges already quaffed, increasingly flowery.

While the sun moved westward and March's raw wind troubled the flag above the square, the celebrants drank to "The President," "The Vice President and Congress," "The Allies of the United States," "The State of New York"—some of the drinkers must have choked a little on that—and "His Excellency Governor Chittenden."

Glasses were filled and filled again. Faces grew pinkly radiant with patriotic fervor. The assemblage drank to "The Union of Vermont with the United States—May it Flourish like our Pines and Continue as Unshaken as our Mountains," "May the New States soon Rival the Old in Federal Virtues," "May the Federal Officers of the State of Vermont Act with Integrity and Merit the Confidence of the People."

Strong men visibly were moved by the historic significance of this occasion. They drank with intervening bursts of impassioned cheering to "May the Patriotism of America Secure It from Venality," "The Union of States, Interests and Hearts," "Art, Science, Manufactures and Agriculture," "The Clergy—May They Dispel the Clouds of Ignorance and Superstition."

The day was waning, but the toast-making continued. They drank to "The Memorable 16th of August on Which was Fought the Glorious Battle of Bennington," "The Conjugal Union and the Rising Generation," and with immense emotion to "May We Never Experience a Less Happy Moment than the Present under the Federal Government."

Here, a pause intruded. An ode, specially composed for the occasion, was sung to "Washington's Birthday," a familiar tune. "A select choir of singers" had been provided to guide the assemblage's voices, which, otherwise, might just possibly have been inclined to stray. It was a long ode. The following is a sample verse:

> *Come each Green Mountain Boy;*
> *Swell every breast with joy;*
> *Hail our good land.*

As our pines climb the air,
Firm as our mountains are,
Federal without compare,
Proudly we stand.

One more toast then was drunk, so that parched throats might be eased—"May the Vermonters Become as Eminent in the Arts of Peace as They Have Become Glorious in Those of War." This was followed by "continued demonstrations of joy."

Men issuing from the inn may have looked up at the banner that moved in the late afternoon breeze. It was a bright new flag of fifteen stripes and fifteen stars.

There still were only fourteen states, but Kentucky stood on the Union's threshold. Vermont had included the state-to-be in her own celebration and her flag. Vermont knew how it felt to wait before a closed door.

The low sun stretched the flagpole's shadow across the square and turned Mount Pico's snowdrifts golden. Level amber light enriched the standard's colors.

The raising of that flag at daybreak had been independent Vermont's last act. The rippling fifteen stripes of white and scarlet, the uneasy constellation of fifteen stars had been the small nation's farsighted and thrifty farewell gesture.

The new banner was the end piece at the close of the final chapter in the Republic's independent history.

The radiant bunting rippled slowly in the unearthly light. It represented not only triumphant conclusion; it also was the emblem of a beginning.

Vermont stood where from the first day of her nationality she had purposed to stand. No compromise had been made; no penalty had been imposed. Together, the land and its people had fulfilled the original, unmodified intention of the reluctant Republic.

Demonstrations of joy continued into the night.

SOURCES

Sources

ALLEN, ETHAN. *Narrative of Colonel Ethan Allen*. New York, 1930.
CHIPMAN, DANIEL. *Memoir of Colonel Seth Warner*. Middlebury, Vt., 1848.
——. *Memoir of Thomas Chittenden*. Middlebury, Vt., 1849.
CHITTENDEN, L. E. *The Capture of Ticonderoga*. Rutland, 1872.
CRANE, CHARLES E. *Let Me Show You Vermont*. New York, 1937.
CROCKER, HENRY. *History of the Baptists in Vermont*. Bellows Falls, Vt., 1913.
CROCKETT, WALTER H. *History of Vermont*. Burlington, 1938.
Documentary History of the State of New York. Albany, 1861.
FISK, FRANK L. *Horace Ward Bailey, Vermonter*. Rutland, 1914.
FISKE, JOHN. *The American Revolution*. Boston, 1894.
FOX, DIXON RYAN. *Yankees and Yorkers*. New York, 1940.
FRENCH, ALLEN. *The Taking of Ticonderoga*. Cambridge, 1928.
——. *The Day of Concord and Lexington*. Boston, 1925.
FULLER, J. F. C. *Decisive Battles*. New York, 1940.
HALL, BENJAMIN H. *History of Eastern Vermont*. New York, 1858.
HALL, HILAND. *Early History of Vermont*. Albany, 1868.
HAYES, LYMAN S. *History of Rockingham*. Bellows Falls, Vt., 1907.
——. *The Connecticut River Valley*. Rutland, 1929.
HEMENWAY, ABBY MARIA. *The Vermont Historical Gazeteer*. Burlington, 1871.
HOLBROOK, STEWART H. *Ethan Allen*. New York, 1940.
JONES, MATT B. *Vermont in the Making*. Cambridge, 1939.
LAMB, WALLACE E. *The Lake George and Lake Champlain Valleys*. New York, 1940.
LEE, JOHN PARKER. *Uncommon Vermont*. Rutland, 1926.
LEFFERTS, CHARLES. *Uniforms in the American Revolution*. New York, 1926.
MANSFIELD, DAVID L. *History of Dummerston*. Ludlow, Vt., 1884.
NICKERSON, HOFFMAN. *The Turning Point of the Revolution*. Boston, 1928.

PARKMAN, FRANCIS. *Frontenac and New France.* Boston, 1909.
——. *A Half Century of Conflict.* Boston, 1909.
——. *Wolfe and Montcalm.* Boston, 1909.
PECK, THOMAS B. *Records of the First Church of Rockingham.* Boston, 1902.
PELL, JOHN. *Ethan Allen.* Boston, 1929.
PETERS, SAMUEL A. *A History of the Rev. Hugh Peters.* New York, 1807.
PERKINS, NATHAN. *Narrative of a Tour through the State of Vermont.* Woodstock, Vt., 1927.
PHELPS, JOHN. *Family Memoirs.* Brattleboro, 1886.
POWERS, GRANT. *Historical Sketches of the Coos Country.* Haverhill, N.H., 1880.
ROBINSON, ROWLAND. *A Hero of Ticonderoga.* Rutland, 1933.
——. *A Danvis Pioneer.* Rutland, 1933.
——. *Vermont, A Study of Independence.* Cambridge, 1892.
SPARGO, JOHN. *The Bennington Battle Monument.* Rutland, 1925.
——. *The Epic of Fort Massachusetts.* Rutland, 1933.
——. *Ethan Allen at Ticonderoga.* Rutland, 1926.
THOMPSON, ZADOCK. *History of Vermont.* Burlington, 1833.
THORPE, WALTER. *History of Wallingford.* Rutland, 1911.
TYLER, MARY PALMER. *Grandmother Tyler's Book.* New York, 1925.
VERMONT HISTORICAL SOCIETY. *Proceedings.* Montpelier.
WALTON, E. P. *Governor and Council of Vermont.* Montpelier, 1873.
WARDNER, HENRY STEELE. *The Birthplace of Vermont.* New York, 1927.
WELLS, FREDERICK P. *History of Newbury, Vt.* St. Johnsbury, Vt., 1902.
WILBUR, JAMES H. *Ira Allen, Founder of Vermont.* Boston, 1928.
WILLIAMS, SAMUEL. *The Natural and Civil History of Vermont.* Burlington, 1809.
WILSON, HAROLD F. *The Hill Country of Northern New England.* New York, 1936.
WOOD, EVELYN M. *History of Royalton.* Burlington, 1911.

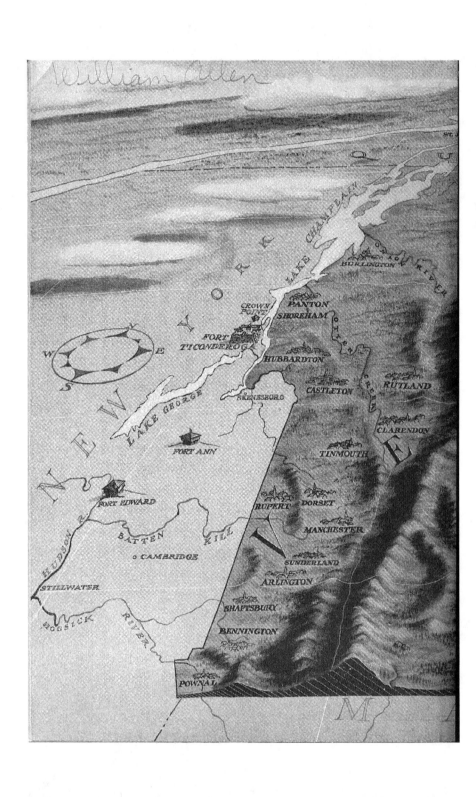

CPSIA information can be obtained
at www.ICGtesting.com
Printed in the USA
LVHW020022150222
711105LV00004B/169